Britain and the
Wars in Vietnam

# Britain and the Wars in Vietnam

*The Supply of Troops, Arms and Intelligence, 1945–1975*

Gerald Prenderghast

McFarland & Company, Inc., Publishers
*Jefferson, North Carolina*

## Acknowledgments

With grateful thanks to the following: The staff of the Public Record Office, Kew. Miss Jessie Webb of the Australian War Memorial Research Center, for her kind assistance in locating the British citizens serving in the Australian military. Mr. Peter Seal, for permission to use the pictures of the Jungle Warfare School on his site www.wingedsoldiers.co.uk.

LIBRARY OF CONGRESS CATALOGUING-IN-PUBLICATION DATA

Prenderghast, Gerald, 1954– author.
Britain and the wars in Vietnam : the supply of troops, arms and intelligence, 1945–1975 / Gerald Prenderghast.
p. cm.
Includes bibliographical references and index.

ISBN 978-0-7864-9924-3 (softcover : acid free paper) ∞
ISBN 978-1-4766-2091-6 (ebook)

1. Vietnam War, 1961–1975—Great Britain. 2. Indochinese War, 1946–1954—Great Britain. 3. Great Britain—Foreign relations—Indochina. 4. Indochina—Foreign relations—Great Britain. 5. Great Britain—Foreign relations—Vietnam. 6. Vietnam—Foreign relations—Great Britain. 7. Great Britain—Foreign relations—1945– I. Title.

DS558.6.G7P74 2015      959.704'140941—dc23      2015028230

BRITISH LIBRARY CATALOGUING DATA ARE AVAILABLE

© 2015 Gerald Prenderghast. All rights reserved

*No part of this book may be reproduced or transmitted in any form or by any means, electronic or mechanical, including photocopying or recording, or by any information storage and retrieval system, without permission in writing from the publisher.*

Front cover: (top) Blackburn B-101 Beverley, RAF Transport Command, 1964 (Adrian Pingstone); Mekong Delta region in Vietnam, 1969 (UK National Archives and Records Administration)

Printed in the United States of America

*McFarland & Company, Inc., Publishers*
*Box 611, Jefferson, North Carolina 28640*
*www.mcfarlandpub.com*

"What we really learned about Vietnam was that we shouldn't have been there in the first place."
—Stanley Karnow, *New York Times*, 8 January 2010

"Comment is free, but facts are sacred."
—C.P. Scott, *Manchester Guardian*, 5 May 1921

# Table of Contents

| | |
|---|---|
| *Acknowledgments* | iv |
| *Preface* | 1 |
| *Introduction* | 3 |
| 1. Britain's War (1945–1946) | 7 |
| 2. Britain's War (1945–1946): Consolidation | 21 |
| 3. France's War (1945–1954) | 35 |
| 4. America's War (1954–1963) | 46 |
| 5. BRIAM: The British Advisory Mission to Vietnam | 53 |
| 6. America's War (1963–1968) | 59 |
| 7. America's War (1968–1973) | 78 |
| 8. The British Government's Political Involvement with Vietnam, or: What the Politicians Were Saying, and What They Were Really Doing | 95 |
| 9. Military Support, or: Did British Troops Fight in the Vietnam Wars? | 111 |
| 10. The British Army | 116 |
| 11. The Royal Navy | 126 |
| 12. The Royal Air Force | 135 |
| 13. Civilians, Conscripts, Mercenaries and R&R | 148 |
| 14. Sales of Military Hardware, or: How Many Guns, Tanks or Bullets Did Britain Sell for Use in Vietnam? | 161 |
| 15. Military Hardware: Sales, Contracts and Tenders | 179 |

16. Intelligence Support, or: What Was Britain Telling the
    Americans That They Didn't Know Already?                    214

17. Medals and Myths                                             220

18. What Was British Involvement in Vietnam Between 1946
    and 1973?                                                    225

*Appendices*
    *I. Chronology of the Vietnam Wars*   229
    *II. People and Organizations Associated with Vietnam: 1945–1975*   254
    *III. Allied Contributions to the Vietnam War: 1963–1973*   278
    *IV. British Forces in South Vietnam (September 1945–May 1946)*   280
    *V. Equipment Lists for Forces Operating in Vietnam: 1945–1975*   282

*Chapter Notes*     309

*Bibliography*     317

*Index*     319

# Preface

This book is concerned with the part Britain played in the wars in Vietnam between 1945 and 1975. It describes the role of the British in that country—first as peacekeepers after World War II, later as intermediaries in the French peace negotiations of 1954 and finally as allies to the Americans, although this last role was not without its hazards, as will be seen. Authors dealing with the French and American wars in Vietnam during this period have concerned themselves almost exclusively with the impact of those conflicts on the political relations between Britain and those two countries and, most especially, their influence on Britain's "special relationship" with the United States. This book is unique in dealing with the military, logistics and intelligence aspects of Britain's involvement and the steps taken by the political establishment to justify and, in some cases, obscure the nature of those activities.

This study is intended to be primarily an account of British involvement; consequently, a complete and comprehensive history of the French and American wars will not be found here, although sufficient detail is given for the reader to understand the context of Britain's role. Nor has any attempt been made to apportion blame or criticize any member of the various administrations described in the text (except in those cases where information obtained later has demonstrated their culpability). That task is left to the reader's best judgment.

The first chapters cover the periods of conflict in Vietnam that took place during the twentieth century and include a discussion of the role of the British Advisory Mission to Vietnam during that period. The succeeding chapters briefly discuss Britain's political stance before going on to give details of the amount of military support, arms and intelligence actually supplied by the United Kingdom and the prevalence of myths in the media concerning Britain's role. The concluding chapter discusses the real nature of British involvement in Vietnam, shorn of conspiracy theorists' hype. The text is based upon academic sources and original documents from the National Archives of Great Britain.

# Introduction

Much has been written about the situation in Vietnam after World War II, from both sides of the conflict, and blame for what happened there has been fairly equally apportioned.

The French began it in 1946, in what became a futile attempt to repossess what had once been one of their colonies. The Americans continued the conflict, with the help of many affluent South Vietnamese, because of what turned out to be the misplaced fear of a combined Russian and Chinese-inspired, Communist takeover of the region. The Vietnamese fought both the French and the Americans, despite appalling casualties, because they wanted their country back and enough rice to eat. Incidentally, they would probably have fought a Russian or Chinese invasion with the same ferocity and dedication.

Britain's role in the region in the immediate post-war period, from 1945 to 1946, was clear enough, although later it was to become more diffuse and even shadowy.

A force composed of Indian and some British troops, commanded by Major-General Douglas Gracey, was given the job of disarming and repatriating the Japanese, rescuing Allied POWs and re-establishing and maintaining law and order in what was later to become South Vietnam, after the Japanese cease-fire in 1945. This role, essentially a peacekeeping operation, had been largely completed when the British returned the region to French control in January 1946. In line with the Potsdam agreement and an Anglo-French accord, the British then left elements of the French Army and Civil Service to continue re-establishing itself in what had been that country's colony.

British overseas concerns immediately after that period centered first on Indian partition (1948) and subsequently on events in Brunei and Indonesia, part of the region later to become Malaysia, where British forces were to become involved in the Malayan Emergency and, subsequently, the Indonesian Confrontation (1948–1966). Britain, and in particular British industry, appears to have had little to do with the French during their operations in Vietnam, which is not unexpected, since arms sales between Britain and France had never been very extensive or lucrative. British political support for France's actions was positive but minimal during this period, although Anthony Eden was one of the major architects of the 1954 Geneva Agreement.

With America's entry into the region, British political and technical involvement became more significant. Products from a number of UK companies were included in the military supplies sent to Vietnam by the Pentagon, and most of this material was supplied to the U.S. military under normal government-approved contracts, despite Harold Wilson's assurance that Britain was not supplying arms for use in Vietnam. However, nothing sold by the British seems to have been designed or intended specifically for use in Southeast

Map of Vietnam ca. 1954 showing principal towns, the DMZ dividing north and south, the Mekong and Red rivers, the Hồ Chí Minh Trail and the site of the Leong Nok Tha air base.

Asia, although (perhaps not unexpectedly) some observers with political interests have attributed sinister motives to these transactions. Large, organized bodies of troops were not sent either, although there were cases of individual British citizens fighting in the region, and many Americans and South Vietnamese were certainly trained by British instructors, particularly at the Jungle Warfare School in Malaysia.

While there may have been individual cases of political bias, successive British governments were very well aware of the political sensitivity of any involvement in Vietnam. In general, they tried to act as a conscientious adviser to the various American administrations on matters involving Vietnam during this period (thus mirroring their stance on other issues), which was hardly surprising, given the potentially explosive postwar environment as well as Britain's increasingly weakened role in world politics and reliance on U.S. trade. However, it would not be unreasonable to claim that British support was sometimes inclined to be noncommittal and even self-effacing, at least in public. This was especially so when such support involved issues that might reflect negatively upon Britain's own colonial responsibilities, although, after 1963, these were becoming increasingly less important. Despite this considered public stance, however, there were certainly a few cases when it was suggested that financial expediency and concern about the U.S. response might be

*From left to right:* **Chiang Kai-Shek, Franklin D. Roosevelt and Winston Churchill during a pause in talks at the Cairo conference, 25 December 1943.**

allowed to quietly override official government policy, particularly when large and very lucrative arms contracts were involved.

Britain's involvement in America's Vietnam War has become one of history's minor myths. Secret deals, clandestine troop deployments, covert arms shipments—all these stories have appeared at various intervals, usually supported by what may be charitably described as flimsy evidence, if any evidence is presented at all. This book attempts to redress the balance and record the facts about Britain's role in Vietnam during the French and American wars, including something of what the British government failed to disclose at the time.

# 1

# Britain's War (1945–1946)

## Postwar Vietnam

Vietnam had been part of French Indochina (FIC) since its formation in October 1887. Initially, the colony consisted of North, Central and South Vietnam (then named, respectively, Tonkin, Annam[1] and Cochinchina) and the Kingdom of Cambodia, with Laos added in 1893, after the Franco-Siamese War. France was in control until Japan invaded in 1940 after being granted military access by France's Vichy government, and Japanese troops occupied the region until Japan's surrender in September 1945. British involvement in Vietnam officially began during World War II,[2] although the colonial administration in Burma and Malaya probably knew a significant amount about the political climate in those countries bordering their colonies prior to this period.

With the end of the war in Asia imminent, Allied representatives at the Potsdam Conference in July 1945 agreed that reoccupation of what had been French Indochina would be best achieved by simultaneous invasions from the north and south. The northern assault was to be conducted by Nationalist Chinese troops, while the British would push up from the south, with the two forces meeting and thus ending their respective troop movements at the 16th Parallel (of longitude). Allied opinion favored at least an interim return to French colonial rule for Vietnam, although Roosevelt himself was initially against even this temporary re-establishment of France's colonial status in the region. Unfortunately, such a neatly packaged solution did not take into account the intense nationalism of the Vietnamese and their leaders, nor their hatred of the previous French administration.

Hồ Chí Mính (president of North Vietnam; 1945–1969) had spent the war fighting the Japanese, leading partisans trained and

U.S. President Franklin D. Roosevelt, America's longest-serving president (four terms, from 1933 to 1945), in 1933. He orchestrated America's entry into World War II, but his anti-colonial convictions and inconsistent attitude toward the French resulted in difficulties at the end of the war in Indochina.

supplied with arms by the American OSS (Office of Strategic Services), forerunner of the CIA. With the Japanese effectively defeated, he prepared to cooperate with the Americans, probably in the hope that they would recognize his government and refuse to allow the French to repossess their former colony. Helped by the OSS and unrest stirred up by the disastrous famine that many Vietnamese rightly attributed to the Japanese, Ho's Việt Minh staged what would come to be known as the August Revolution (16 August 1945), taking over public buildings in a number of cities and culminating in the occupation of Hanoi on 19 August 1945. In response to these military operations, Bảo Đại, the Vietnamese emperor, abdicated, handing over sovereign power to the Việt Minh on 25 August 1945.[3]

Hồ Chí Mính in 1946. President of Democratic Republic of Vietnam from 1954 to 1969, predominantly nationalist in sentiment, he was forced into an unwelcome alliance with the Chinese Communists because France refused to negotiate with him.

Ho entered Hanoi late in August and, on 2 September 1945, declared the establishment of the Democratic Republic of Vietnam (DRV). With him at the ceremony were Archimedes Patti and other OSS officers, all saluting the DRV flag, which was flying over Hanoi's Citadel building, where, despite the American presence, the Việt Minh were still holding French POWs, many of them starving and wounded. Ho must have been intent upon cultivating the U.S. government during this period, because he included part of the U.S. Declaration of Independence in the text of his speech, although the OSS officers (particularly Patti) never seem to have realized the extent to which he was manipulating them.[4] Jean Sainteny, who knew Ho well and negotiated the first abortive agreement with him, wrote of the Americans in Vietnam during this period, "The infantile anti-colonialism of the Americans assisted to power a movement dominated by Communists with incalculable consequences."[5]

According to General Tran Van Dohn, it was not popular sentiment but the visible support of the Americans, in the person of a few OSS officers, that established Ho in government, and Ho himself emphasized the importance of American support during this period.[6] Even when the Việt Minh proclaimed the "Independent Government of Viet Nam" on 17 September 1945, they did not have the support of most South Vietnamese, who were nationalist, rather than Communist, in their sentiments.[7] It has even been suggested that without this early American support, the Communist movement in North Vietnam might never have become sufficiently well established to engage both France and, later, America in a series of wars the invading forces could not win.[8]

## China in the North

Using military and administrative powers temporarily granted him under the Potsdam Plan, China's leader, Chiang Kai-shek, dispatched the first of a force of 200,000 Chinese troops under General Lu Han into North Vietnam early in September 1945. Ostensibly there to disarm the Japanese, Han's ragged, starving troops followed the pattern that Chinese invaders had adopted for centuries and carried out a program of systematic looting on their way to Hanoi. This continued on an even larger scale once they arrived in the city, where the Chinese Nationalist soldiers raided Hanoi's markets continually and even forcibly entered private houses, where they stole everything, including door knobs and light bulbs. Without organized troops at his disposal and in a country weakened by years of war, Ho tried to bargain. He used gold donated to his regime by the citizens of Hanoi to bribe the senior Chinese officers, while also beginning political maneuverings to rid his country of the foreign troops and install a coalition government, although he knew the Chinese would force him to include his major political rivals, the Chinese-backed VNQDD, in any administration he formed.[9]

This newly established Hanoi administration was characterized by significant mismanagement, mainly because of internal dissension, which prevented its members from concentrating on North Vietnam's real economic problems. Their actions led to widespread dissatisfaction among the North Vietnamese, who attributed most of their problems to Hanoi's inept government, although Ho himself was still regarded as a hero. In the south, by contrast, a large proportion of the population knew nothing about the north's problems

**Douglas DC-3 Dakota, shown here landing supplies at Zamboanga in the Philippines in May 1945. The Dakota was the workhorse of the British army in Burma and was responsible for most of the supply drops that enabled Slim's men to defeat the Japanese. It also saw service in Vietnam over twenty years later as the AC-47 Spooky Gunship.**

and so welcomed the Việt Minh, who were perceived as a nationalist rather than a Communist-inspired organization. Despite their economic troubles, the North Vietnamese did, however, manage to organize shipments of arms and troops into the south, where they combined with more radical elements of the Việt Minh in a poorly organized guerrilla campaign, which began in September 1945,[10] despite having to accept aid from the Control Commission, in the form of tons of rice, to keep a significant proportion of their population from starvation.[11]

## *Britain in the South*

The nature of operations necessary in Japanese-occupied areas was determined, in part, by President Truman's General Order No. 1, which directed the Japanese to maintain law and order in their occupied areas until Allied forces could relieve and disarm them. In addition, the role of occupying forces in South Vietnam was encapsulated in a second document, Force Plan 1: "The Occupation of French Indo-China," drawn up by the Headquarters, Southeast Asia Command Joint Planning Staff (JPS). Britain and France had already agreed by mid–August that the French were to reassume responsibility for administration in FIC, and the JPS document reinforced that stance.[12] It also included the following statement, which was to dictate the conduct of the whole operation: "The eventual reoccupation of FIC is a matter for the French."[13]

General Slim (then commander-in-chief, Allied Land Forces, South-East Asia [ALFSEA]) based his directives to the generals under his command on Force Plan 1, which he delivered in the form of ALFSEA Operational Directive No. 8, giving all the generals who received it, including Douglas Gracey, particular responsibility for maintaining law and order in their respective areas of operations, along with their other duties.[14]

As a further complication, the JPS plan contradicted the view of the Americans, who, alone of the Allies, were publicly against the return of French colonial rule to Indochina (or anywhere else), although, earlier in the war, Roosevelt had expressly agreed that the French would retain control of their old colonies.[15]

Field Marshall W.J. Slim, shown here around 1950. Slim was given command of the Fourteenth Army late in 1943 and was responsible for the success of this group during the fighting in Burma. In particular, Slim's innovative use of aircraft to supply troops on the ground gave his men the advantage they required to defeat the Japanese. He supported Gracey's actions in South Vietnam and threatened to resign if Gracey were replaced.

Richard Dewey, in charge of OSS operations in Saigon, seems to have been particularly anti-colonial, as was Archimedes Patti, his colleague in Hanoi, which was one of several reasons why relations between the British and Americans in FIC were difficult, to say the least.[16] The Americans were intent upon preventing any return to colonial rule during this period, with one Foreign Office official almost echoing Sainteny's view when he described American foreign policy as apparently based on an event that had occurred two centuries before.[17]

Despite the fervor of these two OSS men, it seems everybody, even the Vietnamese, thought the French were coming back, and most saw their return as an interim arrangement, especially de Gaulle, who wanted Vietnam to become an independent state within the French Republic.[18] The only exceptions to this liberal view, unfortunately, were the influential French colonial residents who had spent their lives in the country and had everything to lose if it was returned to the Vietnamese. Harry Brain, Gracey's political adviser, wrote of them, in his report dated 27 September 1945:

> As I have said, their morale is low. They combine an almost hysterical fear of the Ammonites (which to my mind denotes a guilty conscience), with an intense hatred and desire for revenge. These people will constitute one of the greatest obstacles to the institution by France of a liberal policy and its acceptance by the Ammanites. If at all possible I think that these people should be evacuated from Indo-China at the earliest possible moment.[19]

Brigadier M. Myers, who was ordered by Mountbatten to conduct a full investigation into the situation in Saigon, shared Brain's opinion. He wrote that the majority of Vietnamese nationalists were not Communists and that the problems in Vietnam were mainly the result of French intransigence. Furthermore, the Vietnamese "did not want to become 'second-class' French colonial citizens once again," and Myers felt that the Communists would know how to turn that "nationalistic outburst" to their advantage.[20] Which was exactly what happened.

## Initial Preparations

When the Potsdam Conference divided Indochina at the 16th Parallel, Lord Louis Mountbatten (Supreme Allied Commander, South-East Asia [SACSEA]) was given the task of organizing the British contribution. To effect the surrender of the Japanese and control French Indochina until a permanent French administration could be returned, two separate bodies were created:

- The Allied Control Commission (for Saigon), to be primarily concerned with administration.
- Allied Land Forces French Indochina (ALFFIC), the body actually responsible for military and policing operations and originally intended to consist of an entire infantry division.[21]

Mountbatten appointed Major-General Douglas Gracey to both head the Control Commission and command the ALFFIC, initially dispatching the 80th Infantry Brigade, commanded by Brigadier D.E. Taunton, to serve as the land force. The 80th Brigade had previously been part of the 20th Indian Division, which Gracey himself had raised and subsequently commanded. After his appointment, Gracey was told that the rest of 20th Division would be sent to Saigon as soon as possible, to give him the force necessary to complete his task. (Brigadier Hirst actually commanded 20th Division on a day-to-day basis as Gracey's subordinate, Gracey himself being too preoccupied with the Control Commission to run the division as well.)

Gracey's orders at this point, both as Chief of the Control Commission and Commander of the Allied Land Forces, FIC, were clear.

Operations in FIC were to begin with the introduction of a force into Southern FIC to control the Japanese, evacuate POWs and maintain public order. Later, arrangements were to be made for the French to reassume control. Initially, Gracey, as Chief of the Control Commission, was ordered to:

- assume control of the headquarters of the Japanese Southern Army, supervise the surrender of Japanese forces and transmit Mountbatten's orders to Japanese headquarters.
- obtain information regarding Japanese dispositions and supplies.
- control Japanese communications.
- report on the POW situation and render all possible aid.
- report on FIC's communications, airfields and the port of Saigon.
- open river and sea approaches, using Japanese resources.
- reduce the size of the Japanese headquarters as soon as possible.
- maintain contact with the local French government, keeping Mountbatten informed.

In addition, as Allied Land Forces Commander, FIC (in orders communicated to him by General Slim in ALFSEA Operational Directive no. 12),[22] Gracey was further instructed to:

- secure the Saigon area, including the headquarters of the Japanese Southern Army.
- disarm and concentrate all Japanese forces in accordance with the policy laid down in headquarters' letters 10028/G(0)1, dated 19 and 28 August 1945 (this refers to Headquarters, Allied Land Forces, South-East Asia, *not* HQ, SEAC).
- maintain law and order and ensure internal security.
- protect, succor and subsequently evacuate Allied POWs and internees.
- liberate Allied territory as far as his resources permitted.

These orders also contained the following addition: "You will give such directions to the French Indo-China Government as are required to effect these tasks. In these matters you will consult the senior French Land Forces Commander." (This section of his orders applied most particularly to his decision to stage the coup d'état of 23 September.)[23]

These orders clearly gave Gracey no authority to make any political decisions; in particular, Mountbatten specifically ordered him not to enter into negotiations with, or even acknowledge, any Vietnamese political party, although later Gracey and his staff did oversee the first, fruitless negotiations between the French and Việt Minh. Gracey's instructions also clearly made him responsible for maintaining law and order, although there was concern both on his part and at South-East Asia Command (SEAC) headquarters about how these operations, intended as simple peacekeeping, might be interpreted by the Vietnamese. There was a long history of resistance to French rule in Vietnam, and it would be all too easy for the British to be drawn into fighting the Vietnamese nationalist forces, which were effectively a nationalist resistance movement only aimed at removing French colonial control, with little animosity toward the British. Not only would the British then be doing at least part of the work of the French for them, but, more importantly, such activities would also reflect negatively on their own role in the eyes of the inhabitants of other Far Eastern countries, which were intent upon independence themselves. Some in the Foreign Office felt it was possible that the French might even encourage British participation, by claiming the Vietnamese nationalist forces were inspired and controlled by the Japanese, who would be seen as intent upon causing maximum disruption to the Allies before relinquishing French Indochina. Significant numbers of the Japanese military were, in fact, later found to be encouraging the Việt Minh's guerrilla activities, as well as supplying them with arms.[24]

SACSEA's chief political officer, Esler Dening, was fully aware of these problems and concerned, in particular, about the French attitude and the political capital some in America might make out of Britain's enforced role. He offered a foretaste of the American attitude to Britain's involvement in Vietnam when he wrote, just before Gracey's arrival in Saigon, "I think we should at all costs avoid laying ourselves open to the accusation that we are assisting the West to suppress the East. Such an accusation would arise very readily to the lips of the Americans and Chinese and would be likely to create an unfavorable impression throughout Asia."[25]

Dening's major concern at this point was probably the Indian independence negotiations, although the British position in Malaya and Indonesia would also have been detrimentally affected by anything that reflected negatively on Britain's impartiality in Vietnam. His assessment was later to prove correct, with the production of a flurry of superficially researched newspaper articles and books about Vietnam and America's involvement there. A number of these publications, predominantly those by Americans, were uniformly critical of Britain's earlier Vietnamese operations in general, and of Douglas Gracey in particular.[26]

Gracey's task was problematic from the beginning. As head of the Allied Control Commission, he took his orders from Mountbatten, while as commander of the ALFFIC he was responsible to General Slim, commander-in-chief, Land Forces (S.E. ASIA). Given the level of duplication between the two bodies and their necessarily different perspectives of the operation, he could certainly expect some conflict in his orders. Slim, however, was obliged to further add to Gracey's difficulties with an amendment to his original orders, which was intended to forestall any French requests for armed assistance and limit the British role as far as possible. This amendment ordered Gracey to simply concern himself with the surrender of Japanese and to designate those areas he needed to control to achieve this goal, these sections being defined as "key areas." Gracey, incidentally, claimed that he did not receive this amendment until after the proclamation of 21 September (although the amendment is dated 12 August 1945, it was only a draft memorandum on this date and so was still awaiting approval, so it may well not have been sent to Gracey until its original text was finalized).[27]

Effectively, Gracey was now being ordered to dismantle the Japanese High Command structure, disarm and arrange the repatriation of Japanese troops, and offer humanitarian aid to Allied POWs and internees. However, in line with Slim's latest orders, he could only do this while using troops to maintain law and order in those "key areas" where he found it necessary to operate, and nowhere else. In other words, he was to do the job he had been sent to do, keeping British participation to a minimum, and get out as soon as he could, without contributing more to the French reoccupation operations than was absolutely necessary.

Unfortunately, it was not quite clear what might be appropriately designated a "key area" when there were over 70,000 Japanese troops widely distributed below the 16th Parallel who had to be collected, disarmed and sent home. This situation was to be immeasurably complicated later when, finding himself without sufficient troops of his own for internal security duties (due to the Việt Minh's guerrilla activities and delays in sending the rest of his division), Gracey was forced to allow armed Japanese to continue in this role in areas outside Saigon. Slim's orders to him also reinforced the role France was expected to play in postwar Indochina, even if the return was only a short one.

So, while disarming and removing the Japanese with as little fuss and expense as possible, Gracey was also expected to arrange things so that when the British left, French control would be secure, without, however, alienating the Vietnamese. And nobody, it seems, had given much thought to what role the Việt Minh might play, or included any instructions about how Gracey was to deal with them. As Maunsell himself said later, "All talk was once they got the Japs under control in those various places, there wouldn't be any more trouble…. It never entered our heads that there would be any problem caused from any other source than the Japanese."[28]

## Disarming the Japanese and Operation Masterdom

Japan announced its capitulation on 15 August 1945; by the end of that month, Gracey and his men were ready to move in the first stage of the British reoccupation, codenamed Operation Masterdom. Their departure for Vietnam was prevented, however, when General Douglas MacArthur ordered that no reoccupation should take place until he had received the formal Japanese surrender in Tokyo Bay aboard the battleship USS *Missouri*. This decision had disastrous consequences for French Indochina, delaying the British until 11 September and allowing the Việt Minh, in particular, the time they needed to establish themselves as a political entity in Saigon.[29]

When British troops finally began to arrive in force, they found the south, especially Saigon, in chaos, with rioting and every form of civil disorder widespread. The original Vichy French administration had disappeared, as a consequence of losing the vital support of the Japanese after their surrender, and armed Vietnamese police had been back in control since 25 August. They were proving ineffectual, however, and armed nationalist mobs were still out in force on the streets. What minimal organization there was came from a Việt Minh group, the Southern Committee, although its members lacked experience and were also proving ineffective, being unable to control even their own armed guerrillas. In particular, they had failed to prevent the rioting of 2 September, in which a number of French civilians were killed by members of the South Vietnamese police and armed forces; only the intervention of unarmed British and Australian POWs prevented further bloodshed. Alongside the Việt Minh, religious factions such as the Cao Dao and Hòa Hảo and political groups and criminals like the newly emerged Bình Xuyên were also maneuvering for power in the political and economic vacuum left by the Japanese. And as a final complication, both the Việt Minh and Japanese were still armed, the Việt Minh having been issued weapons by the Japanese in March 1945, in an attempt to use them to control dissident French residents. Some Japanese troops had even joined the Việt Minh and were acting as military advisers, although this was not confirmed by the British until some weeks later.[30]

The first small detachment of British troops (1/19 Hyderbad Regiment of India [1/19 Hyderbad])[31] flew into Saigon on 6 September 1945, escorting the advance party of the 20th Indian Division, consisting of an intelligence team, some engineers, medical staff, and an RAF detachment.[32] This group did not have the 9-man American signals unit that had been promised,[33] although the troops were equipped with radio sets, from which they sent back firsthand reports of the situation to Gracey, who was still in Rangoon. The main body of troops did not begin to arrive by air until five days later, on 11 September, and the full force was not on the ground until the next day. They consisted of two companies of 1/1 Gurkha Rifles (1/1 GR) and two companies of 1/19 Hyderbad, together with 80th Brigade headquarters staff and a tactical headquarters. The Hyderbads took control of the airfield and the Gurkhas posted guards on what was to be Gracey's residence, the mission compound and the signal exchange. 80th Brigade headquarters was established in the former Japanese staff quarters, which was in south-west Saigon and just across the road from the headquarters of the Japanese Southern Area Army.[34] By 13 September, there were still only 1,302 men and a meager 37 tons of stores in Saigon (Gracey eventually had over 20,000 troops in South Vietnam engaged on security and repatriation duties). Slightly less than a third of the troops were infantry and they had only small arms, rifles and a few Bren guns. The company mortars and heavy machine guns had been left behind because Headquarters thought their role would be purely ceremonial. This body of troops was tasked with beginning to disarm the 71,000 Japanese soldiers listed as present in French Indochina. In reality, they were insufficient even to establish complete control over Saigon itself.

Gracey arrived on 13 September to find himself faced with the bewildering complexity of Saigon's religious and political situation and an airfield perimeter guarded by armed Japanese troops. The Việt Minh's Southern Committee had sent a delegation to greet him, but he ignored them, having been expressly ordered by Mountbatten to recognize no political factions, and he acknowledged only the senior Japanese officers drawn up on the tarmac. Gracey initially had no specific orders concerning the Việt Minh, whom he and his superiors thought would be a problem for the French after the British had left the country.

The day after Gracey's arrival, 14 September, life in Saigon seemed to be proceeding normally, despite claims of complete control by the Việt Minh. At least that was how one of Gracey's subordinates, Brigadier M.S.K. Maunsell, saw things when he returned from a trip through the city, and he felt the Việt Minh claims of complete control were unlikely to be accurate, the first of several examples of Việt Minh exaggeration. On 15 September, in an attempt to win over the city's population, pamphlets were circulated by the Control Commission, condemning recent attacks on Europeans and explaining how the criminals responsible would be caught and punished by the authorities. General Slim arrived for an inspection tour on 16 September and, to his credit, quickly appreciated Gracey's difficulties. He recommended that the rest of the 20th Division should be sent to Saigon as soon as possible, although the whole division did not arrive until a month later (17 October). By then, this delay had caused the situation to deteriorate so much that Gracey was forced to utilize the Japanese, who had retained their weapons, and the French POWs.

In accordance with his responsibilities for organizing the Japanese surrender, the next day, 17 September, Gracey made a formal visit to the Japanese commander-in-chief, Field-Marshal Terauchi, to discuss plans for the formal surrender ceremony. In particular, he stressed that Terauchi himself should be personally responsible for controlling Japanese behavior (a sensible precaution, given the previous human rights record of some Japanese junior officers). On the same day the British also began turning over their captured arms dumps to the French, who, in turn, started using the weapons to rearm members of their colonial forces who had been POWs.

While Gracey was visiting the ailing field-marshal, the Việt Minh, having made little progress in their negotiations with the French, tried to force matters by declaring the establishment of "The Independent Government of Vietnam" from their base in Hanoi, claiming the right to govern the whole of Vietnam. Phạm Văn Bạch, who was part of the negotiating team, although not a member of the Việt Minh, also called for a general strike, to begin at midnight. The strike was intended to paralyze the city, with all Vietnamese ordered to cease any cooperation with the French, although the British, after negotiation with the Việt Minh, kept both the power station and the port operating. This was thought by many, including Gracey, to be the start of a planned insurrection, which had been timed to suit the Việt Minh perfectly. With the British and French still only present in small numbers and the Japanese willing to supply arms and experienced military personnel to the Việt Minh, this was that organization's best chance to seize control, and possibly prevent the return of the French, by confronting the British and showing the South Vietnamese in particular the extent of their power. To achieve this goal and obtain maximum propaganda value from their operations, their first objective had to be gaining control of Saigon.[35]

Gracey was forced now to take action against the Việt Minh, a step that had not been foreseen by anyone at SEAC, because, in his judgment, until the country was pacified and law and order re-established, it would be impossible to begin safely repatriating the Japanese and Allied POWs. In addition, the continued breakdown in security would involve unnecessary risk for his troops and vastly complicate the planned re-establishment of the French. Finally, and of no small importance, he believed that any indecision on the part of the British might be seen as an opportunity for further disruption by the Japanese military. Even an unsuccessful coup attempt in Saigon by the Việt Minh might have had a deleterious effect on the attitude of the Japanese, who were still armed and vastly outnumbered the British.[36]

He described the situation to Mountbatten in a telegram dated 19 September. In this report Gracey explained that, although the situation was not serious, in his view the Ammanite government constituted a direct threat to law and order through its armed Police Gendarmerie and Garde Civile, although it was exercising no real control in Saigon, even over its own members. He also noted that the Vietnamese press was daily becoming more violently tour anti–French (the reason he later banned the Vietnamese-owned newspapers) and Vietnamese propaganda was being distributed, aimed at subverting British troops. He proposed to calm the situation, initially by declaring martial law, although he does not appear to have specifically informed Mountbatten of his intentions.

Gracey began his campaign against the Việt Minh by giving instructions to restrict the press, banning the publication of some Vietnamese newspapers and ordering their leader, Trần Văn Giàu, to stop requisitioning buildings, return property that had been misappropriated, and keep his forces inactive and furnish a list of armed Việt Minh police and militia personnel.

Gracey also supplied Mountbatten with a copy of the proclamation he intended to issue on 21 September. This proclamation has attracted a certain amount of controversy, although, when read dispassionately, it is a relatively innocuous document that simply warns dissident groups that the Japanese were responsible for internal security. Moreover, it is similar to material issued by occupying forces in Thailand and the Dutch East Indies, and was almost standard procedure in areas under British control in Southeast Asia.[37]

In his proclamation, Gracey first explained that he was in command of all British, French and Japanese forces, as well as all police forces and armed bodies in FIC below the 16th Parallel, with orders to maintain law and order in that area.[38] He then went on to say he wanted to achieve this with minimal disruption and called on all citizens to cooperate in that aim, warning that all looters, saboteurs and other criminals would be summarily shot. Finally, he issued four orders, to go into immediate effect:

- No demonstrations or processions would be permitted.
- No public meetings would take place.
- No arms were to be carried, except by authorized personnel.
- A curfew would be enforced in Saigon and Cholon between 21:30 and 5:30 hours.

It was the sentence about maintaining law and order that caused trouble, but, contrary to the opinion of many observers (including Mountbatten, apparently), it only reiterated and reinforced President Truman's General Order No. 1, in that it made the Japanese responsible for law and order in their immediate vicinity. Gracey did not say that only British troops would be responsible for law and order, but rather that it was the task of *all* troops under his command (British, French and Japanese). In addition, Gracey made it clear to Mountbatten that he had no intention of trying to use his small force to control any area outside Saigon, although Mountbatten felt obliged to repeat this instruction to him.[39] In fact, Gracey had already decided to use mainly Japanese troops to control the Việt Minh. This was a shrewd decision, since the Việt Minh would be reluctant to fire on their former allies, more especially because some of the surrendered Japanese were supplying most of their arms.

Gracey issued this proclamation as planned on 21 September 1945 and subsequently, on 23 September, he telegraphed Mountbatten full details

Mountbatten's reply (also dated 23 September) criticized Gracey over the wording of the first paragraph, implying that he should not have claimed that the British were responsible for law and order in the whole of South Vietnam (which Gracey had not said), but only in key areas. However, the SAC said he would support Gracey, since he was "the man on the spot."[40] He also sent a telegram to the Chiefs of Staff (although, perhaps characteristically, not without first consulting Generals Slim and Leclerc), which said that he (Mountbatten) "considered that Major-General Gracey, in issuing his proclamation, had acted with courage and determination in an extremely difficult situation." Furthermore, Mountbatten claimed, if the riots Gracey feared had developed, his small force and the French population might well have been in grave danger. Gracey and his men, of course, had been in considerable danger since their arrival, and there can be no doubt that if he had waited and trouble had resulted, with further casualties on both sides, he would have been even more severely criticized. He was in a position familiar to most British officers and soldiers in general—"damned if he did and damned if he didn't."

Unfortunately, this view of the situation was not taken in the later report written by SEAC staff, in which Gracey was blamed for everything that went wrong in South Vietnam during 1945–1946 and Mountbatten given credit for all that went right.[41] Many in the Foreign Office and at SEAC headquarters, however, including Leclerc, agreed with Gracey's assessment of the situation in Saigon and his action in issuing the proclamation.[42] In addition, Leclerc was also concerned about the lack of French involvement in FIC and wrote a letter explaining his fears and criticizing American interference in the region.[43]

Mountbatten now reported to the Joint Chiefs of Staff that Gracey's actions left him only two options: either increase the troop numbers in FIC up to a division and try to control the whole of the country below the 16th Parallel or concentrate on the Japanese Supreme Headquarters only, leaving control of the country outside the key areas to the French. Mountbatten favored the second approach and Leclerc agreed but explained that he could achieve control only when enough French troops were in FIC. The French also favored this alternative because it was important to their own postwar plans to be seen as the real liberators of FIC.[44] However, those responsible in the Foreign Office understood that Gracey could not even safely repatriate the Japanese and POWs unless he was allowed to establish control in the south, and after consultation, the Joint Chiefs of Staff released him from Mountbatten's restrictions.[45]

The Việt Minh responded to Gracey's proclamation by trying to intensify the strike, but they also sent him a letter, claiming they desired to cooperate with the British but asking for some relaxation of Gracey's controls. Gracey responded positively, saying that he would renew publication of those newspapers owned by "men of integrity and high repute," in addition to looking at how Radio Saigon might "best serve the interests of the country."

Despite these assurances, it had been clear from the arrival of the Control Commission on 13 September that the Việt Minh had to be removed from any position of authority in South Vietnam, because a returning French administration could not function in association (or, more probably, in competition) with them. In addition, although it had originally been the intention of the British to negotiate such a change with the Việt Minh, it was soon clear that no single body or individual had overall executive control of that organization in and around Saigon, as Gracey had previously reported to Mountbatten (in a telegram dated 19 September 1945). This meant that any agreement entered into with the Southern Committee was worthless, as it would be ignored by some of their own men as well as by the equally strong groups then maneuvering for control, such as the Trotskyites.[46] Moreover, the Việt Minh had tried once to wrest power from the occupying forces, and there was no reason to suppose they, or some other independent group, would not make a second attempt. In response to this situation, and with French agreement, Gracey decided to stage a coup d'état, replacing the inept Southern Committee of the Việt Minh with French civil servants.[47] This would involve disarming those Việt Minh still in Saigon, removing the Southern Committee's representatives from the city's public buildings and then reinstating the French civil servants remaining in the country. Gracey, incidentally, was not confident about the quality of these French officials, doubting their ability to run even Saigon's civil administration. In this, along with his other criticisms of French attitudes, he was, unfortunately, proven to be all too correct.

Even before the issue of the proclamation, Gracey's troops had begun the operations necessary to return control of Saigon to the French. They started by systematically disarming the Việt Minh police, a task that should have been done by the Japanese, and on 20 September, they carried the plan forward by seizing Saigon's central prison. On the night of 21/22 September, 1/19 Hyderbad took over two police stations and the civil jail, where they relieved and disarmed the Việt Minh in charge. At the same time, a detachment of 1/19 Hyderbad troops also occupied the Treasury, while 1/1 Gurkha Rifles took over the post office, removing the Việt Minh officials then in charge from both buildings.

The *coup d'état* proper began on the night of 22/23 September, with rearmed French forces (a total of 300 men, composed of 5th RIC, 11th RIC and some armed civilians) occupying the Việt Minh police posts and the Town Hall before placing guards on the five bridges over the Arroyo de l'Avalanche. During the same period, 1/19 Hyderbad had taken control of both the Bank of Indochina and the nearby Japanese-owned Yokohama Specie Bank, which they subsequently turned over to the French. On the morning of 23 September, 1/1 GR turned over the post office, which also contained the telegraph and telephone exchange, to the French, while the city prison was handed over by 1/19 Hyderbad at 1100 hours. Unfortunately, when the prisoners saw the French resuming control they tried to escape, along with a number of warders, and order did not return until 1/1 GR reoccupied the prison at 1400 hours.

With control apparently well established in Saigon, the operation should have concluded peacefully, but now the French, apparently incensed against their Việt Minh captors, began a series of reprisals. No Vietnamese were killed during the coup or as a result of the subsequent French actions, contrary to some accounts (the only casualties were two Frenchmen), but there was violence and "rough handling" by the French against Vietnamese civilians. This so incensed Gracey when it was reported to him that he ordered Jean Cédile and the other senior French officials to his HQ, where he summarily ordered the perpetrators be disarmed and punished, stating that he would have nothing more to do with the French until this was done. Their actions after the coup seem to have finally confirmed for the Việt Minh and many ordinary Vietnamese that the French were intent upon re-establishing the prewar status quo, aided by the British, and many Vietnamese historians date the beginning of their county's fight for independence from the day of the coup.

With the French back in power, Gracey divided the city into two sectors, North and South, in order to achieve better control. The northern sector (bounded in the north by a waterway, the Arroyo de l'Avalanche, and in the south by the Rue Verdun) was the responsibility of an advance party of 100 Brigade (under Lt. Col. Murray), along with 1/1 GR, some French forces and two armed Japanese regiments. The southern sector became the responsibility of Lt. Col. Purcell, commanding his own 3/1 GR, 1/19 Hyderbad, some men of 4 Dogra, a number of French police and an armed Japanese regiment. Despite this armed presence, on the night of 24/25 September, a group of Vietnamese (probably Trotskyites) managed to penetrate the French residential district of Cité Heyraud and murder 150 French civilians, including some women and children. They also captured approximately 100 more people, many of whom were subsequently tortured and killed. In perhaps the worst aspect of this situation, the area was guarded by Japanese troops, who simply allowed the Vietnamese to pass through into the residential quarter. It was this massacre of French civilians that enabled Cédile to later persuade Gracey to allow French POWs to be rearmed and returned to the streets (no date for this found).

Events at SEAC Headquarters were also starting to affect the situation in FIC, with Gracey being warned on 25 September that the whole of 20th Division might not be available for deployment there. Mountbatten had even signaled the Joint Chiefs of Staff that he wanted to stop the build-up of British forces in FIC, so as to force the French into resuming their responsibilities more speedily.[48] To facilitate this development, Gracey was now ordered to restrict the activities of British forces to a specific perimeter, large enough to ensure the safe working of the port of Saigon and the airfield, while allowing the rapid concentration and disarming of the Japanese.[49] Mountbatten also told the Joint Chiefs that "I have re-affirmed my orders to Gracey that he is not to employ British Forces outside key areas unless called upon by the French, in which case matter is to be referred through me to HMG."[50]

This appears to be the first indication Gracey had that he was to confine himself to operations only within "key areas," and it cannot have been very welcome because the Việt Minh were now attacking in force and British troops were involved in heavy street fighting in Saigon starting 24 September, with both British and Việt Minh forces suffering a number of casualties. British troops in Saigon were still only three infantry battalions, plus one company and the noncombatant Control Commission (1/1 GR, 1/3 GR, 4/10 GR and a company of 1/19 Hyderbad).

# 2

# Britain's War (1945–1946)
## *Consolidation*

When reports of the coup reached SEAC HQ, Mountbatten sent an experienced officer, Brigadier Myers, to report on the situation. Myers arrived following an eventful journey, and on 25 September, after consulting him, Gracey send a report to SEAC, reiterating what he now considered his main tasks. Gracey told SEAC bluntly that the Southern Committee (a.k.a. Southern Republic of Vietnam), which had been acting as the provisional government, was controlled from Hanoi, and that it was a menace to law and order and had needed to be removed to allow the re-establishment of the French and the return of proper administrative control. This, he explained, was the reason for his implementation of the coup d'état of 23 September. He then described how French provocation had resulted in a violent response by the Việt Minh and, as a result, just the appearance of French troops was now resulting in further violence by Saigon's residents. Gracey finished by making a number of recommendations, which included speeding up the deployment of the remainder of the 20th Division and the introduction of better-quality, experienced French troops. He also suggested that the British needed to remain until all the Japanese were out of the country.[1]

On 26 September, Gracey sent another report via telegraph. This one contained an apology for the trouble his proclamation had caused and thanked Mountbatten for his support. He assured the SAC that he had never intended to use his troops outside the Saigon-Cholon area and then went on to describe the increasing deterioration of the situation in Saigon and its outlying districts.

He explained how roadblocks were being set up around Saigon and Cholon by the Việt Minh, in some cases 30 kilometers (20 miles) from the city, and that mob violence was increasing. Gracey stated that the Japanese were reluctant to either protect French civilians or fire on the Việt Minh, so he had instructed Field-Marshal Terauchi to report to his HQ, where he ordered Terauchi to improve Japanese efficiency and ensure the safety of French civilians. Gracey stated that Terauchi was genuinely angry at his men's behavior and passed on stringent orders that improved the situation dramatically, ensuring the safety of French citizens and the security of vital installations from that time forward (this remained the situation until both the British and the Japanese left Indochina). In his telegram of 26 September, Gracey also sent a list of incompetent French colonial officials he wanted replaced and then went on to outline his future plans. He described these in five parts:

- Keep clear the northern approaches to Saigon, using Japanese troops.
- Keep Saigon secure, this time using British and Indian troops, while deploying the French as little as possible.
- Reopen the markets and encourage trade.
- Reopen Saigon Radio and urge the French to broadcast a prepared liberal policy statement.
- Clear the southern approaches to Saigon.

Finally, he repeated his request for the rest of 20th Division and some "good quality" French troops.[2]

British and Japanese forces combined to begin clearing Việt Minh roadblocks around Saigon on 26 September, and after releasing a number of French captives in an operation in the Dakao area, a company of 3/1 GR received a call to go to the assistance of the OSS detachment in the north of Saigon. Upon arriving at the OSS building, it transpired that the Việt Minh had fired on an American vehicle, killing the head of OSS in South Vietnam, Lt. Col. Peter Dewey.[3]

Violence in Saigon was increasing, making the situation for the British troops there increasingly desperate. Gracey still had only three battalions (1/1 GR, 1/3 GR, 4/10 GR and a company of 1/19 Hyderbad) to control the whole city, in collaboration with the Japanese and French, and between the intransigence of some of the former and the incompetence of the latter, his men were becoming worn out. Gracey appealed again to be sent the rest of 20th Division and, in the meantime, ordered trucks loaded with Indian, Gurkha and Japanese soldiers to patrol the city, dispersing mobs, shooting snipers and dismantling any roadblocks they found. The two area commanders, Lt. Col. Murray in the north and Lt. Col. Purcell in the south, maintained control, but mob violence and rioting still occurred almost nightly, and it was clear that the Japanese were also cooperating closely with the Việt Minh and, in some cases, leading their forces. In addition, Murray and Purcell's men had to respond to daily calls to rescue French and Indian civilians. These operations, with their casualties, civilian atrocities and especially clandestine Japanese involvement, also brought about a hardening of attitudes among Gracey's Indian and Gurkha veterans, which was reflected in their treatment of the Việt Minh in the following months.[4] The difficulties British troops endured following the coup and the subsequent Việt Minh uprising were described at the time in the plain words of the 3/1 Gurkha Rifles newsletter, here reproduced in full:

During the whole of this period, bazaars, factories and "go-downs" (shacks) were burnt nightly. French women, children and irregular troops were murdered and altogether the French com-

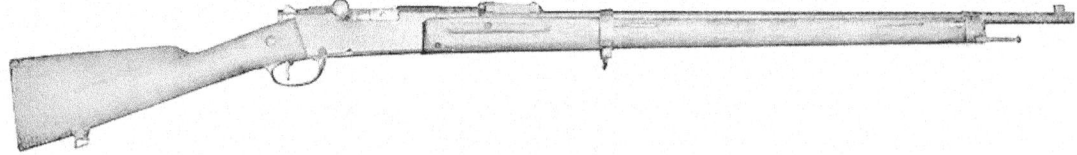

**Lebel M1886 bolt-action rifle, extensively used by French forces in Indochina and by the Việt Minh. Chambered for the early 8×50mm R Lebel cartridge, it possessed several obsolete features—most importantly, the tubular under-barrel magazine, into which cartridges could only be loaded singly, unlike the later Lee-Enfield and M-1 Garand, which were both designed for clip-loading.**

munity lived indoors in terror of their lives. The Battalion was roughly disposed to keep open Boulevard de Gallieni, the streets up to the Arroyo Chinois, and to protect vital points such as the fire station, leaving a small mobile force which was used exhaustively, dashing from the scene of one place of lawlessness to another.[5]

This account shows clearly that most of the troops' problems stemmed from a lack of personnel, which would not have been the case if the 20th Division had arrived as planned.

In addition to problems of internal security, the Japanese Headquarters organization, which it was the Control Commission's job to dismantle, was becoming problematic. Even before Gracey's occupation, Japanese staff organization had been poor because the system operated in small, self-contained departments. This meant that only officers within specific departments knew what was going on there, and Harry Brain, Gracey's chief political adviser, also claimed that even the most senior officers knew very little about their own departments, relying instead upon their immediate subordinates for information and even decisions. In addition to this kind of inefficiency, Brain wrote that he had no doubt there was some kind of underlying organization intent upon making the change to Allied control (with its consequent return to a stable administration) difficult, if not ultimately impossible.[6] The British had previously confirmed the existence of this covert operation to their own satisfaction after observing uniformed Japanese soldiers leading Việt Minh groups attacking their units and finding Japanese weapons in use by captured Việt Minh. Despite a number of setbacks, however, the Control Commission finally managed to complete its examination of the Japanese Headquarters and arrange for its closure by the middle of October.

Gracey, Cédile and Brain were summoned to a meeting in Singapore with Mountbatten on 28 September, where Gracey was once again obliged to explain his reasons for issuing the proclamation, which he did with some force.[7] He added that he was sure the Japanese were behind most of the disorder in Saigon and that he was preparing a list of those responsible, which included members of the Kempeitai, who could be brought to trial at a later date. Gracey then asked for the rest of his division to be sent to Saigon. With the notable exception of Mountbatten, he received the support of all the generals present, including Slim and Leclerc, and it was after this meeting that a firm decision was made to dispatch the rest of the 20th Division. In addition, on 30 September, the Joint Planning Staff (JPS) in London sent a report to the Joint Chiefs of Staff, strongly suggesting that Gracey be authorized to control the Saigon area and assist the French, so long as, by doing so, he did not compromise the security of Saigon.[8] The Joint Chiefs forwarded these instructions to SEAC and Gracey was then released from the restrictions (the key areas, Saigon perimeter, etc.) previously imposed upon him by Mountbatten. The SAC also allowed Gracey to make a statement to the effect that, although he had no wish to interfere in the internal politics of FIC, he would not tolerate activities that impeded either the orderly administration of his major tasks or the internal security of the country. Incidentally, when Gracey returned from Singapore, he reported that Mountbatten had decided to relieve him of his command, only to be told by General Slim that "if he [Gracey] goes, I go!"

Saigon continued in turmoil, with rioting taking place almost every night, often until dawn, and, since he was still without sufficient troops to ensure control of the city, Gracey compromised. On 1 October, he met with the Việt Minh leaders to organize a truce and arrange for the French representatives and South Vietnamese leaders to meet for discussions, with a British representative present. The meeting resulted in the declaration of a

**Members of France's 6th Commando CLI entering Saigon in November 1945 while surrendered Japanese soldiers salute them.**

cease-fire starting at 1800 hours on 2 October and a meeting between the Việt Minh and the French on 3 October, although Gracey privately informed Mountbatten that he was not optimistic about the possibility of any progress between the two parties or the long-term prospects for the truce.[9] The meeting took place as arranged, but afterward one of the Việt Minh negotiators, Dr. Thach, spoke with Gracey's representative, Harry Brain, informing him that he felt that the Việt Minh's political negotiations would be detrimentally affected, perhaps fatally, by the activities of extremists in his party. However, things were at last beginning to move in the right direction, because on 5 October, Leclerc and the first contingent of French troops arrived in Saigon.

## The French Arrive

Upon his arrival, Leclerc was met as he left his Dakota by Gracey and members of his staff. A French proclamation was issued to coincide with Leclerc's arrival, in which it was stated, among other things, that France intended to "build on your ruins, work for the well being and prosperity of your families whose great traditions are the best guarantees of peace and prosperity; this can only be achieved if order reigns." Significantly, the whole focus of this document was on the past glories of Indochina, under the French, without any mention of future independence, a fact that could not have escaped even observers less critical of French foreign policy than the Việt Minh.

On 6 October another meeting took place between the French and the Việt Minh, which again resulted in no further progress being made, as did a second, subsequent meeting on the 9th.[10] Gracey sent Lt. Col. Murray to Cambodia on the same day, 9 October, as Commander, Allied Land Forces, Cambodia, with orders to take control and disarm the Japanese; also at this time, Brigadier Hirst informed the Việt Minh of Gracey's intention to move troops into the northern suburbs of Saigon, with a clear warning that they were there only to disarm the Japanese and that they should be received peacefully. Gracey's reinforcements were also beginning to arrive at last—32nd Brigade had come, together with an additional 7,150 troops and 507 vehicles arriving by sea at intervals between 6 and 11 October, although this was overshadowed by an event that marked a change in the attitude of the British to the Việt Minh, when the truce was broken without any warning on 10 October.

A Royal Engineer reconnaissance party, with an escort from "B" Company 2/8 Punjab and drivers from 9/14 Punjab, had been sent to inspect water lines between Saigon and Ton Son Nhut airfield. On their return journey, they were ambushed by a large group of Vietnamese; four men were killed and the rest wounded. The airfield at Ton Son Nhut itself was also attacked, although the Gurkhas in possession repulsed the attack with mortar fire, killing six Việt Minh.[11] There were also a number of other attacks, which seemed to indicate that these operations were part of an organized series intended to incite British retaliation.[12] The Việt Minh justified this resumption of violence by claiming that the British were acting simply as a screen for the build-up of French forces; in this context, it may be significant that the attacks began soon after Leclerc's arrival. The Việt Minh further claimed that the British were not impartial, but had always intended that the French reassume *permanent* control of the whole of FIC. Gracey and Ernest Meiklereid, the new political adviser, wrote to Mountbatten of the new conditions.[13] Gracey, incidentally, had said as early as 1 October that unless the French offered the Vietnamese some form of autonomy, fighting was inevitable. These incidents put an end to the truce and, more importantly, gave further proof (if it was needed) that the Việt Minh leaders in reality exercised little control over their forces, whatever their claims to the contrary.

32nd Brigade, together with some Japanese, deployed as planned into Saigon's northern suburbs on 11 October and established themselves in Gia Định, after overcoming strong Việt Minh resistance. With the end of the truce, fighting intensified, culminating in a Việt Minh attack on the Tan Son Nhut airfield on the night of 12/13 October, which was beaten off by the 16th Cavalry, with heavy losses for the Vietnamese forces. In addition, the British found further evidence of formed bodies of Japanese troops fighting with the Việt Minh.[14]

Having failed to dislodge the British by direct assault, the Việt Minh now returned to their attempts to isolate Saigon from the surrounding countryside. Reconnaissance by the RAF revealed roadblocks and demolished buildings on all roads out of the city, with large concentrations of Vietnamese troops in certain areas. British forces were still involved in heavy fighting, especially in the northern suburbs of Saigon, where they were gradually pushing out the Việt Minh, while the Japanese bore the brunt of the anti–Việt Minh operations, although the arrival of the French 9 RIC (Colonial Infantry Regiment) was imminent.

The military situation for the Allies now began to improve rapidly, with the British moving out of Saigon to control the country to the north and the French going south.

Gracey's plan was to establish complete control over the rough triangle formed by the northern towns of Thủ Đức, Biên Hòa and Thủ Dầu Một, and then concentrate most of the Japanese troops there for processing and subsequently transfer them to Cap St. Jacques for shipment home. Unfortunately, the Control Commission's intelligence officers had reliable information from both Japanese and local sources that most of the Việt Minh troops were also in this triangle, and if it was to be used for processing the Japanese, it would have to be made secure and the Việt Minh driven out. This task was given to the newly arrived 100th Brigade, under Lt. Colonel C.H.B. Rodham, who had reached Saigon on 17 October.[15]

The British began their move north on 23 October, with elements of 100th Brigade occupying Thủ Đức that day, Biên Hòa on the 24th and Thủ Dầu Một on the 25th. Fighting was light and sporadic in all three locations, as the main bodies of Việt Minh troops had left the towns sometime in the previous 24 hours. Col. Rodham had already informed the Japanese officer previously in control of these areas, the inept General Manaki, that the British were coming and, once they arrived, Japanese troops in those towns would come under the command of British officers. The Việt Minh now appeared to be drawing back from the expanding Allied perimeter, confining themselves to minor guerrilla operations, which allowed the British to begin patrolling beyond their designated border, with the intention of encouraging the rural Vietnamese to resume their normal lives. The French, commanded by Lt. Col. Jacques Massu in their first postwar operation in FIC, went south on 24 October, supported by the British and Japanese, and captured Mỹ Tho.[16]

Back in Saigon, on 25 October, part of Cholon was accidentally burned down after the death of a 92 Field Company sentry, guarding an essential well, made necessary the destruction of some neighboring huts that the Việt Minh had been using for cover. Only one hut had actually been set alight by the British troops, but a strong wind moved the fire into an adjacent block, which, being made largely of thatch, immediately caught fire, creating an inferno half a mile long and a quarter of a mile deep. The whole of Cholon, Saigon's Chinese quarter, seemed threatened, because there was no time to make a fire break and the Việt Minh had removed all the fire appliances. Fortunately, the wind suddenly dropped and it began to rain, quenching the flames. It was this incident that apparently served as the basis for the accusation that the British had deliberately burned down great sections of the native quarter of Saigon, which was not what happened.[17] Those who made this argument also failed to mention the Việt Minh's own arson campaign, in which they incinerated much of South Vietnam's most valuable commercial property (rubber dumps, warehouses, etc.) on an almost daily basis, their activities being further exacerbated by their theft of all Saigon's fire appliances.[18]

With the British northern perimeter now well established and the French gaining control of the south, Gracey instructed Rodham to extend his operation offensively, so as to consolidate the triangle he intended to use to concentrate the Japanese, by removing or rendering ineffective the Việt Minh guerrillas. In order to achieve this objective, Rodham was ordered to organize a group, under the command of a reliable officer, to move out of Biên Hòa and attack the Việt Minh in their rural bases. Rodham selected Major L.D. Gates (14/13 Frontier Force Rifles) to command the detachment, now designated "GATEFORCE," which would consist of 500 Japanese infantry (Sato *butai*, or battalion), a squadron of armored cars from 16th Cavalry, and a company of 14/13 FFR, together with field ambulance, machine gun, mortar and Royal Engineer detachments.

Gates was ordered to establish a patrol base some miles east of Biên Hòa at Xuân Lộc, patrol the adjacent Baria road and then return to Biên Hòa. He was to use maximum force against enemy opposition, disarm all armed Vietnamese and burn any village in which opposition was encountered. This abrupt approach had a simple purpose: to inform the Việt Minh that there was no safe place from which to conduct offensive operations and convince the villages that harboring guerrillas would result in punishment. Most of GATEFORCE left Biên Hòa on 29 October, collecting the Japanese from Trảng Bom on their way east and arriving outside Xuân Lộc as darkness fell. Gates had received information that 300 lightly armed Việt Minh had left Trảng Bom a day before his arrival, so he remained outside the city and asked for a company to be sent out to establish a base at Trảng Bom, thus protecting his line of retreat. Trảng Bom was occupied early on the morning of 30 October; at 13:30 on the same day, Gates reported that his force had been attacked at dawn and that they had returned fire, forcing the Việt Minh to withdraw, pursued by a company of Japanese. GATEFORCE then entered Xuân Lộc and began using their armored cars to patrol. The next day, despite the only bridge between Trảng Bom and Xuân Lộc having been destroyed, GATEFORCE attacked the Việt Minh again, this time in a plantation area near Xuân Lộc. In the two days of GATEFORCE operations, approximately 250 Việt Minh were killed and many more wounded or captured, almost wiping out the Việt Minh's organized force in that area. More importantly, transport difficulties and French counter-guerrilla operations meant that it was many years before the Việt Minh had a significant body of troops in the Xuân Lộc district again. Despite this resounding success, Gracey received yet another letter from Mountbatten criticizing his wording of a propaganda leaflet, demanding to know why it was necessary for British troops to burn down areas of Saigon and asking if the French could not be given the job instead. Gracey replied by explaining the nature of the pamphlet and providing an explanation of the other incidents.[19]

Back in Saigon, the Việt Minh had stopped trying to fight the Allied troops in conventional engagements and settled down to a pattern, which was to become very familiar in later years, of sabotage and small-scale operations against isolated patrols. Gracey's men, however, achieved considerable success in this type of warfare against the Việt Minh irregulars, being both highly experienced and well led by competent professionals, from division down to platoon and section level. In addition, many had experience in controlling civil disorder in India and on the northwest frontier, and they were also greatly helped by the antagonism within the Việt Minh between the northern Tonkinese troops, recently brought in as reinforcements, and the southern Ammanites,

From the beginning of November, as a consequence of the activities of GATEFORCE and the French, Gracey's troops were increasingly able to shift the emphasis of their operations from general peacekeeping to pacifying and controlling those areas they needed to use for concentrating and disarming the Japanese. Gates returned to Biên Hòa on 2 November, leaving the Japanese infantry as a garrison in Xuân Lộc to prevent the remaining Việt Minh from returning to the area. On the other side of the city, the activities of the 32nd Brigade and another mobile column (designated "CLARKOL") under the command of Major R.W. Clarke (second-in-command 1/1GR), operating around Ben Cat from 8 November, had also pushed the Việt Minh out of Saigon to the northwest and well away from Gracey's triangle. The French participated in this operation, advancing from Mỹ Tho to Tay Ninh and then sending patrols toward Ben Cat to drive the Việt Minh in that direction.

Clarke's men captured 106 prisoners and the Japanese Yamagashi *butai* remained to garrison Ben Cat and prevent the return of the Việt Minh.

Clarke was unenthusiastic about the French troops he saw in action.[20] He wrote, "They really were a band of pretty unruly cut-throats and it was subsequently no surprise to me that they were not accepted in the country by the Vietnamese." Giving just one example of French military operations, he wrote:

> Their method of "pacifying" a village, without any provocation or indication that the place might be hostile, was to drive through in American 3-ton trucks, .300 machine guns on the cab, all guns firing on alternate sides of the street at first floor level, in case someone might be about to snipe at the column. They seldom hit anyone but if that is the way friends arrive it is little wonder that the Vietnamese threw them out.

The important Thủ Đức, Biên Hòa and Thủ Dầu Một triangle was now well protected and relatively safe. The nearest Việt Minh were some miles distant from the towns and two Japanese garrisons offered further protection, in the east at Xuân Lộc and in the west at Ben Cat. This meant Gracey could finally begin his original task of concentrating and disarming the Japanese with reasonable confidence that the unarmed troops would not be molested.

## *The British Depart*

There were still significant problems, however. The Japanese were becoming increasingly difficult about working with the French, referring to their plans as "scheme less." Gracey agreed with them and, in addition, predicted that "the French troops are leaving a pretty good trail of destruction behind them ... which would result in guerrilla warfare, increased sabotage and arson as soon as we leave the country."[21]

However, British anti-guerrilla activities and the increasing French presence meant that the Japanese could be relieved and disarmed in some areas. This began to happen with increasing frequency from mid–November onward, with the relief of British units also beginning on 23 November. In addition, large quantities of Japanese ordnance were being collected, although, because of the nature of the country, much more was probably stolen by or supplied to the Việt Minh. There were also problems with Vietnamese currency being hoarded by the Japanese.[22] Mountbatten formally received Field-Marshal Terauchi's surrender on 30 November in Saigon. While in the city, the SAC conducted a meeting with Leclerc and d'Argenlieu in which the program for British departure was eventually agreed on, although Gracey and Leclerc were left to organize the details.

Col. Woodford's 32nd Brigade was relieved by the French between 18 and 19 December, being declared non-operational on 20 December, prior to their move to a new deployment in North Borneo. The French were now assuming control of Saigon and finding themselves continually engaged by Việt Minh guerrilla forces. By contrast, in the south around Cap St. Jacques, the Việt Minh were cooperating with 9/12 FFR, which was controlling the area. On 6 and 7 December, the 9/12 FFR Adjutant, Japanese representatives and local Vietnamese met to decide on the distribution of the Japanese before their departure from FIC and discuss the evacuation of certain areas by the Vietnamese to allow the arriving Japanese to occupy them. The Vietnamese even went so far as to say they were willing to cooperate with the British as long as no French troops returned to the area.

Gracey and his men were still having trouble with the French, and the general became so incensed by the attitude of the French rank and file toward his Indian soldiers that he wrote to Leclerc, demanding that the French show his men proper respect, criticizing them in particular for their constant reference to his troops as "black men."[23] Meiklereid, Gracey's chief political officer, had more to say about their behavior in his report to Dening on the 15 December, explaining the problems being created by the new arrivals' arrogant behavior and lack of discipline, as well as their conduct of the clearing operations they were involved in. The colonial French (colons) did not like them, and, to make matters worse, the Saigon Vietnamese were refusing to cooperate with the French civil administration, with many in both groups perturbed by the thought that the British departure would be a signal for the Việt Minh to step up their guerrilla activities.

The first contingent of British troops (32nd Brigade) departed from Saigon between 25 and 27 December. The 80th Brigade was also moving, in the process of withdrawing from Cholon (Saigon's Chinese section), which left 100th Brigade to deal with the Việt Minh and disarming and repatriating the remaining Japanese. Brigadier Rodham, commanding 100th Brigade, received intelligence on 31 December that the Việt Minh were planning a coordinated operation between 1 and 10 January as "a last grand offensive before the British leave." In order to discourage this, 100th Brigade carried out a series of preemptive strikes against Việt Minh concentrations[24] between 1 and 5 January 1946. Rodham had good intelligence that the locals were tired of military operations and the Việt Minh were becoming discouraged, so he hoped that action now might prevent the Việt Minh from attacking the British in the period before their final withdrawal.[25] Just prior to this operation,

De Havilland DH-98 Mosquito multi-role combat aircraft. Operated in Vietnam between 1945 and 1946, principally against Việt Minh roadblocks.

however, British patrols confirmed that Việt Minh activity in the countryside at night was increasing and becoming more extensive, with armed bands very common and moving around at will. Numbers were increasing, too, and there was at least one attack, directed against 14/13 FFR on 3 January, by Việt Minh troops in battalion strength. Tactically, the Việt Minh were also becoming more knowledgeable; the attack on the 14/13 FFR was carried out by five separate units attacking simultaneously, although the attack itself proved ineffective because the Việt Minh were still poorly armed.

The French were now well on course to assume complete responsibility for FIC and they informed the British to that effect. 80th Brigade was finally relieved of all commitments in Vietnam on 11 January. The rest of the 20th Division was also rapidly moving out of South Vietnam, with 114th Field Regiment, RA, leaving on 10 January, followed by 16th Light Cavalry (except "C" Squadron) on 12 January. 80th Brigade finally departed Saigon on schedule on 22 January aboard the SS *Ordana*.

Command of all French forces in FIC was assumed by General Leclerc on 28 January, the day Gracey left Saigon for good (French troops had previously been under Gracey's authority since their arrival, despite Leclerc's presence), and from this date, violence between the French and Việt Minh began to intensify. Before his departure, Gracey was accorded a singular honor, being made a Citoyen d'Honneur of Saigon, in addition to receiving compliments on his actions from many Vietnamese. Command of the remaining British troops in Saigon was now the responsibility of Brigadier Hirst; these troops consisted of 4/10 GR (due for relief on 5 February), one company 2/8 Punjab and a single Jat machine gun (MG) company. All Japanese troops in Vietnam were due to be relieved by 15 February, when

**Super-marine Spitfire. Although deployed by the RAF in South Vietnam, RAF pilots flew no sorties against the Việt Minh. Some of these aircraft were turned over to the French when the RAF left the region (Wikipedia; Creative Commons).**

**Douglas DC-3 Dakota, with U.S. Air Force markings.**

they would proceed to Cap St. Jacques. 100th Brigade left Saigon on 8 February, in the SS *Cameronia*, followed the next day by their headquarters staff. This left only 9/12 FFR guarding the Japanese at Cap St. Jacques and 2/8 Punjab in Saigon; battalions were relieved and left Vietnam on 30 March 1946, the 9/12 receiving a particularly emotional send-off from their Japanese captives. The Japanese remaining in Cap St. Jacques then became the responsibility of the French, their repatriation being completed by 15 May 1946; only the Japanese Naval HQ remained until 24 July, when it was disbanded, as well as some Japanese war criminals awaiting trial. Maunsell also left on 15 May 1946, followed by the last company of British troops—B Company, 2/8 Punjab. All that now remained of the British organization was the Liaison Department of the Control Commission, which became the military attaché of the British Embassy.

Britain's official role in Vietnam was over.

## RAF, Far East Air Force (RAF, FEAF) Operations

An RAF headquarters was set up near Saigon on 8 September, at the Tan Son Nhut airfield, where hard standing was available for approximately 70 Dakotas. The other aircraft at the airfield were Spitfires of No. 273 Squadron RAF and a detachment of photo-reconnaissance Mosquitoes. RAF pilots did not generally fly in a combat role in South Vietnam during this period; such operations were carried out by French Armée de l'Air pilots using Spitfires on loan from the RAF. The bulk of RAF personnel were withdrawn in mid-February 1946, when the Air Headquarters was disbanded, although a small RAF presence was retained for a few more months to help direct military transport aircraft using the airfield.

## *Perspectives*

The main problem for the British in French Indochina was the unexpected speed with which the Việt Minh emerged as a major military and political force in the south, with a large, well-equipped guerrilla contingent. Gracey and his superiors expected it to be necessary only to organize the removal of the Japanese and the return of the French; instead, British forces found themselves also involved in fighting a totally unexpected third element, which outnumbered them significantly. It was the presence of this substantial, hostile and very active force that complicated matters to such an extent that Gracey was forced to act in the way he did, issuing the proclamation of 21 September and involving the Japanese. Moreover, this expedient might not have been forced upon him if all the troops he was promised had been available from the start.

It was also implicit in Gracey's instructions that the French should return and, moreover, be left in the strongest possible position when the British withdrew. So, if the French were going to be responsible for administration in FIC, as had been agreed at Potsdam, it was clearly desirable that they be put back in control as soon as possible and the Southern Committee removed. This was seen as especially important since the committee members had proved themselves incapable of efficient administration and were unable to control even the Việt Minh guerrillas they claimed to command. Gracey himself was dubious about the advisability of using officials who had been in power under the Vichy administration, although these were the only suitable personnel available, the Gaullists being both too few and insufficiently experienced in colonial administration. For those reasons, Gracey organized the coup d'état of 23 September, which achieved the transition to French administrative control efficiently and with no loss of life on the Vietnamese side, although there were two French casualties. With French civil servants now responsible for the country's infrastructure and French troops starting to arrive, Gracey should have been able to begin work on his other tasks, mainly the disarming and repatriation of the Japanese.

However, the coup, and French reprisals in its wake, incensed the Việt Minh so much that they began a campaign of bombing and shootings, aided and supplied by both the Hanoi government and a small but very significant number of Japanese. With the French subsequently proving incapable of operating their administration efficiently, nor allowed to get enough troops into the country to resume control, Gracey's men were forced to concentrate on maintaining law and order in Saigon. Moreover, until the French were present in sufficient force for Gracey to assign them a meaningful peacekeeping role, he had to retain all Japanese troops under his command, allow them to keep their weapons and use them to control certain areas outside Saigon.[26] The proclamation of 21 September, incidentally, simply emphasized this aspect of the Japanese troops' role, which corresponded with President Truman's General Order No. 1. It did not imply that British troops would be responsible for security anywhere outside Gracey's key areas, which he explained in a signal to Mountbatten. He did not have the troops to pursue such a course, even had he wanted to, and his report to Mountbatten also makes it very clear he never intended the British should adopt this role. To have tried to maintain law and order with just his own troops would have meant spreading his available manpower so thinly that he could not have retained control even of Saigon and the surrounding areas. This, in turn, would have meant losing control of the whole country. Saigon was the key, because it controlled the only major airport, Ton Son Nhut, as well as the road and rail networks and the only deep-water harbor in the south capable of accepting ocean-going freighters and tankers.

Gracey really had no option but to use the Japanese, and even with this addition, the occupation forces were still so badly outnumbered that, initially, Gracey's men could do no more than fight a holding action, maintaining control of key points in Saigon such as the ports, railways and airfield. By the end of October, however, Leclerc had sufficient troops under his command to begin relieving the 20th Division of security duties, and the arrival of the rest of Gracey's troops (32nd Brigade and 100th Brigade) also meant he could begin the Japanese repatriation.

The British were able then to finally move out of Saigon and establish safe areas for disarming and subsequently repatriating the Japanese in the loose triangle formed by the towns of Thủ Đức, Thủ Dầu Một and Biên Hòa. As a consequence of this consolidation and their subsequent operations, particularly those carried out by GATEFORCE and CLARKOL, the British and Japanese were also instrumental in reducing the numbers of Việt Minh in the south to a negligible level, which had far-reaching effects on the subsequent history of that region.

With the exception of certain Việt Minh elements, the response of ordinary South Vietnamese to the British troops occupying their country seems to have been a positive one, perhaps, at least in part, because they were beginning to realize the disastrous way things were being run in the Communist North.[27] The British, in general, seem to have had no particular bias toward either side, although they were largely sympathetic to the cause of Vietnamese independence and, in contrast to the French, had been moderate and tactful in their operations.[28] Major Charles Blascheck (CO, "D" Company 3/1 GR) wrote some time after his service in South Vietnam, "We had no antagonism towards the Việt Minh on our arrival. We knew that independence was coming for India and thought that the Vietnamese should also have their independence—and we were all largely sympathetic to them."[29]

It was only when it became clear that the British would be obliged to hand control over to the French that the real trouble started. Moreover, the especially vicious engagements resulting in high casualties were invariably between the French troops and Việt Minh during the period from November 1945 to March 1946, although, when they were attacked, the Indian and Gurkha troops dealt ruthlessly with their opposition, whoever they were.

Most of the British participants, including Gracey, had no doubt that the attitude of the French was the cause of the failure to resolve the conflict in FIC through negotiation. The SEAC assistant director of intelligence summed up the problem as follows: "Provided the French are prepared to deal with the Ammanites as human beings and not as chattels for exploitation as in the past, there is every reason to believe that the leading Ammanites will not only listen to them but will help them."[30] This view was echoed by the British soldiers, with Christopher Buckley of the *Daily Telegraph* quoting one British officer as saying of the French, on the morning of the coup, "They have the opportunity of a lifetime for starting with a clean sheet a liberal policy for the joint running of the country."[31]

Once the French were back in control, however, they reassumed their prewar colonial stance, attitudes on both sides hardened and war became inevitable. What many of the French and Americans who came after seem not to have understood at the time was that most Vietnamese, from both north and south, did not want the Communists, or anyone else, in control. They wanted national government, a Vietnam run by Vietnamese, and with a little constructive help and good will, devoid of political doctrine, they might well have succeeded. In addition, such a government would have served as an effective buffer against the Communist Chinese, thus removing one of the permanent nightmares of succeeding postwar Washington administrations (see Eisenhower's "domino effect," for example). Hồ Chí Mính himself had never wanted Chinese help and only turned to the Communists after his requests for negotiation and aid were ignored by both the French and Americans.[32]

Unfortunately, no succeeding administration in either the north or the south could ever operate efficiently enough to appease the forces professing to offer them help. The Soviets and Chinese sent military hardware to Ho but did not, or perhaps could not, offer him what he really needed—advice on stabilizing and extending the economy in a way that was acceptable to the independent-minded, land-hungry Vietnamese. And the south found itself dominated by a series of incompetent soldiers, politicians and patriots, concerned only with keeping American aid flowing and the Việt Minh out of power, whatever the price.[33]

# 3

# France's War (1945–1954)

While Gracey dealt with the problems imposed by his role in Britain's operations in South Vietnam, General de Gaulle, serving as prime minister of France for the first time, was implementing plans to install a new French colonial regime in Indochina. To his credit, the general seems to have been perfectly well aware of the impossibility of restoring French prewar political control there, and he saw Vietnam as eventually becoming an independent part of a French Union, although just how that would have worked in practice is not clear. One of his first actions was to appoint Admiral Georges Thierry d'Argenlieu as high commissioner and give command of France's land forces in the country, which consisted of the Far East Expeditionary Corps (CEFEO), to General Jacques Philippe Leclerc.

The surviving units of the CEFEO and its commander arrived in Saigon on 5 October, and, having organized his men and consulted Gracey, Leclerc broke out of Saigon and drove through the Mekong Delta, via Mỹ Tho, and up into the central highlands. The Việt Minh retreated before the well-organized French advance, terrorizing the population and destroying the infrastructure as they went. By February 1946, Leclerc claimed to have control of

**Fairchild C119, *Flying Boxcar*. Supplied to the French air force by the Americans, this aircraft was operated with French markings but flown by CIA pilots.**

**H-21C Shawnee transport helicopter, this one shown air-lifting a 105mm howitzer during the 1960s. Supplied by the United States for use in Algeria, some Shawnees saw service in Vietnam.**

the south, although he was later shown to have been overly optimistic in his estimate of military success. Certainly, the French could drive the Việt Minh out of any area of rural South Vietnam with little difficulty, but they could do nothing to prevent the guerrillas' almost immediate return. A French historian, M. Philippe Devilliers, who served with Leclerc's army, explained the situation:

> If we departed, believing a region pacified, the Vietminh would arrive on our heels... There was only one possible defense, to multiply our posts, fortify them, arm and train the villagers, coordinate intelligence and police. What was required was not Leclerc's thirty-five thousand troops but a hundred thousand—and Cochinchina was not the only problem.[1]

By the end of January 1946, the French had assumed responsibility for most of the areas previously controlled by the ALFFIC. With many of the British troops gone and the French re-established below the 16th Parallel, Hồ Chí Mính now learned that the Chinese had previously entered into a pact with the French, whereby Chinese troops would leave Vietnam, allowing the French back into Tonkin, in return for French evacuation of Shanghai and other Chinese ports. This agreement was signed in February 1946, and it left Ho trapped once again without any allies among the major powers. The United States was supporting France, while the Russians were simply ignoring him, having not even sent an observer to Hanoi.

Once more, Ho sought an accommodation and opened negotiations with de Gaulle's representative, Jean Sainteny, who had been sent to Hanoi by Leclerc, then acting as high commissioner in d'Argenlieu's absence. Leclerc seems to have realized quite soon after his arrival that a diplomatic solution would be a far better result than beginning a war he might

Bell Aircraft Corporation P-63 Kingcobra, single-seater fighter/short-range bomber, supplied to the French air force by the Americans.

Sikorsky UH-19D helicopter. Supplied to the French army by the United States, its main role in Vietnam was CAS-VAC (casualty evacuation), although in 1956 a few trials were conducted with armed UH-19s.

never be able to bring to a successful conclusion. However, unsure about the outcome of these talks, and probably wanting to protect his position with de Gaulle, Leclerc took the precaution of also dispatching a large number of French troops to the north, aboard ships carrying sufficient munitions and heavy weapons to ensure Việt Minh compliance.

Ho and Sainteny entered into a vigorous discussion and soon found themselves faced with a single point of contention: the problem of Cochinchina (effectively, what was going to happen to South Vietnam). Sainteny was under pressure from French colonial interests in Saigon to ensure that Cochinchina remained separate from the Communist north, while Ho was determined to see Vietnam wholly and finally united. Compromise was only reached as Leclerc's troopships entered the Gulf of Tonkin, with the two men deciding that the administration of Cochinchina should await a referendum. Additionally, Vietnam would become a free state within the French Union; in return, Ho would allow the presence of 25,000 troops in Vietnam for five years.

To Ho it must have seemed like a victory. Certainly not complete, but he had been recognized as Vietnam's leader by the French and, most importantly, was rid of the Chinese, whom every Vietnamese loathed. He made his views clear when describing the situation to some critical colleagues at a meeting in Hanoi, in the spring of 1946, after concluding his negotiations with Sainteny:

**OH-23 Raven helicopter. Multi-role light helicopter, mostly used for CAS-VAC.**

## 3. France's War (1945–1954)

**M2A2 "Terra-Star" 105mm howitzer. Supplied by the United States to the French army, this particular weapon is an original prototype (Wikipedia; Creative Commons).**

You fools! Don't you realize what it means if the Chinese remain? Don't you remember your history? The last time the Chinese came, they stayed a thousand years.

The French are foreigners. They are weak. Colonialism is dying. The white man is finished in Asia. But if the Chinese stay now, they will never go. As for me, I prefer to sniff French shit for five years than eat Chinese shit for the rest of my life.[2]

Unfortunately, the Vietnamese were to be disappointed again. D'Argenlieu refused to honor the agreement, insisting that these terms could only be discussed at another meeting, arranged to take place in Paris. Ho reluctantly agreed and left Hanoi for Paris on 31 May 1946.

As soon as Ho was out of the way, d'Argenlieu ignored the previous agreement and declared South Vietnam to be the Republic of Cochinchina and under French control. Ho remained in Paris but found himself moved from location to location and involved in pointless conferences with minor officials. After eight weeks of uninspired haggling, a draft accord was formulated, which simply reinforced France's economic power in the north without resolving the Cochinchina problems. Ho sent his delegation home and, on 19 September, signed a document that was referred to as a *modus vivendi*, or interim understanding. The French still had Cochinchina, without effectively conceding anything. Small wonder that Ho told his bodyguard on leaving that final meeting, "I've just signed my death warrant."

**M101 105mm howitzer in action. It saw widespread use in Vietnam with the French and SVN as well as the Việt Công, who were supplied with howitzers and ammunition by the Chinese.**

By October 1946, Ho was back in Hanoi, calling for moderation in the country's dealings with the French. Most Vietnamese seemed satisfied with the agreement, although some militants claimed it was a surrender to the French. This fragile peace was soon threatened from both sides. Leclerc's replacement, General Étienne Valluy, began circulating a secret memo to his officers proposing that Ho be deposed in a coup d'état, while in the north Ho's army commander, General V.N. Giáp, was training and arming the Việt Minh.

War finally broke out again between the French and Việt Minh in the northern port of Haiphong, bizarrely over a dispute about customs duties. Fighting began on 20 November 1946, and although a cease-fire was declared the next day, on 23 November, the French commander, Colonel Debes, was ordered to clear the city. French troops went through Haiphong, supported by tanks, aircraft and the cruiser *Suffren*, which shelled the town and some of the fleeing civilian population. Estimates of the death toll vary, although reliable Vietnamese sources claimed, in 1981, that there were "between 500 to a 1,000 dead."[3]

Ho tried to negotiate, and for a time it looked as if he might succeed, when Léon Blum was elected prime minister, on 16 December 1946. Blum declared that he favored a "sincere reconciliation" with Vietnam that would be based on independence, which must have seemed hopeful to Ho.

Both sides had now deployed major troop numbers around Hanoi, however, and on the evening of 19 December, fighting broke out again. Although they fought back desperately, the Vietnamese troops and Việt Minh had few weapons, most of them old and poorly maintained, with which to fight a modern French army equipped with tanks, artillery and automatic rifles. Inevitably, the Vietnamese forces were driven out of the city.

Unfortunately, French domestic politics was in a volatile state during this period, and yet another new prime minister, Paul Ramadier, replaced Léon Blum on 22 January 1947. Ramadier began by dismissing d'Argenlieu and appointing Émile Bollaert in his place. Ho proposed another cease-fire and negotiations were opened once again. However, Ramadier quickly found his position in a coalition made up of Socialists, Christian Democrats and Communists increasingly precarious. Faced with opponents in his own cabinet like Georges Bidault and the defense minister Paul Coste-Floret, who were intent upon preventing any negotiations with Ho, Ramadier was forced to concede, and his representative and adviser, Paul Mus, was instructed to deliver to Ho what was effectively a demand for his surrender. Inevitably, Ho refused, and, in response, Maurice Thorez, a deputy prime minister in Ramadier's cabinet, countersigned a directive ordering military action against the Việt Minh. Leclerc, a voice of sanity in the prevailing atmosphere of patriotic fervor, suggested a more cautious approach, warning that "anti–Communism will be a useless tool unless the problem of nationalism is solved."

The French had made the same mistake the Americans would repeat years later in not understanding that Ho and the Việt Minh were more concerned with freeing their country than becoming involved in what was seen increasingly as Communism's dogmatic ideology.

Fighting was now confined to the north and continued during 1947, with the French achieving a major victory during Operation "Lea," when they attempted to capture the Việt Minh communications center at Bac Kan, along with Ho and his chief advisers. They missed Ho but killed 9,000 Việt Minh troops and auxiliaries. This year, however, marked a turning point in the French campaign. Unable to send any more troops to the region, the French military had to content itself with establishing outposts on the important roads in an attempt to hold the Việt Minh in the eastern part of Tonkin, although this quickly proved ineffective. The Việt Minh easily infiltrated these lines, moving supplies and reinforcements where they were most needed without significant French interference, and it was this forced retrenchment by the French that ensured the later Việt Minh victories. With their country's economic situation making a military solution unlikely in the foreseeable future, the French authorities in Vietnam began to look for a political solution, especially one that would renew their weakening ties with the Americans.

## American Intervention

Although Soviet activities in Western Europe after World War II had led President Truman to institute what came to be known as the "Truman Doctrine,"[4] the U.S. administration was not concerned about Vietnam during this early period.[5] U.S. officials were more interested in China, where the Communists, led by Mao Zedong, were in the final stages of defeating Chiang Kai-shek's Nationalists. General George Marshall had gone there to mediate on behalf of the United States in 1946, but had argued against any intervention. He took a similar view of Vietnam, saying to the U.S. ambassador in Paris, soon after his China visit, "We have fully recognized France's sovereign position in the area, but it is a matter for the French and the Việt Minh to work out for themselves."

It is also significant that, during this period, Ho's previous Communist sympathies were not seen as a cause for concern. In a U.S. State Department analysis from 1948, it was concluded that "the Vietnamese Communists are not subservient to Kremlin directives and … it is rather the French colonial press that has been strongly Anti-American … to the point of *approximating the official Moscow position*"[6] (author's emphasis).

U.S. policy was therefore that Indochina, including Vietnam, should become a self-governing nationalist state closely associated with the West, particularly France, but not under Communist influence. Ho, unfortunately, was not an acceptable leader within this neat framework, so the French, wishing to cement relations with the Americans, returned to the idea of a "traditional monarchy," by which their later actions showed they meant a "puppet" monarch whom they could control. And the French government had what seemed the perfect candidate in the person of the former emperor, Bảo Đại. His postwar position as Ho's adviser had lasted barely a year and he had left Hanoi in 1946 to live in Hong Kong, where he was leading a dissolute life among its bars and nightclubs.

Although the consensus of Western opinion later concluded that he was weak, unpredictable and corrupt, Bảo Đại was astute enough to see through the motives of the French representatives who tried to entice him back to the throne early in 1947. He insisted that France agree to the unification and independence of Vietnam before he would accept any role in government. While these negotiations were being conducted, Émile Bollaert, the French high commissioner, made Ho an offer, in September 1947, effectively to dissolve d'Argenlieu's "Republic of Cochinchina" in favor of what he termed a "self-governing" Vietnam, with the French controlling its defense and administration. Ho professed himself willing to bargain, but Bảo Đại now found himself trapped into signing a "protocol" in which France acknowledged Vietnam's independence but kept control of its administrative services and the armed forces. Bảo Đại refused to participate in the farce, and although he remained as emperor, the French appointed General Nguyễn Văn Xuân prime minister and head of its new puppet government.

By 1950, despairing of any reconciliation with the French, Ho had induced both Moscow and Beijing to recognize his regime as the "Democratic Republic of Vietnam" (DRV), which completely changed his status in the eyes of the White House. Ho's government was now perceived as part of the "Soviet Empire," so the Americans in response officially recognized Bảo Đại's regime and American financial support began, with a large portion of the money going to the emperor as his personal allowance.[7]

Ho had also managed to secure major military support from the Chinese and Russians, and it was in the period immediately after 1949 that the Việt Minh changed from a poorly equipped guerrilla force into a conventional army, organized along divisional lines and equipped with modern artillery and military engineering equipment. Using these forces, Ho's most senior general, Võ Nguyên Giáp, began an organized campaign of harassment against the French.

Giáp's first move, made during 1949, was to surround and cut off the most isolated French outposts in the north, which allowed his forces to operate in the surrounding countryside without interference. As the strength of his forces increased, Giáp began to attack larger garrisons, beginning with the capture of Đông Khê in September 1950, followed in rapid succession by Cao Bang, Lang Son, Lao Kay and finally Thai Ngu Yen. These military successes left the Việt Minh in possession of the vital Chinese border region, which ensured that, by the end of 1950, the French had no chance of securing victory in French Indochina. However, de Lattre, the French commander, halted the Việt Minh advance by building a fortified line across the Red River Delta, from Hanoi to the Gulf of Tonkin (the de Lattre line), which stabilized the situation temporarily and allowed the French to consolidate their position.

Instead of contenting himself with the steady gains he had previously made, Giáp now tried to precipitate matters by attempting to force his way through de Lattre's fortifications in January 1951 and occupy the Red River Valley, one of Vietnam's main rice-producing areas (Battle of Vinh Yen). When that attack failed, Giáp assaulted the east coast port of Haiphong in March (Battle of Mao Khe). In both of these operations, Giáp made the mistake of sending his troops against heavily fortified positions where artillery and automatic weapons gave the French defenders an overwhelming advantage. The Việt Minh lost heavily, but Giáp was undeterred. He launched another offensive in May 1951 along the Day River, southeast of Hanoi at Phu Ly, and, once again, the French drove his men back with appalling casualties. The war now became a series of small-scale engagements, with neither side able to make significant progress, despite the Americans giving the French large supplies of military equipment. The French did make one significant gain, however, in November 1951, when they occupied Hòa Bình, a key position southeast of Hanoi, temporarily extending their westward perimeter.[8]

The situation began to change again in February 1952, when Giáp forced the French to withdraw from Hòa Bình, leaving them immobilized behind their static defenses and with major supply problems due to Việt Minh activity on the roads to Hanoi. To alleviate this situation, the new French commander, General Raoul Salan, launched Operation "Lorraine" on 29 October 1952. Lorraine was designed to capture the Việt Minh supply dumps at Phu Yen and force the Việt Minh to withdraw from the area immediately adjacent to the de Lattre line, making their attacks on Salan's supply columns much more difficult. Unfortunately for the French, although they captured Phu Yen on 13 November, their supply lines were again overextended and vulnerable to Việt Minh attack, which Giáp had expected and now planned to take full advantage of. To his credit, General Salan realized Giáp's intention and canceled Lorraine on 14 November, immediately ordering his men to withdraw to their original positions on the de Lattre line, which they achieved despite a Việt Minh ambush at Chan Muong on 17 November.

During the early part of 1953, the emphasis of the Việt Minh campaign changed. Ho and Giáp knew that if they could make the French pay a high enough price in men and material, public opinion would force the French government to negotiate, but they also needed a spectacular military triumph to precipitate these negotiations. Accordingly, Giáp looked around for a battlefield where he could tie up the French, in an area that would stretch their supply lines to the breaking point and so defeat them with minimal losses to his own troops. The place he chose for his trap was neighboring Laos (whose ruler was sympathetic to the French), which presented him with several strategic advantages. He guessed that the French could not allow him free access to Laos, if only because they would never endure the damage such an action would do to their international prestige. This assessment proved correct, and action would later center on a little village near the border between the two countries called Dien Bien Phu, which gave easy access to the border for large bodies of troops and where the French mistakenly decided the Việt Minh could be stopped easily.

Giáp's campaign opened in October 1952, when three Việt Minh divisions first occupied the tiny hamlet. From here, in April 1953, he moved into Laos, reaching the outskirts of the capital, Luang Prabang, before pulling back, just prior to the onset of the rainy season. He had shown, however, that he could move into Laos with little risk of attack by French forces, and the French commander, General Henri Navarre, and his advisers decided that Dien Bien Phu was a significant strategic point for their own campaign as well as the place where Giáp's forces could be conveniently destroyed. Consequently, the French campaign focused on occupying the village and protecting Laos, despite the newly elected French president, Joseph Laniel, being more concerned with stabilizing the Vietnamese situation so that peace talks could begin, rather than fighting on to ultimate victory, whatever the cost.

By May 1954, the Việt Minh had driven the French out of Dien Bien Phu. On the morning after their occupation, 8 May 1954, negotiations began in Geneva regarding the future of Indochina at the instigation of the new French prime minister, Pierre Mendès France, who had set himself a deadline of four weeks to end the fighting. The details of these negotiations are interesting, if only for what they reveal about how the fate of Indochina was thought to affect world security as a whole.[9] It is sufficient to say, however, that the end result, arbitrated by Molotov, the Russian foreign minister, resulted in an agreement to split the country at the 17th Parallel into Communist North (Democratic Republic of Vietnam), administered by Hồ Chí Mính, and anti–Communist South (State of Vietnam, or South Vietnam), under the control of Bảo Đại, with Ngô Đình Diệm as prime minister. Both countries were to have separate but temporary governments, because the agreement included a plan to hold a reunification election in two years. This was a temporary division, not a political settlement, pending the national election in 1956, which presumably was intended to settle the question of who governed Indochina. The only documents signed were the cease-fire agreements, ending hostilities in Vietnam, Cambodia and Laos, with the French agreeing to withdraw from the north while the Việt Minh would leave the south.

**Ngô Đình Diệm, prime minister of South Vietnam from 1954 to 1963. His intransigence and refusal to delegate responsibility outside his family led to his assassination in 1963, in which it is claimed the Americans colluded with his murderers.**

## Perspectives

French operations in Vietnam between 1946 and 1954 were characterized by the failure of multiple military commanders to appreciate the flexibility, military expertise and, most importantly, sheer determination of the Việt Minh to be rid of their former colonial masters. The Việt Minh could move at will through the jungle and crippled the French logistic efforts through a series of well-organized attacks that left French garrisons cut off and without food or munitions. It was only when Giáp abandoned his policy of stealthy clandestine attacks, at Vinh Yen and Mao Khe that the French military achieved any notable success. Giáp clearly learned his lesson from these reverses, and during Operation Lorraine and the attack on Bien Dien Phu, he reverted to his original approach of steadily wearing down French resistance via continually applied pressure rather than spectacular frontal assaults, which resulted in the Việt Minh's ultimate success—at least on the battlefield.

Political negotiations during that period were notable for Ho's early willingness to reach an agreement and the French government's inability to honor any bargain it made (for example, d'Argenliou's declaration of a Republic of Cochinchina, despite the Ho/Sainteny agreement, and Bảo Đại's coercion into signing a document he did not agree with). Moreover, Ho was not even treated seriously by the Paris administration until it had suffered significant military reverses, particularly the ultimate disaster of Dien Bien Phu, when the French were forced to negotiate a final peace. Even then, the Vietnamese lost at the Geneva conference table because Molotov, Zhou Enlai and Sir Anthony Eden persuaded the Việt Minh representative, Phạm Văn Đồng, to accept terms more favorable to the South Vietnamese, who were largely influenced by the French and Americans.

British activity in French Indochina during the French military operations was minimal, although Eisenhower did propose a joint Anglo–U.S. military operation shortly before the Geneva Conference. Churchill, then prime minister, refused to participate, and Anthony Eden, who was foreign secretary and co-chairman of the conference with Molotov, was even more emphatic, refusing to be "hustled into injudicious military decisions."[10]

# 4

# America's War (1954–1963)

America had some involvement in what was then Indochina both during and soon after World War II, but its major political and military entanglement really began after the French left in 1954 and Ngô Đình Diệm was appointed prime minister of South Vietnam. Between February 1955 and May 1964, organization of U.S. military activity in South Vietnam was the responsibility of the Military Assistance Advisory Group (MAAG) Vietnam.

## The Diệm Years

After the fall of Bien Dien Phu, the emperor, Bảo Đại, needed continued American aid both to sustain his regime and to meet his own expenses, which meant he required a leader for his government who would be acceptable to Washington. Ngô Đình Diệm was popular with Eisenhower's regime principally because he was seen as a committed anti–Communist, so, with a view to appeasing his American allies, Đại first appointed Diệm's brother, Ngô Đình Luyện, as part of the 1954 delegation to the Geneva peace talks, and then subsequently named Diệm himself as prime minister on 26 June 1954.

Diệm's administration was unstable from its very beginnings. Bảo Đại is said to have disliked him personally and had appointed him only to satisfy the Americans, while the French certainly saw Diệm as hostile to their plans. The French Expeditionary Corps was still the most powerful military force in the south; in addition, the Vietnamese National Army (VNA) had been trained and organized by the French, who had also appointed its officers. Among these appointments was the chief of staff, General Nguyễn Văn Hinh, a French citizen who is said to have loathed Diệm and frequently disobeyed his orders, which naturally affected Diệm's ability to deploy the country's armed forces effectively.

Diệm's problems with the army, however, were only one of a catalog of difficulties. He was also faced with two religious sects, the Cao Đài and the Hòa Hảo, which both had private armies in the Mekong Delta, while the Việt Minh were still estimated to be in control of approximately one third of the rural areas. In Saigon, the Bình Xuyên had grown into a criminal organization with 40,000 active members, financed by prostitution, gambling, extortion and drugs on a scale bigger than anything yet seen in Asia during that period. To make matters even worse, Bảo Đại had also sold control of the national police to the Bình Xuyên, which left them in control and the prime minister effectively powerless.

Instead of capitulating in the face of these problems, Diệm acted resolutely, helped by the CIA's representative in Vietnam, Col. Edward Lansdale. A number of Hòa Hảo and Cao Đài commanders were bribed into amalgamating their units with the VNA, and in April 1955, Diệm ordered the Bình Xuyên to relinquish control of the police and either join this augmented national army or disband. The Bình Xuyên and its leader, Bay Vien, ignored him, and on 27 April 1955, the VNA moved against them in what became known as the Battle for Saigon. Fighting was predominantly confined to Cholon, Saigon's Chinese quarter, and after a week of action, which left between 500 and 1,000 people dead and 20,000 homeless, the VNA had captured the Bình Xuyên's Saigon headquarters and effectively driven them out of the city, despite the French Army giving support and intelligence to the group. Bay Vien escaped but never returned to Saigon, fleeing the country and living the remainder of his life in Paris, financed by the profits of his criminal activities.

With both his political and military position vastly strengthened, Diệm moved against Bảo Đại and, in consequence, his French allies. On 15 May 1955 he disbanded Bảo Đại's Imperial Guard and enrolled its 5,000 men into the VNA as the 11th and 42nd Infantry Regiments. Bảo Đại was then stripped of both his lands and his executive powers; Diệm subsequently had himself declared president by the Council of the Royal Family at Hue, and two months later, on 16 July, apparently now sure of his position, he announced that he would not take part in the reunification elections. Instead, Diệm declared, on 6 October, that a referendum would be held in South Vietnam on 23 October to determine whether he or Bảo Đại would rule the country. Diệm won the election by an overwhelming majority, having enforced a ban on all pro–Bảo Đại and anti–Diệm activity, while basing his own campaign on a well-organized personal attack on the emperor, possibly orchestrated by the Americans.[1] He also appears to have manipulated the voting. In Saigon, for example, the returns showed Diệm had polled more votes than there were registered voters—605,025 votes for Diệm, out of only 450,000 registered voters. In the country as a whole Diệm received an astonishing 98.2 percent of the vote, although with only 5,335,668 people eligible to vote (consisting of men and women aged 18 or over), final returns showed that 5,784,752 ballots had actually been recorded.

Three days later, on 26 October 1955, Diệm announced the formation of the Republic of Vietnam, with himself as president. He also confirmed once again that he would not take part in the reunification elections, which had been part of the 1954 Geneva agreement. The Americans supported Diệm, declaring that the election had been properly run and hailing Diệm as a "new hero of the free world" (although documents later released show that they not only knew about the electoral manipulations but also had advised Diệm to be content with a smaller margin for victory to make the result more convincing).[2] Diệm severed economic relations with France and withdrew from the French Union in December 1955, leaving America as the sole foreign power with influence in the country.

## The North

Ho had returned to Hanoi in October 1954, where he found the French Army leaving, together with thousands of ordinary Vietnamese, evacuated under America's "Passage to Freedom" initiative (estimates of the exodus range from 600,000 to 1,000,000 persons). He also found economic chaos, with essential services, such as railways, harbors, libraries, hospitals and factories, either destroyed or useless. More importantly, the north no longer had access to the south's important rice-producing regions, and only emergency imports from Burma prevented a famine during 1955. Ho made matters worse by immediately introducing an ill-considered land reform, which classified the rural population into five classes ranging from "landlord" to "farm worker." Landlords were automatically enemies of the state and arbitrarily considered to constitute 2 percent of the population by Hanoi's bureaucrats, who dispatched political cadres into the countryside to arrest, imprison or shoot sufficient individuals to fulfill the government's quotas.

Unfortunately, in devising his new system, Ho had largely ignored a major difference between farmers in the north and those in the south. Unlike the more affluent south, with its big landowners who might justifiably be classified as landlords, most northern farmers held only three or four acres, and it was ludicrous to accuse the owner of such a tiny holding of being a landlord, especially since most of the northerners lived barely above the subsistence level. Despite this major difference and the clear difficulty of finding anyone resembling a landlord among the northern farmers (i.e., someone who was exploiting his fellow Vietnamese, which is what the term was intended to imply), the political cadres still implemented these land reforms, liquidating or imprisoning all those considered to be in this higher class. Corruption was widespread, and officials were later shown to have used their positions to settle old scores and terrorize and rob the defenseless peasants.

By August 1956, Ho had realized his error and released all those who had been interned in forced labor camps, although he could do nothing about the thousands more who had been killed, among them many Việt Minh veterans. Ho and his colleagues exhorted the nation to "forgive and forget," but reprisals were widespread and Ho sent troops to quell the subsequent rioting, which resulted in more civilian deaths and escalating chaos.

## The South

South Vietnam was also undergoing a period of political "cleansing." In anticipation of the 1956 reunification elections, the Hanoi government had encouraged large numbers of Việt Minh activists to remain behind in the south when the country was partitioned. Diệm now began a purge of these dissidents, organizing so-called security committees to try Việt Minh suspects, which included anyone who had fought against the French or even had a relative in the resistance. As in the north during the land reforms, corruption was widespread. Initially, however, Diệm was able to claim that his policy was working because by 1956 his government had published figures showing that 90 percent of former Việt Minh cells in the Mekong Delta, the center of Việt Minh activity in the south, had been destroyed.

Unfortunately, just when he might have consolidated his control of South Vietnam, Diệm made a series of fatal blunders. His first major mistake came almost immediately upon assuming office, when he refused to delegate power or even place his trust in anyone outside his close family. His government thus came to be seen by many as a family concern, run by himself and his brothers for their personal profit, which, together with the later land reforms and ill-advised "Strategic Hamlets" program, made both Diệm and his regime extremely unpopular. Many educated Vietnamese also criticized him because his massive spending on security meant there was little left for schools, hospitals or other essential social services, and Diệm came under immense pressure to carry out reforms. He ignored this public outcry, even when it was supported by members of his own cabinet, and responded by closing newspapers opposed to his regime and arresting a number of prominent Saigon journalists and intellectuals, whom he accused of having Communist affiliations. In November 1960, dissatisfaction with Diệm reached a climax when his palace was surrounded by paratrooper and marine units intent on forcing reform on the president. Led by Lt. Col. Vương Văn Đông, the coup was launched at 5 a.m. on 11 November 1960, but Diệm slyly prevaricated over agreeing to the group's demands until his own loyal troops had reached Saigon. The rebels had failed to take even the most elementary military precautions, such as blocking the roads into the capital, and Diệm's troops quickly scattered them, forcing the senior officers responsible to seek asylum in Cambodia. Although the coup had failed, Diệm became mentally more unreliable than ever, even accusing the Americans of being his enemies (the American ambassador, Elbridge Durbrow, had refused to intervene with the rebels on Diệm's behalf when he was trapped in his palace during the early hours of the coup). From that time onward, even Diệm's most loyal subordinates began to plot against him.[3]

Diệm's troubles multiplied still further when, at the end of 1960, the Hanoi government formed a new organization, the National Liberation Front for South Vietnam, largely replacing the earlier Việt Minh, which Diệm's publicists called the Vietnamese Communists, or "Việt Cộng." The Việt Cộng were based in South Vietnam and recruited mainly from that population. Consequently, the group's representatives were quickly able to infiltrate southern villages, including the strategic hamlets, promising a better future for the peasants (although, because of their indiscriminate violence, many Vietnamese peasants appear to have felt that there was little difference between the two sides).[4] The Communists also took advantage of Diệm's paranoia by terrorizing and murdering government officials so that, as a direct consequence of their actions, Diệm appointed army officers rather than government officials to replace his dead civil servants. These appointments caused the situation in rural areas to deteriorate even more and further increased Diệm's unpopularity (if that were possible), because the majority of his officials were Catholics from the northern or central provinces and acted as though the villages they were administering were enemy territory. They lived in fortified camps and only ventured out under heavy guard, often accompanied by their American advisers, which lent substance to the Việt Cộng accusations that Diệm was intent on allowing the Americans to enter the country as a neocolonial replacement for the French.

By December 1960, the Americans were beginning to regret their wholehearted support of Diệm. They had given him billions of dollars in arms, equipment and cash, sent "advisers" to train his army and supported him internationally, even when his policies became openly subversive. Now, however, Diệm obviously felt that he was the one in control, "a puppet pulling his own strings," as one American diplomat called him, and could afford to ignore the recommendations of his American allies, because he was sure they could find no one to replace him. In the White House, however, opinion was divided about Diệm's future, with some members of Eisenhower's staff suggesting that Diệm was the only viable option while others stated bluntly that he had to go.[5] Durbrow, still U.S. ambassador and usually a moderate where policy was concerned, suggested that in the not too distant future the Americans might need to find and support an alternative leader for South Vietnam. This

American disquiet was reflected by many of Diệm's close associates, who were especially concerned with his refusal to face the realities of the situation his intransigence was forcing him into.

In 1961, Britain had also begun giving more support to the RVN by establishing BRIAM (British Advisory Mission to Vietnam) under the leadership of Robert Thompson, who had previously advised Diệm on security matters. In the wake of Thompson's "Delta plan," which he had shown to Diệm, the Vietnamese president began to play the British off the Americans, further inflaming the political situation in Saigon. Later that same year, when U.S. advisers began implementing Roger Hilsman's "Strategic Hamlets" program, based upon Thompson's "Delta" plan, subsequent disenchantment with this policy (particularly its inherent relocations) added to Diệm's unpopularity.[6] Despite misgivings about Diệm, on 8 February 1962 the U.S. government created the MACV (Military Assistance Command, Vietnam) to oversee the military aid being given to the Saigon government. This organization later absorbed the MAAG Vietnam in May 1965 and was responsible for all U.S. combat unit deployments until it ceased operations in March 1973.

## The End of Diệm

Diệm's exit, when it came, was sudden, predictable and assisted by the U.S. government.

By the beginning of 1963, Diệm was being assailed on two fronts, and he found himself unable to deal with either the mounting Communist threat from the north or the turbulent South Vietnamese factions within his own government, alienated by what they considered his abuse of power. It was this southern faction, comprising mainly disaffected senior army officers, that staged the coup d'état which resulted in Diệm's removal and death, although the coup would never have succeeded if it had not been for American complicity, especially the involvement of the U.S. ambassador in Saigon, Henry Cabot Lodge.

The end of Diệm's regime began with a religious controversy. Diệm was a strict Catholic and the regime had strongly favored its Catholic supporters, often preferring them over better-qualified non–Catholics, particularly the Buddhists, who were their main organized religious rivals. This situation was further exacerbated because, under the French, Buddhism had acquired a "private" status, which required its adherents to obtain official permission for public acts of worship. Quite naturally, the Buddhists resented Diệm's bias and his restrictive laws, but they were content to continue working quietly to increase their influence, in the hope of one day being able to pressure the government into more reasonable behavior. Unfortunately, once again, Diệm's intransigence precipitated matters.

On 8 May 1963, large numbers of Vietnamese Buddhists gathered in Hue to celebrate the birthday of the Lord Buddha. With the crowds assembled, the deputy province chief, Major Dang Xi, enforced an old decree banning them from displaying their flag. Upset and angered by this discrimination, a large crowd gathered in front of the radio station to listen to a speech to be broadcast over its public address system by one of their most influential leaders. The station manager canceled the address and contacted Dang Xi, who immediately dispatched five armored cars to the scene. Upon arrival, the commander ordered the crowd to disperse, then ordered his men to open fire, killing nine people—a woman and eight children.

In the wake of the attack, the Buddhists began a series of organized protests. Diệm responded by becoming increasingly intransigent, even encouraging his sister-in-law, Madam Nhu, to allege that the Buddhists were being manipulated by the United States. The Americans, in turn, warned Diệm that he would lose all their support if he did not stop his attacks on the Buddhists. Diệm responded to this threat by forming a committee, effectively a powerless charade, to investigate the Buddhist complaints, although it never appears to have reported on the situation. On 11 June 1963, however, the initiative was savagely snatched from Diệm's grasp when an elderly Buddhist monk, seated at a busy Saigon junction, allowed himself to be set on fire and burned to death in protest of the government's policies. Diệm remained unmoved and the self-immolations continued, despite pointed suggestions from the Americans that Diệm change his methods and his approach to the religious controversy, which the Việt Cộng were also exploiting for propaganda purposes. Hostility toward Diệm was mounting, even among the moderate, rural South Vietnamese, and clearly, from the U.S. point of view, he was becoming a liability.

The man who eventually orchestrated his removal was the new U.S. ambassador, Henry Cabot Lodge. Just before Lodge's appointment, a group of senior army officers, including the commander of the SVA, General Trần Văn Đôn, had already begun planning a coup against Diệm, with the help of a veteran CIA operative, Lt. Col. Lucien Conein. Diệm himself inadvertently encouraged the conspirators when he allowed them to declare martial law, which they claimed would let them prosecute the war against the Communists more effectively, although their real reason for the move was simply to strengthen their own position. Diệm also had his own reasons for the action. His brother Nhu had devised a scheme that involved disguising Diệm's own loyal troops as regular soldiers and then using them to attack the Buddhist temples and sanctuaries, which Diệm hoped would set the army and the Buddhists against each other, thus diverting public attention and reducing pressure on his own administration.

Unfortunately for Diệm and Nhu, the plan backfired badly. On 21 August, Nhu's men attacked temples in Saigon, Hue and other major cities, rounding up over 1,000 monks, nuns, radical students and ordinary citizens before ransacking the temple precincts. Unfortunately, the disguises do not seem to have worked, and many quickly realized that the attacks were the work of Diệm's own troops. The response by ordinary Vietnamese was fearsome. Thousands surged into the streets to protest, and a number of Diệm's own associates in the government condemned his actions. For the Americans as well, this was seen as Diệm's final and most disastrous miscalculation.

Lodge was en route to Saigon to take up his new post as U.S. ambassador when Nhu launched his operation. Upon arrival he found a telegram from the State Department, asking for an assessment of the situation. After gathering information from his advisers, Lodge correctly named Nhu as the culprit, with Diệm's active support, and confirmed the generals' plans for a coup. On Saturday, 24 August, Lodge received a telegram instructing him to tell the generals that the American government would support them in a coup against Diệm, unless the president was willing to remove his brother Nhu from office. This decision was controversial, to say the least, because it implied that the Kennedy administration was prepared to orchestrate the demise of a dependent government simply because that government would not conform to what the White House had decided its policy should be.[7] Regardless of its original intent, this action sent a clear message: Do what we say ... or else.

Whatever the long-term effects of this decision on White House policy and political thinking, in Saigon, Lodge was finding Diệm increasingly difficult. The ambassador made repeated demands to Washington, insisting on approval for the generals' coup. Finally, after weeks of delay and prevarication, the U.S. leaders decided that, while they could not support the generals (that would raise far too many political and even moral difficulties with the public), they could agree not to thwart the proposed coup, without offering any advice or financial support. With this assurance the generals finally agreed to act, only insisting that the Americans confirm, once again, that they would not interfere with the operation. This, of course, provided Cabot and the Americans with the perfect escape clause, in that they could now insist with perfect truth (as Cabot actually did a year later in an interview with the *New York Times*), "The overthrow ... of the Diệm regime was purely a Vietnamese affair. We never participated in the planning. We never gave advice. We had nothing whatever to do with it."[8]

The coup took place on 1 November 1963 and succeeded more because of the ineptitude of Diệm and Nhu than the organizational skill of the generals involved. By the morning of 2 November 1963, Diệm and his brother were dead, assassinated in the back of an armored personal carrier they believed was transporting them to the freedom promised by General Đôn.[9]

South Vietnam rejoiced over Diệm's fall, and Lodge congratulated the generals on their actions before jubilantly telegraphing President Kennedy personally that "the prospects now are for a shorter war."

Three weeks after Diệm's murder, on 22 November 1963, President Kennedy was assassinated in Dallas and Lyndon Baines Johnson replaced him in the White House.

**John F. Kennedy, 35th president of the United States from 20 January 1961 until his assassination on 22 November 1963.**

# 5

# BRIAM

## *The British Advisory Mission to Vietnam*

Although Harold Macmillan and most of his government were dubious about the political acumen and effectiveness of the men controlling the regime in Saigon, in July 1961 the prime minister sanctioned the formation of a British advisory mission to Vietnam. It was to be referred to as BRIAM, and its role in supporting the South Vietnamese was "to provide expert assistance in the field of administrative co-ordination and police matters.... The British Advisory Mission to Vietnam ... consists of three officers and a small administrative staff led by Mr. R.G.K.Thompson."[1]

## *The British Advisory Mission (BRIAM)*

Thompson left London on 17 September 1961 on a flight to Washington, with the intention of establishing good relations with the Americans, many of whom were opposed to British involvement in Vietnam's affairs. After meetings with a number of influential figures in the Kennedy administration and discussions of the way British operations in Malaya could be adapted for Vietnam, Thompson's expertise in counter-insurgency began to be accepted by the U.S. government, with many American officials believing his advice to be worth serious consideration. Having established his credentials with the Americans, Thompson left Washington, arriving in Saigon on 29 September 1961, where he was soon joined by the three other senior members of BRIAM: Dennis Duncanson, an expert in psychological warfare; Jock Hindmarsh, who had trained Malayan police contingents; and Desmond Palmer, an intelligence officer. They set up a temporary office in Saigon's Hotel Majestic and immediately started to tour the country by car and helicopter to assess the situation in the south.

Despite American sensitivity to BRIAM's activities and candid advice from the Foreign Office about the need to placate the MAAG, Thompson showed little regard for American feelings. Although he was supposed to be concerned only with the details of policing and administration, he produced a paper after only a month in the country that described an initiative based on his Malayan experience and centered on a series of strategic operations in the Mekong Delta. This was Thompson's "Delta" plan, which he claimed might bring success in as little as six months, and which would later be used by the Americans as the basis for their unsuccessful "Strategic Hamlets" policy.[2]

## The "Briggs" Plan

During its operations in Malaya, the British army had defeated the Communist guerrillas by implementing the "Briggs" plan, which had been devised by the British director of operations, General Sir Harold Briggs. This had dealt effectively with the guerrillas through the construction of what were termed "new villages." These were essentially new, heavily fortified settlements that protected and contained the indigenous Chinese population, thus depriving the guerrillas of their main sources for food, information and, most crucially, fresh recruits. Thompson was convinced that a similar operation would be effective in Vietnam. After touring the Mekong Delta for a scant five days, he concluded that a similar plan was feasible because he felt conditions in the Delta were similar enough to Malaya to ensure its success.[3]

Thompson's "Delta" plan had four main objectives:

- The formation of what Thompson called a "Super State War Executive Committee." This body would be responsible for directing all emergency measures from an integrated civil and military command center.
- The building of "strategic hamlets," similar in scope to the Malayan "new villages," which were to be built to provide security for the population from Việt Cộng attack and influence.
- The existing self-defense corps, which lived in the villages, was to be expanded and re-equipped.
- After the establishment of the hamlets, with their properly trained self-defense corps installed, the Việt Cộng were to be encouraged to attack the villages, so that RVN forces could react against them, thus providing government forces with their main opportunity for killing "terrorists." Once areas were confirmed as free from Việt Cộng control, the population would benefit from a program of social improvements and a relaxation of military controls.[4]

By now, however, Washington's policy was leaning strongly toward a solution in Vietnam that involved the deployment of large bodies of troops. Consequently, the Foreign Office instructed Britain's ambassador in Washington to pass Thompson's paper to Gen. Maxwell Taylor, then Kennedy's primary military adviser, and other members of the administration, in the hope that they would consider it as an alternative, since it required only material aid and no massive injection of manpower. This may also have been seen as desirable by the British government, which was intent upon avoiding inclusion in any troop commitments made by the Americans. Unfortunately, as these recommendations were not in accordance with U.S. government policy, they were not well received, particularly in the U.S. Embassy in Saigon. Thompson was seen as having clearly gone beyond his original remit agreed between British and U.S. embassy officials in Saigon. Even worse, on 11 November 1961 Thompson sent a copy of his report to Diệm. Two weeks later, the two men met, and after the meeting, Thompson concluded that Diệm was in agreement with his proposals and even prepared to trust British advice over that supplied by the Americans. Diệm was thought to have particularly liked Thompson's plan because it called for a "super executive council," which the South Vietnamese president felt he could manipulate to give him effective operational control of any force in the delta, rather than requiring him to delegate responsibility, which he almost paranoid about avoiding. This sort of delegation was one of the conditions the Americans were keen to impose on Diệm, because his insistence upon a closed, family-run government was seen as contributing significantly to the failure of his regime.

Late in 1961, Kennedy decided against deploying combat troops to Vietnam, and since General Taylor had already told Kennedy that "the present war cannot be won by direct action; it must be won by the Vietnamese," it appears unlikely that Thompson's plan influenced this decision. But even though Kennedy had decided against direct military intervention, he insisted that the proposed expansion of military aid should be accompanied by the appointment of political advisers to every level of Diệm's government. Naturally, Diệm welcomed the military and financial aid but resented what he saw as American political interference and, using Thompson's "Delta" plan, he began to try and play the British against the Americans. This considerably increased the difficulties faced by the U.S. ambassador, Frederick Nolting, when dealing with Diệm, who was slippery enough at the best of times. Ultimately, Nolting summoned Thompson and the British ambassador, Harold Hohler, to the Saigon Embassy. The result of this meeting was that Nolting felt Thompson and Hohler seemed to accept that they would play only a minor role in the advisory effort in Vietnam, and Thompson even offered to revise the Delta plan to preserve a unified command structure, which would force some form of delegation upon Diệm. As a result, Nolting felt able to inform Washington that Thompson was working "closely and amicably" with MAAG, although Thompson still insisted that operations should concentrate on the Mekong, while the Americans were intent upon moving into the country north of Saigon, where they felt a series of quick victories would improve the morale of the Army of the Republic of South Vietnam (ARVN). Despite these differences, the Americans felt that BRIAM should remain in the country, although they were also desperate for a military contribution from other countries, such as Australia and New Zealand.[5]

Throughout 1962, Thompson was seen by many in Britain and America as the most reliable expert on counter-insurgency activities in Vietnam in either government, although the lower echelons of the U.S. military, who were gaining considerable Vietnamese experience of their own, were less complimentary. Despite the concerns of the U.S. military, by the end of January 1962, Hohler felt confident enough to write that a new "special relationship" was developing between Britain and the United States in the region, due to their mutual involvement in a common enterprise. In Washington, Thompson's ideas were about to find a new advocate, in the shape of Roger Hilsman, director of the State Department's Bureau of Intelligence and Research, the man who would originate America's "Strategic Hamlets" policy.

## The Strategic Hamlets Policy

On 15 January 1962, Hilsman attended a conference on Vietnam in Honolulu, and afterward he immediately moved on to Vietnam, where he stayed for five days, meeting with American advisers and Robert Thompson. Returning to Washington, he briefed Kennedy and Taylor, and the president asked Hilsman to produce his own counter-insurgency plan for Vietnam. Hilsman's final document, "A Strategic Concept for Vietnam," owed much to Thompson's original "Delta" plan, especially the three elements at its core: the adoption of both a "Strategic Hamlets" initiative and guerrilla tactics by the ARVN, together with some form of civic action.

Originally, the strategic hamlets program was to intended to concentrate on reorganizing existing villages to make them more defensible, with relocation kept to a minimum and the villagers themselves supplied with weapons and trained in self-defense. Moreover, the villages were not to be left in isolation but were to be part of an expanding, self-protecting network, which would then establish the basis for economic, social, political and cultural reform.

Unfortunately, the speed with which the Saigon government implemented the plan and constructed the villages was not matched by a corresponding ability to support and protect them; consequently, Việt Cộng easily infiltrated the hamlets and intimidated the residents. Instead of initially restructuring existing villages in secure areas, which was a principal feature of both Thompson's and Hilsman's plans, Diệm and his brother Nhu ordered wholesale relocations. This resulted in religious objections from the rural population, who were mostly Buddhist and so practiced a form of ancestor-worship closely associated with ceremonial observances at the graves of their relatives. Relocation made this sort of observance impossible and, in some cases, villagers who resisted relocation on these grounds were summarily executed by government troops. Corruption was also rife, with government officials pocketing both the money allocated to compensate villagers for the loss of their homes and what had been promised to them for working to build the new villages. Even worse, some officials forced the villagers to buy materials intended for the protection of the new villages that had been provided without charge by the Americans as part of their aid program.

Most problematic was the question of security. Instead of establishing new villages in secure areas and then spreading out from those centers in an organized way, the Saigon government began building at random, without considering defense priorities. This meant the new hamlets were isolated and easy targets for the well-organized Việt Cộng, especially because ARVN units, which were supposed to answer radio calls for support from the villages, frequently failed to respond. Once the villagers realized that the army was indifferent to their requests for assistance, they usually surrendered to whatever Communist force attacked them, even if it was relatively small.[6]

Despite its obvious shortcomings, coupled with the incompetence of Diệm's regime in implementing the program, in April 1963 Thompson returned to Washington and gave Kennedy a glowing report on progress in Vietnam, emphasizing the success of Hilsman's strategic hamlets initiative. In particular, Thompson expressed his conviction that by the end of 1963, the United States could begin withdrawing its advisers from South Vietnam, which would show both that Saigon was not a satellite in an American war and that "we are winning." Unfortunately, by July 1963, it was clear to the Americans serving in South Vietnam that the program had little chance of success, and its demise began a corresponding decline in Thompson's reputation with the Americans. Kennedy's death and Johnson's entry into the White House accelerated this process, and by the beginning of 1964, Thompson's advice was being largely ignored and even seen as unwelcome by many U.S. officials, both in Saigon and in Washington.

BRIAM's role between 1964 and early 1965, when Thompson and his associates retired from the organization, was mainly concerned with police training, which included recruitment of some British police officers to the South Vietnamese Special Branch. When Thompson left BRIAM in 1965, its activities and personnel were transferred to the USOM (United States Operations Mission), with salaries and other expenses being paid by the Americans from that time forward. A summary of the activities of the five officers remaining in Saigon is included in a confidential memo from the Saigon Embassy to the Foreign Office, dated 14 May 1965, after Thompson had left BRIAM. One officer was responsible for civil disturbance control, another was compiling a national police manual of procedures and two more were assigned to the Bureau of Resources Control, which was responsible for denying food, weapons and other necessities to the Việt Cộng. The remaining officer was assigned to the South Vietnamese Special Branch.[7] All these officers liaised closely with both American and South Vietnamese officers during their part in these operations.

Lyndon B. Johnson, 36th president of the United States, in 1964. Responsible for the initial escalation of the Vietnam War and the $31 billion debt that resulted from his policies.

## The Montagnard Operation

In addition to BRIAM's activities, in early 1963 a British intelligence officer, Richard Noone, was appointed to lead a small team of Malayo-Polynesian tribesmen, whose role was to train and organize the Montagnard tribes of Vietnam's Central Highlands into teams of guerrillas. His intention was to disrupt communications along the Hồ Chí Minh Trail and harass the Việt Cộng, but, unfortunately, the operation proved unsuccessful and Noone's team had to be removed.[8]

## Perspectives

The establishment of BRIAM and subsequent sponsorship of Thompson's "Delta" plan were undertaken by the British government both to support American efforts in the Far East and, perhaps, as a way of quietly avoiding too much further involvement of their own in the region. Certainly, one of their aims seems to have been to influence American policy by emphasizing the success of their early "hearts and minds" policy in Malaya, thus preventing both the Communists' incursion and any military escalation in Vietnam, which Britain might have been called upon to support and, in part, pay for. Macmillan himself had said that part of Britain's role was to "guide the power of the U.S.," and the threat by the U.S. Secretary of State, John Foster Dulles, to use tactical nuclear weapons against China during the 1958 dispute over the islands of Quemoy and Matsos may have confirmed him in this opinion, although he was certainly not an advocate of peace at any price.[9] Secondarily, the establishment of BRIAM was also a means of reassuring Australia and New Zealand that Britain was still to be relied upon for military support, despite Macmillan's plan to grant independence to a number of British colonies in the Far East and Africa. Certainly, if Kennedy had lived and Thompson and Hilsman's combined plan had worked, it was intended that Vietnam would have needed little, if any, military aid from either Britain or America. Although Thompson and his ideas had been found acceptable to the Americans initially, after Kennedy's death the emphasis in Washington changed. With the inevitable troop commitments and the failure of the strategic hamlets program (seen by many as at least partly his fault), Thompson became less credible and his advice was no longer valued by the Americans.

# 6

# America's War (1963–1968)

## Johnson's War

President Johnson's entry into the White House coincided with the establishment of a new regime in South Vietnam, and it also marked the beginning of an escalation of American military operations in Southeast Asia. Initially, however, his first concern was, of necessity, to establish himself firmly in the government by winning the 1964 presidential election, so as not to be seen simply as a poor substitute for John Kennedy.

Unfortunately for Johnson's election hopes, within days of Diệm's assassination, South Vietnam was once again in chaos. The country was being ruled from Saigon by a military revolutionary council, made up of 12 members, although the council was really controlled by General Dương Văn Minh. This group faced major problems. Diệm's strategic hamlets program was in ruins and many of the hamlets had been destroyed in the summer before his death by their inhabitants, on the orders of the Việt Cộng. More importantly, much of this enforced resettlement had been in the Mekong Delta, Vietnam's principal rice-growing area, and the destruction of the new hamlets and subsequent movement of the villagers threatened the rice harvest. The council, however, did nothing, its members being more concerned with internal squabbles than untangling the formidable administrative, economic and social problems with which the country was beset. In January 1964 Minh was replaced by General Nguyễn Khánh, who was equally incompetent, but much more manipulative and expert at conspiracy.

During this period, Johnson received increasingly discouraging reports from a number of sources about the competence of both the South Vietnamese government and his official American team in Saigon. He did seem inclined to try and avoid too deep an entanglement in Vietnam during this early period before his election, but these unfavorable reports only added to his problems because his position was not simple, nor were his options particularly clear cut.

His military advisers, the Joint Chiefs of Staff, were convinced that South Vietnam was "pivotal to America's world-wide confrontation with Communism"[1] and had developed a series of suggestions designed to escalate the conflict and "Americanize" the struggle, with a U.S. commander assuming responsibility for the direction of the war. Johnson was not convinced, but he was experiencing difficulties with both chambers of Congress, for if he was seen as "soft" on Communism, much of the necessary social legislation for his "Great Society" initiative would be blocked by conservative politician.[2] Many of these were still worried about Eisenhower's "domino effect" and consequently wanted a tougher U.S. stance in Southeast Asia to discourage the Chinese and Soviet Union. Johnson, however, was an adept politician and he circumvented the problem by making promises to the generals and hardline conservatives that he never intended to fulfill. At a Christmas Eve reception in 1963 at the White House, for example, he told members of the Joint Chiefs of Staff, "Just get me elected, and then you can have your war."[3]

The North Vietnamese, however, were intent upon making President Johnson's decision for him.

## *The Việt Cộng: Supply and Organization (1964–1967)*

In Hanoi, by December 1963, Ho and his advisers had concluded that the Americans would neither abandon South Vietnam nor negotiate a settlement acceptable to both sides. In response to this assessment, they decided that their only chance of success lay in increased military operations involving North Vietnam's entire population. Although their involvement was never admitted by the North Vietnamese leaders until after the war, Ho always maintained that the north was entitled to help the people of the south because "Vietnam is one and the Vietnamese people are one."

North Vietnamese troops secretly infiltrated the south long before Johnson seriously considered sending large bodies of troops there, the old Hồ Chí Minh Trail being widened and improved to send weapons, ammunition, military supplies and thousands of troops into South Vietnam to aid the Việt Cộng. The trail had always been an important strategic asset for the North Vietnamese and had been in almost continual use during their war with the French, but in its present state it was really only suitable for foot traffic. Consequently, after an initial survey, the North Vietnamese leaders began a new project in 1964—enlarging the old jungle paths into a modern highway, down which all the paraphernalia of warfare could reach the south, most of it supplied by the Chinese and Soviet Union.[4]

During 1964, ten thousand troops moved into South Vietnam by this route, increasing Việt Cộng strength to a total of one hundred and seventy thousand men. This included a central formation of fifty elite battalions, containing approximately thirty thousand men, and specifically intended to destroy the South Vietnamese army. By 1967, this figure for reinforcements had increased dramatically, with over twenty thousand North Vietnamese moving south down the trail every month. These units contained many North Vietnamese officers and were controlled by the Hanoi government, although they had their own southern headquarters, the Truong Uong Cuc (Central Office for South Vietnam, or COSVN).

The Việt Cộng were not, as many Americans then believed, an indigenous and wholly separate insurgent movement, but in fact had firm links with Hanoi and took their orders from North Vietnamese generals.[5] The COSVN, incidentally, bore no resemblance to its Pentagon counterpart, being simply a collection of individuals who held their meetings and made their command decisions sheltered by whatever huts and tunnels they found available. In addition to reinforcements, the Việt Cộng were also supplied with sophisticated new weapons, mortars, anti-tank guns and anti-aircraft rockets, as well as AK-47 automatic rifles and machine guns, which both used the same 7.62×39mm cartridge. The South Vietnamese army was no match for well-equipped troops in these numbers, and as early as the end of 1964, the Việt Cộng were beginning to dominate the military situation.

## America and the South (1964–1965)

In Saigon, the political situation had also continued to deteriorate, largely as a consequence of the continuing military success by the Việt Cộng, and many in the Pentagon and White House were desperate for an excuse to intervene and appoint their own commander to conduct the war. This excuse arrived, ready made, early in August 1964, following U.S. naval action in the Gulf of Tonkin. Details of the operation (usually referred to as the "Gulf of Tonkin Incident") and the controversy surrounding it have been dissected at length elsewhere, and it is sufficient to say that on 2 August 1964, a U.S. Navy warship, USS *Maddox*, fired upon and damaged a number of North Vietnamese torpedo boats, which the American captain alleged were stalking the ship while it was engaged in intercepting North Vietnamese military radio traffic in the Gulf of Tonkin. Two days later the Americans claimed their ship had been attacked again, although it is now believed that the ship's crew was mistaken and there was no second attack. Johnson used the incident as an excuse to launch air attacks on the torpedo boat bases before requesting a resolution from Congress allowing him to use conventional forces in Southeast Asia without a formal declaration of war by Congress. This would effectively enable Johnson and his successor Nixon to conduct military operations in Southeast Asia in any way they thought fit, deploying troops and conventional weapons without reference to either the House of Representatives or the Senate. Significantly, Johnson's aides had begun preparing just such a resolution before the election, in May 1964, but Johnson had decided against proposing it, feeling that it might detract from his moderate image and detrimentally affect his chances of being elected.[6]

The Gulf of Tonkin Resolution was approved by Congress on 7 August 1964. It authorized the president "to take all necessary steps, including the use of armed force, to assist any member or protocol state of the South-East Asia Collective Defense Treaty requesting assistance in defense of its freedom." Incidentally, this resolution also effectively silenced Senator Barry Goldwater (the candidate opposing Johnson in the forthcoming presidential election), who had been claiming that Johnson was soft on Communism.

Johnson won the 1964 presidential election on 3 November by a huge majority of 22 percent, the biggest majority since 1820 and still the largest achieved by any president since then. Equally important, his overwhelming victory in the election not only was a boost to his own administration but also gave the Democrats huge majorities in both chambers of Congress, which made passing any major legislation, particularly that for Johnson's "Great Society" initiative, significantly easier. His personal confidence thus rejuvenated, he now began to claim increasingly that direct American intervention had become inevitable in response to the situation in South Vietnam, in order to push the Việt Cộng north of the De-Militarized Zone (DMZ) and keep them there.[7] This would compel the nationalists to give up their efforts to unify the country under a Communist-inspired regime led by Hồ Chí Mính, although it does not seem to have been clear what Johnson or his advisers expected to put in place as an alternative once such a fragile stalemate had been achieved. More importantly, from Johnson's viewpoint, intervention would also shield him from charges of being the first American president to lose a war.

Despite Johnson's undeniable sincerity, his approach to the war failed to achieve the expected result because no one in his administration, least of all the president himself, appreciated the intense level of commitment that the North Vietnamese, and particularly the Communists, brought to their fight for unification.[8] Perhaps even more important than his lack of sympathy for the Vietnamese viewpoint, however, was his refusal to sanction serious diplomatic efforts, which, inevitably, left only military options available.

Even in the period before Johnson's election, despite it being characterized by military escalation and bombastic rhetoric from both parties, war was not seen as inevitable by either side. On 13 August, the Johnson administration had offered the North Vietnamese peace terms that included economic aid and other benefits if they abandoned their insurgency activities in the south, although they were also threatened with "consequences, if they pursued their present course." The North Vietnamese, in turn, replied with threats of their own, warning that if American attacks continued, the war would spread throughout Southeast Asia, although their spokesman, Phạm Văn Đồng, then secretly asked for alternative U.S. proposals, based on the 1954 Geneva agreement, which had specifically proposed unification based on free elections. Even U Thant, then UN secretary-general, and Khrushchev, the Russian premier, tried to arrange a meeting between the two sides, but without success. Johnson, concerned that his anti-Communist position might be compromised with voters before the presidential election, would not bargain without a significant battlefield advantage and, unfortunately, the North Vietnamese, who controlled the Việt Cộng, took exactly the same view. Inevitably, therefore, no compromise of any sort was possible or even expected, and the negotiations again degenerated into futile posturing by both sides. Johnson's aides were so firmly against any weakening of their leader's resolve that they even withheld information about U Thant's meeting from the president, which was arranged for some time in September 1964.[9]

## *The Saigon Coups (1964–1965)*

Although Johnson was not enthusiastic about conducting a war in Indochina, the decision was quietly made in the White House to assume management of both the war and the Saigon government. The unenviable task of implementing this decision fell to the new American ambassador, General Maxwell Taylor, who was, unfortunately, to prove wholly unsuitable for the job. Taylor was a former chairman of the Joint Chiefs of Staff and Johnson had only appointed him to placate potential opponents in the military. Taylor's previous career had been exclusively with the military and, despite his best efforts, the complexities, vendettas and convolutions of Vietnamese political life proved beyond his grasp and experience.

Soon after Taylor was appointed, on 25 August 1964, Nguyễn Khánh resigned as prime minister and the government's advisory body, the military revolutionary council, appointed Khánh and two other generals, Tran Thien Khiem and Duong Vanh Minh, to rule as a coalition. This arbitrary allocation of power resulted in wholesale rioting between Catholics and Buddhists, which continued into September, despite intervention by the military. On 13 September, another coup attempt was made, this time only lasting 24 hours, because Air Vice Marshal Nguyễn Cao Kỳ threatened to bomb the headquarters of the organizers if they did not surrender, which they promptly did. By October, Khánh was again in control, having exiled his two rivals and formed a puppet council. This council, in turn, proclaimed the creation of a civilian regime formed to do exactly as Khánh told them, headed by an elderly politician, Phan Huy Quat, as president, and with a contemporary of his, Tran Van Huong, as prime minister. The chaos continued, with riots, demonstrations and hunger strikes, until the situation had deteriorated so much that Huong was forced to declare martial law, giving Khánh and Kỳ, who had joined forces, the opportunity to resume their plotting for a return to power. Taylor warned Kỳ and the other generals that any further disorder might result in withdrawal of American aid, but they ignored him and on 20 December deposed Quat and Huong in yet another coup attempt. Taylor, in perhaps his worst blunder so far, called the architects of the coup to the embassy and berated them, causing a loss of "face" that in turn alienated the very officials whose good will the Americans were most dependent upon.

By 27 January 1965, Khánh had maneuvered his way back into power, but the Americans distrusted him and encouraged his colleagues, who were plotting against him once more. Saigon was besieged in yet another coup on 16 February 1965, and Khánh was expelled from office and left Saigon—this time for good. A civilian administration was put in place for a few months before being replaced in early June by a military regime, with Air Vice Marshal Nguyễn Cao Kỳ as prime minister and General Nguyễn Văn Thiệu as head of state.[10] In the summer of 1965, Johnson was more convinced than ever that the ineptitude and unreliability of the South Vietnamese military meant that the only way forward lay in the American military continuing to conduct the war.

*Left:* **Nguyễn Cao Kỳ in 1967. Coming to prominence as a flamboyant air vice-marshal in the 1960s, he staged a military coup that made him prime minister in 1965; although deposed in 1967, he served as vice-president until 1975.** *Right:* **Nguyễn Văn Thiệu in 1967. Elected president of South Vietnam in 1967, he retained this position until 1975, when Saigon was overrun by Communist forces from the north.**

## Escalation (1964–1968)

Even before Johnson's election, from August 1964 onward, military operations had been gradually scaling up, and although Taylor, the Joint Chiefs of Staff and the president's civilian advisers were still dubious about committing ground troops to Vietnam, all felt it necessary to continue the campaign of air strikes. Johnson was also hoping to avoid, or at least delay, sending U.S. troops and so prevaricated over any major commitment of the navy or air force. In one instance, he ordered the navy into the Gulf of Tonkin, and then abruptly withdrew the ships six days later, although, in the same period, he did approve a contingency plan allowing retaliation against any Communist attack on American troops (a plan that later had a lethal significance for the U.S. troops it affected). Even more inexplicable, however, was the Pentagon staff's reaction to their own planners' projections. In September 1964, the joint chiefs organized a war game code-named "Sigma II," designed to show the effects of a prolonged air offensive against North Vietnam. The results were predictable, clearly demonstrating that no amount of bombing would stop the North Vietnamese, principally because their rural economy was flexible enough to carry on with a minimum of resources, with an infrastructure that bombing could not damage sufficiently to render inoperable. Despite the result of these simulations, Johnson's aides continued planning for a massive series of bombing raids, which they already knew would be ineffective. During this later half of 1964, however, the Hanoi regime had also continued its military and logistic operations.

Bell UH-1 Iroquois helicopter, used extensively in Vietnam by American, Australian and New Zealand armed forces. They were deployed for general support, air assault, cargo transport, CASVAC, search and rescue, and ground attack, becoming one of the most enduring symbols of American involvement in Southeast Asia.

In that period (June–December 1964), the North Vietnamese had continued the improvements to the Hồ Chí Minh Trail, and in October 1964 the Việt Cộng proved their efficiency by attacking a U.S. air base at Biên Hòa, damaging or destroying with mortar fire 26 B-57 jet bombers that had been lined up on the tarmac and killing five Americans and two Vietnamese, as well as wounding over a hundred more. Taylor, still U.S. ambassador, wanted to escalate the bombing, but with the election pending, Johnson decided to wait. Immediately after his election, however, Johnson's aides began to present him with a new set of options for continuing the war, despite many in the CIA and government beginning to doubt a successful outcome. These objections were brushed aside. The question was not whether the Americans should stay or go; that was decided. Their perceived role in the global conflict meant, in the words of William Bundy, that they had to "maintain our position in South-east Asia."

General William Westmoreland in January 1969. Commander of MACV from January 1964 until June 1968, when he was replaced by General Creighton Adams.

Now it had become a simple question of what to do in order to win and defeat the "Communist Menace."

The Việt Cộng continued their attacks, striking a series of devastating blows against the South Vietnamese army, culminating, on Christmas Eve 1964, in the bombing of the Brinks hotel in Saigon, which was being used to house U.S. officers. Johnson responded by ordering an escalation of the air raids in January 1965, and the United States now began regularly bombing bridges, railways and oil storage depots in North Vietnam as well as mining Hai Phong harbor, despite the previous "Sigma II" simulation showing that this would be largely ineffective.

After a period of prevarication, conflicting advice from his closest aides and another major Việt Cộng attack (this time at Plei Ku), Johnson initiated a further escalation of the bombing campaign. "Flaming Dart I," which attacked North Vietnamese army bases near Đồng Hới, began on 7 February 1965, and it was followed by a second series of attacks on 11 February, codenamed "Flaming Dart II," focusing on bases near the DMZ. A series of jet strikes against targets in the south followed "Flaming Dart" before the commencement of a new offensive, code-named "Rolling Thunder"—a campaign of aerial bombardment using B-57 bombers, originally intended to last for 8 weeks but which in fact continued for 44 months, from 2 March 1965 to 2 November 1968.[11] One consequence of this attack, unforeseen by the Americans, was that Alexei Kosygin, the new Soviet leader, was forced to capitulate to North Vietnamese demands for increased military aid. Kosygin was in Hanoi during the air strikes, trying to extract a compromise from the North Vietnamese to prevent a wider war that would jeopardize a peaceful Soviet-U.S. coexistence. Unfortunately, he found himself in a position similar to that faced by Johnson, unable to refuse aid to the victims of "imperialist aggression" because of intransigent anti–American politicians in his own party. Some observers have suggested that the Plieku raid was deliberately timed to precipitate American retaliation and in turn force the unconditional Soviet military aid package that resulted.[12]

The war now began to gather momentum, and as the bombing escalated, another problem arose, which was to generate the war's most serious, long-term consequences. Carrier-borne aircraft used in bombing raids were safe from attack by the North Vietnamese, but those based at Danang were still extremely vulnerable, as had been clearly demonstrated by the Biên Hòa raid. To deal with this problem, on 22 February 1965, General Westmoreland, commanding American troops in Vietnam under Taylor, asked for two Marine battalions to defend the base. Taylor objected, seeing this as "an ever increasing U.S. combat involvement in a hostile, foreign country."

Johnson ignored Taylor, and on the morning of 8 March 1965, the first American Marines came ashore at Danang. Westmoreland, however, wanted more troops and asked for another division to protect the other U.S. bases. Taylor disagreed again, saying first that an increasing U.S. troop commitment would only encourage the South Vietnamese to leave the war to the Americans, and, second, that the United States would, yet again, be open to the criticism from Hanoi that they were simply replacing the old French colonial administration with its American equivalent. Johnson agreed with Taylor, but also increased the bombing raids on North Vietnam.

By late March, Johnson's Washington aides were intent upon further escalation; consequently, on 1 April, Johnson agreed to Westmoreland's request, sending two more Marine battalions and twenty thousand logistical troops to South Vietnam. More significantly, on Westmoreland's advice, he also sanctioned a more aggressive approach. Instead of simply defending the U.S. bases, the Marines would now send out combat patrols to actively engage the Việt Cộng, in line with Johnson's pre-election commitment to allow retaliation against any Communist attack on American troops. American military operations had really begun in earnest now, but Johnson concealed the deployments, because U.S. political opposition was also finally and belatedly beginning to gather momentum. It was led by William Fulbright, chairman of the Foreign Relations Committee, who had categorically warned Johnson late in March 1965 that "a massive air and ground war in Southeast Asia would be a disaster for the United States."[13]

Johnson would not discuss the matter with Fulbright, who was a long-time friend, but instead gave a speech at John Hopkins University, Baltimore, in which he called for the North Vietnamese to agree to "unconditional discussions" in return for a share of a huge development project in the Mekong Delta, to be financed by the Americans. The president himself was not optimistic about the proposal, even telling members of his staff, "If I were Hồ Chí Mính, I would never negotiate."

Phạm Văn Đồng, then North Vietnam's prime minister, agreed to discussions, but only if the U.S. bombing ended and a neutral coalition government (which would include Việt Cộng representatives) was created in Saigon, conditions the Communists would continue to insist upon until the final peace talks in 1972. The North Vietnamese had learned bitter lessons from their abortive attempts to negotiate with the French, who had often used peace agreements to gain time for a build-up of military forces, and they now transferred this legacy of distrust to their dealings with the Americans.

Việt Cộng forces began another series of attacks in May 1965. This time, they were more widespread, decimating the South Vietnamese army and causing the civilian government of the elderly Phan Huy Quat to be replaced by a military regime led by Air Vice Marshal Nguyễn Cao Kỳ as prime minister and General Nguyễn Văn Thiệu as chief of state. By June, with Taylor subdued and acquiescent, Johnson had agreed to send another forty thousand U.S. troops to Saigon, double the number already there, with further deployments possible. Westmoreland, however, was concerned about the rapid and complete disintegration of the South Vietnamese army during the Việt Cộng's May offensive and appealed to Johnson for still more reinforcements, sufficient to increase the total American forces in the country to 180,000 men, with another 100,000 more needed in 1966. Now, whether Johnson and his aides liked it or not, the conflict had truly become an American war. And Westmoreland, for one, was clear about the consequences, telling Johnson bluntly, "We are in for a long pull. I see no likelihood of achieving a quick, favorable end to the war."

Unfortunately for Johnson, there were still dissenters, once again led by Senator Fulbright, who said in Senate speech that the Communists should be offered a "reasonable and attractive alternative to military victory" through negotiations. Some of Johnson's closest aides were also concerned, but the president ignored them all and sent the troops Westmoreland had requested.

## Westmoreland's Strategy

Westmoreland had conceived a long-term strategy to deal with the Việt Cộng even before Johnson agreed to his troop requests. Initially, he would use his troops to protect U.S. installations around Saigon and along the coast, while simultaneously sending detachments into the central highlands to block any attempt by the enemy to reach the sea and effectively divide the country in two. With his position consolidated in this way, he then proposed to launch a series of operations (later termed "search and destroy" missions) to destroy enemy troop concentrations, after which he would simply kill or capture the remaining Communists, thus achieving final victory. Once again, what would happen after this "final victory" does not seem to have been discussed or even considered. Westmoreland's military initiative, together with the intensive bombing of the north and U.S. "pacification" program aimed at controlling the South's rural population, was thought to be all that was needed to produce the desired result, whatever that was to be.

The Americans began with a gigantic logistical effort, pouring equipment and material into the country on an unprecedented scale. By 1967, approximately 35,000 tons of supplies a day (a million tons per month) were being shipped into Vietnam to maintain the U.S. troops there—over 100 pounds a day for every American stationed the country.[14] This was in contrast to the Việt Cộng, who were using only fifteen tons per day to maintain the whole of their effort in the south and were receiving nearly six thousand tons of aid a day from the Chinese and Soviet Union (although this was still less than 20 percent of what the Americans were supplying). This explains why, despite continual air bombardment and attacks by ground forces, traffic down the Hồ Chí Minh Trail was more than sufficient for the Việt Cộng's logistical needs.[15] As well as being able to operate without luxuries like shaving foam, beer, cigarettes and toilet paper, which seemed to be a necessity for the

American GIs, the Việt Cộng were also not so dependent upon motorized transport. When the trail became impassable to vehicles, the Vietnamese resorted to bicycles, mules and porters to move vital supplies, and because their logistical requirements were so slight, this primitive transportation system sufficed to maintain the momentum of their military operations.[16] Moreover, the industrial capacity of the North Vietnamese was so limited that, even when American attacks reduced its electricity-generating capacity by 85 percent, the shortfall was easily made up by about 2,000 World War II vintage diesel generators, the whole country's power requirements being only 20 percent of that required by a small American town. Even without the war game's predictions, the Americans might have guessed that destroying industrial centers would not have affected North Vietnamese and Việt Cộng military activities significantly, because the country's minute industrial capacity was the reason all the Communists' military supplies had to come from China or the Soviet Union in the first place!

Bombing was not very economic, either. By the end of 1967, the Americans had inflicted approximately $300 million worth of damage on North Vietnam—in exchange for the loss of over 700 aircraft conservatively valued at approximately $900 million. And that takes no account of wages, the cost of ordnance or the expenses involved in operating the carriers that the majority of these aircraft flew from. Clearly, the predictions from "Sigma II," the war game staged back in September 1964, were coming true, much to the Pentagon's embarrassment.

These huge levels of bombing, attacks with chemical defoliant and shelling resulted in other problems, however. The constant air strikes drove approximately four million South Vietnamese (around one quarter of the population) from their homes and into a twilight existence on the fringes of cities such as Saigon, Danang and Biên Hòa. And, incredibly, it was *American* strategists who encouraged this exodus on the grounds that this "forced urbanization," as they clinically termed it, would deny peasant support to the enemy and so hamper their ability to operate in the countryside. Predictably, it had little effect. Việt Cộng units quickly returned to those areas that the Americans believed they had rendered uninhabitable, as they did, for example, at the end of Operation "Cedar Falls."[17] The only real victims were the farmers and their families; many young South Vietnamese from rural backgrounds were forced to live in the cities, with no recourse but prostitution or the drug trade to avoid starvation. Consequently, such activities flourished, encouraged by a Saigon administration in which corruption was widespread, if not universal, and fed by the influx of money that accompanied the immense American military machine now destroying the country and people it was intended to save. Moreover, it was becoming increasingly clear, even to some in Washington, that the American forces in Vietnam were grinding themselves to pieces, trying to fight a war they had not the slightest hope of winning.[18] Unfortunately, even the colossal level of waste that this policy was engendering could not deter the American planners. For example, when it was suggested to Robert Komer, Westmoreland's civilian deputy in charge of the pacification program, that it would be cheaper to buy the Việt Cộng off at $500 dollars each, rather than continue to waste money in the way they were currently doing, he replied, quite seriously, "We've staffed it, it's more like twenty-five hundred dollars a head."[19]

The Americans were now unequivocally running both the country and the war, with the wholehearted support of the Saigon regime and its rural subsidiaries, although, ironically (and perhaps predictably), it was this complete dependence on American resources that would be responsible for the later collapse of the South Vietnamese administration.[20]

Saigon's politics remained in an uneasy flux in the years between 1967 and 1973, with factions and alliances between the army, the Buddhists and the Saigon administration forming, shifting and reforming in a seemingly endless (and largely pointless) procession. In April 1966, Kỳ, then prime minister, even attacked his own forces in Danang and Hue, claiming they were controlled by the Buddhists, who, according to him, were now dominated by the Communists. The situation was calmer by June, and with the situation in Saigon temporarily stable, Johnson, driven by American public opinion, asked Kỳ to hold a national election, based on a new constitution written by a White House aide, John Roche. The polls were duly opened in September 1967, and, predictably, General Nguyễn Văn Thiệu was elected president, with Kỳ as his vice-president. To compensate Kỳ for this subordinate position, he was also appointed head of a military council empowered to clandestinely shape government policy.[21] This uneasy alliance was to remain in place until peace talks halted the war in 1973.

The North Vietnamese were also having trouble with their Chinese allies during this period. They had changed their strategy late in 1965, deciding to wage a conventional war in South Vietnam, with the initial intention of wholly destroying the South Vietnamese army, but the massive American military effort in support of their opponents had ruined any hope of that, at least for the foreseeable future. In response to the American economic "invasion" and the demands of their Chinese allies for a more modest use of resources, the Nationalists consolidated their position, continuing to move material down the Hồ Chí Minh Trail on foot and by bicycle when the road was destroyed by bombs, but not beginning any major offensives.[22] They also dug miles of shelters in the city streets and even into the fields, so farmers could work their farms with minimal risk from air raids. American bombing actually helped the Communists far more than the Americans, because it angered the population so intensely that even many who disliked the Communists joined with them to resist the American invaders.[23]

Despite losing over 500,000 troops in the period between 1967 and 1973 (compared to American losses of 58,000), the Việt Cộng and North Vietnamese leaders refused to negotiate, bolstered by a commitment to driving the invaders from their country that was shared universally by their troops.[24] Many American analysts of the period simplistically labeled this phenomenon "indoctrination," implying that some form of psychological coercion or "brainwashing" was involved. They refused to believe that what drove the ordinary Vietnamese soldier was a simple desire to have his country unified and returned to an elected Vietnamese administration. As one North Vietnamese private explained under questioning, "I knew that I might be killed, but I was committed to the sacred salvation of the nation." It was that level of commitment that the Americans wholly failed to understand or, if they did understand it, refused to believe in. And they were to spend billions of dollars and 58,000 American lives before it was clearly brought home to them.

## The American Soldier in Vietnam

Surveys conducted after the war have shown that, in many respects, the Americans who were sent to Vietnam were as patriotic as their enemies. In a study conducted among

Vietnam veterans by the Veterans Administration in 1980, 71 percent of participants said they were "glad" to have gone, with 74 percent claiming to have enjoyed their tour and 66 percent saying they would be willing to serve again. That does not mean that their enthusiasm for the war did not diminish as it went on, however. In another poll, 82 percent said they felt that it was "the political leaders in Washington who would not let them win," which Stanley Karnow suggests is a major contribution to the average American's currently waning faith in public institutions.[25] Despite this lack of trust, a significant number of civilians and veterans, when asked, also subscribed to President Reagan's view of the war as "noble."

Many U.S. troops went to Vietnam suffering from what some more flippant observers have referred to as the "John Wayne" complex, expressed in both an overconfidence in the ability of their army to defeat any opponent and their own view of themselves as the stereotypical hero portrayed by the American media. As Ron Kovic explained in his book *Born on the Fourth of July*, when describing his meeting with two recruiters prior to his own enlistment, "As I shook their hands and stared up into their eyes, I couldn't help but feel that I was shaking hands with John Wayne and Audie Murphy."[26]

This seems to have been a commonly held view among the first recruits sent to Vietnam early in the war, but their optimism and enthusiasm was to be gradually eroded by the reality they found awaiting them.

Unlike the solidarity and impressive commitment of the Việt Cộng detachments, even after suffering the most horrendous casualties, once in combat, many American soldiers felt isolated, even within their own units, and there seems to have been little mutual support or camaraderie among American troops. Moreover, they were made to feel wholly unwelcome, even by the South Vietnamese, whom they had been told they were in the country to help. This generally unfriendly reception was exacerbated by a difficulty complained about by many who served there—first, in telling friend from foe, and then how frequently such a mistaken perception resulted in injury or death. Việt Cộng booby traps were also ingenious and widespread, which together with the difficulty of knowing the difference between a friend and an enemy, increased the stress and fatalities of normal jungle patrols out of all proportion to their importance. All these factors were a continuing, damaging influence on the troops' morale, which, for many, had been ebbing from the time of their arrival in the country.[27] As one American soldier put it:

> It was less the fear of death that nagged us than the absurd combination of certainty and uncertainty—the certainty that the mines were everywhere, and the uncertainty about how to move or sit in order to avoid them. The Việt Cộng had so many ways to plant and camouflage mines.... I'm ready to go home.[28]

The Americans had been losing the war from its beginning, for reasons that were incomprehensible to those running it. Most of the soldiers were only required to serve for a single tour, lasting a year, but that was enough to make many doubt their government's reasons for subjecting them to what was coming to be seen as an increasingly pointless and dangerous war. One GI summed up the feelings of many who served there:

> After a few months, it began to seem crazy, but you didn't dare to draw conclusions that might point in terrifying directions. Maybe we Americans weren't the guys in white hats, riding white horses. Maybe we shouldn't be in Vietnam. Maybe I'd gotten my ass out in these bushes for nothing. Still, it never occurred to me to lay down my rifle and quit.

**Phantom F-4, destroyed at the Tan Son Nhut airbase during the Tet Offensive. Photograph taken 18 February 1968.**

> Instead, you develop a survival mentality. You stop thinking about what you're doing, and you count the days. I knew that I was in Vietnam for three hundred and ninety five days, and if I was still alive at the end of those three hundred and ninety five days, I'd go home and forget the whole thing. That's the way you operated.[29]

One way in which the American soldiers' disenchantment was reflected was in the widespread use of illegal narcotics.[30]

## Media Influence

Although the media bore much of the blame from politicians and generals for turning American public opinion against the war, the press had usually followed U.S. public opinion rather than leading it. Until late in 1966, that is, when Harrison Salisbury of the *New York Times* sent in a series of dispatches about the bombing in North Vietnam, describing the wholesale slaughter that the American attacks had caused. Later, in October 1967, Hedley Donovan, the editor of *Life*, also decried the conflict, describing it as "not worth winning." Johnson was furious with both journalists and even used his influence to exclude Salisbury from a well-deserved Pulitzer Prize.

More then ever, despite overwhelming logistical, numerical and especially financial advantages, it was becoming clear that the Americans would never defeat the Việt Cộng, because the Việt Cộng would simply not admit that they could be defeated. The GIs were fighting an enemy with superior psychological and physical characteristics, in a country beyond their generals' experience and where, increasingly, the ordinary American soldier did not want to be and did not understand why he should have to remain. The only chance America had to save face was a negotiated peace. But that seemed further away than ever.

## Johnson's Demise

Despite progress in the war slowing to a crawl by the beginning of 1966 and its growing unpopularity with many Americans, Johnson was adamant that it should continue.[31] He made his viewpoint clear in a speech given at this time: "We will stay until aggression has stopped because in Asia and around the world are countries whose independence rests, in large measure, on confidence in America's word and in America's protection."

Clearly, Johnson was still publicly advocating America's role as global policeman, despite changing conditions that made it increasingly untenable. In addition, Vietnam was now dominating American domestic politics in a way that would have been inconceivable even a year before and, most importantly, poisoning Johnson's attempts to pass his "Great Society" initiatives. The electorate was also becoming increasingly unhappy about the number of Americans killed during operations in Vietnam, despite figures showing that approximately ten Việt Cộng were dying for every American soldier who was killed there.

At the end of 1965, in order to implement his "seek and destroy" strategy, Westmoreland again asked for even more troops to match the Communist build-up. It was effectively a demand for an open-ended troop commitment, and Johnson prevaricated. He wanted to win—in fact, he could hardly afford not to at this point—but he needed to make the price of victory politically acceptable, so, once again, he sent his secretary of defense, Robert McNamara, to review the situation. McNamara came back to Washington convinced that America could not win without sustaining unacceptably high casualties, and as Johnson shrewdly commented, after hearing McNamara's pessimistic conclusions, "the weakest chink in our armor is public opinion. Our people won't stand firm in the face of heavy losses and they can bring down the government."

**Robert McNamara, secretary of defense from 1961 until 1968, when he was removed for advocating a policy of conciliation in South Vietnam, 22 November 1967.**

In mid–December, faced with the realities of the report from his secretary of defense, Johnson began to discuss the possibility of a cease-fire with his aides. After two days of discussions, he decided to call a halt to the bombing and try to open negotiations, beginning a spectacular "peace offensive," sending emissaries to more than forty countries to plead his sincerity. But it was a sham. Although the air war had been halted, the truce on the ground only lasted a single day before American troops renewed the fighting, and by the end of January 1966, with no results from his feigned diplomatic initiative, Johnson renewed the bombing.[32] In response, the North Vietnamese continued to insist that the bombing must stop before talks could begin, even if the halt was accepted as temporary.

By now, however, Johnson was starting to experience rising political pressure at home, forced to placate both sides in the political conflict in the hope of securing, or at least maintaining, his increasingly precarious position. This was made progressively more difficult by attacks on his Vietnam policy from many in Congress, most notably Robert Kennedy and William Fulbright. Moreover, the cost of the war had been rising astronomically. In 1965, it had cost $8 million a year, and this number would rise to just over $21 billion by 1967. Johnson, concerned that this increase might acquaint the public with the real cost of the war and result in the sacrifice of some of his domestic programs, had repeatedly concealed its actual price by manipulating the financial statistics, until he quite literally ran out of money in the summer of 1967 and was forced to order tax increases. Congress delayed passage of his proposal until 1968, at which point the 1967 deficit of $10 billion had increased to over $30 billion and America was beginning a dizzying spiral into crippling inflation and massive debt. Incidentally, at any time during Johnson's presidency, members of Congress could have refused to allow the president's appropriations for the war and thus brought the conflict to an end. They did not, apparently due to fear of the president's ability to withhold grant aid to their constituencies if they dissented and also because they might be seen as unpatriotic, a certain vote-loser in the maelstrom of American domestic politics. So, Johnson got everything he asked for and he never encountered more than a token resistance to his Vietnam policies during the whole of his presidency.[33]

McNamara was sent back to Vietnam in October 1966 and returned with a plan based on a holding action and possible negotiation.[34] The Pentagon was not impressed and called for an increase in air and naval attacks. Johnson, however, rejected this advice and decided to scale down operations, although the bombing continued. White House opinion continued to be divided, with one group, mostly but not wholly military, advocating a new, tougher campaign, while a second group, led by McNamara, favored a less belligerent approach. This dichotomy was reflected in other areas of the Washington political scene as well, although, significantly, no group suggested calling a halt to the bombing or that joint concessions might be mutually agreed with the Communists.[35] The only patriotic response was to be seen supporting actions that would result in a clear victory in Vietnam, and this was an attitude shared by both White House and public alike. Any other view was still political suicide.

Westmoreland came back to Washington in the spring of 1967, and his assessment of the situation was even less optimistic than previously. He warned Johnson that the war could go on indefinitely, and even with the 470,000 men he had been promised he could do little more than maintain the present stalemate. Given another 200,000 men, he might "finish" the war in two years, but, as Johnson pointed out, what would happen if the enemy

**Vietnam protesters at the March on the Pentagon on 21 December 1967, in a picture taken near the Lincoln Memorial.**

organized a proportionate increase? Westmoreland had no answer. Yet, despite the general's uncertainty, Johnson once again agreed to send more troops, an additional 45,000 troops this time, with the vague possibility of still more being made available.

Bombing continued to prove ineffectual, much as "Sigma II" had predicted against a largely rural population not dependent upon modern conveniences like fuel and electricity for its existence. More crucially, the South Vietnamese were still apathetic about their own fate and quite content to leave the war to the Americans, which was seen as the major obstacle to victory by many Washington analysts, such as Alain Enthoven.[36] By May 1967, McNamara was advocating a de-escalation of operations in Vietnam, which served to end his political career in a series of maneuvers orchestrated by Senator John Stennis and supported by the Pentagon generals, both convinced that they only needed to hit the Việt Cộng harder in order to win.[37] Johnson capitulated to the Pentagon, approving fresh air strikes, many against heavily populated areas and several in a sensitive area near the Chinese border. He also got rid of McNamara, sending him on his way to a job as president of the World Bank late in February 1968.

Peace talks were still seen by many outside America as the only rational solution to the impasse that Vietnam had become, but several attempts to begin negotiations came to nothing during 1967, including a joint attempt by Harold Wilson and Alexei Kosygin.

In Vietnam, Westmoreland continued his campaign of attrition, and by the end of 1967, there were nearly 500,000 U.S. troops in Vietnam. American casualties now stood at over 9,000 killed, with 1.5 million tons of bombs having been dropped; yet the Americans were no nearer to any sort of solution than they had been in 1963. Despite this stalemate, Johnson ordered an impressive public relations exercise intended to convince ordinary Americans that the war was being won. He even called Westmoreland home in November 1967 and sent him on a tour of the country, although he was carefully steered away from areas that might generate unsympathetic questioners. In Vietnam, however, the Communists had quietly been preparing for a major offensive since the summer, timed to coincide with the celebration of Tet, the lunar New Year. The Tet Offensive, as it came to be known, although largely unsuccessful for the Communists, was to spell the end for Johnson.

## The Tet Offensive

Previously, apart from the low-level clandestine bombing operations, all the Việt Cộng's military activity had been confined to rural areas, although by January 1968 Communist forces in South Vietnam were estimated at six hundred thousand men.[38] On the evening of 31 January 1968, the Việt Cộng changed the arena. In an offensive of huge scope, 70,000 North Vietnamese and Việt Cộng troops surprised the Americans by attacking over a hundred cities and towns, including Saigon, Hoi An, Danang, Qiun Hon, Hue and the military base at Khe Sanh. Action at Khe Sanh and in other parts of the hinterland began first and was well coordinated, being specifically intended to draw large numbers of American troops away from the cities and thus leave them more vulnerable to Communist attack.[39] American intelligence about the assault appears to have been both confused and poorly interpreted.

The offensive was characterized by an unprecedented ferocity on both sides, with the Americans and South Vietnamese mercilessly and indiscriminately crushing Việt Cộng resistance wherever it was found, while the Communists murdered hundreds of innocent civilians who could have done them no possible harm, particularly in the coastal town of Hue. The attacks went on until March; by then, it was estimated that fifty thousand Communist troops, mainly the southern Việt Cộng, had been killed, along with four thousand South Vietnamese and two thousand Americans. For the Việt Cộng, it was close to a military disaster, although, typically, the whole operation had been planned with parallel political and diplomatic objectives, and it was to have some unforeseen future benefits for the hard-pressed Việt Cộng in the way it affected American public opinion.

Võ Nguyên Giáp, who had overall command of the Communist forces during the campaign against the French, had organized the Tet Offensive himself. He admitted, in an interview conducted after the war, that the offensive was not intended to be a decisive victory, but only the first "episode" in a campaign intended to bleed the overextended Americans into granting a settlement that suited the Hanoi regime (an objective they achieved five years later).[40] Most importantly, one of Giáp's main objectives in the Tet Offensive was to alienate the Americans and South Vietnamese. His intent was to show the war-weary southern population both that they could not depend upon the Americans and their Saigon allies and that, ultimately, they would be defeated and the country returned to a nationalist administration. Finally, the Communists considered that the offensive might at least persuade Johnson to stop the bombing and open negotiations, a "fight and talk" strategy they had used before. This could have also led to a further weakening of the ties between the United States and Saigon, if the Saigon regime thought the Americans might reach an agreement with the Communists that excluded the Thiệu government (this is exactly what happened in October 1972, when Henry Kissinger and Le Duc Tho achieved a compromise without consulting the Saigon administration). To encourage the Americans to come to the negotiating table without South Vietnamese participation, on 30 December 1967, at reception in Hanoi, the North Vietnamese foreign minister, Nguyễn Duy Trinh, modified his country's negotiating stance, demanding only that the American bombing stop before discussions were opened.

In America, well-constructed (but almost wholly untrue) reports of American success during Tet, particularly regarding the defense of Khe Sanh, were having unexpected repercussions, especially on Johnson's popularity. Opinion polls at the time showed him to be disliked by the voters and his credibility had all but disappeared. Many both in and out of government were also openly saying the conflict was futile, principally because of Johnson's conduct of the war.[41] Westmoreland was demanding more troops, his request endorsed by General Earle Wheeler, who was using the Tet Offensive to force Johnson to call up the military reservists, an option the president had consistently rejected because of its political repercussions. McNamara having been pushed aside late in February, his place was taken by a Washington lawyer, Clark Clifford, whom Johnson now ordered to find him a way out of the mess he was in. The president's instructions to his new secretary of defense were simple, if plaintive: "Give me the lesser of the evils." Clifford responded by producing a document that, as one of its compilers said, "really attacked the fundamental motives behind U.S. policy in Vietnam."[42]

In brief, Clifford's proposal recommended that no more troops be sent and that the efficiency and training of the South Vietnamese army be improved until they could assume the Americans' combat role—effectively Nixon's later "Vietnamization" policy. Predictably, the Pentagon demanded more vigorous action, but when Clifford tried to extract any form of precise assessment from the Joint Chiefs about the probable time frame of operations, total troop numbers or even a coherent plan for defeating the Communists, he found no one capable of giving satisfactory answers. By early March 1968, Clifford was certain that America could not win in Vietnam, and he set about manipulating Johnson toward the same conclusion.[43] In his initial step in that direction, he included two proposals that might herald America's withdrawal. First, he suggested that Westmoreland should stop trying to destroy the Communist forces and withdraw to the U.S. coastal bases. Second, the South Vietnamese should be clearly warned that continued American assistance would depend upon them improving their own military performance. As usual, Johnson prevaricated and found himself once again faced by critics such as Robert Kennedy and William Fulbright, who were this time supplemented by John Stennis and Henry Jackson, who had previously supported Pentagon policy unreservedly.

The press was also turning against Johnson, particularly the *New York Times*, which printed a story about Westmoreland's troops requests, while asking why they were necessary if, as the general and President Johnson claimed, the Tet Offensive had crippled the enemy. Political pressure mounted,[44] and, following a meeting on 25 March with a group of eminent advisers (the so-called "Wise Men") who almost unanimously favored withdrawal from Vietnam, Johnson delivered a speech on 31 March 1968 in which he announced he would not seek reelection as president.[45] In addition, he stated that he was restricting air strikes to an area below the 20th Parallel, thereby excluding 90 percent of the north from attack. Averell Harriman was instructed to open negotiations with the North Vietnamese, and these began on 10 May 1968 in Paris.

# 7

# America's War (1968–1973)

## Nixon's War (1968–1972)

The 1968 American presidential campaign was dominated by the war in Vietnam. Anti-war protesters disrupted the Democratic Convention, held in Chicago in August, and although the serving vice-president Hubert Humphrey received the Democratic nomination, splits over Vietnam within his own party doomed his election campaign almost from its inception. Humphrey, along with many both in and out of the White House, clearly understood that some compromise with the North Vietnamese had to be reached. He advocated halting the bombing and transferring responsibility to the South Vietnamese (Clifford's original proposal), first privately at the convention (although Johnson's influence was enough to keep it from becoming public knowledge there), and later in a speech he made in September at a meeting in Salt Lake City.

By then, however, it was too late, despite the North Vietnamese delegation in Paris offering to broaden the talks to include the South Vietnamese and Việt Cộng if bombing raids were unconditionally stopped. This offer was mainly intended to confer official status on the Việt Cộng and humiliate the Saigon government, although the Communists later admitted they also thought it would strengthen Humphrey's position, having decided they would prefer to deal with him than with Nixon. Not wishing to be seen as rejecting a chance of peace, Johnson announced a halt to the bombing on 31 October 1968, just too late to influence the vote sufficiently to ensure Humphrey's election.[1]

Nixon was elected the 37th president of the United States on 5 November 1968 on a platform that had included a promise to "end the war and win the

**Richard Milhous Nixon, 37th president of the United States.**

peace," although he had definitely realized long before his election, and in light of Johnson's futile escalation, that a military solution in Vietnam was impossible. Politically, however, he could not afford to be, in the words of Johnson, "the first U.S. President to lose a war." So, in a curious parallel with his enemies, for Nixon the war became a matter of political "face," and he initially considered trying to scare the North Vietnamese into reaching an agreement with the implied threat of nuclear weapons, which he called his "Madman's Theory."[2]

At the same time, Nixon also opened negotiations with the Soviet Union and China, offering major global concessions in return for reducing tensions in a number of areas, such as the Middle East, Berlin and, most especially, Vietnam, in a policy he termed "linkage." To turn these concepts into reality, he appointed Dr. Henry Kissinger as his national security adviser.

In contrast to Johnson, whose main political concerns had been domestic, predominantly his "Great Society" legislation, Nixon had already decided to confer upon himself an international role. To ensure his success in this venture, he wanted clear authority to make decisions without reference to anyone else, an approach that suited his introverted, solitary personality.[3] In order to achieve this, he authorized Kissinger to curb the influence of the State Department, Pentagon and CIA, in order to ensure that governmental authority returned to the White House, where both men believed it belonged.[4]

While dealing with these mutual domestic antagonists, Kissinger also began to consider how he might approach negotiations with the North Vietnamese during this early period of Nixon's first administration. Finally, he simply adopted Johnson's approach. Briefly, Johnson had emphasized that military and political issues should be separated, the Americans and North Vietnamese confining themselves to negotiations about a cease-fire and eventual withdrawal of troops, thus leaving responsibility for a political agreement with the Việt Cộng and Saigon administration. Kissinger also agreed that the South Vietnamese should have what he called a "major voice" in any talks, but he refused to concede their right to veto an agreement that they found unsatisfactory. Naturally, this looked very much like an American decision to force the Saigon government into a settlement that allowed the United States to get out of the country, having obtained "peace with honor," while abandoning the south to the mercies of the northerners (eventually, of course, that is exactly what happened). Kissinger anticipated this result, saying later that he had hoped only for an agreement that allowed the Saigon government a "reasonable chance to survive—a decent interval."

Once established in the White House, and paralleling his campaign against the State Department, Pentagon and CIA, Kissinger began his peace negotiations by commissioning a massive series of reports about the future of the war in Vietnam. Predictably, opinions ranged from optimism about the progress of the southern army to doubts about the political leadership in Saigon. The consensus was that there was no end in sight, and nobody had a solution to offer. Even the introduction to the final document summarizing the views contained in the mass of reports emphasized what it called "emphatic differences" between the various experts. Clearly there was no genuine consensus, and this was exactly what Kissinger wanted. Now he used the summary to dramatize the divisions between the experts, which would justify Nixon in ignoring the bureaucrats and, more importantly, allow him to act without consulting them. The president grasped this opportunity with both hands, and late in February 1969 he ordered the bombing of Việt Cộng bases in Cambodia to begin (he already had Johnson's "Gulf of Tonkin" resolution in place, which allowed him to do this without involving Congress). Officially, this was in retaliation for a renewed Communist offensive in the south, although Nixon really intended the bombing as a signal to the North Vietnamese that tougher measures, including an implied nuclear threat, were available if necessary—effectively the first step in the implementation of his "Madman's Theory."[5]

Many of Nixon's closest aides, including Kissinger, were worried about the speed and lack of consideration involved in this decision, but Nixon was adamant that something had to be done "on the military front … something they will understand."

Operation "Menu" (the designation given the bombing raids on Cambodia) began on 17 March 1969. Intended as a short-term operation, the raids continued for fourteen months, initially without any information about this new offensive reaching the American public, or even Pentagon officials, until May 1969, when the news was broken by William Beecher, a journalist working for the *New York Times*. There was no discernible public reaction, but Nixon and Kissinger were incensed by what they saw as betrayal by the American media and possibly their own staff. In consultation with J. Edgar Hoover, head of the FBI, Nixon authorized the illegal monitoring (tapping) of the telephones of a number of people, including journalists and some of Kissinger's aides. Kissinger, in particular, was determined to use whatever means necessary to discover the informant; Hoover quoted him as saying that the administration "will destroy whoever did this." The first abuses of presidential authority, which would eventually result in the scandal of Watergate and Nixon's resignation, began with these illegal wiretaps.

**B-52 bomber, used extensively in bombing campaigns against Hanoi and Cambodia.**

Unfortunately, by the summer of 1969, both parts of Nixon's grand plan were starting to unravel. The Vietnamese were not deterred by the Cambodian bombing and its implied threat of nuclear deployment, and, more importantly, despite intense diplomatic maneuvering, the Soviets could not, or (perhaps more probably) would not, exert any influence on the North Vietnamese. Nixon's plan to link all these considerations—Vietnam, disarmament and trade negotiations—into one single, self-regulating pattern had failed. Apparently undeterred, the president fell back on an alternative strategy: endeavoring to transfer responsibility for the war to Saigon (a technique advocated during Johnson's administration, which was later formalized by the Americans and termed "Vietnamization") while at the same time excluding the Saigon regime from secret peace talks with the North Vietnamese. The Communists, however, were sanguine over the American overtures. To them, negotiation was pointless. If the United States carried out its Vietnamization program, the GIs would leave anyway, so no concessions need be made, since, with the Americans gone, the north would quickly overwhelm the south and take control of the whole country. Nixon, however, had no intention of taking American troops out of Vietnam entirely. Or at least they were not going to leave during *his* presidency. His aim in these negotiations was to gain political plaudits for bringing home both the 400 Americans then held prisoner by the Việt Cộng and most of the half a million U.S. GIs who had been sent to Vietnam during Johnson's administration. In conjunction with this withdrawal, he would strengthen the ailing Saigon regime with enough advisers and equipment to make it look as if he was intent upon preventing a Communist takeover. Thus he was safe. *He* would not be the first president to lose a war. That could be safely left to the Saigon administration or, at worst, one of his successors.

**B-52 bomber, this one shown dropping bombs from a high altitude. Photograph taken between 1965 and 1966 during Operation Rolling Thunder.**

By June 1969, public opinion was pushing Nixon to announce at least some token troop withdrawals to begin that year. In response to this changing mood, American tactics were modified, with limited, small-unit actions replacing Westmoreland's huge "search and destroy" sweeps (Westmoreland himself having been replaced by General Creighton Abrams on 10 June 1968). The emphasis now had definitely shifted. Instead of considering how to win, Nixon's aides, including Kissinger, were looking for a cheap way out.

Kissinger, however, still thought that the troops should stay, if only so that America could retain a strong bargaining position. In September 1969, he went so far as to order the preparation of plans for another major bombing campaign, designed to drive the Communists into a new set of peace negotiations. This time, however, even his aides and the men preparing the plan were dubious. Kissinger sent it to Nixon anyway, but the new secretary of defense, Melvin Laird, intervened, advising against any escalation by claiming that it would inflame American public opinion and delay the intended "Vietnamization" of the South Vietnamese army, which was Laird's own solution. Nixon, unfortunately, had been previously confirmed in his more aggressive stance by the English counter-insurgency expert Sir Robert Thompson, who advised him that, given sufficient American aid, Saigon could contain the Communists. Thompson also claimed that "the future of western civilization is at stake in the way you [the Americans] handle yourselves in Vietnam." Given Nixon's already inflated view of his status as a world leader, he could only make one response to such flattery.

The Paris peace talks were deadlocked again, with the Americans, as usual, insisting on a mutual withdrawal and the North Vietnamese, in turn, adamant that the Saigon government be dissolved. Consequently, in July 1969, Nixon sent a message to Ho, via M. Jean Sainteny, stating that unless a diplomatic compromise was reached, he would resort to "measures of great consequence and force." Predictably, Hanoi responded by reiterating the Việt Cộng's previous terms (Ho was too ill to work by August 1969). Ho's death on 2 September reinvigorated the nationalist cause, reasserting the North Vietnamese goal of reunification, although Nixon was still convinced he could compel them to abandon this plan by force and make them accept a permanently divided country, organized in ways similar to Korea and Germany.[6]

In September 1969, Nixon announced further troop withdrawals and a reduction in draft requirements, which temporarily served to quiet both public anxiety and his political opponents. Soon, however, the anti-war faction in the country and both chambers of Congress began to gain momentum again, with organized, nationwide protests beginning in the summer of 1969. Nixon and Vice-President Spiro Agnew both denounced the protesters, Agnew referring to them as "Communist dupes" and "an effete corps of impudent snobs who characterize themselves as intellectuals."

Unfortunately for Nixon, this strength of feeling meant he was now in difficulties over implementing his "measures of great consequence and force" threat. Any escalation at this point would inflame American public opinion and weaken his bargaining position with the North Vietnamese even further, because finally, and fatally for Nixon, the Hanoi regime had realized the importance of propaganda aimed at the American public as well as at their own people.[7]

The first organized anti-war protest, or *moratorium*, held on 15 October 1969 demonstrated even more clearly the extent of Nixon's problems. Instead of being led by violent student activists, the protests were peaceful, with thousands of ordinary, mostly middle-class people assembling in cities as far apart as New York, Detroit and Miami to listen to speakers expressing genuine, acutely reasoned opposition to any continuation of the war. Nixon blustered in public, mouthing platitudes and claiming that "policy made on the streets ... amounted to anarchy."

Beneath his pose, however, Nixon was frightened and ordered his staff to draft a rebuttal of the moratorium arguments, which he delivered on 3 November 1969. In it he spelled out his plan to end the war. Once again he claimed to be able to strengthen the South Vietnamese so that they could defend themselves and then elicit a compromise from the Communists, while still ready to take "strong and effective measures" if they intensified the military actions. However, and this was the catch, he needed time and public backing. At the end of his address, he played his trump card, finishing with the words, "Let us understand: North Vietnam cannot defeat or humiliate the United States. Only Americans can do that."[8]

Certainly, after that speech, it is clear why the American press later resurrected his infamous nickname. He certainly did not become "Tricky Dicky" again without very good reason.[9]

The response to this address, orchestrated by the Republican party machine, was predictable. Supportive telephone messages, telegrams and letters poured into the White House from all parts of the country, and with this level of popular support, Congress also registered cross-party support for Nixon's policy in Vietnam. Nixon's ratings in the opinion polls soared and, along with Spiro Agnew's denouncement of the media, the speech served to temporarily contain the anti-war movement, despite the reports coming out of Vietnam describing war crimes carried out by American troops (especially the My Lai massacre) and the forty thousand U.S. troops killed there by the end of 1969.

Early in 1970, deadlocked on the battlefield and infiltrated by South Vietnamese trained under the U.S. "Phoenix" program, the North Vietnamese and Việt Cộng switched their emphasis back to small-scale operations, aimed at wearing down American morale and forcing Nixon to keep his promises about troop withdrawals The situation was, for the first time, beginning to look promising from the American viewpoint. Communists in both the north and the south were disenchanted, the South Vietnamese were beginning to assume responsibility for their own future and Nixon had already repatriated 100,000 troops during 1969, with another 150,000 set to return home by December 1970. Unfortunately, Nixon was unable to resist trying once again to coerce North Vietnam into accepting peace on American terms, and, in order to do this, he embarked on a series of military operations in Cambodia, which turned out to be ill advised in the extreme.

## Cambodia

In Cambodia, the situation had deteriorated severely since the optimistic days of the 1960s. The economy had been ruined by the extravagance and mismanagement of the country's ruler, Prince Sihanouk, and he had also alienated both the army and the country's professional middle class. Moreover, after he allowed the Americans to bomb the Communists in their Cambodian sanctuaries, the North Vietnamese had also turned against him, training huge numbers of the Khmer Rouge (KR)[10] and then sending 12,000 KR guerrillas into the country. In January 1970, while Sihanouk was on the French Riviera, taking his annual "obesity" cure, his prime minister, General Lon Nol, tried to eject these Communists and their North Vietnamese supporters from their border camps. The attempt escalated out of control and finally ended in Prince Sihanouk's removal from the throne, prompting a suggestion by the French that he might be reinstalled by force. They likewise proposed that a new version of the 1954 Geneva Convention be convened to discuss the Cambodian situation, and perhaps also the possibilities of peace in Vietnam.

Reaction from both the Soviet Union and China was muted, if not entirely negative, but both North and South Vietnam, rightly foreseeing that such a conference would allow others to decide their future for them, quickly rejected the idea. The White House officials were also cautious, anxious to avoid becoming entangled in a situation that might prevent their promised troop repatriations, although Nixon was secretly considering intervention in Cambodia.

By March 1970, the country was becoming increasingly difficult to govern. Rival Cambodian gangs were killing each other, and the North Vietnamese and their Khmer Rouge allies were driving the ineffective Cambodian army into the interior of the country, while the South Vietnamese army, accompanied by covert U.S. forces, surreptitiously infiltrated the border areas. Lon Nol, watching his country's descent into anarchy and powerless to stop it, had at first pathetically asserted Cambodian neutrality, despite the terrible upheaval in the capital and rural centers. By 14 April 1970, however, his American advisers, acting on Nixon's orders, had persuaded him to issue a plea for outside help, to which the American military immediately responded. They had, in fact, only been waiting for an excuse, conveniently provided by Lon Nol's call, because Nixon had already decided to intervene in Cambodia at the beginning of March, even before Sihanouk's removal.

Nixon during this period was under considerable mental stress. At best, he was an isolated, tense individual who took criticism badly, with few, if any, close friends, and some observers believe that he saw Cambodia as a final, very personal test.[11] He feared the country was on the brink of collapse, the generals were telling him that more troop withdrawals from Vietnam would imperil those troops remaining unless the Việt Cộng's Cambodian sanctuaries were destroyed, and he remained convinced that he could drive the North Vietnamese to a peaceful compromise with just one more display of force. Cambodia could be the answer—firmness here might solve everything. On 25 March 1970, Nixon ordered Kissinger to devise a plan to aid the new government of Lon Nol, and by the middle of April, arms and American-trained Cambodian troops were beginning to arrive in Phnom Penh.

As usual, the White House aides and Pentagon staff were not in agreement. The military, including General Abrams and his army colleagues in Saigon, wanted escalation, while many in the White House rejected that option, convinced it would interfere with the "Vietnamization" program they still favored. Nixon, however, decided upon a massive incursion into Cambodia, using both South Vietnamese and American troops, which he unveiled on 30 April 1970 in another of his famous televised addresses. Kissinger was later to call it "vintage Nixon." Pious and strident, Nixon trumpeted America's role as global policeman against "the forces of totalitarianism and anarchy [which] will threaten free nations and free institutions throughout the world."

As his speech was being broadcast, 20,000 American and South Vietnamese troops were attacking the two main Communist bases in Cambodia. Some arms and equipment were destroyed, but at the price of the Americans now being forced to prop up the weak Cambodian regime as well as the increasingly enfeebled Saigon government. Instead of moving closer to peace, Nixon had expanded the war, and the American anti-war movement erupted in fury.

Domestic opposition mounted, led predominantly by influential newspapers such as the *New York Times* and *Wall Street Journal*, and Nixon reacted with his customary intellectual violence. Anti-war protests and the strength of the official response mutually escalated, finally culminating in the deaths of four student protesters at Kent State University in Ohio, on 4 May 1970, shot by members of the National Guard. Protests against this heavy-handed response to the Kent protests sprang up country-wide, briefly sobering Nixon, although this mood did not last. When a group of senators tried to restrict his military activities in Cambodia, he decided to deal summarily with his opponents both within the government and without. He ordered the formation of a covert surveillance team to monitor his critics, headed by Tom Huston, formerly an army intelligence specialist. Later, when told that this project demonstrated a "Gestapo mentality" and, furthermore, that such internal espionage was illegal, Nixon replied, "When the president does it, that means it is not illegal."

Despite his pledge to "end the war and win the peace," Nixon had now reversed the trend begun with American troop withdrawals and extended the war into Cambodia. Unfortunately, it would soon be made clear to all concerned that he was not going to be able to extricate himself without significant concessions to the North Vietnamese.

## Peace with Honor?

Covert peace negotiations between Kissinger and Le Duc Tho, the North Vietnamese representative, had begun some months before the Kent State incident, on 21 February 1970. These talks were held without the knowledge of either the Saigon administration or the Việt Cộng, which gave both sides more flexibility than would otherwise have been the case.[12]

Le Duc Tho began by unrealistically demanding that any agreement must simultaneously resolve both the military and the political situation. The 1954 Geneva conference had embittered the North Vietnamese, and they were not going to agree to stop fighting without strong assurances that political gains would follow.[13] Kissinger rejected this proposal and responded by offering a slightly modified "mutual withdrawal" package, which was rejected in its turn. The two men then settled down to negotiations that would last, with intervals, for the next three years.

American troops had been moved out of Cambodia by the summer of 1970, but this did not serve to silence protests at home, by both students and, significantly, many of the discharged troops returning from Vietnam. A special commission appointed by Nixon found the country, particularly on university and college campuses, deeply divided over the war. Its director, William Scranton, claimed the divisions were "as deep as any since the Civil War," insisting that "nothing is more important than an end to the war." Opinion polls also showed that Americans wanted a firm deadline for troop withdrawals, and this attitude was reflected by the politicians when a Senate bill to bring all American troops home by 31 December 1971 was only narrowly defeated.

Nixon was worried by this new turn of events, concerned principally that he might not be elected for a second term as president, but he was trapped in a dilemma of his own making. He had to continue the troop withdrawals, but now, instead of just defending Vietnam, his invasion of Cambodia and the activities of the North Vietnamese in Laos meant the American army was fighting a war throughout the whole of Indochina. With the election looming, he needed a quick resolution or, at the very least, some form of innocuous postponement that did not look like complete American capitulation, prior to an ignominious withdrawal. As an interim measure, he and Kissinger returned to an old initiative, the "standstill cease-fire." Under this arrangement, the two sides would simply stop shooting and remain where they were while an international conference reached a fair solution. This plan had numerous disadvantages, but Nixon was desperate. Protest movements in America were gathering momentum again and Le Duc Tho had made it plain to Kissinger that North Vietnamese troops were staying in the south.

Nixon unveiled the plan for his standstill cease-fire on 7 October 1970 and once again managed to fool the vast majority who listened to the standard, elegantly written, televised address. Congress and the media agreed unanimously that it was the best way forward, but, unfortunately, the North Vietnamese delegation disagreed and rejected the offer. They had good reason to do so. A day after Nixon gave his speech he confirmed to reporters that removal of American forces would be "based on principles ... previously outlined," and one of those principles was the old stumbling block—"mutual withdrawal by both sides." As Kissinger said, the offer had been simply a device that "at the minimum ... would give us some temporary relief from public pressures," and, as such, it was solely intended to soothe the American voter before the congressional elections. Nixon was effectively offering nothing new and, unfortunately, the North Vietnamese had spotted it. Dicky had not been quite tricky enough.[14]

However, the beginning of 1971 saw the possibility of a peaceful resolution, although the opportunity was generated by American overconfidence in the South Vietnamese army. Nixon and Kissinger had earlier predicted a massive Communist offensive during 1972, timed to coincide with the American presidential election and damage Nixon's standing with the voters. This would necessarily entail a major logistical operation during the spring of 1971, before the rains made the Hồ Chí Minh Trail impassable to vehicles. Since the Americans in Saigon assumed that the trail would be the main route used to transport supplies to the Việt Cộng, it was believed that if the trail was cut, supplies could not move and there could be no offensive.

American troops were prevented from entering Cambodia (where the trail lay close to the border) by a 1970 congressional amendment, so the operation was delegated to a force of South Vietnamese infantry, with American air support. Code-named "Lamson 719," the entire operation, which began on 8 February 1971, was a complete disaster, reflecting, according to Kissinger, "myopic American planning, poor South Vietnamese execution and even Nixon's warped leadership."[15] Everyone else was clearly to blame, except Kissinger, the national security adviser and the one, perhaps, who might have been expected to oversee the operation and prevent it from descending into the debacle it became.

"Lamson 719" marked the beginning of the disenchantment many South Vietnamese came to feel for their erstwhile allies. This disaffection spread through the American army, finding expression in fights and a general feeling among all ranks that the conflict had become pointless. Its most serious manifestation, however, was the rapidly mushrooming drug problem, which may have been the result of better communications with the "Golden Triangle" (Laos, Thailand and Burma) via Cambodia.[16] By March 1971, one opinion poll recorded that those retaining confidence in Nixon had dropped to 50 percent, while only 34 percent supported his conduct of the war. Perhaps even more worrying was that the same poll showed that 51 percent of Americans now saw the war as "morally wrong." Street protests resumed and Nixon found himself faced with further media opposition when extracts from the "Pentagon Papers" began to be published by the *New York Times* on 13 June.[17] His problems were not confined to the media either, because just over a week later, on 22 June 1971, the Senate also showed its mood. This time, Nixon's opponents managed to pass a resolution calling for the repatriation of all U.S. troops by the end of the year.

Nixon, however, thought he could use the release of the Pentagon Papers to discredit liberal and Democratic opponents of the war—in fact, everybody he saw as an enemy. And his paranoia was starting to show him enemies in the most unlikely places. As one of his assistants, Egil "Bud" Krogh, put it, "Anyone who opposes us, we'll destroy. As a matter of fact, anyone who doesn't support us, we'll destroy."

Nixon gave orders to mount an investigation into Daniel Ellsberg, the source of the Pentagon Papers leak, and a special unit was established for this purpose, whose members included Krogh, David Young (a lawyer), and two experts in covert operations, E. Howard Hunt (formerly CIA) and G. Gordon Liddy (formerly FBI). A description of their activities, which ranged from forgery to burglary, is included in the relevant literature.[18]

From the middle of 1971 onward, Nixon began to show increasing signs of mental instability, which took the form of depression and associated mood swings. The Paris peace talks were stalled, held up by the North Vietnamese refusal to negotiate while Nguyễn Văn Thiệu remained president of South Vietnam, because he refused to try and work out a political compromise with the Việt Cộng. An opportunity to remove Thiệu from office arose with the election of 3 October 1971, but Thiệu skillfully manipulated the circumstances surrounding the vote and gained another term, with the connivance of the CIA, which was acting under Nixon's orders. The North Vietnamese claimed that this represented a missed opportunity by the Americans, but Nixon and Kissinger were sanguine over the result, because Thiệu represented security and fresh convulsions in Saigon were to be avoided at any cost. With U.S. troop numbers in Vietnam down to approximately 100,000 at the beginning of 1972, support for the Saigon regime would have to be drastically cut. Moreover, Nixon, via Kissinger, was exploring a new peace initiative with the Chinese and Soviets, which might also be broadened to include Vietnam.

By the early 1970s, support for Vietnam in both the Soviet Union and China was dwindling. The two Communist giants were involved in several minor border engagements between March and December 1969, which gave the Americans the chance they had been looking for to improve their own security. A long series of negotiations began between the United States and China, culminating in Nixon flying into Beijing on 21 February 1972 for talks with Mao Zedong and his prime minister, Zhou En-Lai. Zhou, under pressure to prevent the Vietnamese from turning to the Soviets and in danger from his political rivals, urged a quick peace but would not endorse Vietnam's political demands. Predictably, the North Vietnamese saw Nixon's visit and the resulting Chinese-American cordiality as clear evidence that the two countries had reached an agreement without consulting them.

Despite these Vietnamese suspicions, the Chinese had actually increased their aid to North Vietnam in 1971, as had the Soviets. The North Vietnamese were still planning their new offensive against the Americans, timed to coincide with the 1972 American presidential election and had demanded increased logistical support. They had become increasingly adept at playing the two major Communist powers against each other, and the political consequences were such that neither China nor the Soviet Union could refuse them. The North Vietnamese had other motives for the attack as well, principally a desire to show the Americans that "Vietnamization" was not working and that negotiation with the Hanoi administration was, quite literally, their only way out of the war and the country.

The attacks began on 30 March 1972, with the Communists deploying one hundred and twenty thousand North Vietnamese regulars and thousands of Việt Cộng, synchronized to strike in three successive waves. The first swept over the northern provinces and the second drove across the central highlands to the coast, while the third was concentrated in the area to the north of Saigon. The south, particularly the Mekong Delta, was not attacked, which seemed strange to a number of commentators at the time, especially considering the importance of the Mekong as a rice-growing region. Attacks continued until June and resulted in the deaths of unprecedented numbers of participants on both sides. The North Vietnamese were most successful in the north, capturing the provincial capital of Quang Tri on 1 May and holding it until September, which gave them control of that northern sector. They achieved similar gains in their central and southern operations despite being outnumbered almost five to one by the South Vietnamese.[19] And although action in the Mekong Delta was light compared to other regions, the Communists soon showed their strategy here. When Thiệu moved his main strength away from the Mekong to defend other areas of the country, the area was quickly infiltrated by Việt Cộng guerrillas, who occupied many of the government posts in that region and rendered ineffective the government "pacification" programs, which had been put in place with American guidance.

Although this operation cost the Communists over one hundred thousand dead and wounded, resulted in no permanent territorial gains and had no significant effect on the Saigon administration or the south's army, they had exploded the myth of "Vietnamization" and, more importantly, showed up the dependence of the South Vietnamese army on the stiffening effect of a relatively small number of American "advisers." This heightened Thiệu's anxiety about the Americans leaving, which coincided with Nixon's view that complete American withdrawal would result in the destruction of Thiệu's regime and, more importantly, his own reputation. The day after the Communist offensive began, on 31 March 1972, he ordered air raids to begin against targets in North Vietnam, including Hanoi, intent upon showing his support for Thiệu and his intention to bomb the North Vietnamese if they violated any resulting peace agreement. Significantly, given his state of mind, Nixon had fallen back on his old favorite, the "Madman Theory." It was also, most obviously, the option with the least chance of proving effective, as had been shown on more than one occasion in the past.

Once again, however, Vietnam was influencing more important matters on the world stage. Kissinger was due to fly to Moscow to arrange for Nixon to meet Leonid Brezhnev, the Soviet premier, for vital talks on arms control. Nixon, his thoughts still inflexibly dominated by Vietnam, instructed Kissinger to cancel the meeting if the Soviets did not persuade the Vietnamese to commit themselves to what he called an "acceptable peace settlement." Kissinger, more realistically, advocated a less rigid approach. He arrived in Moscow on 20 April 1972 and, ignoring Nixon's frantic instructions, avoided discussion of Vietnam, concentrating upon the arms control summit, which he later claimed Brezhnev wanted "at almost any cost." He treated Vietnam as a side issue, telling Brezhnev that the Americans would adhere to the "standstill cease-fire" scheme, but that North Vietnamese troops must return to positions held before the 1972 offensive.

Nixon, unfortunately, had decided that further offensive action was necessary and ordered B-52 attacks against Hanoi and Haiphong, to begin on 5 May 1972, regardless of the outcome of Kissinger's Paris negotiations, due to start three days earlier. Kissinger was nervous, fearful about the fate of his carefully nurtured summit. His state of mind was not helped when, three days later, on 8 May, Nixon decided to mine Haiphong harbor and escalate the bombing of North Vietnam. Opinion among his aides was mixed, and Kissinger awaited an anti–American outburst from the Kremlin. This never came, because, as one Soviet embassy official explained, "We've done a lot for those Vietnamese, but we're not going to let them spoil our relations with the United States."[20]

Nixon seemed vindicated and the North Vietnamese began to get nervous, worried by the increasingly cordial relations between the United States and both Beijing and Moscow. More than that, however, it seemed that Nixon was now sure to be elected for a second term and, given his recent political success, he would be more certain than ever that the north could be bombed to the peace table. Peace talks continued, however, with the North Vietnamese showing increasing flexibility, even dropping their condition that Thiệu be deposed as president. On 8 October 1972, the climax came, when Le Duc Tho offered what he called a "very realistic and very simple proposal."

The United States and North Vietnam would arrange a cease-fire, American troop withdrawals, prisoner exchanges and other military matters. Political problems would be resolved by the opposing Vietnamese within an interim council, termed "the Council of National Reconciliation." It would include representatives from both the north and the south, as well as certain "neutral" figures, and its purpose would be, initially, to supervise national elections and then move toward achieving a permanent, stable peace. Both sides would also remain in control of the areas they had occupied at the time of the cease-fire.

Kissinger was jubilant. Unfortunately, his aides were less confident, but Kissinger rejected their legitimate concerns, his own aims becoming clear when he shouted at his aides, who included John Negroponte, "You don't understand…. I want to end this war before the election!"[21]

Despite his apparently earnest desire to achieve a realistic peace, Kissinger was still covertly manipulating the situation. He telegraphed President Thiệu, telling him to seize as much territory as possible before peace talks were concluded, while the Pentagon received orders to rapidly deliver over $2 billion worth of supplies to South Vietnam (Operation Enhance Plus). All the American bases in the country were also transferred to South Vietnamese ownership, in an attempt to circumvent a clause in the draft agreement that specified that all U.S. installations would be dismantled. Despite these American maneuvers, South Vietnam's President Thiệu was not reassured and began to show distinct signs of panic and an increasing distrust of his American allies, which was reflected in Nixon's ambivalent attitude toward Thiệu.[22]

On 21 October, the North Vietnamese approved the draft agreement. Nixon promptly and cheerfully acknowledged U.S. assent and Kissinger traveled to Saigon to persuade Thiệu to accept it. What the Americans assumed was a formality proved to be nothing of the sort. Thiệu accused them of colluding with the Chinese and Soviets, paving the way for the Communists to assume power in Saigon. He insisted that any agreement should include the removal of North Vietnamese troops north of the DMZ and that the zone itself should be a secure border. Furthermore, South Vietnam had to be recognized as a sovereign, independent state, thus nullifying the most important principle that the Communists had been fighting for. Thiệu, despite his other shortcomings, had grasped the most significant point: Despite having fought the Communists for nearly ten years to *defend* South Vietnamese independence, the United States now refused to protect or even recognize it when negotiating their peace terms with the North Vietnamese. Any price now seemed to be acceptable if, by paying it, Nixon could win over his electorate.

The Saigon government refused consistently to accept the terms of the Paris draft agreement; as a result, the North Vietnamese grew restless and the situation became increasingly complex until, on 14 December 1972, Nixon decided to resort to force again.[23] Four days later, on 18 December, he ordered a new bombing campaign, Operation "Linebacker Two." This went on for eleven days, with American aircraft flying more than 3,000 sorties, mainly over the heavily populated strip between Hanoi and Haiphong, and dropping approximately 40,000 tons of bombs. With most of the American troops now out of the country, American public reaction to the bombing was muted, almost indifferent. American newspapers and media commentators were revolted, however, as was much of the rest of the world, although later reports clearly showed that the damage and loss of life had been surprisingly moderate, with a total of approximately 1,800 killed in Hanoi and Haiphong. Moderate, that is, compared to Vietnam's bloody past.

On 3 January 1973, talks began again, and this time all differences between the Americans and North Vietnamese were quickly resolved. This time Nixon was determined there would be no last-minute problems. He sent Thiệu what amounted to an ultimatum: "You must decide now whether you desire to continue our alliance or whether you want me to seek a settlement with the enemy which serves U.S. interests alone." Thiệu capitulated, saying that he could not allow himself the luxury of resisting America.

Nixon's response was predictable: "We have finally achieved peace with honor."

In reality, the North Vietnamese had got all they wanted, what they had set out to gain ten years before. The intervening period, which included 58,000 American deaths, 500,000 Vietnamese casualties and billions spent by both sides, had resulted, fundamentally, in the settlement agreed on at the 1954 Geneva conference—a united Vietnam, governed by an administration placed in office as a result of a free election. Significantly, North Vietnamese troops would remain in the south, so there would be no possibility of denying the Communists their participation in the affairs of that region.

The full cease-fire began on 17 January 1973, and by March of that year the last Americans, including the returned POWs, had left Vietnam, and the country settled down to determine its fate without American involvement. Just over two years later, on 30 April 1975, the first Việt Cộng tanks entered Saigon and took control of the city, later to be renamed Hồ Chí Mính City, uniting the country and establishing Communist control, after a fight that had lasted nearly three decades.

## Perspectives

U.S. involvement in Southeast Asia was initially driven by an overestimation of their Communist opponents' political ability and the influence Communist doctrine would exert on what succeeding American administrations considered the "unsophisticated" rural populations of Laos, Cambodia and, most importantly, Vietnam. Most of the officials involved had barely even a superficial understanding of the region and its people, and, consequently Washington's approach to the problem was based on a deep-rooted anxiety, inherited from the Eisenhower years, that the only alternative to Western democracy was Eastern bloc Communism, which would take over and contaminate unprotected peoples of those regions if allowed to spread unchecked.

Fear of Communism, the so-called Red Menace, drove America to war in Korea, and it was President Eisenhower (1953–1961) who originally exacerbated American paranoia, justifying early intervention in Indochina by explaining that it was to protect the countries of Southeast Asia, which he claimed would "topple like a row of dominoes"[24] if the Communists took over Vietnam. Then, the Pentagon litany ran, nothing could save, in turn, Malaysia, Indonesia and finally the whole of the Philippines (which had already experienced one unsuccessful Communist-inspired insurrection), leaving Hawaii hardly a step away. So, the specter of defending their homeland on "the beaches of Waikiki" came to haunt the military and politicians alike, fueling the diplomatic intransigence that subsequent administrations showed over Vietnam and infusing (even directing) much of the country's foreign and internal policy during the 1950s and 1960s. In addition, many ordinary Americans, in the aftermath of World War II and fearful of the consequences of atomic warfare, saw their country as a self-appointed global policeman, a role they considered essential for their own survival. Henry Kissinger later decried this view of American responsibilities when he warned his countrymen that they must dismiss the idea that they could "rebuild the world to American specifications."[25]

Superficially, Eisenhower's fears must have seemed justified. By 1950, the Soviet Union and Communist China were certainly supplying military aid to Vietnam from the north, a situation that seemed to justify all the American government's original concerns about Communist domination of the region.[26] Unfortunately, this convenient scenario ignored two important factors.

First, Hồ Chí Mính was only ever concerned with the freedom and unity of Vietnam. A French Communist who knew Ho during his wanderings in the 1930s said of him, "He was taut and quivering, with only one thought in his head, his country, Vietnam."

When the Japanese invaded Vietnam in 1941, Ho fought on the side of the Allies, contravening Moscow's orders, because he feared the Japanese more than the French. He said many times that his objective was Vietnamese independence, and he was forced to deal with China and the Soviet Union in 1950 only because first the French and then the Americans refused to negotiate on that basis, although he made numerous appeals to both countries for a compromise involving such an agreement. He even confided to an OSS agent that he would welcome "a million American soldiers ... but no French."

Võ Nguyên Giáp, Ho's military leader, echoed these sentiments after Ho's 1945 declaration of independence, when he told a Hanoi crowd to regard the United States as "a good friend because it is a democracy without territorial ambitions." Even the Americans themselves appeared to have reached the same conclusions about Ho's aims, because a 1948 State Department memo recorded that "the Vietnamese Communists are not subservient to Kremlin directives," although, after Ho was forced to deal with the Communists, the American attitude toward Ho changed, instantly according him the status of a "Soviet satellite," apparently without taking into account their previous analysis of his political motives.[27]

Even more important than Ho's convictions, centuries of successive invasions by the rapacious Chinese had left all Vietnamese with a deep-rooted hatred of their northern neighbor. China's Nationalist leader, Chiang Kai-shek, was well aware of this. When Roosevelt literally offered him Indochina, in 1945, he politely declined, explaining simply that the Indochinese "would not assimilate into the Chinese people." If the American counterinsurgency experts had realized the importance of these factors and exploited them, some observers believe that the war which cost the lives of 500,000 Vietnamese and 58,000 American servicemen might have been avoided.[28]

The Americans began operations in Southeast Asia with the claim that they were opposing Communist aggression toward a small, defenseless democracy, although, clearly paralleling this declaration of policy, their primary concern was also to protect themselves. They can hardly be blamed for that, but was their intervention a huge mistake or a necessary evil?

With hindsight, always such an invaluable historical tool, it seems unlikely that the Americans needed to go as far as they did. Even a wholly Communist government in Vietnam probably would not have shifted the balance of power in Southeast Asia enough to allow its countries to have "toppled like dominoes" and settle the whole region happily under a Chinese Communist regime, because Ho and the Vietnamese hated their northern neighbor more than any white invader. Moreover, after the takeover in 1975, the Vietnamese government soon found the Chinese Communist system of communal farms to be unworkable for their land-hungry people, and they were forced to revert to what were essentially traditional farming practices, although not before their experiments had caused yet another nationwide famine.

Unfortunately, the effects of the war were not confined to Vietnam, although the wider, international conflict frequently influenced events in that country. To successive American administrations, Vietnam became the focus of their fight against Communist aggression, personified by China and the Soviet Union. Even many ordinary Americans during this period were convinced, mainly by their government and media, that the war was nothing short of their patriotic duty. This attitude, which at times bordered on hysteria even among professional politicians who might have been expected to know better, drove much of the ensuing legislation, frequently assisted by the Pentagon, whose members were almost wholly behind a military solution in Vietnam. More importantly, with this viewpoint being adopted and exploited by both Democratic and Republican politicians, successive presidents, particularly Kennedy and Johnson, could not be seen as softening their attitude to the Communist bloc, whatever their private misgivings may have been. Often dependent on the anti–Communist elements in Washington for the passage of legislation aimed at social reform, they were forced to continue military escalation to appease these political opponents, although Johnson, in particular, seems to have had little reluctance about adopting a military solution, *if* it could be made to work.[29] Beginning in Johnson's administration, however, there were many in the government (such as MacDonald Bundy, William Fulbright and Robert McNamara) who became convinced that America could not win a military victory in Vietnam, and that negotiations should be started with the North Vietnamese, with or without agreement from Saigon. It is indicative of the mood in both the White House and the Pentagon that, without exception, these men were ignored and castigated until it became obvious, during Nixon's first term, that they were right and there was no way forward, except through negotiation.

The role of America's military personnel also changed as its commitment deepened, although their main objective (driving the Việt Cộng and North Vietnamese army out of the south) remained consistent. Kennedy, the first president to sanction major involvement in the country, was intent upon keeping troop commitments and expenditures to a minimum, while still effectively supporting Diệm against the Việt Minh. His administration, however, was not above manipulating the Saigon government, and it was Lodge and the CIA who were instrumental in Diệm's removal and murder by a group of his own generals, just before President Kennedy was assassinated in Dallas.

Johnson began in the same supporting role, although with a gradually increasing military presence. After Kỳ became prime minister, however, Johnson became more dissatisfied with the competence of the military and political factions in Saigon, and his generals began to assume control of the war themselves. This was the period of the massive troop commitments, widespread "search and destroy" missions and blanket bombing of North Vietnam, although, by 1968, when he decided not to pursue reelection, Johnson was wavering and had begun to scale down the bombing campaign and even authorized the Paris negotiations.

Nixon began to change the emphasis of American involvement in the war after his election in 1968, by initiating a process of what came to be termed "Vietnamization." This was intended to force the South Vietnamese army to take over the responsibilities previously assumed by the Americans, thus allowing the United States to withdraw without seeming to abandon their anti–Communist stance, although he also ordered the bombing to be widened to include Cambodia and parts of Laos. Operations were scaled down and major troop withdrawals began during Nixon's first term as president, as did the final peace negotiations, which eventually saw an agreement reached in January 1973. The last U.S. troops left Vietnam on 29 March 1973, eighteen years after American involvement had begun. Significantly, this period also marked the beginning of improving relations between the West and the two major Communist countries—the Soviet Union and China.

War broke out again on 4 January 1974, and just over three months later, on 30 April 1974, Saigon was a Communist-controlled city. The Communists certainly made significant mistakes in the early years, but their regime has sufficiently mellowed so that, in 2008, the *Economist* could describe them as "ardently capitalist Communists." The Vietnamese also have good international relations with over 170 countries, including the United States, and a thriving industrial and scientific base.

Graham Greene, writing in 1955, when the French were on the verge of defeat and the CIA was beginning its involvement in Vietnam, described the attitude of Southeast Asia and its peoples to the fighting and the invaders, acutely summing up the aim of their long fight: "They want enough rice.... They don't want to be shot at. They want one day to be much the same as another. They don't want our white skins around telling them what they want."[30]

Of course, that analysis, with minor changes to the wording, might serve as a fitting postscript to any number of wars.

# 8

# The British Government's Political Involvement with Vietnam, or:

## *What the Politicians Were Saying, and What They Were Really Doing*

The relationship between Britain and the United States is of long standing and steadily increasing complexity. It has not always been a comfortable association (partnership, in this context, would be entirely the wrong word), and this was especially true during the period of America's involvement in Vietnam, when it was always complicated, sometimes acrimonious, and occasionally approached incendiary. This period, together with its political ramifications and the relations between the two governments, has been discussed fully, not to say exhaustively, in the relevant literature.[1] Consequently, British involvement with the Americans and its consequences are described here only in terms of each prime minister's foreign policy, emphasizing in particular Britain's relationship with America, both political and economic, and how this affected relations between successive prime ministers and presidents and, as a consequence of those relationships, how Britain's general policy on Vietnam developed.

## *Winston Churchill (1945)*

With VE celebrations over, the task of reconstructing a postwar Britain had to begin, although, whatever Mr. Churchill's intentions were in this direction, they were cut short when he lost the General Election of July 1945 to Clement Attlee. With India desperate for independence, the British government at that period had little time or appetite for any further colonial complications. Unfortunately, they had the only experienced troops available to achieve a reasonably humane end to the war in Southeast Asia, and it was SEAC, headed by Lord Mountbatten, to which the task of reoccupation fell.[2]

### THE WAR IN ASIA

The Japanese occupied French Indochina in July 1941, subsequently sweeping through a large part of Southeast Asia during the early part of 1942 after their attack on Pearl Harbor

(7 December 1941). By April 1942, they had driven the British out of Burma and Malaya, only to be halted almost on the border of what was then British India. By the end of 1942, the Japanese had consolidated their occupation of much of the Far East, and in French Indochina (FIC) the Vichy government was cooperating fully with the occupying forces, although in some areas French citizens were forming resistance groups.

Organized French resistance in Vietnam began as a cooperative effort with the British in 1941, when General de Gaulle sent François de Langlade to Delhi, where he joined Force 136 and collaborated with its director, Colin Mackenzie, in that department's plans for the reoccupation of the region. De Langlade was a rubber planter who had worked in British Malaya for nearly 20 years, and so he knew the people and was fluent in the various dialects used in the rural areas. During the same period in North Africa, the French were also forming a guerrilla and insurgency force called the Corps Léger d'Intervention (CLI), later renamed the 5th RIC.[3] The men who formed this group were specialists, many fluent in the various dialects spoken in Indochina, and it was intended that they would be transported into the area in small groups, where they would form resistance cells to oversee and organize the military and political objectives of the Allies.[4]

**Sir Winston Churchill, in a characteristic wartime pose, 1942.**

With de Langlade and the personnel of Force 136 working from India and liaising with the men of the CLI, it looked possible that an effective resistance movement might be organized without too much difficulty, especially since both the Japanese and Vichy forces in the region were not very efficient. Mountbatten was also well aware of the possibilities offered by the development of such a resistance "net," especially for the planned reinvasion of FIC, and he approached Chiang Kai-shek about just such a possibility in November 1943.[5] Unfortunately, the Americans were unable to cooperate with the French forces or support Mountbatten's initiative, which meant that the CLI sat out the war in North Africa and never participated in the covert operations in Indochina for which its members had been trained. Moreover, this was only the beginning of the difficulties between the Americans and their allies in the Far East, one consequence of which was that none of the available Free French forces were ever properly utilized at a time when they could certainly have made a significant contribution. These partly self-imposed difficulties with the CLI were characteristic of American relations with the French, particularly those between Roosevelt and de Gaulle, and they were continually problematic for both the SEAC and the British government until the end of the war in the Far East.[6]

Inconsistent and often openly derisory in their dealings with the French, the Americans' responses were primarily dependent upon what they needed from their allies during any given period.[7] Of particular note in this context is Roosevelt's abrupt change of attitude toward de Gaulle when the American military needed to use ports on the French Pacific islands to implement their plans for the eventual invasion of the Japanese mainland.[8] One of the U.S. president's particular concerns during this period was to deprive the French of their colonial possessions and, as a direct consequence of this, as well as Roosevelt's failure to understand the important part the French would have to play in postwar Europe and his derogatory comments about their role in the war, relations between the French and Americans began to deteriorate. This was still evident almost thirty years later when the French remained indifferent to American requests for aid during their involvement in Vietnam. This Franco-American antagonism also influenced many of the postwar negotiations between the NATO partners and was directly responsible for de Gaulle's veto of Britain's early attempt to enter the EEC, because he perceived the British as being too closely allied with the Americans.

It was not just the French that Roosevelt was intent upon depriving of their colonies, either. Earlier in the war, at the Atlantic Conference of August 1941, he had tried to obtain postwar access to British colonial and dominion areas, in order to weaken British control in those regions, and had only been forced to compromise when Churchill refused categorically to negotiate on those terms. Although the two men were said to be close personal friends, Roosevelt still felt able to tell Chiang Kai-shek in 1942 that "Churchill is old," and that a new British government without him would be more sympathetic and might even return Hong Kong to the Chinese. Upon hearing this, Anthony Eden, then foreign minister, noted that he had not heard of the Americans offering similar concessions, and, apparently in response to what he saw as British intransigence, Roosevelt said later, "We shall have more trouble with Great Britain after the war than we are having with Germany now." As one of his biographers explained, "FDR's anti-colonial idealism was firmly rooted in the determination to protect American spheres of influence with military force."[9]

After Roosevelt's death in 1945, the succeeding Truman administration seemed to take a more balanced view of American relations with the French, and South Vietnam was eventually handed over to French colonial forces in January 1946.

## Clement Attlee (1945–1951)

Foreign policy during Attlee's time in office focused broadly on three major areas: the establishment of the United Nations and NATO, decolonization and Europe's involvement in the Cold War. After Stalin had taken political control of most of Eastern Europe and begun his attempts to influence a number of Balkan governments, Attlee's government was instrumental in the creation of the new NATO alliance, formed to protect Western Europe against what was seen as the Communist threat. Augmenting the NATO-based military response, the British were also deeply involved with plans to implement what came to be called the Marshall Plan, organizing American aid for a number of countries that the Western powers felt might otherwise have become Communist "satellite" states. Although a significant number of the most influential Labour MPs favored adopting a policy of armed neutrality to both the United States and the Soviet Union, as a direct consequence of the Marshall Plan, Britain became generally supportive of American foreign and economic policy. Britain's later political support for America's involvement in Vietnam, as well as in other areas, had its beginnings in this early postwar relationship, although the association was, of course, reinforced later by a continuing mutual dependence over arms deals and other economic, political and military accommodations.

Attlee's government also oversaw the negotiations for the independence of India, Burma and Ceylon during this period, and, perhaps as a consequence of the need to concentrate its efforts in these regions, its political involvement in Indochina was muted, although a monthly report on the situation in Vietnam was dispatched from the British Embassy in Saigon.[10]

Clement Attlee, Britain's first postwar prime minister and responsible for much of the legislation that finally developed into the Welfare State.

## Sir Winston Churchill (1951–1955)

Churchill's second term of office saw a lessening of Britain's global role, arising from a change in international attitudes after World War II, Britain's waning military establishment and the increasing intensity of the Cold War. Significant events included the Mau-Mau uprising, the Iranian coup d'état (which, it has been suggested, Britain and America orchestrated so as to maintain control of Iranian oil), and the Malayan Emergency. Malaya was to prove particularly significant, with the lessons learned here by the British military authorities later being applied to Vietnam in the form of the American "Strategic Hamlets" program, although without the same degree of success.

### INVOLVEMENT WITH VIETNAM

French involvement in Vietnam came to an end in 1954, with Britain and the Soviet Union appointed co-chairmen of the Geneva Peace Conference in that year. These meetings resulted in a series of agreements, known as the Geneva Accords, which included a cessation of hostilities, excluded foreign involvement in Indochina's internal affairs and made provision for a process of unification based on internationally supervised free elections, to be held in 1956. The country was to be temporarily divided at the 17th Parallel into North and South Vietnam, with the Việt Minh withdrawing north of the parallel, while the French were to occupy the south, although, in fact, most of the French troops were evacuated soon after the agreement was ratified. Although France and the North Vietnamese (as the Democratic Republic of Vietnam) signed the agreement, significantly, both the South Vietnamese and America declined and so were not legally bound by it. Ngô Đình Diệm was helped to power as the president of South Vietnam in 1955 by the United States, and once he had consolidated his position, still with considerable American support, any thought of unification elections was abandoned.

During this period of his last premiership, Churchill delegated much of the day-to-day running of the government to his deputy, Anthony Eden. This was particularly true of the government's foreign policy, and Eden was largely responsible for the solution achieved at the Geneva Conference, where he showed himself diametrically opposed to any armed intervention by the major powers.[11] In accordance with its policy on foreign aid, Britain also began to give technical assistance to Cambodia and Vietnam under the Colombo Plan, along with a number of other countries in the Far East.

Although his relationship with President Eisenhower was less cordial than his relationship with Roosevelt, Churchill still devoted much of his time in office to trying to maintain what he saw as Britain's "special relationship" with America, a phrase he had coined for his "Sinews of Peace" address on 5 March 1946.

## Sir Anthony Eden (1955–1957)

Foreign affairs during Eden's premiership were overshadowed by the catastrophic events that occurred after Gamal Abdel Nasser's nationalization of the Suez Canal and America's support for Egypt.

In 1955, Nasser, the Egyptian president, after a series of confrontations with Britain and France, concluded a major arms deal with the Soviet Union, America having previously refused to supply him with the arms he wanted, assuming that he was intent upon using them to attack Israel. This deal bolstered Soviet standing in a region where previously the Soviets had little influence and resulted in Britain and the United States withdrawing their promised funding for a project to construct a new dam at Aswan on the Nile. Nasser retaliated by nationalizing the Suez Canal on 26 July 1956, closing both the canal and the Straits of Tiran to Israeli shipping and paying off the shareholders. The canal was a vital link to the Middle Eastern oil fields, with over 60 percent of the oil supplies for Western Europe passing through it, and it was widely believed that if Nasser succeeded in his nationalization plan, this might lead to the oil-producing Middle Eastern countries threatening to cut off oil supplies to their European customers. Britain was almost wholly dependent upon oil from the Middle East, and so Eden and the French prime minister, Guy Mollet, secretly agreed to neutralize Nasser by encouraging an Israeli invasion, giving Britain and France an excuse to move into the region, repossess the canal and expel Nasser from office. Unfortunately, although the invasion was a military success, it had disastrous diplomatic repercussions.

Eden had initially enjoyed good relations with Eisenhower because of their wartime association, but with the Americans largely unaffected by Nasser's planned nationalization and fearing that the invasion might push the Arab nations into a closer association with the Soviet Union, Eisenhower sided with the Egyptians. The United States began applying pressure by denying Britain financial assistance via the IMF (International Monetary Fund) when its ally experienced financial difficulties after its Middle Eastern oil suppliers suspended deliveries. Eisenhower also threatened to sell part of the U.S. government sterling bond holdings, which would have resulted in a steep devaluation of the pound and financially crippled Britain, perhaps permanently. Saudi Arabia also began an oil embargo against Britain and France, and the United States, acting in unison with the Saudis, refused to supplement their oil supplies until both countries withdrew from Suez. The Soviet Union also intervened, threatening to begin rocket attacks on Britain, France and Israel on 5 November if they did not withdraw from Egypt.[12]

Assailed internationally from all sides, Eden unilaterally announced a cease-fire on 6 November 1956, without warning either France or Israel, despite British forces being within 24 hours of capturing the entire Suez Zone. With the cease-fire in place, the UN demanded that British and French forces immediately begin their withdrawal, which they were ordered to have completed by 22 December 1956. America and the UN confirmed Egyptian ownership of the Suez Canal, but it was the Soviet Union that received Nasser's thanks as Egypt's protector. This strengthened Krushchev's belief that nuclear blackmail was an effective tool for implementing Soviet foreign policy and led indirectly to the insanity of the Cuban Missile Crisis.[13]

Perhaps not unexpectedly, Vietnam does not appear to have figured prominently in Eden's foreign policy commitments during his time in office. Britain was a founding member of SEATO (South East Asia Treaty Organisation) in 1957 and sent a certain amount of foreign aid and technical expertise to the region, but appears to have had little involvement beyond that, although the embassy in Saigon submitted the usual monthly status reports.

Interestingly, America's actions toward its most important Western ally during the Suez Crisis did not result in a significant long-term deterioration in their "special relationship." Macmillan, who succeeded Eden as prime minister, worked diligently to improve the association and was even consulted daily by Kennedy during the later confrontation with the Soviets in Cuba.

## Harold Macmillan (1957–1963)

Macmillan's foreign policy was successful in a number of key areas, with his visit to the Soviet Union in February 1959 probably his most influential contribution. This was the first visit to Russia by a British prime minister since World War II, and the talks he had there with Krushchev eased the tensions in East-West relations and ultimately led to the Partial Nuclear Test Ban Treaty of 1963. Macmillan was also responsible for Britain's major drive to grant independence to its former colonies, implementing a policy that removed support from the white minorities in those countries, as well as ignoring a number of eminent right-wing conservatives in Britain (most notably the Monday Club). Nigeria, the Southern Cameroons and British Somaliland were granted independence in 1960, followed by Sierra Leone and Tanganyika in 1961, Uganda in 1962, and Kenya in 1963, with Zanzibar merging with Tanganyika to form Tanzania in 1963. All remained within the Commonwealth apart from British Somaliland, which merged with Italian Somaliland to form Somalia. South Africa's government responded to this drive toward independence by leaving the now multi-racial Commonwealth in 1961, with Macmillan acquiescing to the dissolution of the Central African Federation by the end of 1963. In Southeast Asia, Malaya,

Sabah (British North Borneo), Sarawak and Singapore became independent as Malaysia in 1963.

In addition to being an advocate of colonial independence, Macmillan acted forcefully to restore the confidence of Britain's Middle Eastern allies, which had been badly shaken by the humiliation of the Suez Crisis. He supported the Sultan of Oman with aircraft and troops when he was attacked by revolutionary troops in July 1957 and also sent military aid to the governments of both Jordan (1958) and Kuwait (1960). When trouble began between Malaysia and Indonesia in 1963, Macmillan sent British forces to the region, at the beginning of what escalated into the Indonesian Confrontation.

## Relations with America

Despite the problems America's actions had caused Britain in the Middle East, Macmillan acted quickly to smooth over the difficulties and bad feeling created by American actions during the Suez Crisis. Whatever his views on American foreign policy (he was quoted as saying that it was Britain's historical duty to guide the power of the United States as the ancient Greeks had done for the Romans), he certainly tried to broaden the "special relationship" beyond Churchill's conception of an English-speaking union into a more inclusive "Atlantic Community." He also realized America's inherent potential for influencing world events, and his main preoccupation was to bring about "the interdependence of the nations of the Free World and the partnership which must be maintained between Europe and the United States."[14]

Prime Minister Harold Macmillan at No. 10, Downing Street, in 1957. Dubbed "Super MAC" by the media, he was responsible for the 1963 Test Ban treaty and largely orchestrated the improving relations between the West and Russia that were a feature of the late 1960s.

Macmillan and Kennedy in particular appear to have shared a mutual respect, even a liking for each other, and Kennedy consulted Macmillan almost daily during the difficult days that marked the height of the Cuban Missile Crisis. On Macmillan's enforced retirement in October 1963, Kennedy declared, "In nearly three years of cooperation, we have worked together on great and small issues, and we have never had a failure of understanding or of mutual trust."[15] Macmillan was equally complimentary, confiding to the widowed Jackie Kennedy in February 1964, "He seemed to trust me—and, as you will know, for those of us who have had to play the so-called game of politics—national and international—this is something very rare but very precious."[16]

The "special relationship" was not always as harmonious as these exchanges make it appear, however, and both Eisenhower and Kennedy acted in ways that strained this "mutual trust."

Difficulties first arose at the Paris Peace Summit in May 1960, when Eisenhower, embarrassed by the U-2 spy plane incident, blocked Macmillan's attempts to introduce a Partial Nuclear Test Ban Treaty between Britain, America and the Soviet Union (Macmillan eventually orchestrated the treaty in 1963). Even more significantly, in 1962, Kennedy and his secretary of defense, Robert McNamara, tried to divest the United Kingdom of its nuclear deterrent when they cancelled the joint UK–U.S. "Skybolt" guided missile project without consulting Britain. Kennedy made this decision despite Macmillan having already agreed to allow the United States to station Polaris submarines at the Royal Navy submarine base at Holy Loch, effectively in exchange for the missile deal. Directly on the heels of Kennedy's unilateral declaration, Dean Acheson, a former U.S. secretary of state, also chose this moment to publicly deride the "special relationship" and minimize Britain's contribution to the Western Alliance:

> Great Britain has lost an empire and has not yet found a role. The attempt to play a separate power role—that is, a role apart from Europe, a role based on a "Special Relationship" with the United States, a role based on being the head of a "Commonwealth" which has no political structure, or unity, or strength and enjoys a fragile and precarious economic relationship—this role is about played out.[17]

Macmillan responded forcefully to Acheson's speech:

> In so far as he appeared to denigrate the resolution and will of Britain and the British people, Mr. Acheson has fallen into an error which has been made by quite a lot of people in the course of the last four hundred years, including Philip of Spain, Louis XIV, Napoleon, the Kaiser and Hitler. He also seems to misunderstand the role of the Commonwealth in world affairs. In so far as he referred to Britain's attempt to play a separate power role as about to be played out, this would be acceptable if he had extended this concept to the United States and to every other nation in the Free World. This is the doctrine of interdependence, which must be applied in the world today, if peace and prosperity are to be assured. I do not know whether Mr. Acheson would accept the logical consequence of his own argument. I am sure it is fully recognized by the U.S. administration and by the American people.[18]

The imminent possibility of the collapse of the Anglo-American alliance forced Kennedy into an immediate change of policy at the Nassau Summit meeting, where he agreed to sell the submarine-based Polaris as a replacement for the canceled Skybolt. Later, however, after the test ban talks of June 1963 at Macmillan's country house, Birch Grove, Kennedy and his advisers described Macmillan and Alex Douglas-Home as "fuddy-duddy." Their subsequent remarks became so offensive that Macmillan's private secretary, Phillip de Zulueta, complained to Kennedy's adviser on foreign affairs.

These periodic manifestations of American ill will probably exacerbated Macmillan's disenchantment with the "special relationship" and may have led to his attempt to find an additional military and economic power-base in Europe by joining the EEC (European Economic Community). Despite Macmillan's obvious distrust of American motives and his moves toward new alliances, Kennedy still felt able to assure him "that relations between the United States and the UK would be strengthened not weakened, if the UK moved towards membership [of the EEC]."[19] Unfortunately, Macmillan's machinations were unsuccessful, and de Gaulle vetoed the British application precisely *because* he mistrusted the Anglo-American relationship and wanted the EEC to remain a French-German coalition. There were also significant problems revolving around America's refusal to sell nuclear technology to the French while sharing nuclear secrets freely with the British.

Macmillan was generally supportive of U.S. policy in the Far East, although he refused to consider sending British troops to fight in that region and was also instrumental in preventing U.S. military intervention in Laos, which might have precipitated a third world war. When Kennedy began increasing the number of American advisers in Vietnam in 1961, Macmillan authorized the formation of BRIAM as a means of advising the Americans on ways of countering the techniques of urban and rural terrorism that the Việt Cộng were becoming adept in, without increasing their military commitments. During this period, although a conventional military solution was perceived as being extremely difficult to achieve by the British, it was thought that the Americans could succeed there by adapting the techniques Britain had used in Malaya. Consequently, Macmillan may have instituted BRIAM as a means of covertly giving a more experienced British direction to U.S. efforts to defeat the Việt Minh, as well as providing an outward show of support. While offering this practical support, his government also continually tried to convince both the Eisenhower and Kennedy administrations that large-scale military intervention in Indochina would be unsuccessful. This advice was never accepted, although, if Kennedy had lived, U.S. involvement in Vietnam might well have had an entirely different outcome.[20]

## Sir Alex Douglas-Home (1963–1964)

During Douglas-Home's premiership, the colonies of Northern Rhodesia and Nyasaland became independent, although this was as a result of negotiations previously carried through by Iain Macleod during Macmillan's time as prime minister. Most significantly, John F. Kennedy was assassinated on 22 November 1963, which marked the beginning of another period of deterioration in relations between Downing Street and the White House. Douglas-Home had been able to work constructively with Kennedy but failed to establish a similar cordial relationship with Johnson (this lack of accord was also typical of the relationship between Johnson and Harold Wilson when the latter took office on 15 October 1964).

Alex Douglas-Home, prime minister for slightly less than 12 months from 19 October 1963 until 16 October 1964, in 1963. He was thought by many Tories to be a poor choice when he became leader after MacMillan fell ill, but he achieved a certain amount of success, and his term of office saw a growth of 4 percent in the British economy *(Wikipedia; Creative Commons)*.

## Harold Wilson (1964–1970)

During Labour's time in opposition, Wilson had been vehemently opposed to any British involvement in Vietnam, whether to aid the French or the Americans, stating categorically in a speech in February 1952 that "it must be the duty of the British Parliament, and the British Labour Movement in particular, to make it clear that if any section of American opinion sought to extend the area of fighting in Asia, they could not expect us to support it." Two years later, on May Day in Manchester, he went a good deal further:

> The Government should not further subordinate British policy to America. A settlement in Asia is imperiled by the lunatic fringe in the American Senate who want a holy crusade against Communism.... Asia is in revolution and Britain must learn to march on the side of the peoples in that revolution and not on the side of their oppressors.[21]

By 1964, and the election of Labour into office with its scant majority, Wilson's public stance had softened, apparently influenced by his reserved admiration for John Kennedy. After Kennedy's assassination in November 1963, Wilson, strongly believing that the next general election would bring his party into office, was optimistic about the possibility of working with Johnson because the new president's stance on social justice seemed to parallel Labour's own socialist principles. Unfortunately, once Johnson had committed America irrevocably to winning the ground war by dispatching large numbers of U.S. troops to Vietnam in April 1965, he began to become obsessed by both the war and especially its effect

Harold Wilson, prime minister during the most intense period of the Vietnam War, No 10, Downing Street, in 1974. His maneuverings were largely responsible for avoiding a major British troop commitment.

on American public opinion. Johnson's views became increasingly unbalanced as the war progressed, centering on the loyalty of those in Congress who opposed his increasingly intransigent stance on Vietnam for what seemed to them perfectly sound reasons. This attitude was ultimately transferred to America's allies, particularly Britain and its prime minister, despite Wilson consistently supporting Johnson diplomatically throughout his time in office, often in opposition to a considerable number of MPs in his own party.[22]

Wilson's most important single instance of public criticism of Johnson's policy came on 29 June 1966, when Wilson was forced to voice his government's disapproval of the U.S. bombing of Hanoi and Haiphong. In a statement from Downing Street, later repeated in the House of Lords, he announced "with regret that United States aircraft have attacked North Vietnamese targets touching on the populated areas of Hanoi and Haiphong," and that "we must dissociate ourselves from any action of this kind."[23]

Wilson acceded to this necessity only because he was under overwhelming political pressure to do so, both from the members of his own party and from the opposition. His statement, however, also reaffirmed British support for the United States, and it is clear from an examination of the original sources that the White House knew in advance what the prime minister intended to say—Johnson himself even made changes to the text. Apparently Johnson did not like the word "dissociate," but the vice-president, Hubert Humphrey, and the defense secretary, Robert McNamara, confirmed that "the Prime Minister's position was well understood" and "there would be no hard feelings."

During much of Johnson's term of office, Wilson was also desperately resisting the president's increasingly strident calls for the commitment of British troops, with McNamara at one time even insisting that the United Kingdom should "pay the blood price" by sending troops to Vietnam as part of "the unwritten terms of the Special Relationship."[24]

Although Wilson continually avoided sending troops to aid the Americans, he was vocal in supporting their anti–Communist role in Southeast Asia, while still urging them to negotiate peace with the Việt Cộng and their numerous, powerful allies, as well as organizing a number of peace initiatives himself.[25] In return for this support and Wilson's agreement to continue maintaining military bases in areas like Malaysia, Borneo and Singapore (the "East of Suez" commitment) and UK forces in West Germany, despite independence making the presence of the Far East garrisons unnecessary, the Americans gave financial support to the UK economy, which delayed the pound's devaluation by several months. The original agreement had also included some form of troop involvement in Vietnam at brigade strength, with McGeorge Bundy (then national security adviser) trying to include a firm commitment to Vietnam, telling the president categorically on 28 July 1965 that it made "no sense whatsoever for us to rescue the pound in a situation in which there is no British flag in Vietnam ... a British brigade in Vietnam could be worth, say, a billion dollars at the moment of truth for sterling." Although he agreed to the "East of Suez" proposal, Wilson was careful to give no firm commitment on Vietnam, probably knowing what his political future was likely to be in the event of promising to send troops to help the Americans.

Unfortunately, Britain's balance-of-payment crisis and the weakness of sterling during this period meant that maintaining large overseas troops commitments became unrealistic. Consequently, in July 1967, Dennis Healey, then defense secretary, announced that Britain would give up its military bases in the region "East of Suez" by 1977. Further financial constraints, most notably the devaluation of the pound on 18 November 1967, forced Wilson to accelerate this timetable in January 1968, declaring that British troops would be withdrawn from these areas by 1971 and that the purchase of the F-111K would be canceled (Wilson's successor, Edward Heath, kept small numbers of troops in those areas until 1977).

Despite Wilson's forced withdrawal from their original agreement, Johnson publicly showed him no animosity, apparently realizing that, although he was forced to make the occasional public gesture, Wilson had little choice but to remain a staunch supporter of America's foreign policy.[26] The president was, however, disappointed over the withdrawals and cancellation of the F-111, and he had no compunction about telling Wilson just how badly he felt. He wrote to the prime minister of his deep dismay "upon learning this profoundly discouraging news ... tantamount to British withdrawal from world affairs.... The structure of peace-keeping will be shaken to its foundations."

In the period after the Tet Offensive (31 January 1968), Wilson and his cabinet, along with many other world leaders, became even more firmly convinced that the U.S. position in Vietnam was wholly untenable and advocated that the United States find some way to seek a Vietnamese solution to the country's problems.[27] After his election in November

1968, Richard Nixon appears to have taken much the same view, beginning significant troop withdrawals in 1969. At this point, the question of British troop involvement became meaningless, especially as Australian troop withdrawals were also beginning.

## *Edward Heath (1970–1974)*

Heath's foreign policy was an attempt to reverse many of Wilson's changes, being especially desirous to maintain Britain's military presence in the Far East. He also began developing a constructive relationship with the Chinese and figures in the Iraqi Ba'ath Party. Heath particularly favored stronger links with Europe and a lessened dependence upon the Americans, describing the association as a "natural relationship, based on shared culture and heritage," and stressing that the "special relationship" was "not part of his own vocabulary."

Despite this lack of warmth, Heath publicly supported Nixon when the U.S. president ordered the massive U.S. bombing campaign of Hanoi and Haiphong in April 1972 and continued to maintain a working relationship with Nixon throughout his time in office. Anglo-American relations during Heath's premiership were dominated by the implications surrounding Britain's entry into the EEC (European Economic Community). Although the two leaders' 1971 Bermuda communiqué restated that entry would serve the interests of the Atlantic Alliance, many American political commentators suggested that Britain's membership might impair its role as America's unofficial advocate. Moreover, because the eventual goal of the EEC was the formation of a pan–European political system, Britain's special relationship with the United States would only survive if it included the whole community.

Heath was to be proved right in his assessment of the "special relationship" as something decidedly not so special. Some political commentators criticized Nixon for impeding the EEC's inclusion in the "special relationship" through his economic policy, which dismantled the postwar international monetary system and sought to force open European markets for U.S. exports. The personal relationship between Heath and Nixon was also unraveling, some alleging that the prime minister hardly dared communicate with Nixon for fear of offending his new EEC partners.

Heath, however, was hardly conciliatory toward the Americans, either. In October 1973, he placed a British arms embargo on both sides in the Arab-Israeli Yom Kip-

Edward Heath, prime minister of Britain during much of Richard Nixon's term of office. This photograph was taken while he was leader of the opposition, 1 May 1966.

pur War, which most severely affected the Israelis, America's most important allies in the Middle East, by preventing them from obtaining spare parts for their Centurion tanks. He also refused to allow U.S. intelligence gathering from British bases in Cyprus, resulting in a temporary halt in the U.S. signals intelligence tap, and prohibited U.S. forces from using any British bases for resupply purposes. The "special relationship" was strained even further during this period when Nixon failed to inform Heath that U.S. forces had been put on DEFCON 3 in a confrontation with the Soviet Union over the war in the Middle East, with Kissinger subsequently also misleading the British ambassador in Washington over the nuclear alert. Heath, who learned about Nixon's actions from a press report some hours later, confessed, "I have found considerable alarm as to what use the Americans would have been able to make of their forces here without in any way consulting us or considering the British interests."

## Harold Wilson (1974–1976)

The 1972 general election resulted in neither of the major parties gaining a clear majority, effectively a "hung" Parliament, and marked the first time since World War II that an election had not produced a majority for the winning party. Wilson succeeded Heath on 4 March without a working majority, and he called another election on 10 October 1974, managing to secure a majority of just 3 seats. By now, however, the Americans were out of Vietnam, Nixon had resigned and the world scene and America's place in it had undergone some radical and long-term changes.[28]

**Table One: British Prime Ministers, American Presidents and Their Terms of Office**

| Prime Minister | Term of Office | U.S. President | Term of Office |
|---|---|---|---|
| Winston Churchill (Con) | 1945 | Harry Truman (Dem) | 1945–1953 |
| Clement Attlee (Lab) | 1945–1951 | | |
| Sir Winston Churchill (Con) | 1951–1955 | Dwight Eisenhower (Rep) | 1953–1961 |
| Anthony Eden (Con) | 1955–1957 | | |
| Harold Macmillan (Con) | 1957–1963 (resigned due to ill health, succeeded by Douglas-Home) | John Kennedy (Dem) | 1961–1963 (assassinated 22 November 1963) |
| Sir Alex Douglas-Home (Con) | 1963–1964 (succeeded Macmillan) | Lyndon Johnson (Dem) | 1963–1969 (succeeded Kennedy after assassination, then elected November 1964, with large majority) |
| Harold Wilson (Lab) | 1964–1970 | | |
| Edward Heath (Con) | 1970–1974 | Richard Nixon (Rep) | 1969–1974 (resigned in 2nd term on 9 August 1974 ) |
| Harold Wilson (Lab) | 1974–1976 | Gerald Ford (Rep) | 1974–1977 |

## *Perspectives*

The "special relationship" between Britain and America probably achieved its most useful form during World War II; certainly it became increasingly less cozy in the postwar environment. Even Churchill, who was the major advocate of this association and coined the phrase "special relationship" to describe it in the early years of the Cold War, must have felt, after his wartime experiences with Roosevelt, that "special" was, at best, an optimistic way to describe it.

Successive British prime ministers became increasingly disenchanted with the political and financial consequences of Britain being seen by the world as America's junior partner, and this was brought to a head by Eisenhower's actions during the Suez Crisis, which saw Eden's resignation and a widespread disenchantment in Britain with all things American. Although Macmillan worked hard to restore the special relationship after the Suez Crisis, he never fully trusted Americans motives and sought to dissipate their influence in Britain by forming a stronger relationship with Europe. He also began the economic and military withdrawal from Britain's former possessions, which Wilson continued, through his policy of African decolonialization, dismantling the military and administrative infrastructure in those regions for which the British government had been responsible and so reducing the financial burden that their upkeep had imposed upon British taxpayers.

British foreign policy in both the Macmillan and the Wilson governments contrasted strongly with that of the contemporary American administrations, particularly in Southeast Asia. While Kennedy and Johnson had both sought to widen the sphere of American influence in the Far East, the British, drawing upon a wider colonial experience, recognized and reacted positively to the growing nationalist sentiment in their former colonies, although successive governments were also increasingly concerned about the rising financial burden of those commitments. Macmillan's government began the process in that region by establishing the Federation of Malaysia, a strongly based association of states that Britain later supported in withstanding the attacks of President Sukarno, the Communist-backed leader of Indonesia. Potentially, Britain and its Commonwealth allies might have found Malaysia turning into a disaster similar to Vietnam if they had been less sophisticated in their approach, although circumstances certainly helped them eventually achieve a favorable settlement. Despite Macmillan's success with foreign policy, however, it was the problems arising from Britain's balance of payments during his term in office that became a disastrous inheritance for successive governments. This contributed significantly to the economic crisis in 1967, which resulted in the devaluation of the pound and might have given the Americans sufficient leverage to force Wilson to order the deployment of British troops to Vietnam.

Wilson's period as prime minister saw an acceleration in the continuing decline of Anglo-American relations. Like Macmillan, Wilson was concerned with greatly reducing the cost of Britain's role "East of Suez," although he was also intent upon pursuing a conciliatory policy on Vietnam, in order to both involve the Soviet Union (as co-chairman of the 1954 Geneva Conference) in bipartisan peace negotiations and enhance British trading relations in the region. Naturally, this policy was unpopular with Johnson, who, like Kennedy, wanted the British to have a much greater role in military operations in Vietnam, if only for the propaganda value such a move would have. Consequently, Britain's subsequent withdrawal from the Persian Gulf and East Asia was widely criticized in the United States, where it was seen by many, particularly in the White House, as an act of betrayal. In reality, however, Wilson's realistic scaling back of Britain's global commitments went some way toward correcting the United Kingdom's balance-of-payment problems and gave Britain a more European emphasis, and this eventually proved more beneficial than Johnson's reckless spending in Southeast Asia, which caused significant problems for the U.S. economy.

Johnson is said to have despised all of the postwar British prime ministers. He came to be especially critical of Wilson in private, particularly when the prime minister advocated restraint in Vietnam and insisted that little needed to be done to bridge the gap between the Americans and Việt Cộng and so achieve peace. The president and his administration were especially incensed over the British refusal to send troops to Vietnam, an attitude expressed by Johnson's secretary of state, Dean Rusk, when he told Louis Heren, the *London Times* American editor, "All we needed was one regiment, The Black Watch would have done. Just one regiment, but you wouldn't. Well, don't expect us to save you again. They can invade Sussex and we wouldn't do a damn thing about it."[29]

Another example of the deteriorating relations between the two men over the question of troops occurred in February 1965, when Wilson, suspecting that the Americans might use nuclear weapons against the North Vietnamese, telephoned Johnson to suggest he visit Washington to discuss the matter. Johnson, believing that Wilson was trying to appease the left-wing activists in his own party, replied, "If you want to help us some in Vietnam send us some men.... Now, if you don't feel like doing that, go on with your Malaysian problems."[30] Understandably, American disenchantment with Britain was only further exacerbated by the "East of Suez" troop withdrawals in January 1968.

Nor did Edward Heath's appointment as prime minister help matters very much. Heath was most concerned with establishing strong links between Britain and the rest of Europe, and he was clear that there was nothing "special" about the relationship between Britain and America, referring to it as a "natural relationship" based on ties of culture and language, rather than economics and mutual military aid. Although Heath was instrumental in delaying Britain's withdrawal from the Far East, his motives were firmly based on what he saw as Britain's advantage and had little to do with supporting the Americans, who by this time were clearly intent upon getting out of Vietnam with as little fuss as possible.

Wilson's last period in office saw the Communist invasion of South Vietnam and the establishment of a country-wide political system based on Communist doctrine. Its effects were catastrophic for the Vietnamese, but Britain maintained equable trade relations with Vietnam throughout the long period of transition to a healthy economy, now judged by many observers to be among the strongest in Asia.

Britain's relationship with America survived the U.S. withdrawal from Vietnam, and subsequent British prime ministers have been more or less enthusiastic about the association, depending upon their perception of the relative advantage that cooperation with the Americans gave them. Margaret Thatcher and Tony Blair were perhaps the two outstanding enthusiasts for the "special relationship" during this later period, although many in Britain seem to feel now that it has outlived its usefulness and, with economic problems becoming the main government concern, that there is a need for wider partnerships to ensure economic protection in a rapidly changing global theater. The stock market may yet become the battleground of the future, in an unceasing war fought out in tariff agreements and exchange rates, and one might be forgiven for wondering what use any sort of "special relationship" will be then, especially given America's tendency to consult its own interests, regardless of the consequences for its less fortunate associates and former allies.

Perhaps the most honest appraisal of the "special relationship" came from President Truman's secretary of state, Dean Acheson, when he said, "Of course a unique relation existed between Britain and America—our common language and history ensured that. But unique did not mean affectionate. We had fought England as an enemy as often as we had fought by her side as an ally."[31]

# 9

# Military Support, or:
## Did British Troops Fight in the Vietnam Wars?

### France's War (October 1945–April 1954)

Aside from the early consolidation, there is no official government record of Britain sending any military personnel to support the French in Vietnam during this period, nor of Attlee's or Churchill's governments offering any other form of assistance. There may, however, have been private citizens who fought there, as either volunteers or mercenaries, although no record of any such involvement has so far been found in any file held in the Public Record Office.

### America's War (April 1954–August 1973)

Small numbers of American military advisers had been operating throughout South Vietnam in support of Diệm's government since the French army evacuated in 1955, sent there by President Eisenhower to counter the possibilities of a Communist threat inherent in the White House's "domino" theory. Macmillan was prime minister (1959–1963) when Kennedy slowly began to increase American involvement, and he and his cabinet were generally supportive of what was seen as the American stand against Communism, although neither the prime minister, cabinet, labor opposition nor many in the country were in favor of giving military support to the South Vietnamese.[1]

Kennedy began his escalation in 1961 circumspectly, initially creating a "Task Force Vietnam" to prepare military, economic and social programs for South Vietnam that could be introduced to counter the influence of the northern Communists. He also began to steadily increase the number of advisers working in the south, from 700 in 1960 to 16,000 by 1963. This was in conjunction with an increase in both Vietnamese troop numbers and the amount of American equipment provided to supply those troops, although such an increase was contrary to the Geneva Agreement, which specified that foreign military personnel could only enter South Vietnam as replacements. The Americans sent their advisers anyway, at the same time failing to inform either Britain, as co-chairman of the Geneva Conference, or the International Control Commission about the deployments, this type of secrecy being a distinct feature of Anglo-American relations at the time.[2] Kennedy, however, was not comfortable with using American troops in South Vietnam, believing that Diệm's forces, the ARVN (Army of the Republic of Vietnam; also the South Vietnamese Army [SVA]), should be helped to defeat the Việt Minh without any obvious American military assistance, although he had accepted the need for covert aid.[3] The president and his team were also intent upon involving the British in the defense of Southeast Asia and, in an attempt to help the Americans decrease Communist influence in the country (and probably to forestall demands for more substantial assistance), Macmillan authorized the establishment of BRIAM in July 1961.[4] At the end of November 1961, Edward Heath, as Lord Privy Seal, added to the controversy surrounding British military aid to Vietnam, and support for the American troops already there, by declining to give an assurance that no British troops would be used or stationed in Vietnam.[5] Macmillan and his cabinet were still opposed to any deployment of British troops to Vietnam, however, as well as being concerned that the Americans' potential use of nuclear weapons in Vietnam might also involve China and so precipitate a third world war.[6] Consequently, Britain confined itself to diplomatic support and advice on counter-insurgency and policing, via BRIAM, evading the question of any joint military intervention if it arose.

America's involvement began to gain significant momentum after Kennedy's assassination (22 November 1963) and Lyndon Johnson's entry into the White House. Troop numbers and financial aid to South Vietnam from America increased enormously during Johnson's time in power (1964–1968), deployments reaching a peak in 1968, the year Nixon replaced Johnson as president, when over 500,000 American troops were stationed in Vietnam. In conjunction with American financial and military aid, Johnson attempted to gain international support for the American anti–Communist stance in Vietnam by adopting what came to be known as his "more flags" policy, asking friendly countries to also begin sending non-military aid to the South Vietnamese.[7] With the election of the Labour Party and appointment of Harold Wilson as prime minister, however, British government policy on American military operations in Vietnam began to become less openly supportive, although the cabinet was reluctant to be seen as uncooperative for both financial and political reasons, maintaining what George Brown called a "policy of committed detachment." Certainly, many in Whitehall were sure by the end of 1968 that only diplomacy would resolve Vietnam's problems, perhaps mediated by Britain and the Soviet Union; the Americans were seen as having little chance of winning the war, either on the ground or in the air.[8]

## British Service Personnel in Vietnam

The last official deployment of British troops in organized units to Vietnam took place as a result of Operation "Masterdom," which ended with the withdrawal of the last members of the 20th Division in 1946. After that period, the policy of succeeding British governments was to decline to send troops there in support of either the French or the Americans.

However, the Americans consistently tried to persuade the British to commit troops to Vietnam, particularly during Harold Wilson's premiership (1964–1970), when General Westmoreland was organizing his huge "search and destroy" missions and the long-term bombing campaign had begun (Operation "Rolling Thunder," which started in March 1965

**Troops of the Royal Australian Regiment after arrival at Tan Son Nhut Airport, Saigon.**

and lasted 44 months, until November 1968). Wilson refused all these requests on the grounds that Britain was the co-chair of the Geneva Peace Conference, and so had to remain impartial.[9] More importantly, the British army also had extensive commitments in Malaysia, with 30,000 troops stationed there during the Indonesian Confrontation (1962–1966). This gave the prime minister another good excuse for refusing military aid to Vietnam, most especially since British involvement in Malaysia was seen by the White House as an important, additional bulwark against Communism in Southeast Asia as a whole. Although Wilson's stance was clearly defensible, during this same period the other co-chair of the 1954 Geneva Conference, the Soviet Union, was known to be sending arms worth millions of dollars to the North Vietnamese every year, which may have been one reason for Johnson's disenchantment with Britain's policy of non-involvement. He certainly felt pressured and, under his "many flags" policy, even offered to pay all the military expenses of any country that would join the Americans in their war against the Việt Cộng.

American demands for some British involvement were not primarily concerned with the numbers of troops that might be sent, however. More important, from the Americans' point of view, were the propaganda effects of Britain taking America's side.[10] Britain was still a leading social democracy with important roles in NATO, the UN Security Council and especially SEATO. Despite a diminishing world status, its opinion counted, and any condemnation or wavering of support for America by Britain might be seized upon and exploited by North Vietnam and its sympathizers, particularly the left-wing, liberal American voters whom Johnson and his team were to come to loathe so much in the years that followed.[11] William Bundy, Johnson's assistant secretary of state for foreign affairs, said as much when he stated that a British troop commitment "would have made a considerable psychological difference ... particularly in liberal circles, which is where the main criticism of the war came from." Johnson agreed vehemently with Bundy, asking Wilson at their meeting in Washington in December 1964 if the Black Watch could be sent to Vietnam, adding that "a platoon of bagpipers would be sufficient, it was the British flag that was needed."[12]

Undoubtedly, this assessment was correct and the presence of British forces would have prolonged, and possibly escalated, the fighting. Both the Chinese and Soviets might even have entered the war on the side of the North Vietnamese, with effects too disastrous to contemplate.[13] Wilson's response, however, may not have been wholly motivated by a desire to be the unbiased "honest broker" he was portraying to America and the rest of the world. Although he was under pressure from Johnson, some members of his own party and the Conservative opposition to make a stronger commitment in Southeast Asia, the overwhelming mood of the Parliamentary Labour Party and the country was against any military action there.[14] It was probably concerns about possible repercussions in a general election that led to the government's stance, rather than any worries over the eventual fate of the people of South Vietnam or the consequences for America of its involvement there.

## British Government Policy on the Deployment of Troops to Vietnam

Wilson's official position on troop deployments during Johnson's presidency, the most intense period of the war, was made consistently clear in his replies (as well as those of Secretary of State for Defense Denis Healey) to numerous questions on the subject that were raised in the House of Commons.[15] Wilson also confirmed this stance in his reply on 16 June 1965 to a letter from Mrs. Anne Kerr, MP, who represented a large group of Labour MPs opposed to British participation in the Vietnam War. It contained this passage: "Thank you for your letter of June 3, signed by yourself and a number of your colleagues, about the situation in Vietnam. I have made clear in the past and can certainly confirm again that there is no question of the Government sending British troops to Vietnam."[16]

Of course, this had been the British government's overall policy since operations in Vietnam began in 1946 and had been constantly reiterated by Wilson's predecessors. However, the increased pressure exerted by the Johnson regime meant that the United Kingdom did find it expedient to help the United States in a number of minor ways during this period.[17] Not surprisingly, this support appears to have been given only to forestall American demands for a more major, public show of solidarity, and official records show that it was government policy during this period to avoid (and at times actively discourage) publicizing these activities.[18] Edward Heath continued this policy of minor, unpublicized support when he became prime minister, although the pressure for British military involvement was reduced during Nixon's first term, which saw the beginning of major American troop withdrawals. By 1973, the president was able to announce that Kissinger had achieved the "peace with honor" for which he had been negotiating, which would allow the United States to escape from Vietnam and pave the way for the Communist occupation of the south.

## Secondments

The British government's main problem with its military personnel serving in Vietnam was not over the deployment of large, organized bodies of troops, which Wilson always simply refused to sanction, but rather revolved around men on secondment. Secondments, in general, involve serving military personnel being attached to a unit in the armed forces of another country, and during the period of the Vietnam War, decisions had to be made about the conduct of British servicemen seconded to the armed forces of America, Australia and New Zealand, which all had units fighting in Vietnam. Official policy had always prohibited service personnel on secondment from fighting alongside the armed forces of any country deployed in Vietnam, but it was not until 1968 that officials felt the government's position to be awkward enough to cause them to properly formalize such arrangements.[19]

Previously, the conduct of British troops serving with another country's armed forces fighting in Vietnam had, in many cases, been governed by what the MOD (Ministry of Defence) referred to as simply "gentleman's agreements." This had led to a certain amount of embarrassment for the government during Parliamentary Questions; consequently, in 1968, formal instructions to seconded personnel were embodied in a DCI,[20] which included the following clauses:

1. British Service personnel are forbidden to visit Vietnam either on duty or on leave unless they have first obtained permission from their controlling Service authority....

2. This instruction applies to all personnel whether they are serving in established posts, or on loan, exchange, advisory, attachment or secondment posts with Commonwealth or foreign military, diplomatic or other services, and covers all forms of visits in any capacity whatsoever (e.g., as an observer) to Vietnamese territory including Vietnamese airspace and territorial waters.[21]

This prohibition officially included all personnel serving with the armed forces of America, Australia, New Zealand and Canada, although exceptions were occasionally made. When this sort of flexibility was exercised, however, the government officials responsible were very careful to see that it attracted as little publicity as possible.

British military and civilian personnel did visit South Vietnam during the war for a variety of purposes other than combat, and a number of British ex-service personnel and civilians also fought with the U.S. and Commonwealth forces deployed there. Their involvement is described in the succeeding chapters, using information obtained from government records and newspaper articles, although this cannot be considered a complete list.

# 10

# The British Army

## *Recruitment from the British Army to the Australian Army*

Although officers and men from Britain's armed forces could not participate in the fighting in Vietnam, that did not prevent the Australians from trying to make use of this pool of experienced manpower. The Australian army seems to have been particularly short of experienced personnel during this period, because in November 1967 it issued recruiting literature aimed at serving officers in the British army. The requirement was for 250 natural-born British subjects of European descent to be appointed to short service commissions of five years, possibly becoming permanent after two years, subject to review and satisfactory service. Applicants were required to be under 32 (to satisfy pension requirements), although those with specialist qualifications could be appointed up to 42 years of age. No special financial incentives were offered, pay remaining on the normal scale, but it was intended that only officers with a substantive rank of captain or major would be recruited. Officers were required to serve anywhere "within and beyond the limits of the Commonwealth" (clearly, this stipulation was intended to include Vietnam).[1] No information is available regarding the number of officers who either responded to this advertisement or were subsequently recruited.

## *Recruitment from the British Army to the U.S. Armed Forces*

No records exist in the National Archives indicating that any serving personnel in the British army, Royal Navy or RAF were ever recruited by the United States between 1963 and 1973. However, some individuals may have resigned their posts in the British armed forces in order to join the Americans and subsequently fight in Vietnam. Consequently, there may have been occasions when this happened that are not the subject of a government record, although technically, if those persons remained British citizens, they would have been violating the Foreign Enlistment Act of 1870, which prohibits British subjects from serving with a foreign power not at war with Great Britain (Chapter 13: Mercenaries).

## *British Citizens Conscripted or Volunteering for Service in the Australian Army*

Although figures recording the success of the Australian army's 1967 recruiting campaign are not readily available, a number of serving Royal Navy, Army and RAF officers certainly did resign before transferring to the corresponding branches of the Australian armed forces while the fighting continued. As well as these serving officers, retired members of the British military are also recorded as having served with the American, Australian and New Zealand armed forces (some were even believed to have emigrated so as to participate in the fighting).[2]

Unfortunately, complete, detailed records of British citizens who served in Vietnam with all the countries fighting there are not readily available. Australian government figures for enlistment, however, show that over 2,700 men who served in Vietnam gave Britain, England, Great Britain or the United Kingdom (hereafter referred to as "British citizens") as their place of birth when joining the Australian army between 1963 and 1972, when the last Australian soldier left the country. Their service numbers were in a variety of series, beginning at 15200 and ending at 5710000, with no clear correlation between these numbers and the date of enlistment or unit the man joined. Of these men, 24 died in service with the Australian army.[3]

## British Citizens Conscripted or Volunteering for Service in the New Zealand Army

Records for the New Zealand army between 1965 and 1971 show that 20 British citizens volunteered for service—four who had immigrated to New Zealand as children and 16 others, although most of the remainder were between 16 and 20 years of age when they joined and so were probably also immigrants. However, of these 16 men, three had been in the British army previously and one had served in the Royal Navy, so they may have come to New Zealand specifically to fight in Vietnam. Three of the twenty were either killed in action or died in service during their period of enlistment. National servicemen in any branch of the New Zealand armed forces were not required to serve in Vietnam.[4]

## Training and Secondments

### VISITS BY SENIOR BRITISH SERVICE PERSONNEL

Senior British officers from the Royal Navy, Army and RAF regularly made a small number of visits each year to American units in South Vietnam. These trips were of varying duration and specifically intended to improve their knowledge of modern combat techniques. The usual restrictions applied, especially that prohibiting officers from acting as observers, and from February 1967, visits were limited to roughly four in any given year, although between 1965 and November 1967 there were 19 such visits. This information is contained in a Commons answer of 8 November 1967, in which Denis Healey gave some details of the numbers of British servicemen who had visited Vietnam in the previous two years: "Visits to South Vietnam by Service officers to gain information have numbered 19, involving 42 officers in all, in the last two years."[5]

### SECONDMENTS AND EXCHANGES

The extent of secondments and exchanges between U.S. and Commonwealth forces fighting in Vietnam was described in part by Mr. Healey in the House of Commons on 4

May 1966. He revealed that 158 British servicemen had been exchanged with U.S. servicemen since October 1964, which covered the preceding period of 20 months, and he also confirmed that none of these men were serving in Vietnam. No information seems to have been made available subsequently on later secondments, although if they took place to the same extent, approximately 650 service personnel (i.e., 8 per month, over 82 months) would have been seconded or exchanged at various times between May 1966 and March 1973, when the last U.S. troops left Vietnam.[6]

In his Commons answer of 8 November 1967, Mr. Healey also supplied information about men seconded to the Australian or New Zealand armed forces:

> Since 1965 some 30 British service personnel who have been on loan or exchange with Australian or New Zealand forces have been to South Vietnam for short visits, mainly in ships. The arrangements under which they are exchanged or loaned preclude involvement in active military operations, and the Service men in question have not been so involved.[7]

If later secondments took place to the same extent, estimated figures show that a further 60 secondments to Australian and New Zealand forces (15 per year, over four years) would have taken place between November 1967 and December 1971, when Commonwealth forces were leaving Vietnam.

These exchanges went both ways, however, and there had been a significant number of visits to the British by both U.S. and South Vietnamese personnel that had become matters of routine, especially those to the Jungle Warfare School in Johore, Malaysia.[8] Such routine visits were not publicized, and impromptu or unofficial trips were also severely discouraged because of the possible diplomatic complications.[9]

## Jungle Warfare School

The British army's Jungle Warfare School (JWS) in Johore, Malaysia, was initially established to train British soldiers in jungle warfare and prepare them for operations in that environment. The school consisted of about 50 square miles of jungle, which was used for the teams' training exercises, as well as a sophisticated base camp, organized into three wings, along with a technical section or "cell." These facilities also included an air-conditioned cinema and lecture hall; accommodation for students, staff and their families; and a cricket and hockey pitch.

### THE JUNGLE TACTICS WING

This section ran courses of four weeks' duration for British, Australian and American jungle commanders ranging in rank from major to sergeant, with an average intake of 40 students for each course. Between 1966 and 1970, this included a number of American Special Forces officers.

### THE "STAP" (SERVICES TRAINING AND ASSISTANCE PROGRAM) WING

Courses here were also of four to six weeks' duration for officers of the Army of the Republic of Vietnam and offered basic training in jungle warfare. Average course size was

The sign that trainees encountered upon arrival at JWS (courtesy Peter Seal).

45. These courses were also provided to a number of other participating countries, and participants were subsidized by funds from the United Kingdom.

## The War Dog's Training Wing

This section was commanded by a major in the Royal Army Veterinary Corps, its purpose being to train tracker dogs and their handlers. American trainees were funded by their government.

## The "Technical Development" Cell

As its name suggests, this cell devised and tested new techniques and equipment that might be useful in jungle warfare operations.[10]

American troops began jungle training at JWS in January 1964, following a request from the American government to provide such training for some of their personnel who were being sent to Vietnam. From the very beginning, this training was not publicized; Americans who attended the school went to Malaysia on official government passports, and, as an additional security measure, they carried no U.S. Army equipment, traveling in civilian clothes and being issued with British uniforms and equipment to use while at the school.[11] The emphasis on secrecy was so great that when three American trainees died in a river accident in January 1967, it was suggested in one newspaper report that their bodies had been taken from Malaysia to Saigon, where they were treated as conventional casualties of the war.[12]

Average course intake varied, up to a total of 48, with an average yearly intake of approximately eighty (two courses each year). Between 1964 and 1966, these men were only trained in jungle warfare, with 74 entrants completing such a course by 1968. From August 1966 onward, however, entrants were also trained specifically for service with U.S. Army Combat Tracker teams; a total of 199 men completed one of these courses by the end of 1968. These Combat Tracker teams were first operated by the British army in Malaysia. They consisted of a dog trained to reveal the presence of enemy troops, its handler, a team leader (usually an officer), a visual tracker, a radio operator and, finally, one or two armed soldiers to provide cover for the rest. Training for the visual trackers lasted approximately 65 days, while that for the dog handlers was longer, usually 95 days; in the last two weeks the men from both courses worked together. The British had initially agreed to train a total of 140 men as Combat Trackers in a program that would conclude in mid-1967, but the Americans later asked for the original program to be extended to November 1968 and include another 70 servicemen, and this was agreed.

**Plaque of the Jungle Warfare School (courtesy Peter Seal).**

Training of South Vietnamese troops had begun even earlier than that for the Americans, in 1961, during Macmillan's premiership and the period of BRIAM's most critical operations. The usual course intake was 45, resulting in a yearly average intake of 170 (four courses each year). These men were given training in basic jungle warfare tactics, and government records show that a total of 1,125 servicemen completed one of these courses in the period between 1964 and 1968, although these figures may have also included men trained between 1961 and 1964.[13]

## Public Notice

The training of these forces in the JWS first came to public notice when a Commons question on the subject was asked on 13 June 1966. This question only referred to the training of South Vietnamese troops and how this reflected the government's policy of non-involvement. Mr. Healey's reply was noncommittal, specifying that out of a total of 55 instructors, only three were concerned exclusively with courses for the South Vietnamese, and making no mention of the American trainees. Harold Wilson sanctioned the additional training for American Combat Tracker teams on 8 August 1966, and the first students arrived at the JWS soon afterward.

Unfortunately for the government, a story about the training of U.S. dog handlers at the JWS was published by the *Daily Telegraph* on 25 December 1966, and the Russian newspaper *Ixvestia* also included the story in a front-page article; however, it appears to have attracted little attention or comment in Britain, except at the Foreign and Commonwealth Office (FCO) and, momentarily, in Hanoi. The British news company ITN (International Television News) also requested permission to be allowed to film at the school in March 1967. The British advised the Malaysian government that permission for filming should be refused, and no record of such a film being made has been located. The confidential MOD memo concerned also contains a passage giving "general guidance" about publicity:

> Although we are not averse to general publicity for our training of Malaysian and third-country troops we do not want to encourage it in respect of the training of South Vietnamese troops or U.S. tracker dog teams as this would stimulate embarrassing political attention here. Equally, though, we do not want to give the impression we have anything to hide.

Later in the same memo:

> We must leave it to you to handle each journalistic inquiry in the light of this general guidance, but whenever possible we should like you to discourage interest provided you can do so without stimulating irresponsible and uninformed speculation.[14]

Interest in the story appears to have diminished by the spring of 1967, when it was inflamed once more by two articles describing the training and naming the school, which appeared in two U.S. Army magazines: the *Army Reporter* (13 May 1967) and the *Army Times* (31 May 1967). These stories again evoked no response from the press in Britain except for a brief paragraph in two British provincial newspapers, the Sheffield *Morning Telegraph* and *The Press and Journal* of Aberdeen. However, at approximately the same time, a British reporter from the *Daily Express*, acting on information from a different source, did request to be allowed to visit the school. The response of the MOD and FCO had clearly always been to avoid answering questions about American training at the JWS and to supply as little factual information as possible without actually being untruthful.[15] Consequently, the officials responsible were less than sanguine about this request and the subsequent discussion between Downing Street and the Office of the Political Advisor to the Commander-in-Chief, Far East, reflects the sensitivity of the British government to questions about Vietnam in general and the JWS in particular during this period. The confidential memo quoted here is dated 28 May 1968:

> [Name omitted] explained that he had met some South Vietnamese officers who stated they had been trained at the Jungle Warfare School in Malaysia. As a result he asked for arrangements to be made for him to visit the school. As you know we have never concealed the fact that South Vietnamese officers are trained by us at the school, though clearly we do our best to avoid publicity.... We were consulted and agreed that it would not be possible to keep [name omitted] away from the school to which he could go by taxi from here.

It concludes:

> No figures of the total number of foreign students will be given and emphasis will be laid on the British and Commonwealth troops who have used and are using the school. We shall have to hope that any story he files is along those lines.[16]

Once again, this story does not seem to have been widely publicized, and although there was some ongoing press interest and the occasional Commons question, both MOD and FCO continued to supply little factual information while minimizing the contribution the school made to American training.

## Justification and the Reason for Training the Americans

The response of these departments (and hence the government) to questions about the JWS always took the same line, playing down the importance of the training and emphasizing the difference between simply training a country's armed forces and, to them, the infinitely more serious business of supplying that country with troops and weapons. The conventional justification for continuing this training was embodied in a reply made by Denis Healey to a senior member of the Congregational Church of England and Wales, who had written to Healey asking about the role of the school in the Vietnam War. Part of the reply the churchman received included the following:

> We have said many times that we have no intention of participating ourselves in the fighting in Vietnam. What the training at the Jungle Warfare School achieves is to enable those trained to profit by the experience in fighting in jungle conditions that our troops have built up over the years. We see no moral objection to assisting in the training of a free country to defend its freedom in this way and there would be no logic in refusing to assist the United States in the same way.[17]

The British response does not appear to have been entirely altruistic, however. In a memo from the FCO, dated 8 September 1967, the real reason for British cooperation becomes a little clearer: "The Americans clearly value the training and it is a useful response to the periodic American appeals to increase our 'non-involved' aid to Vietnam." This passage strongly suggests that the JWS training was provided as a convenient diversion to distract the Americans and make it harder for them to demand more concrete military assistance, although it would perhaps be going a little far to insist that such manipulation of the Americans was official government policy.

Government statistics concerning the numbers of troops trained at JWS and the cost to the United Kingdom are also slightly contradictory. In a written Commons reply to Mr. James Dickens, Denis Healey admitted that, between 1 January 1964 and November 1967, 240 U.S. troops and 1,035 South Vietnamese had been trained by the British at the JWS, "at a cost to the British tax-payer of £132,364." South Vietnamese troops had actually been trained at JWS since 1961 and the Americans themselves paid for their soldiers' training, which Mr. Healey failed to mention.[18] In another confidential memo, this time discussing the possibility of officers from JWS visiting Vietnam, it is estimated that "slightly more than 300 South Vietnamese troops are trained annually by British instructors at our Jungle Warfare School … at a cost … of approximately £38,000." This gives an expenditure of £152,000 for 47 months, for training just over 1,200 troops, a figure higher than the estimates in Mr. Healey's written reply, which were for both American and South Vietnamese trainees, although the same file contains another memo estimating South Vietnamese training for the same period as costing £162,000.[19] Even this is an underestimate, because statistics from the S.T.A.P. program, which covered training for just the South Vietnamese, give the actual costs as £43,175 for April 1967 to March 1968—a total of £172,700 for four years.[20] The difference between these three sets of statistics has probably little or no significance, except that the Wilson government may have been attempting to downplay the amount of financial aid it was giving the South Vietnamese. With British help, the Americans established their own training school at Fort Gordon, Georgia, which opened in 1969; from then until 1971, American Combat Tracker teams were trained there.

The Americans may also have tried to use this training provision in yet another attempt to involve the British army in Vietnam.

On 9 December 1967, the Vietnamese Ministry of Defense invited the commandant of the JWS, the chief of Vietnamese training and two instructors to visit South Vietnam, in order to see the conditions their trainees were experiencing firsthand. The FCO examined the proposal and then drew up this list of objections:

- The visit could not be kept quiet. In fact, it was considered that the Vietnamese would want to publicize it as much as possible.
- To be effective, the officers concerned would have to visit operational areas—that is, act as observers and thus contravene government policy.
- It might encourage MOD to increase the number of yearly visits to Vietnam requested for British service personnel.

Not unexpectedly, the invitation was declined, with one FCO official writing on the bottom of a confidential memo that suggested a polite refusal, "If the Vietnamese find our help in jungle warfare training useful they should have no difficulty in understanding that it would be folly to publicize it." But the Vietnamese knew that already, so why ask for this visit when it was clear that conditions made it undesirable, to say the least, and everyone concerned, even the Malaysian government, had always adopted a policy of "no publicity" over this use of the facility?[21]

One possible explanation suggests itself: Did the Americans suggest the visit to their allies, perhaps as a way of increasing the pressure on Britain to move away from its policy of "non-involved" aid? Publicity of this sort could only work in the Americans' favor, even if it resulted in facilities at JWS being withdrawn, because they were setting up their own training center for Combat Tracker teams by this time, and evidence that the British were helping them, even clandestinely, would have certainly improved the credibility of their Vietnam operations in the eyes of the world. Johnson would have had his "platoon of bagpipers." No evidence of any sort exists to suggest that this was what happened, and, of course, the invitation may well have been, and in truth probably was, exactly what it appeared—simply an ill-advised suggestion from the South Vietnamese.

## Special Forces Personnel and Instructors

Information from at least one unofficial source contains claims that among the men seconded to Australian and New Zealand units while those countries were fighting in Vietnam were members of Britain's SAS (Special Air Service), and that, while attached to Commonwealth SAS units as instructors, these men saw combat in Vietnam. It is also suggested that some members of the SAS Regiment served there with American Special Forces units.[22]

Denis Healey had admitted in 1967 that service personnel were seconded to the armed forces of Australia, New Zealand and the United States. These placements may have included members of the SAS Regiment seconded as instructors to both the Australian and New Zealand SAS as well as U.S. Special Forces units, and so it is possible that these men accompanied their trainees on active service.

The Summary of Events for 22 SAS Regiment for 1 July–31 December 1965 confirms SAS involvement in this training, but records only that "a small party engaged in training troops in the Commonwealth completed its task and was withdrawn in December."[23] Consequently, it is difficult to make even an approximate estimate of how many individuals (if any) might have been involved, although, since Australian troops began to serve in Vietnam from June 1965 onward, SAS involvement there alongside their trainees is not impossible. However, no official documentary evidence exists to show that any of these seconded personnel ever saw action with the forces they were training, and their involvement, of course, even as observers, would have contravened both the 1968 DCI and earlier government policy.[24]

Although information on men serving on secondments is unavailable, Australian government records show that 26 British citizens served with the 1st, 2nd and 3rd Australian Special Air Service squadrons between 1963 and 1972. Some of these men may have served previously with the British SAS Regiment, which could explain the rumor suggesting *official* SAS involvement.[25]

## Royal Army Medical Corps

At least one member of the RAMC (Royal Army Medical Corps) visited Vietnam during the war, sent by the Australian Army HQ in 1968 to investigate the unexpectedly high incidence of malaria among the Australian troops garrisoned there. The officer concerned had been seconded to the Australian Army Headquarters as army health liaison officer, although he actually filled the appointment of Directorate of Army Health, and official concern over the visit is indicative of what a sensitive topic Vietnam was at that time.

The FCO and MOD eventually agreed that the trip should go ahead but insisted that "every effort should be taken to avoid publicity for the visit in general and particularly for the fact that the officer concerned is seconded from the British Army." The officials involved also went so far as to preempt any criticism from opponents of the government that they were allowing British involvement in the war by preparing their response in advance, stressing the following points:

• The visit was short and consultative (FCO insisted it should be less than a week; otherwise, it would cease to look like a consultative visit and more like a secondment to combat forces).
• The officer assigned this duty was concerned with medical matters and the saving of life, not the direct prosecution of the war.
• Medical experience gained from the visit would be useful to UK forces.
• The FCO and MOD were consulted about the visit and permission was given for these special reasons.[26]

Why did this relatively minor change in the status quo result in such an absurdly sensitive reaction? After all, despite the fears of the officials at FCO, such a secondment would be seen by most people for what it was: a humane, routine response to a difficult situation. Was there something more going on that those involved felt should remain hidden? Or (and this certainly seems more likely) was it simply extreme caution engendered by the depth of feeling that was starting to be felt by British voters against the Americans and their actions in Vietnam?

# 11

# The Royal Navy

Government files contain no record of any ship of the Royal Navy being involved in action against the North Vietnamese during the period of the Americans' operations in Vietnam in a combat role. As with the army, however, there were a number of minor, poorly publicized operations, some of which were interpreted as military assistance by some observers. Those recorded in the relevant government files and various newspaper articles are included here, although this may not be a complete list.

## *British Citizens Volunteering for Service in the Royal Australian Navy*

Australian government figures for enlistment show that over 1,200 British citizens joined the RAN (Royal Australian Navy) between 1963 and 1972 and subsequently served on ships in Vietnamese waters, with one of these men dying in service. National servicemen did not serve in the RAN.[1]

## *British Citizens in the Royal New Zealand Navy*

Records show that only one British citizen served with the RNZN (Royal New Zealand Navy) in Vietnam. He did not have previous military experience with British forces and did not die in service, although he was a volunteer, because New Zealand's national servicemen did not serve in the RNZN or in Vietnam.[2]

## *Royal Navy Personnel Seconded to RAN, RNZN and USN Ships*

Eighteen ships from the RAN served in Vietnamese waters from 1965 to 1970 as part of a series of USN (U.S. Navy) operations under the collective designation Operation "Sea Dragon." These operations were intended to intercept WBLCs (waterborne logistic craft) being used to supply the North Vietnamese from South Vietnam and to destroy land targets with naval gunfire. Ships of the RAN were also used to escort USN aircraft carriers engaged in Operation "Rolling Thunder."[3]

Denis Healey's answer in the House of Commons on 8 November 1967 also described

**HMAS *Melbourne* off the coast of Vietnam, in company with the American carrier USS *Midway*. Although she escorted HMAS *Sydney* (the Vung Tau ferry) on some of her transport voyages, *Melbourne* was never involved in combat in this region.**

the involvement of British service personnel with the RAN. He admitted that some of the men seconded to serve in RAN ships had made short visits to South Vietnam, but denied that any had been involved in military operations there.[4] Healey had previously admitted on 4 May 1966, in answer to another Commons question, that there had been exchanges between British and American servicemen. Consequently, Royal Navy personnel may have been seconded to USN ships, although Healey confirmed that none of these men had served in Vietnam.[5]

### Table Two: RAN Ships Deployed to Vietnamese Waters (1965–1970)

*Aircraft Carriers*

HMAS *Melbourne* (R21): Escort duties only.

HMAS *Sydney* (R17): Used as a troopship and known as the "Vung Tau Ferry"; made 25 voyages to the port of Vung Tau, transporting approximately 16,000 troops.

*"Gunline" Destroyers* (involved in bombardment of land targets)

HMAS *Brisbane* (D41): Two deployments, March to September 1969 and 1971.
HMAS *Hobart* (D39): Three deployments, March to September 1967, 1968 and 1970.
HMAS *Perth* (D38): Three deployments, September to March 1967, 1968 and 1970.
HMAS *Vendetta* (D08): One deployment, September to March 1969; subsequently escort duties.

*Escorts* (escorts for HMAS *Sydney* and USN carriers engaged in "Rolling Thunder")

HMAS *Anzac* (D59)
HMAS *Derwent* (DE49)
HMAS *Duchess* (D154)
HMAS *Parramatt* (DE56)
HMAS *Stuart* (DE48)
HMAS *Swan* (DE50)
HMAS *Torrens* (DE53)
HMAS *Vampire* (D11)
HMAS *Yarra* (DE45)

*Logistic Support* (200,000 tons of cargo delivered)

MV *Jeparit* (commissioned into RAN as HMAS *Jeparit*): 43 voyages, from June 1966 to March 1972.
MV *Boonaroo*: One voyage, March 1967.

No British government records are available to show to which RAN ships serving members of the Royal Navy were seconded, nor the dates of such service.[6]

## Visits by Royal Navy Ships and Exercises with the South Vietnamese Navy

A number of Royal Navy ships visited Saigon in 1962 and 1963, including one of the largest ever to use the port, the cruiser HMS *Lion* (C34).[7]

HMS *Lion*, a "Tiger" class cruiser of 12,000 tons displacement and over 500 feet (~160 meters) in length, visited Saigon between 5 and 9 April 1963. The ship's complement also included a rear-admiral from the Far East Fleet and the first day of the visit was taken up with visits by this officer and the captain of the *Lion* to various South Vietnamese dignitaries. Subsequently, the visit followed normal diplomatic lines, with receptions given by the British ambassador at the embassy on the first night, a similar ceremony hosted by the Vietnamese navy on the following evening and a reception on board the night before the ship's final departure. Formal dinners were also given and informal activities included a children's party hosted by the ship's company, as well as a number of sporting events. The visit seems to have concluded amicably enough, and the ambassador even felt able to write:

As H.M.G is inhibited by Your Lordship's position as Co-Chairman of the Geneva Conference from offering much direct help to the Vietnamese Government in its struggle against the Việt Cộng, it is particularly valuable to be able to demonstrate British friendship towards Vietnam in this way.

The Communists were not slow to realize the propaganda value of the visit, and the North Vietnamese news agency described a letter sent by the North Vietnam Military Mission to the International Commission drawing attention to the *Lion* and including this passage:

> The sending of a war vessel and troops to Saigon by the British Government can only be construed as a token of approval and encouragement for the U.S. Imperialist's frantic acts against the Vietnamese people.... This act brazenly violated the 1954 Geneva Agreements and further complicates the situation in South Vietnam.

This seems to have been a typical response by the North Vietnamese to any publicized visit by British military personnel to Saigon and was simply a means to extract maximum propaganda value from such an event.

Unfortunately, relations between Saigon and the United Kingdom were to deteriorate significantly less than a month later, when the South Vietnamese army fired on a peaceful Buddhist festival, killing nine civilians. This was given as the reason for the cancellation of a visit and joint exercise with the South Vietnamese by the Royal Navy's Inshore Flotilla (HMS *Manxman*, *Houghton*, *Maryton*, *Woolaston* and *Fiskerton*), to be accompanied by the fleet replenishment ship RFA *Gold Ranger*, which had been scheduled for 12–18 September 1963.[8] No record exists of subsequent visits before 1975, and this was probably a response to Diệm's assassination and American escalation of the fighting.

## Clearance Divers

On Monday, 23 October 1967, London's *Evening Standard* featured a story with the headline "Sunk Ships Blown Up," which included the following passage:

> Frogmen of the Royal Navy's Combined Operations force, especially trained in underwater demolition, have been used to clear deliberately laid obstructions in Vietnamese creeks and inlets. These operations have been carried out secretly from Hong Kong. Yet secrecy or no, some of the British men engaged have worn the ribbons of U.S. medals given to them by the American forces for their part in the Vietnam campaign.

The article went on to say:

> The British ships from which the frogmen operated have been seen in Saigon and other South Vietnamese ports, though the men themselves wear civilian shirts and shorts while they are ashore.... No trained men were available to the American Navy to deal with these obstructions. So the Royal Navy was called in from Hong Kong.

Not unexpectedly, the official Russian newspaper *Izvestia* picked up the story and used it as the basis for another accusation of increased British support for South Vietnam, but once again the facts, when they emerged, differed significantly from the newspaper report. It may also be significant that the report did not include any interviews with the men who were supposed to be conducting these operations.

The basis for the story was that the Vietnamese had blocked a number of waterways where the Americans needed to operate, some of the obstructions being sunken ships of over 200 tons. Consequently, considerable expertise was required to ensure their safe removal, and since the Americans did not have sufficient trained divers immediately available for this sort of work, they employed a number of specialist salvage and diving companies. These civilian firms were based in Singapore, Hong Kong and the United States, and, inevitably, they employed both Australian and British civilian divers and some ex–RN divers whose training ideally suited them for such work. (Royal Navy clearance divers learn to use underwater explosives and carry out the removal of wrecks as part of their general training and would probably have been seconded to any unit that needed such expertise. The British Combined Operations headquarters had ceased to exist in 1947, and it had been a department of the War Office, not the navy.)

One of the firms also used small craft similar to the American military's MPVs (Motor Patrol Vessels), with armed U.S. Marines on board, who periodically threw overboard one-pound underwater demolition charges to discourage the operations of Việt Cộng divers. In addition, the salvers occasionally retrieved grenades or "dud" shells, which they exploded on shore, and, in dealing with ships of 200 tons or more, they were undoubtedly using explosives to break the vessels into pieces small enough to allow for their removal from the waterways.

This is the account included in government files from the period. Clearly, only *retired or discharged* RN divers were thought to be taking part in these operations while working for a collection of civilian firms, and this appears to explain the facts in the *Evening Standard* feature. One anomaly does arise, however, in the description of personnel wearing "the ribbons of U.S. medals." These medal wearers may have been ex–USN divers also employed by the salvage firms, but it is impossible to be absolutely sure.[9]

## Wreck-Lifting Barges

Dissension arose in the House of Commons in early November 1967 over the leasing of four wreck-lifting barges to the U.S. Navy, claimed to be operating out of Hong Kong. It was later revealed that similar vessels had been chartered by the Americans since October 1965, the government's justification for allowing such a charter being:

- the vessels were not warships;
- they flew the American flag; and
- their crews were American or hired by the Americans.

Consequently, no Royal Navy personnel were involved and, despite press reports to the contrary, the barges were not operating out of the Royal Naval Dockyard, Hong Kong. Whether this constituted military assistance or could be classified as a simple commercial transaction is debatable, but it does show how far the British government was quietly prepared to go occasionally to both support the Americans (once again, presumably to forestall them from making greater demands) and earn some U.S. dollars to bolster the balance-of-payment deficit.[10]

## Singapore: The Royal Naval Dockyard and "Non-Warlike" Equipment Contracts

In January 1969, the Royal Naval Dockyard, Singapore, was handed over to the Singapore government. The dockyard was to be operated on its behalf by Sembewang Shipyards, while the more specialized Weapons and Electronics Workshops was to be the responsibility of Singapore Electronics and Engineering Ltd., whose managing agent would be Phillips (Australia). Britain was concerned with ensuring that the changeover went smoothly, so the Royal Navy personnel on secondment, 3 officers and 150 civil servants in the dockyard and 19 civilians in the electronic workshops, remained with the dockyard after the transfer.

Unfortunately, one of the most lucrative contracts Sembewang tendered for almost immediately after the handover involved the repair of U.S. ships damaged during operations in Vietnam. Clearly, allowing RN personnel to repair war-damaged American ships might be interpreted as direct military assistance, although the Singapore government was keen to accept the work, which would bring in much-needed American dollars. In addition to ship repairs, the Americans also established lucrative contracts with firms in Singapore for repair and maintenance of "non-warlike" equipment such as air conditioners, typewriters and transformers. At first, this equipment was moved in by sea, via U.S. ships coming to Singapore for repair, but later it was transported into RAF Changi, where it was stored in a hanger until it could be collected.

Despite initial objections, the declining interest in the Vietnam War in the United Kingdom finally convinced the MOD and FCO that both of these contracts should go forward. Little or no publicity resulted, and the dockyard was even able to undertake a larger repair contract for the U.S. and South Vietnamese navies in December 1969, which appears to have resulted in a similar lack of media interest.

Although these contracts could be interpreted as military assistance, it is a significant indicator of the way public opinion was cooling over Vietnam (the final Paris peace talks were then in progress, and it looked increasingly as if they might eventually result in a solution) that the government decided that encouraging Singapore's fragile economy took precedence over any embarrassment resulting from the employment of British personnel on the refit contracts.[11]

## The Royal Fleet Auxiliary

The RFA (Royal Fleet Auxiliary) is the organization responsible for supplying Royal Navy ships with fuel, ammunition, food and other necessities while afloat, using specialized equipment and techniques for replenishment at sea. Its ships are manned by seamen with the appropriate Merchant Navy training, who are civil servants employed by the Ministry of Defence. They wear naval uniforms with RFA rank insignia and are subject to naval discipline when their ships are on military operations.

### A Possible Supply Role

Although in the context of the war in Vietnam, RFA vessels would be governed by the same rules as Royal Navy ships, the government appears to have sanctioned a number of operations that involved supplying fuel and other requirements to American ships. However, it is not clear whether these operations were a regular feature of British involvement or occasional deployments when ships of the U.S. MSTS (Military Sea Transportation Service, which became the Military Sealift Command in 1970) were unavailable.

A retired RFA officer who served aboard the RFA *Tidespring*, which was designed to supply fuel for ships and aircraft, described such an operation in the Gulf of Tonkin, when his ship was sent to RAS (Replenish at Sea) a U.S. carrier sometime in July or August 1966:

> I was serving aboard RFA "Tidespring" in the Far East when we were requested to RAS USS "Coral Sea," an American carrier, because the two available U.S. oilers were undergoing repair at the U.S. Naval Base, Subic Bay in the Philippines. Our ship was selected because she was closest to the carrier's area of operations.
>
> As we had to enter a war-zone, the crew were requested to vote on it, with an incentive of a month's money being offered for 10 day's work. Inevitably, the vote was to go!
>
> After steaming north for several days, we rendezvoused with "Coral Sea" well inside the Gulf of Tonkin. She had moved south of her usual station near the coast, a change in position which was made to minimize risk during the RAS, although we were still close enough to the coast to hear explosions on the mainland. As she made her approach to us, a military band struck up and the flight deck seemed to be a mass of colored bibs, never seen so many blokes on a ship before. "Tidespring" carried out two pump-overs, although the second one was more of a "top-up" and was carried out at a more northerly position than the first operation.
>
> On our way back to Singapore, we conducted a "pump-over" with a U.S. oiler, so as to replace the fuel we had supplied to "Coral Sea."

Another incident of this sort was described by a member of the crew of RFA *Tarbathness*, an RFA vessel designed for the supply of general naval stores, when the ship was ordered to deliver stores to American forces in Vietnam:

**Refueling at sea (RAS) being conducted between unknown Royal Navy warship and RFA *Olna*.**

Having completed a visit to Japan and Hong Kong, during February/March 1971, RFA "Tarbatness" was returning to Singapore, when, under the watchful eyes of U.S. Forces, she was ordered to enter hostile Vietnamese waters, in order to offload stores. The sky was overcast and the waters grey in color. American Air Force jets flew above us, at some distance from the low lying, tropical tree lined shore. Closer in, Chinook helicopters patrolled the air space, while stores were off-loaded on to pontoons, using the ship's cranes. The whole operation took about six hours, after which "Tarbatness" resumed her passage to Singapore.[12]

It should be emphasized that these are the only records of RFA vessels being involved in supplying American forces in Vietnam that have been located so far. Unfortunately, the log books for both ships (and every other RFA vessel) are no longer available for this period, nor does any official British record exist of fuel or logistics supplied to the USN for those years. Moreover, the last incident occurred in early 1971, when the Americans were intent on leaving the country and not increasing their logistical commitment there. Consequently, *Tarbatness* may have simply been supplying food and other consumables at a time when the MSC did not have a ship available, in much the same way that *Tidespring* had been deployed in 1966, when the two USN oilers were in Subic Bay for repair.

## The Merchant Navy

### Civilian Merchant Vessels and Tankers

During the period between 1963 and 1973, Britain and North Vietnam had reasonably cordial economic dealings, despite American attempts to control their relations. Government records show that British imports in 1966, mostly rush matting and wicker work, were worth about £91,000, and exports, mainly printed matter, about £33,000. Trade in 1967 was comparable, with imports being valued at £75,000, and exports, £66,000. Trade by other countries was significantly more lucrative, however; even France managed exports to North Vietnam worth £77,000 in 1967, while Japan sent goods worth over £2 million to the country in the same year. British-registered merchant ships also frequently transported cargoes, including fuel, to Haiphong, North Vietnam's main port; at least 27 British-registered ships called there between January 1966 and October 1968, although some made several visits.[13] American figures for the first five months of 1968 (January–May), which recorded only visits and so included ships calling more than once, showed an even higher figure. Forty-nine ships, including six tankers, "flying the British flag" were claimed to have carried cargo to North Vietnam, out of a total of 61 ships from free world (non–Communist) countries that visited there. A CIA report further claimed that over 17 percent of its "seaborne petroleum products" (meaning fuel) was brought into North Vietnam by British-flagged tankers. However, these ships were not the property of British ship owners but were operated by Hong Kong shipping companies thought to be under Communist Chinese control, which accepted charters to carry cargoes, including fuel supplies, from Chinese ports to Vietnam. Moreover, the British government had no power to exercise any legislative control over vessel charters and so could not even oppose the activities of shipping companies based in Britain, much less those whose owners were resident in Hong Kong. Consequently, it would not have been possible for Britain to make an effective response to either the American requests for this trade to be controlled in August 1967 or the implied threat from the Gross amendment to the American Foreign Assistance Act in October 1967, although many observers felt the United Kingdom was intended to be the major target for these sanctions.[14]

## The SS Dartford Incident

A claim was made in May 1967 by the North Vietnamese that, during a raid on the port of Haiphong, a U.S. aircraft fired on a British-registered merchant vessel, SS *Dartford*, owned by Ocean Tramping of Hong Kong, while it was moored there. The attack took place at about 2 p.m. on 25 April 1967, and six crewmen were wounded during the course of it, one of whom, Mr. Tye Chun Yung, subsequently died of his injuries on 19 May 1967. Damage was caused to the stern of the vessel, a ventilator and a lifeboat; subsequent investigation showed it to have resulted from the impact of machine gun bullets and anti-aircraft shells. This led to the suggestion from U.S. and UK sources that the damage had been caused by Vietnamese anti-aircraft guns, fired from vessels moored astern of the *Dartford* and from weapons sited on the quay beside her, rather than by the American aircraft.[15]

## USAF Fuel Deliveries

The USAF also used commercial tankers to transport AVGAS (aviation fuel) into ports such as Saigon, Danang and Nah Trang, which had air bases nearby. Such was their difficulty in obtaining sufficient ships that, in October 1967, the U.S. MSTS (roughly equivalent to Britain's RFA) even approached the British Embassy in Washington about the possibility of chartering thirty British-flagged tankers to transport "clean petroleum products." Almost certainly, that meant AVGAS, but tankers were in such short supply during that period that none could be made available, although British-registered ships may have been used in this trade at some other time.[16]

# 12

# The Royal Air Force

During the period when the Americans were fighting in Vietnam, government records do not show the Royal Air Force involved in any actions against the North Vietnamese, in either a combat or a support role. As with the army and Royal Navy, however, there were a number of minor, poorly publicized operations and training visits to study technical improvements.[1] Some of these events were interpreted as military assistance, and those recorded in the relevant government files and as newspaper stories are included here.

## British Citizens Volunteering for Service in the Royal Australian Air Force

Australian government figures for personnel serving in Vietnam show that over 390 British citizens joined the RAAF (Royal Australian Air Force) between 1963 and 1972, with one of these men dying in service.[2] Despite these additions, the RAAF was still in need of specialized personnel and even published a comprehensive list of its requirements in the *Sunday Times* during October 1967, describing RAF officers from whom its leaders were keen to receive applications.[3] No information is available regarding the number of officers who either responded to this advertisement or were subsequently recruited.

As with the RAN, national servicemen did not serve in the RAAF.

## British Citizens in the Royal New Zealand Air Force

Records show that five British citizens served with the RNZAF (Royal New Zealand Air Force) in Vietnam. None had previous military experience with British forces, and none died in service.[4] As with the RNZN, national servicemen did not serve in the RNZAF.

## The Role of RAF Aircraft in Vietnam

An article published in the *Evening Standard* on 27 October described flights into Vietnam by RAF aircraft, and it was subsequently "picked up" by both the Soviet news agency, TASS (27 October), and the Soviet newspaper *Izvestia*. In a feature dated 30 October, *Izvestia* suggested that these flights were intended to transport military supplies, although the flights were later shown to be either humanitarian relief operations or refueling stops.

B-101 Blackburn Beverley on a landing approach. Aircraft of this type were used for humanitarian relief by the RAF in Vietnam (Wikipedia; Creative Commons).

## The RAF Transport Command Flights into South Vietnam

### Operations by RAF Beverleys

The B-101 Beverley was produced as a heavy transport aircraft by Blackburn and General Aircraft between June 1950 and August 1967, when it left RAF service. It was a high-wing monoplane with a fixed undercarriage and twin tail fins, originally fitted with four Bristol Hercules radial engines. A later version was fitted with Bristol Centaurus engines and reverse-pitch propellers to reduce the distance the aircraft required for landing and takeoff. Range was 1,300 miles with a standard load of 13 tons, while takeoff distance with a full load of 19 tons (20,000 kilograms) was approximately 730 meters, with a landing distance for that weight of cargo of approximately 280 meters. A crew of six consisted of the pilot, co-pilot, flight engineer, navigator, signaler and air quartermaster. The Beverley was loaded through the rear of the fuselage via two side-hinged, hemispherical doors into a main cargo hold that could accommodate heavy equipment including vehicles, bulk cargo or up to 94 soldiers with their equipment. A further 36 men could be transported in the tail boom.

RAF Transport Command placed the first order for 20 Beverleys in 1952, and it entered service as the Beverley C.1 (Cargo, Mark 1) on 29 January 1955. The first operational aircraft went to 47 Squadron RAF (based at RAF Abingdon, Oxfordshire) on 12 March 1956, and then subsequently to 53 Squadron RAF (RAF Abingdon), 30 Squadron RAF (RAF Eastleigh, Kenya, and RAF Muharraq, Bahrain) and 84 Squadron RAF (RAF Khormaksar, Aden). The Beverley was also used in the Far East; Beverley Flight, 48 Squadron RAF (RAF Changi,

**B-101 Blackburn Beverley of RAF Transport Command.**

Singapore) received four aircraft in June 1959, and 34 Squadron RAF (RAF Seletar, Singapore) received their first aircraft in October 1960, which remained with the squadron until December 1967, when it was disbanded.

## Relief Flights

A single Beverley from 34 Squadron RAF flew into Vietnam on four separate occasions: November 1964, February 1966, January 1967 and August 1967. The purpose of these operations was to transport supplies for the relief of civilian casualties and refugees. With most roads too badly damaged to be used, shipping unobtainable and all other available aircraft having higher military priorities, the Beverley flights were an essential link for the distribution of necessary supplies, flying from Saigon to a number of outlying regions, which were otherwise inaccessible. Supplies from a number of sources were transported, including items of British government aid and supplies from charitable organizations (from both the United Kingdom and other countries), as well as material from the South Vietnamese Ministry of Social Action. A London *Times* correspondent went with the RAF on the January 1967 flight, describing how the aircraft transported supplies into Qui Nhon, in Binh Dinh Province. There had been heavy fighting in the province during the previous two years; in addition, the authorities were struggling to cope with an influx of approximately 200,000 refugees into those coastal regions. The Beverley's cargo was intended for the children's convalescent center and widow's training center that "Save the Children" had established in the town, and it consisted of metal cots, six sewing machines and 18 tons of baby food, as well as other essential materials, the cargo being sufficiently bulky so as to require five lorries for transport to the Tan Son Nhat airport, outside Saigon. The Beverley returned to Saigon after this trip to load another cargo, this time sacks of corn flour for the Montagnard district near Buôn Ma Thuôt in the central highlands of Vietnam.[5]

## Operations by RAF Hercules

The Lockheed C-130 Hercules is a four-engined, turbo-prop military transport aircraft, fitted with a rear loading ramp and capable of carrying a payload of 20 tons (92 passengers, 64 fully equipped troops or 2 armored personnel carriers) for 2,300 miles at a cruising speed of 336 mph. The distance required for takeoff with a full load of 20 tons is approximately 1,100 meters (~300 meters more than the Beverley), although with a load of only 10 tons this is reduced to 420 meters. A crew of five consists of the pilot, co-pilot, flight engineer, navigator, and air quartermaster. It is operated by a number of countries, including Australia, Britain and the United States. Adopted by the U.S. military in 1956 and still in service, it is specifically designed to be able to use unprepared runways. This facilitates its usual role as a transport aircraft for the movement of troops, cargo or medical supplies, although the original design has been adapted for a number of other military functions. Those Hercules C-130K planes in service with the RAF were designated the Hercules C-1 and entered service with the RAF on 1 August 1967 with 242 OCU (Operational Conversion Unit) stationed at RAF Thorney Island, Hampshire. Following training, 48 Squadron RAF (RAF Changi) became the first operational squadron in October 1967.

**Lockheed C-130 Hercules military transport aircraft belonging to the U.S. Air Force.**

## 12. The Royal Air Force

**RAF C-1 Hercules (designation changed from C-130 by the RAF) on the runway prior to takeoff.**

### Relief Flights

The first shipments of relief supplies for South Vietnamese refugees were flown into Saigon on 5 March 1968. The 12 tons of cargo were mostly tinned meat, intended to alleviate the chronic protein shortage, and it was moved from Singapore by two Hercules C-1s of 48 Squadron RAF (based RAF Changi). British embassy staff unloaded and distributed the cargo to nominated welfare organizations in Vietnam, the supplies themselves having been purchased in Singapore by British officials, using a grant of £20,000 from the British government's Disasters Emergency Committee. This committee had been previously set up to coordinate the distribution of contributions from organizations such as the Red Cross, Save the Children Fund, Christian Aid, Oxfam and War on Want.

In addition to the relief flights, the RAF had also made an additional 13 flights since January 1968 (the date of the Tet Offensive), with supplies and equipment donated by the British government to a value of £550,000 (£250,000 of that total was to be spent in doubling the size of the pediatric team working in Saigon during that period and improving their equipment and facilities).[6]

The explanatory telegrams sent to Washington and Moscow were essentially charitable about the *Evening Standard* and *Izvestia* features. In these communications, after admitting that the Beverleys were flying into the country, but only making humanitarian relief flights, officials suggested that the accusations made in the articles about RAF operations in Vietnam might have been the result of a mistake in identification between the RAF's Beverleys and the Bristol freighters that were being operated there by both the RAAF and the RNZAF during this period. They also suggested that this confusion could have been exacerbated

Commercial variant of the Bristol freighter, used by the RAAF in Vietnam, showing the similarities, particularly in the front-end silhouette, which may have resulted in confusion among inexperienced observers trying to differentiate between the Bristol and the Blackburn Beverley.

Bristol freighter being loaded through the front cargo doors (Wikipedia; Creative Commons).

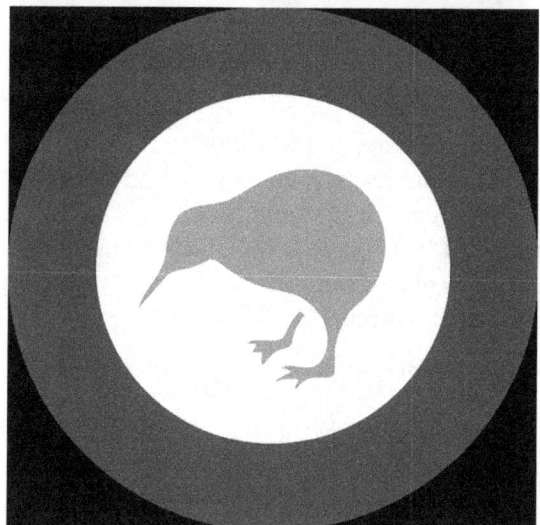

*Above and left:* **RAF, RAAF and RNZAF roundels, showing their similarity. These markings were probably easy to confuse from a distance in poor light, which may partly account for the stories of RAF planes being used for combat purposes in Vietnam.**

by the fact that both RAAF and RNZAF roundels might be easily confused with the similar RAF markings.[7] In addition, the Hercules was being operated by both the United States and the Australians in Vietnam, so confusion about the origin of any C-130 glimpsed quickly was certainly possible, and might have explained the resulting confusion and misinterpretation.

The confidential memos were less forgiving, however. Bad feeling and a desire to make mischief were thought to be behind the whole business, as one government official explained: "The original article in the 'Evening Standard' was, I am sure, given prominent treatment largely because of pique that the 'Standard's earlier sensational article about British Naval frogmen in Vietnam had been shown up as a falsehood."[8]

## Staged Refueling Stops

In addition to the relief flights, short- and medium-range aircraft operated by the RAF had to stage a refueling stop at the Tan Son Nhat airport when flying between the RAF bases at Singapore and Hong Kong. The two cities are 1,611 miles apart, so even the Beverley, with a range of 1,300 miles, could not make the journey in one stage. Tan Son Nhat would

## RAF Stations in Hong Kong

RAF Sek Kong and RAF Kai Tak were the only RAF stations in Hong Kong, although RAF Sek Kong had no aircraft permanently stationed there between 1955 and 1978. Kai Tek was the base for a number of RAF units equipped with helicopters, but only No. 28 Squadron RAF flew fixed-wing aircraft from here, operating with Hawker Hunter jet fighters from 1962 to 1967, when it was disbanded. The Hawker Hunter has a "ferry range" of approximately 1,900 miles, so it would probably not have needed to stage between Hong Kong and Singapore. Both stations were used by the RAF as a refueling stage from Singapore.

## RAF Bases in Singapore

Singapore had several RAF bases in operation between 1963 and 1971, when Britain withdrew from the island. These bases are listed below.

### RAF Changi

Changi, originally a British artillery camp, was used together with the nearby Changi Prison to house Allied POWs from 1942 onward. An airbase was constructed on the site by the occupying Japanese, using Allied POW labor, between 1943 and 1944, subsequently being taken over by the RAF in 1946 and renamed RAF Changi. It was the headquarters of RAF FEAF (RAF Far East Air Force) from 1949 until 1971, and a large number of RAF squadrons operated from the base during this period, including:

- 48 Squadron RAF (1969–1971), operating the Handley Page Hastings (also operated by RNZAF) and Hercules C-1.
- 52 Squadron RAF (1968–1970), operating the Hawker-Siddeley Andover (also operated by RNZAF).
- 103 Squadron RAF (1969–1971), operating the Westland Whirlwind HAR.10 helicopter.
- 205 Squadron RAF (1959–1971), operating the Avro Shackleton for maritime patrol duties.
- 215 Squadron RAF (1963–1967), operating the Argosy C Mk1.
- 41 Squadron RNZAF (1966–1975), operating Bristol Type 170 freighters.

This may not be a complete list.

### RAF Seletar

First established as a base for flying boats in 1928, RAF Seletar was occupied by the Japanese Navy Air Service from 1942 until 1945, when it was returned to the RAF. It was heavily involved in the Malaysian Emergency, finally being handed over to the SADC (Singapore Air Defence Command, later the Republic of Singapore Air Force) in 1971.

RAF Squadrons operating from the base between 1963 and 1971 included:

- 34 Squadron RAF (1960–1967), operating the Blackburn Beverley.
- 52 Squadron RAF (1966–1968), operating the Hawker-Siddeley Andover (also operated by RNZAF).
- 66 Squadron RAF (1962–1969), operating the Bristol Belvedere helicopter.
- 103 Squadron RAF (1963–1969), operating the Westland Whirlwind HAR.10 helicopter.
- 110 Squadron RAF (1963–1969), operating the Westland Whirlwind HAR.10 helicopter.
- 209 Squadron RAF (1959–1968), operating the Scottish Aviation Pioneer and Twin Pioneer.

## RAF Sembawang

Officially listed as "unoccupied" in March 1940, this base's first operational units were 1 Squadron RAAF and 8 Squadron RAAF, operating the Lockheed Hudson. The Royal Navy occupied the station in 1945, handing it over to the RAF in 1948. The station was recommissioned as HMS Simbang in 1953 and provided shore facilities for visiting squadrons until 1957, when it reverted to "care and maintenance" status. In 1960, it became the operational headquarters for 42 Commando, Royal Marines, and the base for 848 Squadron RAF, operating Westland Whirlwind HAR.10 helicopters. Recommissioned as RNAS Sembawang in 1962, it became a Fleet Amphibious Forces Base in 1966 and provided support facilities for various RMC (Royal Marine Commando) units and Royal Naval Air squadrons, all equipped with helicopters, until its closure in 1971.

## RAF Tengah

Commissioned in 1939, RAF Tengah was occupied by the Imperial Japanese Army Air Force until 1945, when it was returned to the RAF. Between 1960 and 1971, a number of squadrons were based here, including:

- 20 Squadron RAF (1960–1970), operating the Hawker Hunter jet fighter.
- 60 Squadron RAF (1961–1968), operating the Gloster Javelin FAW.7/FAW.9 jet fighter.
- 64 Squadron RAF (1964–1967), operating the Gloster Javelin FAW.7/FAW.9 jet fighter.
- 74 Squadron RAF (1966–1971), operating the English Electric Lightning F.Mk.6 jet fighter.
- 81 Squadron RAF (1961–1970), operating the English Electric Canberra 6 jet bomber.

### Nuclear Weapons (1963–1966)

Between 1962 and 1970, 48 Red Beard tactical nuclear weapons were stored at this station for possible use by elements of Bomber Command's Main Force (a.k.a. V-force), operating V-bombers and comprising these squadrons, deployed individually and in the following chronological order:

- 15 Squadron RAF, operating the Handley-Page Victor B.1A jet bomber.
- 12 Squadron RAF, operating the Avro Vulcan B.1A.
- 9 Squadron RAF, operating the Avro Vulcan B.1A.
- 35 Squadron RAF, operating the Avro Vulcan B.1A.

### RAF Aircraft Operating between
### Hong Kong and Singapore

Clearly, there were a considerable number of different types of aircraft belonging to the RAF that might have been using Tan Son Nhut when staging between Singapore and Hong Kong from 1963 to 1971. These included the Blackburn Beverley, Handley-Page Argosy and the Hawker Siddeley Andover, although the jet fighters, V-bombers and Hercules C-1 had sufficient range to make the trip without a refueling stop. These staged refueling stops must have been of a reasonable frequency because an RAF liaison officer was attached to the British Embassy, responsible for air traffic control and safe dispersal of those aircraft staging through Saigon.[9]

### Parliamentary Comment

Mr. Merlyn Rees, MP, explained this situation, referring to both the Beverleys' operations and the refueling stops in a Commons written answer on behalf of the MOD on 10 May 1966:

Last February, an RAF Beverley aircraft undertook three flights within South Vietnam in order to help with the distribution of relief and welfare supplies provided by various charitable organizations. In addition, certain British military aircraft stage in Vietnam on their way between Singapore and Hong Kong. For short and medium range aircraft there is no suitable alternative.[10]

This was an accurate assessment of the situation, since the only alternatives were Bangkok or Phnom Penh, both of which would have added significantly to the distance flown, thus increasing both fuel costs and journey time.

## *The Crown Air Base at Leong Nok Tha*

Amid the speculation about Britain's role in the Far East during the years of the Vietnam War, a story occasionally surfaces about an airfield built in northern Thailand by the British and used by the Americans for covert military operations, including night raids into Laos.[11] Leong Nok Tha, near Mukdahan, is the airfield usually associated with these stories, although the Americans also used a number of Royal Thai Air Force bases (RTAFBs) in the region, which were commanded by Thai officers. Thai bases used in bombing raids by the Americans into both Cambodia and Vietnam included Udorn in the north; Ubon, near the Thai/Laotian border; Takhli; Korat; U-Tapao; Don Muang; and Nakhon Phanom, which was close to Leong Nok Tha. Since the Americans had unlimited use of all these facilities, it is difficult to understand why they would need to make use of what was essentially a very inferior, British-built base, even for covert operations.

### The Airfield

Construction of the Leong Nok Tha airfield (codenamed Operation "Crown") was undertaken by Britain as part of its commitment to SEATO and transferred to the Thai government upon its completion in June 1965. It was originally conceived in 1962, when

SEATO planning revealed that deployment in brigade strength across the Mekong Delta from Thailand to protect the Mekong crossings in the Mukdahan area would be impossible using the existing airfields. Consequently, another airfield in the region was seen as a necessity for use by SEATO forces, and the site at Leong Nok Tha was selected because it was close to Thailand's eastern border with Laos and only 70 miles from Ubon Ratchathani, which had reliable air and rail communications with the capital, Bangkok. Such a project was also considered a useful political gesture by the United Kingdom, both in support of the Thai government's stance against Communism in the region and to demonstrate solidarity with the Americans, who were then engaged in a massive program of Special Logistic Aid to Thailand (SLAT).

The design of the airfield and, in particular, its runway specification, or LCN (Load Classification Number or, more usually in modern texts, Pavement Classification Number), provided for its use by medium-range transport aircraft, which included the Beverley and Bristol Britannia C-1, a medium/long-range, four-engined, turbo-prop airliner used by the RAF for the transportation of large bodies of troops (up to 115) or an equivalent weight of freight. It was intended that the airfield would consist of a 5,000-meter runway, 120 meters wide, with 1 million square feet of associated apron and parking space, originally to be constructed as a prepared and stabilized strip of compacted sand and bitumen-reinforced laterite, covered with a wearing surface of PSP (pierced steel planking). Laterite is a naturally occurring, softish rock used extensively in developing countries for road building, while PSP was an American product that the USAF had employed on other airfields in Thailand. The total cost of the whole project was estimated at £600,000.

Preliminary work began in December 1963, but a more detailed investigation into the structure of the runway between January and June 1964 revealed problems with the pavement, which necessitated a different design, using only bitumen, laterite and sand, resulting in an eventual pavement depth of 22 inches (56 centimeters). The airfield, including the runway, its associated buildings and the wire perimeter fence, was completed by June 1965, and it was transferred to Thai control in an elaborate ceremony on 17 June 1965. Unfortunately, even before the handover, the runway had experienced a marked deterioration, showing soft patches, even rutting, and when tests were carried out again by UK experts, the runway was found to have an overall LCN of only 13, in contrast to the specified 30. This made it unsuitable, even dangerous, for aircraft such as the Beverley and Britannia, meaning troops could not be deployed from Leong Nok Tha in these aircraft, which had been the whole point of building the airfield in the first place. Following a comprehensive survey that located the problem, and then a certain amount of argument between the MOD and senior officers of the Royal Engineers (RE) over the fate of Leong Nok Tha, the RE returned to begin renovation work in November 1965, at an additional cost of £38,000. The project was finally completed in September 1966, with the runway now having an overall LCN in excess of 50, making it safe for even the Britannias of the RAF. Subsequent work by the RE involved, among other projects, road construction to improve access to the airport for the local community.

## Use by the United States

Since the airfield at Leong Nok Tha had been given to Thailand on 17 June 1965, operations by any military aircraft from there after that date were the responsibility of the Thai government, not the British. Wherever the final responsibility for operations lay, both the Phantom F-4 (PCN: 23–27) and the Corsair A-7 D (PCN: 16–18) could have used the runway safely, as could a fully laden Hercules C-130 (PCN: 24–39), so there was no reason why the USAF could not have flown combat sorties out of that airfield. British government records show that after September 1966, both U.S. and Thai aircraft were using the field, with a total of 27 aircraft landing between 30 August and 23 September 1966. There were no incidents or accidents during this period, which is perhaps a little surprising, because the aircraft using the field between August and September 1966 were operating without any air-traffic control or crash/fire-fighting provision, as the RE detachment responsible for road building advised the British ambassador in Bangkok, via CICFE (Commander in Chief, Far East). This certainly seems to indicate that their operations were considered of less importance than aircraft using the other RTAF and VNAF (Republic of Vietnam Air Force) bases.

However, among the aircraft landing at the field on 20 September, there were 2 Fairchild C-123 Providers, which the U.S. Army was using during that period in Operation "Ranch Hand." "Ranch Hand" lasted from 1962 to 1971 and was concerned with spraying 20 million U.S. gallons of defoliants and herbicides over rural areas of South Vietnam, Laos and Cambodia. The Vietnamese government has subsequently estimated that this operation was responsible for the deaths or injury of 400,000 people and birth defects in a further 500,000 children. No information is available from PRO files on the specific role of the C-123s that used Leong Nok Tha, although C-123 aircraft were deployed in a variety of other

**C-123 Provider conducting spraying operations during the course of Operation Ranchhand in 1962.**

operations during the war, including transport and search-and-rescue, and so were certainly not confined simply to operations involving herbicide spraying. It is, moreover, unlikely that Leong Nok Tha was a covert base for herbicide operations, since the safety requirements at those bases known to have been used in "Ranch Hand" (such as Danang) included storage, mixing, loading, and washing areas as well as a parking ramp, and none of these facilities were described by independent witnesses at Leong Nok Tha. However, aircraft deployed on "Ranch Hand" missions or other operations may have used the airfield for a staged refueling stop.[12]

# 13

# Civilians, Conscripts, Mercenaries and R&R

British citizens were employed in South Vietnam in a number of civilian posts, including some who worked for charitable organizations operating there. Informal arrangements involving civilians operating in a military role were also made during this period, all without any form of official sanction from the British government.

## Government and Civilian Employees

### EMBASSY ANCILLARY STAFF

As well as the usual embassy staff, including military attachés, in Saigon and consular officials in Hanoi, there were a number of British ancillary staff with military connections in Vietnam, carrying out routine duties. The staff included three military police NCOs, one Chancery guard and six retired Gurkhas all responsible for local security, as well as two RAF NCOs (Air Crew), five clerks and four DWS (Diplomatic Wireless Service) personnel, all based at the Saigon Embassy. DWS staff were primarily responsible for communications between British embassies and the United Kingdom as well as being involved in radio interception of SIGINT (signals intelligence) from within the embassy, this intelligence being subsequently passed to GCHQ. In some countries, they also operated and maintained transmitters on behalf of the Foreign Office for the broadcasting of the European Service of the BBC and the BBC Overseas Service, which were combined as the BBC World Service in 1988.

Denis Healey admitted to the presence of some of these members of the British Embassy's staff in Vietnam in reply to a Parliamentary question on 8 November 1967, also recorded in the London *Times*: "Mr. Healey: There are seven attachés and assistant defence attachés on the staff of her Majesty's Ambassador in Saigon, together with a supporting staff of 10 other ranks."[1] However, this total does not include the six Gurkha guards, four DWS personnel and one Chancery guard, who are listed in government records as "Foreign Office" staff, and whose inclusion would bring the total to twenty-one individuals.[2]

### BRITISH CIVILIAN EMPLOYEES

As well as the usual newspaper correspondents operating from the foreign bureaus of British or American newspapers, who numbered over 200 in February 1967, companies from a number of countries with branches or outlets in Vietnam employed British citizens. Civilian personnel were also there as part of official UK government operations, although all these groups contained only small numbers of British citizens. The official British government groups included those giving technical assistance (including the pediatrics team based in Saigon) and civilians working for the British Council and appointed as lecturers and teachers.[3]

### British Charity Workers in Vietnam

British charitable organizations at work in the country during the war included Save the Children, which employed a British administrator and two British nurses at Qui Nhon (Bình Định Province), where they opened a children's convalescent center and civilian widows' training center in February 1967. This center was expanded in 1974 with aid from the South Vietnamese government and welfare agencies in Denmark and Norway.[4] The British Red Cross was also responsible for supporting Vietnamese refugees arriving in Hong Kong and the United Kingdom, while the British charity SOS Children began operations near Saigon in 1967, establishing a village there for orphans and children injured in the war.

## Conscripts and Volunteers

### Australian Conscription

Conscription in Australia was introduced by the government of Robert Menzies in 1964 and took the form of a "birthday lottery" of twenty-year-old men who were registered with the DLNS (Department of Labour and National Service). Registration with the DLNS was required of most men who were older than twenty and "normally resident" in the country, which would have applied to many individuals born in Britain who had subsequently emigrated.

Australian government records include details of 4,432 men who served in Vietnam and gave their place of birth as Britain, England, Great Britain or the United Kingdom when they joined one of the Australian services between 1963 and 1972. Of these recruits, only 938 were men eligible for national service under Australian government regulations.[5] Similar records for New Zealand forces show that 26 British citizens served with the New Zealand Armed Forces in Southeast Asia, New Zealand conscripts not being required to serve in Vietnam.[6]

### American Conscription

In America, all male citizens between 18 and 26 were required to register under the provision of the various Selective Service Acts as eligible for conscription. This also included those who were not citizens but were permanent residents allowed to live and work in the United States ("Green Card" holders), which would have included a significant number of British citizens. Unfortunately, records describing the number of British citizens serving with U.S. forces in Vietnam as either conscripts or volunteers are not readily available, because U.S. government OMPFs (Official Military Personnel Files) are only available for individuals by request (GSA Standard form 180) and not as part of a general archive. Consequently, unlike the comparable Australian official archive, there is no source that can be readily searched to obtain relevant information about the origins of American enlisted men, although one source (the Coffelt Database) lists three individuals killed in action who were described as English.

## *Mercenaries*

Despite government policy being one of "concerned disinterest," some private individuals felt the need for a closer involvement. Communism was the "bogey-man" of the 1950s and 1960s, especially in America, and some in Britain seem to have sincerely felt sufficient concern to offer their services to the Americans or South Vietnamese. A number of these individuals applied directly to the British government for permission to join either the American army or the ARVN, but they were consistently refused on the official grounds that "it would be contrary to the policy of Her Majesty's Government to accede to any request for permission for you or any other volunteer to go and fight in Vietnam."[7]

Individuals who were not put off by this response were subsequently advised to seek information about their legal position upon enlistment with a foreign power, the British government at that time being very sensitive to the effect even unofficial involvement of British citizens in Vietnamese affairs might have on Britain's standing as an impartial observer. In fact, there was (and still is) an Act of Parliament covering this situation—the Foreign Enlistment Act of 1870, which is concerned with the engagement of British subjects in the military service of foreign states. The provisions of the act do allow such enlistments, but only if the country the British subject enlists with is not engaged "against a foreign state at peace with Her Majesty."[8] No person has ever been convicted under this act, and although its provisions clearly prohibited British subjects from serving against North Vietnam (since Britain was not officially at war with that country), a number of individuals apparently ignored the act by serving in unofficial groups, said to have been recruited usually by the Australians.

One band of these mercenaries was described in an article by Henry Brandon, a well-respected *Sunday Times* reporter with an international reputation, which appeared in that newspaper on 1 October 1967 under the headline: "A Tiger like the United States Has Never Been Locked into Such a Cage." The article was concerned with the difficulties the Americans were experiencing with the Việt Cộng, but there was one passage particularly relevant to the unofficial involvement of British citizens, which read as follows:

> How deeply these guerrillas [the Việt Cộng] are entrenched in some places, I learnt at a camp of mercenaries near Da Nang. They consisted of a conglomeration of foreign soldiers—some British, some Australian, some Chinese, some Việt Cộng defectors.

The Foreign Office was naturally concerned, and so the British ambassador in Washington was asked to interview Brandon in order to confirm his facts. Part of the ambassador's reply is included this passage:

> He said what he had written was perfectly true. There were quite a few British subjects who had largely been recruited by the Australians and who were really "adventurers." Apparently,

there are groups of special forces made up of people of this sort from various countries such as Britain, Australia, China and defectors from the Việt Cộng who are by far the toughest and most formidable troops in Vietnam. These special forces are generally held in reserve and flown in as soon as a battle begins to develop. I could not get it quite clear what their exact connection with either the American, Australian or South Vietnamese forces is, but they are under allied command and tended to be grouped together.[9]

No other corroborated reference to foreign nationals serving against the Việt Cộng in Vietnam is recorded in UK, U.S., Australian or New Zealand government records, but the reputation of the reporter concerned makes the truth of the story difficult to dispute.

## Mercenary Units

It was not just individuals who offered to fight in Vietnam; at least three groups are recorded in FO or later FCO records as having been formed specifically to serve there. Paul Daniels is the most significant figure in this collection, claiming to have had between 500 and 1,000 men available for deployment in Vietnam (he had previously offered a force of similar size for service in the African Congo).[10] His offer was gratefully acknowledged, but declined, by both the Americans and the South Vietnamese Embassy in London, as well as being reported in the press.

A second individual also wrote to the FCO, asking for permission for himself and a like-minded group of friends to "actively assist our American and Australian Allies fighting the domination of World Communism in Vietnam." Predictably enough, a member of the Foreign Office staff wrote back, taking the usual line about such involvement being contrary to government policy. However, the individual concerned was persistent and wrote again to the FO on 9 May, asking if there was actually any law or regulation prohibiting British volunteers from fighting in Vietnam. The FO replied by quoting the 1870 Foreign Enlistment Act and advised a consultation with a solicitor, but this did not deter the correspondent, whose last letter claimed that "some 500 [men] should be available to a British Volunteer Battalion and contact will be made with the Australian High Commissioner and U.S. Ambassador." His previous reasons for forming this group were reiterated in his last sentence: "They [the Australians] and the Americans are fighting to protect us and the free world from the spread of Communist domination."

Although his sincerity cannot be questioned, extensive research has not revealed the existence of any organized body of troops calling itself the "British Volunteer Battalion" that fought in Vietnam. One further point does arise from this correspondence, which concerns the previously quoted article by Henry Brandon. The date for Brandon's article was 1 October 1967, while the final letter from the prospective volunteer was dated 26 May 1967. This would certainly be time enough for a small group, although perhaps not as many as 500, to find its way to Vietnam and join the Australians. Brandon's feature does not include names of either individuals or units, but it is just possible that what he met was the remains of this British Volunteer Battalion, serving with "like-minded" Australian, Chinese and Việt Cộng irregulars.

Another group with perhaps slightly less firm intentions was organized in the British Solomon Islands by an employee of the medical department. This expedition came into being at a meeting held in Honiara on 14 June 1967. A total of 137 Solomon Islanders volunteered, although many in the Islands did not take the group too seriously, knowing the organizer of the group to be "erratic and unstable, given to vigorous but passing enthusiasms."

Unfortunately, the group attracted the attention of a passing journalist, who photographed the would-be mercenaries and promised to submit their story to the American magazine *Newsweek*. This generated a certain amount of worry for both the Solomon Islanders and the FO, especially because it seemed that the provisions of the 1870 Foreign Enlistment Act did not apply to the Solomon Islanders, and so they could not be prevented from serving in Vietnam. Fortunately, after British officials had pointed out the disadvantages of service there to the Islanders, their enthusiasm (perhaps understandably) quickly waned and nothing more was heard about them.[11]

## *Facilities for Rest and Recreation*

Men serving in the U.S. Army in Vietnam on a 12-month tour were given seven days of R&R outside Vietnam after they had been in the country six months. Between 1965 and June 1967 this period of leave might be taken in Hawaii, Bangkok, Japan, Taiwan, Singapore or Hong Kong. In July 1967, the U.S. government requested that Sydney be added to the list of cities open to U.S. servicemen on leave. Australia proved extremely popular with these men, and by the end of 1968, the number of R&R flights to Sydney had to be doubled. Between October 1967, when the scheme began, and its termination in 1971, almost 300,000 U.S. service personnel spent their leave in Sydney and the surrounding area.

Bangkok became particularly notorious for the types and variety of entertainment it provided to America's Vietnam veterans. As one young soldier explained, "Bangkok certainly lived up to its name!" This influx of young U.S. servicemen has been seen as the impetus for the beginning of that city's lucrative sex industry. The emphasis servicemen place on these types of service and the health consequences associated with them have become a major issue in military circles. This situation was discussed by a researcher from the University of Washington in 2005, and the abstract of her paper shows just how far the relevant American authorities were obliged to go in condoning such activities, although the U.S. military was certainly not alone in its attitude:

> Military prostitution is frequently cited as a problem around military bases in Korea, the Philippines and more recently in Bosnia. Currently, while all houses of prostitution are officially off-limits, the military implicitly condones the commercial sex industry through a variety of means such as supplying condoms and providing a courtesy patrol that escorts personnel to bars where prostitution is available.
> 
> In September 2004, the Department of Defense proposed a draft amendment to the Uniform Code of Military Justice (UCMJ), which would make it a military offense to frequent a prostitute.[12]

### HONG KONG

The British government made R&R facilities in Hong Kong available to the U.S. government for both servicemen and USN vessels, and there were regular visits to the port for that purpose between 1965 and 1973. The naval visits were the subject of a set of secret guidelines agreed to in May 1966 by the two governments, which covered:

- the purposes for which U.S. forces might visit Hong Kong (R&R only);
- the scale of visits of USN vessels, aircraft and troops;
- the spacing of visits by naval vessels; and
- regular and informal consultations between Hong Kong authorities and U.S. consul-general.

Vessels covered by these guidelines had not included nuclear types—only conventional warships. Unfortunately, by May 1968, the number of visiting USN warships, which now included nuclear-powered vessels, had become a considerable embarrassment to British officials in Hong Kong. Many visits, especially those by the giant nuclear aircraft carrier, USS *Enterprise*,[13] were greeted by some form of protest from the Chinese government, usually a note, and inflammatory editorials in Hong Kong's newspapers, which claimed, among other things:

- Visits by USN warships to Hong Kong posed a military threat.
- The USN and USAF were using Hong Kong as a military and logistical base for operations in Vietnam, by establishing various "Attaché's Offices," a "Naval Procurement Office" and "an assortment of Intelligence Organizations."
- Visits by USN nuclear-powered vessels were a danger to the population because of poor safety precautions, although a British NMT (Naval Monitoring Team) inspected every USN nuclear vessel when it docked or very soon afterward.

Subsequently, British officials asked that visits by USN ships be evenly spaced and that nuclear vessels be confined to six visits in any one year in order to avoid provoking the Chinese government, which, it was claimed, was growing increasingly sensitive and xenophobic. The Americans complied, and visits seem to have been conducted without significant further trouble until the end of the war.[14]

### Table Three: Visits by USN Ships to Hong Kong from 1963 to mid–1968

| Year of visit | Number of ships |
|---|---|
| 1963 | 297 |
| 1964 | 315 |
| 1965 | 332 |
| 1966 | 391 |
| 1967 | 376 |
| Mid–1968 | 176 |

## Perspectives

There is no record in the relevant government files of any British troops serving at unit strength in Vietnam or being sent there in a military role by the British government. Nor does any record exist showing either ships of the Royal Navy or aircraft of the Royal Air Force engaged in military operations against North Vietnamese forces. Even if the government were concealing such deployments from general notice, both MOD and FCO would have had to know about them, since they would have been required to organize transportation, logistic support and all the other details involved in the movement of large bodies of troops, ships or aircraft. Consequently, the relevant files would have contained the documents describing these operations or some record of *each* document's removal and its final destination (either "Destroyed" or "Retained"). Since the relevant files do not contain a significant number of entries of this type, it is probably safe to conclude that no records of such operations ever existed and so, consequently, no deployments of troops or movements of ships or aircraft occurred.

Although serving members of Britain's armed forces did not fight in Vietnam, some individuals who had either retired or left one of the services did go there as volunteers or mercenaries, fighting with U.S. or Commonwealth forces in the region, and a significant number of British citizens were also conscripted into both the Australian and the U.S. military. Secondment from the British Army to the armed forces of a number of other countries was also relatively common during that period, as it is now. Some of the men thus seconded could have served in Vietnam in an advisory role with the troops they had been training, although the British government's policy for such men was that they should not be sent to a combat zone, even as observers, and no record of such deployments has been found so far. At least one RAMC officer serving on secondment with the Australian Army Headquarters went to Vietnam on a consultative visit, but the FCO and MOD were careful to insist that the visit not be publicized, and their response to a Parliamentary challenge, from those members on either the political left or right, was carefully prepared in advance. This is a good example of the care both ministries (and government officials in general) took to avoid any suggestion of British military involvement in Vietnam during this period, as a direct result of hostile attitudes in the United Kingdom, particularly within Parliament, concerning the American role there.

**Document recording withdrawal of papers from a file in the Public Record Office.**

Secondments were not just one way, either, as both U.S. and South Vietnamese personnel were sent to British units for training. One particularly large commitment in this respect was made by the British when they allowed men from both groups to train at their

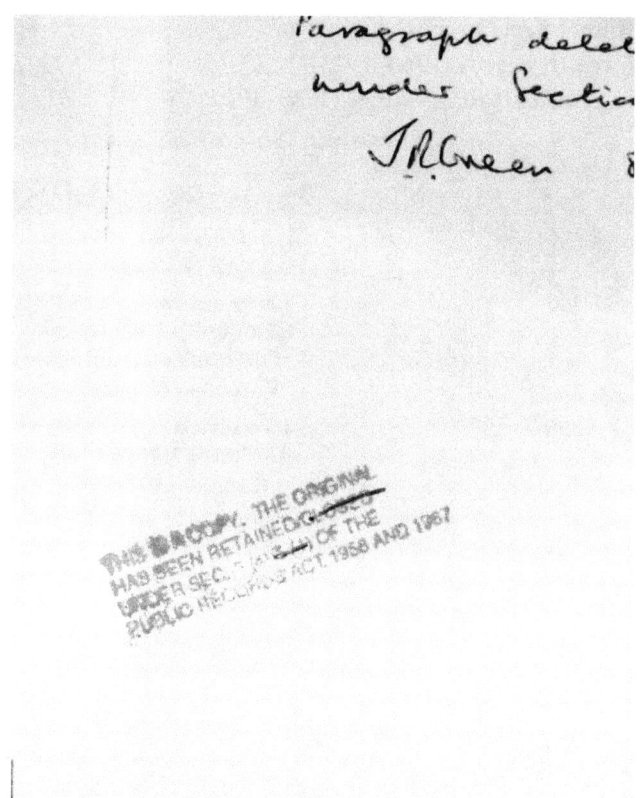

Stamp recording retention of a document under the Public Record Acts of 1958 and 1967, which was included in a file in the Public Record Office.

Jungle Warfare School. Like all of Britain's Vietnam involvement, this training was not publicized, and its major function was apparently to placate the Americans, especially Johnson, over the British government's refusal to either send troops or publicize the sale of military equipment for use there.

Although these records show that there was minor British military involvement in Vietnam while the Americans were fighting there, it cannot be reasonably described as coherent, organized military assistance and was, moreover, characteristic of the British government's attitude to the Americans during the later stages of the war. America was too powerful and useful to lose as an ally, or have even as an indifferent opponent, but U.S. interests, especially during Harold Wilson's time in office, were directly contrary to the British government's desire to be rid of Far East entanglements. Hence Macmillan and Wilson after him remained largely uncommitted to Vietnam, conceding as little in the way of material support to the Americans as possible, and that always covertly. It was not until the devaluation of the pound, and Wilson's subsequent announcement of the "East of Suez" withdrawals, that it became clear to the Americans that Britain's focus was shifting toward Europe and that no significant, material help would be forthcoming for a war in Southeast Asia. While always acknowledging the importance of the Americans' anti–Communist role, the members of succeeding British governments were quite clear, at least in private, that they thought a satisfactory military solution in Vietnam was highly improbable. Consequently, Macmillan, and especially Wilson, encouraged the United States to find a diplomatic answer, although the Americans did not always welcome what they saw as unwarranted interference in their affairs. Concern for the Americans was not the only reason for this lack of enthusiasm, however. Public opinion in Britain was so radically against any involvement in Vietnam, or indeed any war, that it would have been political suicide for the government to send troops there because most of the politicians and the public were agreed that the Americans could not possibly win. More importantly, Britain, struggling with a devalued pound and overstretched military commitments elsewhere, quite simply could not afford another war.

### Table Four: Personnel Serving with American and Commonwealth Forces (1963–1973)

#### British Citizens* Serving in Australian Forces (1963–1972)

| Service/Unit | National servicemen (N/S) | Total (N/S + volunteers) | Died in service | Service number series |
|---|---|---|---|---|
| Australian Regular Army | 935 | 2,766 | 24 | 15100–5710000 |
| Royal Australian Navy (RAN) | 0 | 1,246 | 1 | Three series:<br>R41600–R107000 (ORs)<br>O70–O105600 (officers)<br>V61000–V62000 |
| Royal Australian Air Force (RAAF) | 0 | 396 | 1 | Two series:<br>A33800–A319000 (ORs)<br>O222100–O316400 (officers) |
| Australian Army Training Team, Vietnam (AATTV) | 1 | 85 | 2 | 1630–6710000 (1965–1971) |
| Special Air Service (1st, 2nd and 3rd Squadrons) | 2 | 26 | 0 | 17900–5410000 |
| **Total** | **938** | **4,434** | **26** | |

*In the context of this table, a "British citizen" is a person declaring Britain, England or the United Kingdom as their place of birth. National servicemen did not serve in either the RAN or the RAAF.

Information used in this table taken from www.vietnamroll.gov.au.

#### British Citizens Serving in New Zealand Forces (1963–1972)

| Service | Volunteers (no conscript sent to Vietnam 1964–1971) | Immigrants** | Those with previous UK military service | Died in service |
|---|---|---|---|---|
| New Zealand Army | 20 | 4 | 4 | 3 |
| Royal New Zealand Navy | 1 | 0 | 1 | 0 |
| Royal New Zealand Air Force | 5 | 0 | 0 | 0 |
| **Total** | **26** | **4** | **4** | **3** |

**"Immigrants" are individuals recorded as coming to live in New Zealand before they reached 16 years of age.

Information used in this table taken from "New Zealand's Vietnam War."

#### Seconded Personnel

| Country | Personnel/Date | Unit | Role | Reference source |
|---|---|---|---|---|
| America | 158 service personnel October 1964–May 1966 | All Services | Exchange visits | *Hansard*, 4 May 1966 |
| America | ~650 service personnel May 1966–March 1973 | All Services | Exchange visits | Estimate based on previous statistics |

| Country | Personnel/Date | Unit | Role | Reference source |
|---|---|---|---|---|
| Australia and New Zealand | 30 service personnel November 1965–November 1967 | All Services | Exchange visits | Hansard, 8 November 1966 |
| Australia and New Zealand | ~60 service personnel November 1967–November 1971 | All Services | Exchange visits | Estimate based on previous statistics |
| South Vietnam | 42 officers, 19 visits November 1965–November 1967 | All Services | Visits to obtain information | Hansard, 8 November 1966 |
| South Vietnam | 12 senior officers November 1967–November 1970 (approx. one per quarter) | All Services | Visits to obtain information | Estimate based on official records (PRO. FCO 15/625) |

## Table Five: British Military Personnel Serving in Vietnam

*Some of these accounts are based on uncorroborated sources, and so are not discussed in the text; they are included here only for completeness.*

### Army

| Location | Personnel/Date | Unit | Role | Reference source |
|---|---|---|---|---|
| Vietnam and Cambodia | Serving British Army officers; October 1967 | Australian Army | Various: Advertising campaign to recruit British Army officers (numbers recruited not known). | PRO. FCO 15/583 |
| Vietnam and Cambodia | Ex-British Army personnel, retired or left British Army | U.S./Aus/NZ/Canadian Armies | Regular infantry officers/noncommissioned officers and ORs; served in various combat and specialist roles. | PRO. FCO 15/583 |
| Vietnam | Lt. Col. seconded to Australian Army HQ (1968) | Royal Army Medical Corps (RAMC) | Investigation of high incidence of malaria in Australian troops serving in Vietnam. | PRO. FCO 15/583 |
| British Embassy, Saigon (Ho Chi Minh City) | Military Attaches: 3 Lt. Cols. (Army); 3 Wg. Cmmdrs. (RAF); 1 RN Cmmdr. (1966 onward) | Embassy staff | Collecting and collating information. | PRO. FCO 15/583; FCO 15/660 |
| British Embassy, Saigon (Ho Chi Minh City) | Military Police Guard: Royal Military Police NCOs and retired Gurkhas | Embassy staff | Guarding embassy; noncombatant. | PRO. FCO 15/660 |

| Location | Personnel/Date | Unit | Role | Reference source |
|---|---|---|---|---|
| British Embassy, Saigon (Ho Chi Minh City) | DWS staff | Embassy staff | Dealing with normal signals traffic and intercepting SIGINT. | PRO. FCO 15/660 |
| Crown airfield project; Leong Nok Tha, Thailand | | Royal Engineers | Building airfield and communicating roads. | PRO. AIR 23/8682 Crown airfield website |
| Crown airfield project; Leong Nok Tha, Thailand | | Royal Corps of Signals | Radio/radar provision for air field. | PRO. AIR 23/8682 Crown airfield website. Army Rumour Services (BARC): 3 accounts (unconfirmed) |
| Vietnam, Laos and Cambodia (unconfirmed) | Personnel on attachment to Australian and NZ SAS and possibly U.S. Special Forces | SAS | Training/advisers (prohibited from any involvement, even as observers) | PRO. FCO 15/583 BARC: 3 accounts (unconfirmed) |
| Vietnam, Laos and Cambodia (unconfirmed) | Ex-members of British SAS who joined Australian or NZ SAS | Australian or NZ SAS | Training/advisers in jungle combat. | BARC: 3 accounts (unconfirmed) |
| Laos | | SAS | Special unit tasked with disrupting traffic on Hồ Chí Minh Trail. | BARC: 1 account (unconfirmed) |
| | Alan "Taffy" Brice | SAS | Assassin | *See You in November* (see Bibliography) |
| Cambodia | | Royal Army Ordnance Corps | Dismantling U.S. air ordnance. | BARC: 1 account (unconfirmed) |
| Cambodia | | Royal Engineers | Dismantling U.S. air ordnance. | BARC: 1 account (unconfirmed) |
| South Vietnam | | Royal Tank Regiment | Evaluating Centurion tank performance. | BARC: 1 account (unconfirmed) |
| North Vietnam | Ronald John Dallibar (d.o.b. 17 May 1943) | | Tunnel rat. | BARC: 1 account (unconfirmed) |
| Little Sai Wan, Hong Kong | | GHQ monitoring station (UKC 201) | Signals Intelligence (SIGINT). | BARC: 1 account (unconfirmed) |

## 13. Civilians, Conscripts, Mercenaries and R&R

### Royal Navy

| Location | Personnel/Date | Unit/Ship | Role | Reference source |
|---|---|---|---|---|
| South Vietnam | | SBS | Training and advisory to South Vietnamese Special Forces. | BARC: 1 account (unconfirmed) |
| Mekong Delta and other waterways | Ex-RN divers employed by U.S. commercial diving company. 1967 | Clearance divers | Dredging and clearing operations. | PRO: FCO 15/583 |
| Siahnoukville, Cambodia | November 1968–December 1968 | HMS Albion | Stopping Soviet ships from supplying the Siahnouk trail to the Mekong Delta. | BARC: 1 account (This appears unlikely, as she is listed as part of the Aden Task Force in 1967) |
| Saigon (Hồ Chí Mính City) | RN officer(s) during evacuation (1975) | | Beachmaster(s) during evacuation. | BARC: 1 account (unconfirmed) |
| Seconded to USN ships and air squadrons under Mutual Defense Allocation Program | RN and RM officers | | Various liaison and training duties (prohibited from further involvement). | BARC: 1 account (unconfirmed) |

### RAF

| Location | Name/Date | Unit/Aircraft | Role | Reference source |
|---|---|---|---|---|
| Vietnam | Serving RAF personnel (October 1967) | Royal Australian Air Force (RAAF) | Recruitment from advertising campaign for RAF personnel; numbers not known. | PRO. FCO 15/583 |
| Houston, Texas Vietnam | 1965 | RAF-USAF exchange program | Flying F-4 Phantoms. | BARC: 1 account (unconfirmed) |
| Canh Tho, Ban Me Thout, An Loc, Loc Ninh | 1964–1967 | 34 squadron Flight and ground crews based Seletar, Singapore | Flying Beverley transport aircraft on aid program for flood relief (four operations). | PRO. FCO 15/583 |
| Tan Son Nhat, Saigon City airport | 1966–1968 | Short- and medium-range aircraft, including Blackburn B-101 Beverleys | Refueling stage between Singapore and Hong Kong. | PRO. FCO 15/583 |

| Location | Name/Date | Unit/Aircraft | Role | Reference source |
|---|---|---|---|---|
| British Embassy, Saigon | RAF movement officer | RAF | Responsible for aircraft staging through Saigon en route between Singapore and Hong Kong. | London *Times*: 9 November 1967 |
| Saigon to RAF Changi | Anonymous but claimed log book seen 1966–1969 | Handley-Page Hastings transport aircraft | Evacuation of wounded ANZAC troops. | BARC: 1 account (unconfirmed) |

**Royal Fleet Auxiliary**

| Location | Personnel/Date | Unit/Ship | Role | Reference source |
|---|---|---|---|---|
| Bay of Tonkin | Summer 1966 | RFA *Tidespring* | Two operations to RAS USS *Coral Sea*. | Personal communication to author, 2014 |
| Off coast of South Vietnam, possibly Mekong Delta | NAAFI manager (February/March 1971) | RFA *Tarbathness* | Off-load of various military supplies. Operation, 6 hours duration by Chinook helicopter, covered by U.S. military jets. | Personal communication to author, 2007 |

**Merchant Navy**

| Location | Personnel/Date | Unit/Ship | Role | Reference source |
|---|---|---|---|---|
| Saigon; Danang; Nah Trang | Merchant Navy | Not known | Moving AVCAT into those ports, which were associated with nearby airbases. | BARC: 1 account (unconfirmed) |

**Mercenaries and Other Civilian Forces**

| Location | Name/Date | Unit | Role | Reference source |
|---|---|---|---|---|
| Arrival in Vietnam not recorded | Organizer: Mr. Paul Daniels | 500–1,000 men for operations in Vietnam | Combat | PRO. FCO 15/593 |
| Arrival in Vietnam not recorded | Anonymous organizer: British Volunteer Battalion | 500–1,000 | Combat | PRO. FCO 15/593 |
| Known not to have proceeded beyond first meeting | Hospital technician | Group of Solomon Islanders | Combat | PRO. FCO 15/593 |
| Vietnam | Volunteers | Special Forces units | Combat, logistics auxiliary duties. | PRO. FCO 15/593 |

# 14

# Sales of Military Hardware, or:

## *How Many Guns, Tanks and Bullets Did Britain Sell for Use in Vietnam?*

### *France's War (October 1945–April 1954)*

When the British sailed from Indochina in 1946, they left behind a certain amount of materiel, which the French were able to use later.[1] This included the British uniforms supplied to both POWs and the RIC, together with the loan of some small arms and a squadron of Spitfires. Most of the French requirements were met after this period by the Americans, but the British did sell ammunition to the French, including £1.2 million worth of shells for 25-pounder field guns. In December 1952, the French government complained about the payment terms for these shells, which required 80 percent of the cost to be paid in advance, and the British finally agreed, in January 1953, to an advance payment of only 40 percent for the field gun ammunition because of the size of the order. Britain was also asked for the loan of transport aircraft, pilots and maintenance crews in April 1953, although, with all their Dakota DC3 aircraft needed in Malaysia, the British could not accede to this request. French operations in Vietnam were almost over by this time, however, and the Americans were able to supply sufficient aircraft to meet their needs.[2]

Deliveries of the 25-pounder field gun ammunition were still not complete when, in June 1953, the French Embassy in London submitted a list of requirements for equipment, training services and maintenance facilities to the MOD, with a request to be informed of how much of the equipment could be provided free or at reduced rates.[3] As well as equipment, the French also asked for:

- training for frigate crews in anti-submarine warfare;
- docking and repair facilities for French ships at Singapore and Hong Kong;
- free supply or loan of ships;
- maintenance facilities for Westland S.51 helicopters; and
- training for French pilots in the Far East.

Training and maintenance facilities could not be provided and much of the equipment was not available from British reserve stocks, but those which could be supplied amounted to a total of £128,000. Their own economic problems obliged the British to decline to supply anything either free or at reduced rates, especially since the Air Ministry had unsettled claims for over £1 million outstanding against France (and the French were not seen as reliable payers at the best of times). Subsequently, the British offered to accept an advance payment of only 50 percent for the supply of this equipment, but now (28 July 1953) the French protested that they had been told by a representative of the British government that they would be supplied with most of this equipment from existing War Office supplies and other government stocks free of charge. Ultimately, the deal was canceled on the grounds that the French would not be able to pay until late in 1955 and, moreover, that they had only entered into these negotiations because of assurances that they would get the equipment for nothing, after what they claimed were exchanges between Lord Alexander, then Minister of Defence, and a representative of the French government. This seems to have revolved around the French interpretation of the phrase "give assistance," although a subsequent communication, dated 8 July 1953, had made quite clear the terms under which the French would be supplied.[4] By 1954, the French had negotiated a ceasefire with the Việt Cộng and were leaving Southeast Asia, so they did not require arms for use there.

In addition to the French request for aircraft, the South Vietnamese had also begun discussions with Westland over the purchase of 24 S.51 helicopters in May 1953. The contract would have been worth £800,000, according to Westland's representative, but, unfortunately, French import controls and the need to accept payment in Vietnamese piasters, rather than francs or dollars, caused negotiations to be abandoned at a relatively early stage.[5]

**Westland S-51 Dragonfly helicopter. Negotiations were conducted between Westland and the French government for the purchase of 24 of these aircraft in May 1953. Unfortunately, negotiations were abandoned at an early stage.**

## 14. Sales of Military Hardware

**Westland S-51 Dragonfly in flight.**

### Table Six: French Equipment Requests for Vietnam (1953)

#### Ships, Other Vessels and Naval Equipment

| *Vessels/Equipment* | *Requirement* | *Description* | *Cost/Availability* |
|---|---|---|---|
| Frigates | "Several" | "River" class frigate available; possibly some "Hunt" class frigates but would need refit. | Refit costs for "Hunt" class— £300,000 per vessel |
| Landing craft (tank) Mk IV | 4 or 6 | Landing craft designed for tank transport and landing. | Not available |
| Landing craft gun | 2 or 3 | Landing craft fitted with 2 × 25-pounder guns or 4.7-inch naval gun. | Not available |
| Barbour Defense Motor Launch | 6 | Small (22m) motor vessel, capable of 13 knots and fitted with twin 20mm Oerlikons, twin machine guns and 6 depth charges. | Not available |
| Self-propelled lighter for dredging | 1 | Barge fitted with diesel engine and dredging equipment. | Not available |
| Metal tank | 4 | Collapsible, rigged metal tanks, 10,000 barrels capacity. | Not available |
| Tank barge | 1 | Tank barge, capacity 500 tons. | Not available |
| Tank barge | 3 | Tank barge, capacity 200 tons. | Not available |
| Launch | 2 | Launch suitable for refueling, 2,500–3,000 gallons. | Not available |
| Launch | 2 | Vosper fire-fighting launches, similar specification to that used by the RAF. | Not available |
| Launch | 3 | Suitable for use as tugs. | Not available |

| Vessels/Equipment | Requirement | Description | Cost/Availability |
|---|---|---|---|
| Launch | 3 | Suitable for personnel transportation. | £11,000.00 |
| Buoys | 10 | Large buoys, suitable for flying boats and thus capable of mooring aircraft up to 30 tons. | Not available |
| Nets | Various | Harbor nets for protection of anchorages. | Not available |

## Aircraft and Airfield Equipment

| Aircraft/ Equipment | Requirement | Description | Cost/Availability |
|---|---|---|---|
| Helicopters | 4 | Westland Dragonfly S.51 helicopters, two fitted for cas-vac; complete with spares, including Leonides engines. | Not available |
| Huts | 100 | Prefabricated huts for personnel (Quonset, secondhand). | £2,300.00 |
| Refrigeration equipment | Various | Cold storage equipment suitable for a 500-man complement. | £2,000.00 |

## Vehicles/Railway Rolling Stock

| Vehicle Type | Requirement | Description | Cost/Availability |
|---|---|---|---|
| Workshop vans and trailers | 2 | Van equipped as mobile vehicle workshops with accompanying trailer. | Not available |
| Motorized tankers | 3 | Motorized tanker for petrol, capacity 1,500–2,000 gallons. | Not available |
| Motorized tankers | 3 | Motorized tanker for water, capacity 500–1,000 gallons. | £1,200.00 |
| Emergency cranes | 6 | Crane suitable for emergency rescue work, 10 tons capacity. | Not available |
| Airfield tractors | 4 | Tractor suitable for moving aircraft around airfields. | Not available |
| Jeeps | 10 | Four-wheel-drive utility vehicle, Willis or Land-Rover. | £2,000.00 |
| Lorries | 6 | All-wheel-drive Bedford lorry, 3 tons. | £1,800.00 |
| Fire appliances | 2 | Emergency fire appliance, foam tenders. | Not available |
| Ambulances | 2 | Heavy-duty ambulances. | £800.00 |
| Railway tank trucks | 5 | Tank trucks, 20 cubic meters capacity. | Not available |
| Railway tank trucks | 2 | Tank trucks, 50 cubic meters capacity. | Not available |

## Training and Maintenance Equipment

| Requirement | Description | Cost/Availability |
|---|---|---|
| 2 | Test bench for generator servicing | Not available |
| 2 | Test bench for electric equipment | Not available |
| 2 | Link trainer | Ex–Lend Lease, so no charge |
| 2 | Synthetic trainer for the use of fixed airborne guns | Not available |

## 14. Sales of Military Hardware

| Requirement | Description | Cost/Availability |
|---|---|---|
| 2 | Synthetic trainer for the use of turret guns | Not available |
| 1 | Radar trainer | Not available |

### Ordnance

| Requirement | Description | Cost/Availability |
|---|---|---|
| Various | Spare parts for .303 Lee-Enfield rifle | Available but not supplied |
| Various | .303 caliber ammunition for Lee-Enfield rifle | Available but not supplied |
| 250,000 shells | 25-pounder field gun ammunition | Available but not supplied |
| Various | 25-pounder field gun spares | Available but not supplied |
| 50 | Light series carriers, type E.M Mk III for fitting to Grumman Goose aircraft | £1,600.00 |
| 20 | Selector boxes, 24 volt-type H | £140.00 |
| 2,500 | 1,000-pound HE and MC (medium-capacity) bomb | Not available |
| 5,000 | 500-pound HE and MC bomb | Not available |
| 2,500 | 250-pound HE bomb | Not available |
| 10,000 | 20-pound HE-P, Mk3 | Not available |

### Fuel (for 1953)

| Requirement | Description | Cost/Availability |
|---|---|---|
| 25,000 tons | Fuel oil | Not available |
| 30,000 tons | Diesel oil (heavy fuel oil) | Not available |

### Miscellaneous

| Requirement | Description | Cost/Availability |
|---|---|---|
| Various | Units for construction of Bailey Bridge | Available but not supplied |
| Various | Spare parts for WS.19 mobile radio transmitter | Available but not supplied |
| 25,000 | Electric torches | £5,600.00 |
| 2,000 million | Electric cable, two core and earth, rubberized | £400.00 |
| 50 | Inflatable dinghies, with outboard motors, 10 man | Not available |
| 100 | Inflatable dinghies, with outboard motors, 5 or 6 man | Not available |
| 165,000 million | White drill cloth | £100,000 |
| 50,000 million | Canvas suitable for hammocks | |
| 35,000 million | Canvas suitable for mattresses | |
| Various | Ferrous, non-ferrous metal and steel wire | Not available |

*Estimated total cost of available military equipment—£128,000*

## America's War (April 1954–August 1975)

### BRITAIN'S SALE OF ARMS AND EQUIPMENT FOR U.S. FORCES IN VIETNAM

#### Official Policy

Britain's policy on arms sales to America and the Commonwealth during the period of the Vietnam War on the surface appeared to be quite simple: any weapon that was intended for Vietnam or might be used in that theater would not be sold to any country

TSR 2, the only example of this type that ever flew (Wikipedia; Creative Commons).

U.S. General Dynamics F-111. This aircraft is from 494th Tactical Fighter Squadron and is pictured releasing its load of Mk 82 high-drag bombs over a practice range.

fighting there. Harold Wilson was categorical about this in his reply to a question in the Commons on 17 May 1966, when he said, "We are not supplying arms directly or indirectly for the fighting in Vietnam."[6] George Brown reiterated the government's policy eighteen months later when he gave a written answer in January 1968 to the effect that "although Her Majesty's Government [does] not place any restrictions or conditions on arms sold to the United States of America, it continues to be our policy not to sell arms specifically for use in Vietnam."[7]

That seemed a clear statement of policy, with no change in the government's stance from 1966 to 1968, the period of the off-set agreement—no arms or military equipment sold for use in Vietnam under any circumstances. Unfortunately, that is not quite how the sale of arms between Britain and America was always conducted, especially during the period before the cancellation of the F-111 fighter.

## The Unofficial Stance

The Wilson government's unofficial policy on arms sales to the Americans appeared to owe more to expedience and its need to get out of the financial hole it had inherited from the Macmillan government than to its role as unofficial peacemaker and co-chairman of the Geneva Conference. During Macmillan's time in office and the early part of Wilson's premiership, sales of equipment to both the Americans and the Vietnamese had proceeded quietly, without undue publicity or subsequent public outcry.[8] This situation was helped because the question of sales of military hardware for use in Vietnam had not really arisen

**American F-111s in formation, with wings fully deployed.**

at that time, principally because major American troop deployments in Southeast Asia did not begin until June 1965. Unfortunately, in 1966, the proposed purchase of the F-111K fighter and its associated "off-set" agreement signaled the beginning of a period that would see a need for hugely increased sales of military hardware by Britain to the United States, with a corresponding unwelcome increase in publicity.

## The F-111K and "Off-Set"

In April 1966, the British government ordered 10 F-111K aircraft to replace the defunct TSR-2 that had been undergoing development by the RAF. The sale included options to buy another forty of the swing-wing American jets, at an initial price for each aircraft of £2.1 million ($5.95 million). By April 1967, when the final forty aircraft were ordered, the price had increased to £2.7 million ($7.65 million), resulting in a total of $725 million for the whole sale.

Since this purchase would have been a significant strain on Britain's balance of payments, Britain and America had agreed to an "off-set" arrangement, whereby, in return for purchasing the F-111K, the American embargo on foreign arms contracts (usually referred

**Sequence of wing deployment in F-111.**

to as the "Buy America" Act, which imposed a subsidy of 50 percent on any foreign arms deal) would be lifted to allow British companies to sell arms to the American military, up to the sterling value of the F-111 contract. The first $325 million was to be redeemed in off-set sales to the United States, with the remaining $400 million accounted for by the United States "facilitating" sales to a third country.

Denis Healey described the agreement and its progress for the benefit of the House of Commons in May 1966, in the following terms:

> As the House knows we fixed ... a target of 325 million dollars for direct sales to the United States and 400 million dollars for collaborative sales to third countries. I should, perhaps, make one or two things clear, because they have been raised by hon. Gentlemen opposite. These are separate targets and they are not ceilings. They cover a 12-year period. There is not, as the hon. Member for Woking (Mr. Onslow) seemed to suggest, any limit to what we can sell, but these are targets which both Governments undertake to achieve. I believe that we will succeed in getting well above both of them, particularly since our sales to the United States, unlike our sales to Western Germany—under the German offset agreement—will be free from all artificial preferences imposed by the American Government under the Buy-American Act and balance of payments restrictions.
>
> The target total of 325 million dollars for direct British sales to the United States is, at first sight, a formidable one, but it is to be achieved over a 12-year period and, indeed, represents little more than an average sale of about £12 million worth of equipment a year. Moreover, since our own payments for the F-111A do not become significant under the credit terms until 1969 and 1970, we still have three or four years to make progress before our real need for dollars arises.
>
> I have been asked to give details of concrete progress by way of achievements so far. We have already jointly identified about 50 items of equipment which the Americans think may meet their military needs and which we have, we believe, a good chance of providing on competitive terms. The American Department of Defense has just decided to buy 2 million dollars worth of assault tracking; American tests of our 105 mm. tank ammunition are now nearing completion; the American Navy is testing our 2 inch rockets; a number of invitations to tender are on their way; and the Department of Defense is now considering other items including, I am glad to say, the Hawker Siddeley 125 aircraft, which we are pressing very hard on them. It is perfectly true that we have had a disappointment over the first small batch of naval tugs, but, contrary to what has been suggested, this small batch represents only £750,000 out of the potential £17 million which we hope to earn through the sale of naval auxiliaries to the United States in the current program. We have already learned a good deal from our experience, and I hope that the House will have noted that Brooke Marine Ltd., the British firm which put in the tender, said that it had every assistance from the Americans in making the tender; and are willing to try again. But there will always be difficulties. I do not disguise this fact.[9]

Mr. Healey seemed optimistic about the future of the agreement, but, unfortunately, his confidence proved misplaced. The history of relations between America and Britain over the F-111 deal, particularly the introduction of a lower price limit in May 1967, which precluded many smaller British companies from benefiting from the agreement, is described elsewhere.[10]

Even before the off-set agreement was finalized, America's major military involvement had begun in Vietnam, and when Harold Wilson defined Britain's role in supplying arms for use there in May 1966, certain difficulties obviously became inherent in these arrangements. Clearly, if Britain was going to obtain maximum financial benefit from the off-set agreement, a way would have to be found to allow sales that might be interpreted as covered by Wilson's statement. Denis Healey offered a solution in a memo to the OPD (Overseas

Policy and Defence Committee of the Cabinet) dated 27 June 1966, suggesting that a "more realistic interpretation" of the term "arms" might be employed.

He began by explaining the situation as he saw it:

> If we interpret it [the definition of arms] to include all military hardware our offset arrangements with the United States, and indeed all serious prospect of military sales to the United States, will be in jeopardy since virtually all potential sales are hardware, and virtually all kinds of hardware might finish up in South Vietnam should the war be protracted. This interpretation would allow us to refute completely any allegation that we had failed to honor the undertaking given by the Prime Minister. I suggest, however, that the cost of taking this course would be disproportionate, both in political and financial terms, to the gain.

He continued:

> The alternative course is to place the more usual and realistic interpretation upon "arms," and to be prepared to defend it against Parliamentary criticism.
> A possible interpretation is:—
> "All equipments whose specific purpose is to inflict death or injury, together with live ammunition for such equipments; except where the equipments are only capable of being used for the purposes of air defense."

Healey then went on to explain how even this stance might be modified:

> It would, nevertheless, be unwise of us to interpret our responsibilities (as Geneva co-chairman) so rigidly that we are not free to judge individual requests to supply equipment on their merits. In particular, even if we adopt the interpretation of "arms" suggested above, we should retain the freedom to supply if we are satisfied that the item of equipment is unlikely to be used in Vietnam because we know it will be used in Europe or that the war in Vietnam is likely to be over before it is delivered.[11]

Appended to this memo were lists of both "Unrestricted" and "Restricted" items. Unrestricted items included aircraft, aircraft engines (as well as transport), radar and communications equipment, while restricted items included guns, guided missiles and artillery. However, if it seemed as though the equipment was not likely to be used in Vietnam, virtually any sale of military hardware could be sanctioned under the terms of Healey's memo. Moreover, there were also special dispensations to allow the sale of spare parts and ammunition for weapons already supplied to Australia and New Zealand.

Some in Parliament were not convinced by these semantic contortions, however, and when Mr. Healey triumphantly announced that a number of contracts had been confirmed under the off-set agreement on 3 August 1966, Mr. Philip Goodhart, MP, asked a question that went to the heart of the matter for many in Westminster and the country. The text of their exchange is included here:

> **Mr. Healey:** As I have made clear to the House, under the offset agreement with the United States we are identifying items of equipment, not only arms and military equipment directly, but also general supplies for military purposes.
> **Mr. Goodhart:** The right hon. gentleman referred to the possible order for Spey engines. If it is wrong to sell bombs to the United States, why is it not wrong to sell engines which fly the aircraft which drop the bombs?
> **Mr. Healey:** I think that many hon. Members would feel that, rather than attempt to make mischief between Britain and the United States, hon. and right hon. Gentlemen opposite might do their duty better by expressing some pleasure at the fact that Her Majesty's Government have enabled British firms to win contracts to a value of about 125 million dollars worth of foreign exchange.[12]

The way Mr. Healey avoided directly answering this question would seem to make the position of the Wilson government on the supply of military equipment, regardless of its destination, quite clear. Sales, it seemed, if they could be finalized without political embarrassment, were apparently more important than any political stance, although, with the economy in such dire need of dollar sales and the consequent pressure on ministers, their attitude was perhaps understandable, even if it was not in complete agreement with the spirit of Wilson's original statement. Britain had profited from the off-set arrangement by around $130 million when Healey announced the "East of Suez" withdrawals in August 1967. Arms sales to the United States continued, however, and on 8 November 1967, Mr. Roy Mason, Minister of Defence (Equipment), was still able to assure the House of Commons that

> we have now received other orders from the United States Department for Defense, and from U.S. defense contractors, worth nearly $138 million. The main items are Spey engine components worth $82 million; three salvage tugs and two survey ships worth $40 million; aircraft equipment worth $6 million; machine tools worth $3 million; and general stores such as fence posts and pipes worth $4 million. The balance is made up of miscellaneous items of naval and army equipment worth $3 million. These orders have been won by 28 different firms.[13]

Unfortunately, before sales reached the value of the F-111K contract, Britain's economic problems and proposed withdrawals from the Far East led to the cancellation of the sale and its associated off-set agreement in January 1968. This, in turn, meant that a number of the American contracts were also canceled, although the government quietly retained its new, conveniently flexible approach to what constituted "arms" in the context of Vietnam.

## Development of the General Policy on Arms Sales within the Government

By the end of 1966 it was clear that the government needed to formulate a policy on arms sales for Vietnam that both incorporated Healey's revised definition of arms and allowed decisions to be made quickly about what equipment British companies could be allowed to tender offers for. The implementation of such a policy and decisions relating to it was the responsibility of a group called the Ministerial Committee on Strategic Exports. At a meeting on 2 February 1967, it was agreed that British companies would be allowed to tender offers for all items considered "non-lethal" under Healey's new definition. Bids for the supply of lethal items would also be allowed, provided the items were not specifically for use in Vietnam or delivery was not made before the end of 1967 (by which time it was suggested the war would have come to an end). This arrangement came to be known in government departments as the "Jay" rule, after Douglas Jay, then president of the Board of Trade, who is said to have suggested its introduction. Although it gave considerable flexibility for sales, there were some departures from its criteria, one example being the government's decision, at the beginning of 1967, to refuse to supply herbicides for use in Vietnam because of the political sensitivity of such material.[14]

Events in Southeast Asia soon made it clear that the Americans were going to be involved there for a considerable period, with the war continuing well after the end of 1967.

This meant the government could no longer rely on its previously imposed date criteria and, at the meeting on 12 June 1967, the Committee on Strategic Exports decided the old strategy should be abandoned. In its place, the group now generated a list of "Sensitive" items, in line with Healey's revised definition of arms and based upon the "Restricted" list from his June 1966 memo, which was slightly modified to include combat aircraft, aircraft engines and combat hovercraft. It was felt this would facilitate the sales process, since only items on this list needed ministerial approval before tenders could be submitted by British companies. Anything not included on the list was considered politically "safe" and so could be sold without either ministerial consultation or reference to a delivery date.

Equipment specifically considered "Sensitive" was as follows:

- combat aircraft, including aero engines for them (but excluding, in particular, transport and ambulance aircraft), and combat hovercraft
- armored fighting vehicles and personnel carriers
- guns, rockets, guided missiles, bombs, mortars
- ammunition (other than practice ammunition) and their components (other than anti-aircraft weapons and their components)
- explosives
- chemical and biological warfare agents of all kinds[15]

This comprehensive collection of prohibited equipment still left a wide range of ancillary military hardware for sale that did not need ministerial approval. These were only "Sensitive" items; however, they were not necessarily excluded from sale and a ministerial decision could still authorize a sale that was otherwise not in line with the government's declared policy. Moreover, although government policy on these sales had been clearly stated, by the summer of 1967 a certain flexibility had begun to influence departmental thinking on what was acceptable. The practical outcome of this policy was described in a confidential memo from FCO, dated 29 April 1969. The relevant passage reads:

> Implementing this policy (on arms sales) has caused some difficulty since it is almost impossible to tell whether arms supplied to the three countries (USA, Australia and New Zealand) will end up being used in Vietnam. In June 1967 it was decided that the export to the United States of certain categories of equipment should be considered by Ministers through the Arms Working Party and in the light of our general policy. This means in effect that when a particular item is clearly destined for Vietnam, the sale is refused. *Where the destination is not clear* orders are considered on the basis of the likelihood of the item going to Vietnam, its lethality, the size of the order, the extent to which the items can be identified as originating from the UK and whether there are any particularly emotive aspects (e.g., gas or napalm). This policy has worked reasonably well in that criticism of our supply of arms to the United States has been kept within bounds and yet our practice has not adversely affected our relations with them [emphasis by author].

With reference to sales to Australia and New Zealand, the memo goes on:

> The export of equipment to Australia and New Zealand is subject to similar scrutiny but also against the background of our traditional supplies to these countries and their relatively small involvement in Vietnam. In practice, orders by these countries have not been refused.[16]

Since the place where a particular arms consignment was to be used was critical to the acceptance of an order, it might be expected that this would be carefully monitored by the officials involved. The effectiveness of this monitoring procedure is described in an earlier, confidential government memo, this one from SEAD (South East Asia Department), which includes the following passage:

> Since in the case of arms supplies to the U.S., Australia and New Zealand, it is almost impossible to tell whether the arms will be used in Vietnam *(and we preclude asking for, and other countries would almost certainly preclude giving, any assurances on this point)* we have tended to authorize military sales where there would be little risk of a serious Parliamentary or public outcry if the sale became public knowledge, even if some of the quantity supplied were to be used in Vietnam [emphasis by author].[17]

Since clearly neither the Americans nor any other arms customers were ever going to be asked to specify where anything they wanted to buy was going to be used, the destination was always a matter of interpretation. Consequently, the passages referring to "the destination being unclear" and, in particular, "the value of such an order" were to become temptations that occasionally were difficult to resist.

## *Miscellaneous, "Sensitive" Equipment*

The U.S. DOD (Department of Defense) produced its first list of requirements under the F-111 off-set agreement for the financial year 1967 (1 April 1967 to 31 March 1968) in September 1966.[18] Details from this list were passed on to British industry via the relevant trade associations, and selected firms were also informed individually after the decision of the Strategic Exports Committee on 2 February 1967. Both the MOD and the DOD facilitated these arrangements, and since the "Jay" rule was then the policy under which tenders were allowed to proceed, most items on the American list were agreed to without demur. The only exception was herbicide, which would not be supplied. No subsequent list appears to have been received by the MOD, although both sides were in continual discussion regarding U.S. requirements that could be supplied by British firms until the off-set agreement was canceled in January 1968.[19]

**Table Seven: "Shopping List" of Politically "Sensitive" Equipment Requested by the United States, Open for Tender by British Companies under F-111K "Off-set": September 1966**

### U.S. Navy

| Equipment | Quantity | Value ($ millions) |
|---|---|---|
| Bomb racks | 1,480 | 3.7 |
| Weapons release sets | 393 | 1.1 |

### U.S. Army

| Equipment | Quantity | Value ($ millions) |
|---|---|---|
| 105mm gun barrels | 995 | 2.45 |
| 152mm gun barrels | 9,631 | 35.9 |
| 175mm gun barrels | 504 | 10 |
| 175mm guns | 100 | 2.5 |
| Bomb racks | 4,500 | 0.6 |
| Rack assemblies for helicopter storage | 20 | 0.09 |

| Equipment | Quantity | Value ($ millions) |
|---|---|---|
| Small arms ammunition: service cartridges | 90 million | 4 |
| Small arms ammunition: practice cartridges | 195.5 million | 2.5 |
| Propellants | 19 million pounds | 2.5 |
| RDX/TNT (explosives) | 5,000 tons | 10 |
| 90mm target practice training projectiles | 310,000 | 1.7 |
| 105mm shells: service rounds | 119,000 | 1.8 |
| 105mm shells: practice rounds | 136,000 | 3.4 |
| 60mm mortar bombs | 3 million | 9.5 |
| Riot control agent [C.S gas?] | 1 million pounds | 4.8 |
| Fuses M 565 for 90mm shells | 497,000 | 2.5 |

**U.S. Air Force**

| Equipment | Quantity | Value ($ millions) |
|---|---|---|
| 2.75-inch rocket warheads | 0.5 million | 30 |
| Bombs and bomb dispensers | 78,000 | 78 |
| Bomb fuses | 333,000 | 69 |
| Weapons release computer sets | 300 | 7.6 |
| Bombing and reference systems | 100 | 1.5 |

**U.S. Defense Supply Agency**

| Equipment | Quantity | Value ($ millions) |
|---|---|---|
| Herbicide (sale not approved due to political sensitivity) | 1 million gallons | 6.5 |

*Projected total value (1966–1978):* ~£108 million ($291.64 million)
*Average yearly value (total/12):* ~£9 million (~$24 million)
*Exchange rate (1966):* approx. $2.7 = £1.00

This list of equipment was presented to the UK government by the Americans in September 1966, sixteen months before the cancellation of the F-111K agreement and while the "Jay" rule was still in operation. It cannot be confirmed that any of the items described were actually supplied by British companies, although at the time the expectation seems to have been that much of it would be.

Information for this table taken from PRO file: FCO 46/205.

## Miscellaneous, "Non-Sensitive" Equipment

In addition to the military hardware Britain sold to the United States, there was also a wide range of what were referred to as "Non-Sensitive" items that were open for tender by British companies under the off-set agreement, on a list received in October 1967.[20] Some of these items were perhaps not so innocuous as they may at first seem, since the list included:

- .22 caliber cartridges, long rifle (these are a standard training round)
- magazines for .30 caliber, 5.56mm and 7.62mm ammunition
- links for 7.62mm ammunition
- metal ammunition boxes
- dynamite

- black powder (another name for gunpowder, the old-fashioned equivalent of cordite or nitrocellulose, which is used as propellant in modern cartridges)
- ball: .45 caliber (presumably for use in cartridges to be manufactured for the U.S. Army's M1911A1 semi-automatic pistols)

The .22 caliber cartridges were probably bought for training, but certainly the 5.56mm magazines specified were in the caliber used in the M-16, then in use only by U.S. Army units in Vietnam. The links may also have found their way to Southeast Asia, since they were an integral part of the M-60 machine gun's operating system. Perhaps needless to say, neither type of weapon will operate without these components, and it is certainly stretching credulity to classify them as not "arms" in the sense implied in Wilson's Commons reply of 17 May 1966. Black powder and .45 caliber balls would seem to fall into the same category, in the sense that, although they are not lethal in themselves, they are components for ammunition that was on the "Sensitive" list, while two million dollars' worth of dynamite cannot readily be classed as anything but munitions. Besides, black powder and dynamite are both explosives and, as such, were also on the Strategic Export Committee's list of sensitive items. The MOD, however, felt the sales were justified, since all these items had a general military purpose; ammunition and black powder were not considered "sharp" in the way ammunition or shells were, and, moreover, there was no indication that any of the items were intended for use in Vietnam, because, as usual, no one had asked the Americans where they intended to use what they were buying. Government files do not contain any information about the success of any of these tenders, although the list of requirements was received before the cancellation of the off-set agreement, so it is difficult to be sure how many of the contracts subsequently went to British companies.[21]

### Table Eight: Politically "Non-Sensitive" Equipment Requested by United States, Open for Tender by British Companies under F-111K "Off-set": October 1967

#### Army Tank Automotive Command (ATAC)

| Date required | Equipment | Quantity | Value ($ millions) |
|---|---|---|---|
| November 1967–February 1968 | Tires (various) | 26,850 | 8.8 |
| July 1968 | Track shoes | 16,350 | 0.4 |
| July 1968 | Engine components (sprockets, governors) | 126,000 | 4.42 |
| July 1968 | Batteries (12-volt, dry cell) | 180,000 | 2.2 |
| July 1968 | Vehicle wheels (113, M-60) | 108,500 | 3.3 |

#### Weapons Command (WECOM)

| Date required | Equipment | Quantity | Value ($ millions) |
|---|---|---|---|
| July 1968 | Sight for M18, mountain trailer | 800 | 0.25 |
| January 1968 | Boroscope (optical device for inspection work) | 30 | 0.09 |
| October 1968 | Telescope | 450 | 1.01 |
| January 1968 | Infrared image converter tube for fitting to armored personnel carriers | 4,300 | 3.39 |
| October 1968 | Periscope | 2,500 | 1.05 |

| Date required | Equipment | Quantity | Value ($ millions) |
|---|---|---|---|
| January 1968 | Housing assembly for tank range-finder | 200 | 0.24 |
| 1968 | Tube for 105mm M68 cannon | 350 | 1.1 |
| 1968 | Tube for 175mm M113 cannon (under evaluation) | 604 | 12.5 |

## Munitions Command (MUCOM)

| Date required | Equipment | Quantity | Value ($ millions) |
|---|---|---|---|
| September 1967 | Cartridge, .22 caliber (long rifle) | 1,549,000 rds | 0.86 |
| September 1967 | Magazine, to take 10 rounds, .30 caliber | 23,000 | 1.04 |
| September 1967 | Magazine filler, 5.56mm caliber | 4,000 | 0.16 |
| September 1967 | Magazine, to take 10 rounds, 5.56mm caliber | 52,000 | 1.5 |
| September 1967 | Magazine, to take 5 rounds, 7.62mm caliber | 68,000 | 1.2 |
| September 1967 | Link, M113, 7.62mm | 510,000 | 5 |
| September 1967 | Link, MB, M12 | 41,500 | 7.6 |
| September 1967 | Link, MB, M17 | 1,000 | 0.19 |
| September 1967 | Metal ammunition boxes | 846,000 | 4 |
| Not known | Dynamite | 3,780 pounds (approx. 1.5 tons) | 2 |
| Not known | Black powder | 500,000 pounds (approx. 103 tons) | 0.25 |
| September 1967 | Hexa-chloro-ethane (possibly for use in smoke grenades) | 629,000 pounds | 0.16 |
| August 1967 | Ball, .45 caliber, M194 | 85,500,000 rds | 4.5 |

## Electronics Command (ECOM)/Mobility Equipment Command (MEC)

| Date required | Equipment | Quantity | Value ($ millions) |
|---|---|---|---|
| October 1967 | Transponder test set, designed to test avionics equipment (ECOM) | 306 | 2 |
| February 1968 | Airborne Data Annotation system: avionics link (ECOM) | — | 1 |
| — | Doppler inertial navigation system (under evaluation) (ECOM) | 4 | 0.07 |
| — | Submarine compass for hand navigation set (MEC) | 155 | 1.1 |

## Army Aviation Material Command (AVCOM)/Missile Command (MICOM)

| Date required | Equipment | Quantity | Value |
|---|---|---|---|
| October 1968 | Cargo slings (various) (AVCOM) | 34,000 | 0.55 |
| October 1968 | Cargo chutes (AVCOM) | 2,200 | 1.2 |
| 1968 | Rotary rack assembly for wing storage (AVCOM) | 40 | 0.2 |

| Date required | Equipment | Quantity | Value |
|---|---|---|---|
| January 1968 | Clevis assembly (cargo securing device) (**AVCOM**) | 1,200 | 0.08 |
| January 1968 | Deployment bags (zip-fastening kit bag with handles) (**AVCOM**) | 1,625 | 0.1 |
| January 1968 | Personnel harness (**AVCOM**) | 180 | 0.01 |
| — | Plastic red-eye missile container (**MICOM**) | 8,300 | 0.3 |

*Total value of potential sales in 1968: £31 million ($74 million)*
*Exchange rate (1968): approx. $2.4 = £1.00*

This list of equipment was presented to the UK government by the Americans in October 1967, three months before the cancellation of the F-111K agreement and in the period after revocation of the "Jay" rule. It cannot be confirmed that any of the items described were actually supplied by British companies, although at the time the expectation seems to have been that much of it would be.

Information for this table taken from PRO file: FCO 46/204.

## British Equipment Considered Suitable for U.S. Forces

In addition to the United States' own requirements, by December 1967 the British had generated a list of equipment it was felt the U.S. armed forces or their allies might find of interest, although not necessarily for use in Vietnam (sales to U.S. allies were included separately in the off-set agreement).[22] This included Decca Navigator equipment (eventually sold to the United States, but not as part of off-set), RAPIER, CYMBELINE and MEXEFLOTE. Unfortunately for the UK government, apart from the Decca Navigator, none of this equipment is recorded as purchased by the Americans or their allies.[23]

### Table Nine: List of Equipment to Be Offered to the United States

| Equipment | Description | Comments |
|---|---|---|
| RAPIER | Low-level surface-to-air guided weapon | A briefing about this weapon was given to the Pentagon Systems Analysis Department prior to December 1967. |
| CYMBELINE | Mortar-locating radar | Demonstrated to the U.S. Services in Washington in November 1967. |
| EMI air reconnaissance system | Electronic air reconnaissance system to be fitted as a pod or pallet to Phantom F-4 or F-111 | EMI representatives gave presentations of this equipment in Washington prior to December 1967. |
| Aircraft simulators | Air defense simulators, specifically as Radar Target Simulators | UK firms were thought to be very competitive in terms of both cost and technical ability. |
| Tank ammunition | 105mm armor-piercing kinetic energy shell with tungsten alloy case (L52A2 APDS) | Proven effectiveness against Russian tanks in Arab-Israeli war. |

| Equipment | Description | Comments |
|---|---|---|
| MEXEFLOTE | A system of pontoons that can be used either as a causeway, by linking units, or as a transport raft. Standard raft (60 ft × 24 ft × 5 ft draft) can carry a Class 60 tank. Capacity: 60 tons at 6 kts. Power unit: two 70 hp outboard motors. | Used by RFA for logistics supply role. May be transported by suspending down the side of a suitable ship (RFA "Knights of the Round Table" Class). |
| English Electric Lightning (F.1–F.7) | Single-seater jet fighter, capable of Mach 2. Rolls-Royce Avon turbojet engine; Weapons pack: 2 ADEN cannon, air-to-air rockets or missiles | King Hussein was believed to want to acquire 12 super-sonic aircraft. Funding for these (16 aircraft at £1.2 million each) could be classed as "collaborative sales." |
| Decca Navigator | Position-locating equipment | Well known in United States, so possible scope for increased sales (two towers subsequently bought for Vietnam). Information from PRO. FCO 46/208. |

## Difficulties with American Policy

Although Harold Wilson continually refused to send British troops to South Vietnam, he was successful for a time in soothing the Americans sufficiently to ensure that the trade in arms ostensibly not intended for Vietnam continued. Unfortunately, some members of the U.S. Congress seem to have been unhappy about the number of contracts placed with British companies and the effect these contracts might have on industry in their own constituencies. Consequently, a bill from the American House of Representatives was passed on 13 September 1967, prohibiting the purchase of ships built in foreign shipyards, which resulted in the cancellation of a group of wooden-hulled minesweepers contracted from British shipyards, worth £35 million. Then, in what seemed like a further piece of retaliatory legislation, early in October 1967 the House tried to introduce an amendment to the Foreign Assistance Act, this time to prohibit the sale or purchase of arms from any country trading with Vietnam or allowing its ships or vehicles to transport goods to that country. This seemed to be aimed particularly at Britain because a number of merchant vessels involved in cargo transport to North Vietnam were owned by Hong Kong shipping companies and British-registered, although there was little the British government could have done to control the activities of these ships or their owners.[24] No direct link was ever made officially by the Americans between these two pieces of legislation and Britain's less than enthusiastic support, but to a number of political observers the connection seemed all too obvious.[25] Whatever Congress's ultimate intentions, with the cancellation of the off-set agreement in January 1968, many of the contracts previously negotiated under this arrangement were never finalized; consequently, much of the military hardware intended to profit British business was finally supplied by American arms companies.

# 15

# Military Hardware
## *Sales, Contracts and Tenders*

Despite the financial and political problems with the United States, British industry still managed to obtain a number of contracts to provide U.S. military supplies. Signed contracts, as well as actual and proposed tenders for material, which might have been intended for Vietnam and form part of official government records, are described here in roughly chronological order, although this may not be a complete list.

## *Hovercraft*

The British Hovercraft Company supplied seven SR.N5 hovercraft hulls to the American Bell Aerosystems Company in 1965, ostensibly for evaluation. After being fitted with

**SR.N5 hovercraft being used as a Patrol Air Cushion Vehicle (PACV) after modification by Bell Aerosystems. The craft is seen from the front in this picture, which was taken in 1968.**

**U.S. Navy PACV patrolling in Cau Hai Bay during 1968.**

General Electric LM-100 gas turbines, the hovercraft was renamed the Bell SK-5 Model 7232, and three were armed with a single .50 cal. M2 machine gun on a rotational platform and two side-mounted M-60 machine guns at the front, with remote-controlled M-60 machine guns and grenade launchers firing astern.

These craft, designated PACVs (Patrol Air Cushion Vehicles), numbers 004, 017 and 018, were sent for testing to the U.S. Navy in Vietnam, where they were stationed at Cat Lo for eight months during 1966. Returned to the United States in January 1967 for overhaul and modification, the craft were sent back in 1968 for a further year to Vietnam, stationed at Danang and Tan My with Coastal Division 17. In 1967, the army also produced its own version of the PACV, called the ACV (Air Cushion Vehicle), using three of the remaining BHC SR.N5 hovercraft. Both PACVs and ACVs proved effective in the difficult terrain American forces encountered in Vietnam, participating in a number of successful operations with both American and South Vietnamese Special Forces units. Despite their success, only the first six PACVs and ACVs saw service in Vietnam.

## The Sale

Under a normal commercial arrangement, Bell Aerosystems obtained a licensing agreement in 1963 from Westland Aircraft (the company that owned Saunders-Roe; Westland merged with Vickers-Armstrong in 1964 to become BHC), giving them sole manufacturing and sales rights in the United States for commercial and military hovercraft. As previously described, seven hulls were exported in 1965; this operation did not require government approval, as export licensing controls were not imposed on hovercraft or hovercraft components until 12 July 1966. Hovercraft were included on the government's "Sensitive" list from June 1967, and subsequent sales of ancillary equipment were prohibited due to the possibility that the U.S. military might use them in Vietnam.

## Aircraft and Ancillaries

### ROLLS-ROYCE SPEY JET ENGINES

Rolls-Royce began selling its first Spey class jet engine, the RB.163, in 1964 for use in some of the smaller commercial aircraft being designed during that period. The engine proved so successful that Rolls-Royce subsequently produced a militarized version, the RB.168–25R Spey, specifically for the Royal Navy's new carrier jet, the Blackburn Buccaneer.

A new aircraft was also accepted into service by the U.S. Navy late in 1966. This was the A-7A Corsair; the first squadrons equipped with it were operational from February 1967 and began combat missions from carriers off Vietnam in December 1967. Subsequently, the U.S. Army also required a close-support aircraft for operations in Vietnam, so the army chiefs, with the collusion of Robert McNamara, pressured the USAF into accepting a new

**Corsair A-7E aboard the USS *America*, being prepared for a combat sortie.**

version of the A-7, designated the A-7D (the order was confirmed on 5 November 1965). Production problems with the Pratt & Whitney TF30-P-6 turbo-fan engine installed in the original A-7 meant the air force authorized its replacement with the more powerful Allison TF41-A-1 engine (the name that the Allison Engine Company had given to the modified Rolls-Royce RB.168–25R Spey, which was being built under license).

The first Spey-powered A-7D flew on 26 September 1968, entering service with the 57th Fighter Weapons Wing at Luke AFB (Air Force Base) in 1970 and with 354th TFW (Tactical Fighter Wing) in 1972. The 354th TFW were deployed in September 1972 to Korat Royal Thai AFB, and subsequently used to replace the older Douglas A-1 Skyraider as air cover for helicopter rescue operations. They also flew combat sorties into Cambodia, to support the Khmer Republic (1970–1975) against the Communist-backed Khmer Rouge. A Spey-engined version of the Corsair, the A-7E, was also operated by the U.S. Navy, first flying on 9 March 1969. It entered service in May 1970, with two strike fighter squadrons, VFA-146 and VA-147, aboard the USS *America*, and it was employed in ground support missions until the end of the war.

## The Sale

Pratt & Whitney began to have delivery problems with the TF30-P-6 engine sometime in 1967, and either Rolls-Royce or its American partner, Allison, offered the USAF the TF41 engine as a replacement. The USAF accepted the new engine for the Corsair A-7D, with Rolls-Royce and Allison signing an agreement to build the engines jointly on 17 November 1966; Allison was subsequently awarded the contract to supply the TF41-A-1 engines to the USAF in January 1967, thus avoiding complications with the "Buy America" Act. Performance considerations led to the development of an improved engine, the TF41-A-2, which would develop 15,000 pounds of thrust compared to the A-1, which only produced 14,250 pounds under equivalent conditions (the Pratt & Whitney engine was rated at 12,000 pounds).

Details of the initial purchase of both A-1 and A-2 types were:

- TF41-A-1: 340 engines for USAF A-7D Corsairs
- TF41-A-2: 410 engines for USN A-7E Corsairs

A final total of approximately 1,400 of these engines were sold to the USAF and USN for their Corsairs, but the percentage of TF41-A-1 and A-2 engines is not contained in UK records.

Although the A-7A had been conducting ground-attack raids from carriers off the coast of Vietnam since December 1967 and the purpose of the new USAF Corsair was specifically to give close support to the U.S. Army, British government officials still professed not to know the intended deployment of the new Corsairs.[1] This was confirmed in a memo from the Ministry of Technology dated 17 April 1969 in which, although the official concerned could not suggest a role for the new aircraft, he was able to specify the date of the aircraft's entry into service, from an entry in *Jane's All the World's Aircraft*.[2]

It is also surprising that the Ministry claimed to have no information on the intended end use of the American Corsairs because previously, in October 1967, Rolls-Royce had sought government approval for a visit to Vietnam on the grounds that "considerable benefit in the field of design for 'survivability' and operational maintainability could be derived from a visit by a senior design engineer to an operational area, such as Vietnam." This was,

**A group of Corsair A-7D aircraft in flight during 1971.**

of course, a perfectly reasonable request, from a company with a thoroughly deserved reputation for producing well-designed, reliable jet engines for both civilian and military aircraft. The visit was allowed, but an official of the Foreign Office's Defence Supply Department was cautious, as always, about publicity. The relevant passage from his memo, dated 5 December 1967, reads:

> (3) However, you will no doubt make it clear to Rolls Royce that they should avoid our "sponsorship" of any such visit being linked with supply or possible supply of any British equipment for Vietnam....
> 
> (4) Foreign Office Ministers (whom we have consulted) attach importance to the point in paragraph 3 above. They also consider that steps should be taken to brief the Rolls Royce representatives on the public relations aspects in case things go wrong and there is publicity about the visit. To be on the safe side they feel that this should be done *before* Rolls Royce send their man to Vietnam.[3]

So, as was to be expected, government officials were pursuing their usual policy of minimal publicity, but they clearly seem to have felt able to make a reasonably accurate guess as to where the Corsairs (and, consequently, the Spey engines) would eventually be used.

## Elliot Automation Ltd. "Heads-Up" Display System

Still concerned with the A-7 Corsair, Elliot Automation Ltd. also supplied "heads-up" display equipment for that aircraft, in an order worth $40 million. The relevant entry in

*Hansard* is a reply by Mr. Roy Mason, Minister of Defence (Equipment), concerned with the orders placed with British companies under the F-111 off-set agreement: "I am pleased to tell the House that proposals made by Messrs. Elliott Automation Limited for the supply of head-up display equipment for the United States A7 aircraft have been accepted. This should mean sales worth about $40 million."[4]

The sale is also referred to in government files, and it was justified on the grounds that the equipment was supplied as part of the aircraft's control and guidance system and so was not directly part of its munitions. Consequently, it would not be considered "sharp" within the limits of Healey's new 1966 definition.[5]

A feature in the magazine *Flight International* for 14 November 1974 is relevant in this context. Initially, the text describes the general operation of HUDWAS (Heads-Up Display Weapons Aiming Systems), before going on to specify the number of units Marconi-Elliot Avionics have already delivered for the USN A-7. It then describes the characteristics of the system: "Marconi-Elliot Avionics claims to provide an accurate and flexible system for air-to-ground and air-to-air weapons delivery."[6] Clearly, without this system, the missiles carried by the A-7D and A-7E Corsairs were just so much scrap metal, and a definition of "arms" that included a missile, but not its delivery system, might be seen more as a matter of convenience for the government authorizing the sale and collecting the tax revenue from it than as indisputable fact.

## THE HANDLEY-PAGE "JETSTREAM"

The Handley-Page HP.137 "Jetstream" was a small, turbo-prop aircraft, capable of carrying up to 18 passengers, and in 1967 the Americans were expressing interest in acquiring such an aircraft for ferrying VIPs and similar communication and liaison duties.

Government records for July 1967 show that there was considerable official interest in selling this aircraft or its equivalent, the de Havilland DH 125 Jet Dragon, to the U.S. military.

**Handley-Page HP.137 "Jetstream" on landing approach. It was intended that 171 of these aircraft would be sold to the United States for use by the USAF and USN. Unfortunately, the cancellation of the F-111 off-set deal meant that the aircraft were never sold (Wikipedia; Creative Commons).**

By January 1968, Handley-Page had secured an order for 171 aircraft from the USAF, with the possibility of subsequent larger orders from both the USAF and the USN. The company estimated these contracts to be worth £95 million for more than 490 aircraft, with a further £10 million each year for spares, extending over a period of at least fifteen years. Although the Jetstream seemed almost certain to be acquired by the U.S. armed forces, before the negotiations were finalized Britain canceled the F-111K agreement and the Americans withdrew from the deal. Government records from that period contain a telegram in which a staff member from the British Embassy in Washington states categorically that members of Congress were insisting that the deal should be canceled in direct retaliation for the cancellation of the F-111.[7]

## Hawker Siddeley Harrier ("Jump Jet")

The Hawker Siddeley Harrier, or "Jump Jet," was the first of a group of military jet aircraft capable of vertical/short takeoff and landing (V/STOL) operations. Originally they were intended to fly from facilities such as car parks or forest clearings, thus avoiding the need for large air bases vulnerable to tactical nuclear weapons, although later the design was adapted to operate from aircraft carriers. General performance and weapons-carrying capabilities were found to be disappointing in the initial design, which led to the development of a group of second-generation aircraft, entering service in the mid–1980s. These included the Boeing/BAe Systems AV-8B Harrier II and the BAe (British Aerospace) Harrier GR5, GR7 and GR9.

A Royal Air Force Harrier GR3 aircraft of No. 233 OCU parked on the flight line during "Air Fete '84" at RAF Mildenhall, Suffolk (UK), 9 June 1984.

## The Sale

The Harrier GR1 began operation with No. 1 Squadron RAF between July and October 1969, with squadrons established later (No. 3 Squadron RAF and No. 4 Squadron RAF) being equipped with the improved GR1A and later the GR3 and GR5. The U.S. DOD seems to have been quick to grasp the potential of the new aircraft, and it made an initial approach to Hawker Siddeley in early December 1968 (date of first correspondence from the British ambassador in Washington: 4 December 1968). This was for a proposed order to supply approximately 100 aircraft at a cost of £80 million for the USMC (U.S. Marine Corps), the first batch of twelve to be delivered in 1971, and the squadron equipped with them to be operational by 1972.

Nixon had been elected barely a month before, on 5 November. This was just three days before the termination of Operation "Rolling Thunder" on 2 November, and although the Paris peace talks had begun in May 1968, they were showing no real signs of progress. In addition, whatever he may have said during the campaign, Nixon had not made his intentions clear so far about the withdrawal of American troops, and there were still over 500,000 stationed in Vietnam. Despite there being no apparent change in the tempo of the war, when the Americans offered to buy the Harrier, those responsible for implementing government policy in the Prime Minister's Office felt justified in allowing the sale. The relevant passage from the government memo reads:

> We have hitherto taken the line that our position as Co-Chairman precludes us from supplying war material to either side in the Vietnam war. On this ground we have foregone a number of orders from the United States forces.

**BAe Harrier GR7, prior to making a conventional takeoff. This is the later, significantly improved version of the GR1, which was originally manufactured by Hawker Siddeley.**

**BAe/McDonnel-Douglas Harrier AV-8B, shown from the front, during a vertical takeoff. This aircraft is equipped with drop-tanks but appears to be carrying no weapons.**

> If the Vietnam war were to continue into 1972, it would be in circumstances markedly different from the present time, almost certainly resulting from Communist intransigence and refusal to meet the United States' determination to negotiate a balanced settlement as soon as possible. While we cannot predict British or world opinion at that time and under those circumstances, it is a fair guess it would be shifted heavily against the Communists. On present timing, therefore, and in the light of the Paris negotiations the Vietnam issue need not be an obstacle to the supply of the Harrier to the American forces.[8]

This must have seemed very reassuring to anyone without a proper grasp of the realities of the situation, although the assumption that conditions in Vietnam would change significantly for the better after 1967, and then subsequently after 1970, had also been advanced as sufficient reason to allow a number of tenders between 1966 and 1969 that might not have been approved otherwise. In light of such vehement justification, Denis Healey also felt able to write to Clark Clifford, the newly appointed U.S. secretary of state for defense, that "you can be assured that, if a decision is taken to purchase the aircraft, Her Majesty's Government will be ready to assist in any way it can."[9]

The real reasoning behind this apparent change of policy is made clear in a memo from the prime minister (Treasury Chambers), dated 17 December 1968, thirteen days after the initial approach. The relevant passage reads:

## HARRIERS FOR THE UNITED STATES

The importance of an export order worth £80 million is clear. I hope we can all agree to confirm the proposal in the Minister of Technology's minute of 9 December to you that Harrier aircraft can be supplied to the United States.

For any defence equipment order of this size we should need an overwhelmingly strong political case to justify a refusal to supply. For the United States the only possible political objection is surely met by the Minister of Technology's point that the Marine Corps would not have a squadron operational before 1972. In the defence sales context it strikes me as exceptionally important to demonstrate both to the United States and *for the benefit of other potential purchasers* that we have fully competitive products which we are able to sell to the United States where domestic competition is formidable and barriers against imports are frequently insurmountable. In this case we have the advantage of a product which the Americans themselves cannot match[10] [emphasis by author].

Perhaps understandably, once again the government seems to have been more concerned with its financial problems and relations with the United States than any previous stance on Vietnam. With devaluation, successive strikes by the larger unions and the ineffective "prices and incomes" policy all deleteriously affecting the balance of payments, this order (and, more importantly, the possibility of future, much larger orders) must have seemed like the answer to a prayer. The press release from the DOD announcing the sale was carefully crafted and government officials had, as usual, prepared a series of answers to potentially embarrassing questions from the press.

**BAe/McDonnel-Douglas Harrier AV-8B, from the underside, showing its armament and the twin engine nozzles that allow it to take off vertically and hover (Wikipedia; Creative Commons).**

Of course, the one question everyone was waiting to ask was: "Will these aircraft be used in Vietnam?" Since the Americans had already emphasized in their press release that they were particularly interested in the fact that "the unique performance of this V/STOL close support jet provides the capability to operate from amphibious ships or extreme forward area sites ashore close to ground troops," which was a role they had been trying unsuccessfully to fill with their helicopters in Vietnam, the answer seemed obvious. What could be better for Southeast Asia than what was effectively a helicopter capable of 780 mph, carrying the weapon load of a combat jet? However, the British government was quite comfortable with the sale, and its careful answer to the Vietnam question made this clear: "I would emphasise that these aircraft will not be delivered until 1971. *But in any case, we regard this sale as within the existing UK policy on the sale of arms for use in Vietnam*"[11] (emphasis by author).

The history of the sale after this initial bargaining was checkered. Initially, Hawker Siddeley produced the first twelve aircraft, but when the USMC ordered another eighteen in January 1970, Hawker contracted with the American company MacDonnell-Douglas to produce them under license, in order to avoid the stringent U.S. regulations governing purchases of military equipment from overseas. Subsequently, the U.S. House of Representatives Appropriations Committee found that, by buying directly from Hawker, they could save $32.2 million, and the order was transferred to the British company.[12] The USMC Harriers were designated the AV-8A for the single-seater version and TAV-8A for the two-seater trainer, with the AV-8A entering service with the USMC in 1971, the year before Nixon ordered the resumption of air raids on Cambodia. Between 1971 and 1976, the USMC received 102 AV-8A and 8 TAV-8A Harriers, all manufactured by Hawker Siddeley at an eventual cost of approximately $400 million. The AV-8A aircraft began to be replaced in 1987 by the much improved AV-8B, produced jointly by BAe and McDonnell-Douglas. The USMC Harrier squadrons do not appear to have been deployed in Vietnam.

## Short Bros. "Skyvan" Aircraft

The suggested involvement of the Skyvan in Vietnam came to public attention initially with a story in the *Observer*, dated 27 April 1969, suggesting that Short Bros. was about to sell the United States a "militarized" version of Skyvan, its STOL aircraft. The facts, when they came to light, proved to be slightly less controversial, as usual.

For some months prior to the appearance of this news story, Shorts Bros. had been discussing with the U.S. Department of Defense the possibility of selling 200 Skyvans to the U.S. military. Such an aircraft was intended to fill the American military's need for a light transport aircraft, predominantly for use in an air-support role with South Vietnamese forces. Although Shorts was offering a militarized version of the aircraft, which it had designated the Series 3M Skyvan, this only differed from the earlier, civilian version by an increase in gross weight from 12,500 pounds to 13,500 pounds. At around the same time, to avoid the financial implications of the "Buy America" Act, Short Bros. had also become involved in discussions with the Cessna Aircraft Co. of Wichita, Kansas, about the possibilities of building the Skyvan under license in the United States. Unfortunately, by April 1969 the planned withdrawal of American troops from Vietnam had made such an aircraft unnecessary, and all negotiations came to an end. The British government, which only

Short Bros. Skyvan. Originally offered to the Americans as a transport aircraft for the SVN, the sale was refused, despite this being a transport aircraft and consequently not covered by UK government restrictions on arms sales.

seemed to have learned about the discussions when they were almost finished, had also informed Shorts that the political implications of such a contract would be unacceptable, whatever the Americans decided. The government response was peculiar, because this type of aircraft (i.e., "transport") was specifically excluded from the list of "Sensitive" items produced by the Strategic Exports Committee and seems unlikely to have provoked much reaction in Britain, whatever the newspapers felt like saying. Moreover, the government had agreed to the sale of the HP "Jetstream," which was in the same category, without any argument. Short Bros. management, however, still felt able to pursue the possibility of a civilian contract with Air Vietnam, but these overtures failed to result in either sales or a leasing agreement.[13]

## Helicopters

### The Westland Wessex

This is a very minor digression to alleviate potential confusion. A number of pictures from the Vietnam War show what many in Britain will recognize as a Westland Wessex helicopter, which might suggest that Westland made this aircraft for the Americans. In fact, the reverse is true. The Wessex was produced by Westland under license from the Sikorsky Aircraft Corporation, which made the same helicopter as the H-34 Choctaw (used in Vietnam by the U.S. Army and, more extensively, the USMC). There is no record in either government files or the relevant literature on the war to indicate that any other British helicopter manufacturer was supplying the U.S. military.

15. *Military Hardware*  191

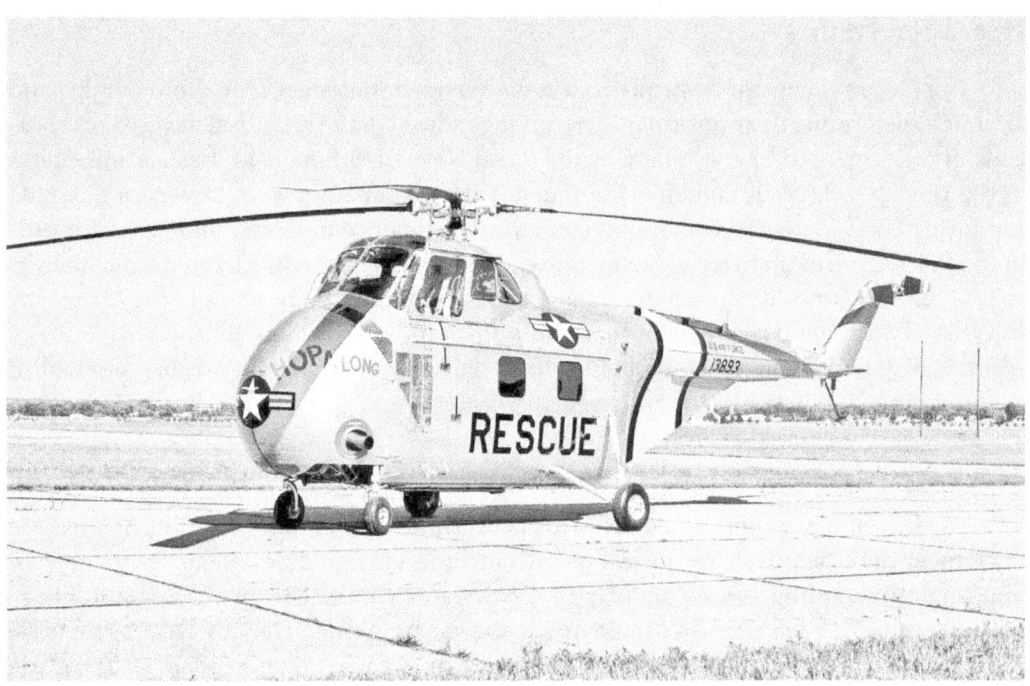

Sikorsky UH-19B Chickasaw helicopter. Used by both the USAF and the USN in Vietnam, this helicopter was also made under license by Westland as the Wessex, which was produced in a number of variations.

Westland Wessex, operating at Ascension Island during Operation Corporate, Falklands conflict, 1982.

## Decca Navigators

The Decca Navigator System was a radio navigation system that allowed ships and aircraft to determine their positions by receiving radio signals from fixed navigational beacons. It was first used operationally by the Royal Navy on 5 June 1944, to clear minefields in the run-up to D–Day, and after the war, a British company, Decca Navigator Co. Ltd., was formed in 1945 to market the equipment, which remained in service until 2000. Records in the PRO confirm that Decca Navigator equipment was in use in Vietnam from as early as 1962, and Decca sold two separate chains of land-based radio beacons to the U.S. Army in 1967.[14] Two radio beacon chains are also known to have been established in Vietnam, and this may have been the equipment sold in 1967, although it is impossible to establish a clear connection between the two events.

## The Sale

The U.S. military approached the British government about the possibility of purchase in October 1968, because government records include a memo describing a telegram from Washington regarding the supply of Decca Navigator equipment for American military helicopters. SEAD felt the sale should not go forward, although Decca was still supplying spare parts for sets sold since 1962, as well as items for what one member of the SEAD called "local assembly" (presumably the production of complete sets under license), during the same period.[15] The relevant government file has no further information about the sale, but, according to another source, Decca Navigator Systems, Inc., was under contract to the U.S. government to train helicopter pilots in Vietnam on the Decca Navigator. The company is said to have employed civilian instructors to conduct the necessary training, and these men traveled between bases, often being transported as "non-manifested" passengers, so as to leave no record of their journeys. Decca Vietnam was based in Saigon at the entrance to the heliport at the Tan Son Nut air base, and the monitor site and control center for both the Central and South Chains was in Qui Nhon, Platoon North HQ.[16] Clearly, this equipment was eventually sold to the Americans and fitted to helicopters deployed during the Vietnam War, despite there being no record in the relevant government files.[17]

Decca was also awarded a contract by the Ministry of Technology in May 1967 to supply "Navigator" equipment for the F-111, although when the agreement was canceled in January 1968, presumably, so was this order.

# *Vehicles*

### Armored Cars and Personnel Carriers

In March 1967, MOD officials were approached by the U.S. DOD about the possibility of buying Ferret and Saladin armored cars and the Saracen armored personnel carrier from their British manufacturers. The Saladin and Saracen were both made by Alvis, while the Ferret (usually referred to as a "scout" car) was produced by Daimler.

The British government had authorized that work should begin on the design of an FV600 series of six-wheel-drive armored fighting vehicles in 1946. They were specifically

**Saladin armored car, requested by the Americans but apparently never sold to them.**

intended to meet the operational requirements of the British army, and Alvis of Coventry was given the contract to produce the prototypes, which went into full production in December 1952.

First of the group to go into production, and subsequently deployed during the Malayan Emergency, the Saracen FV603 was the armored personnel carrier of the design series. It was fitted with a Rolls-Royce B80 8-cylinder petrol engine, giving it a top speed off-road of 20 mph (50 mph on-road). A squad of 8 soldiers plus a troop commander, together with the driver and commander, was the usual complement, and most models were fitted with a small turret on the roof, armed with a Browning .30 caliber machine gun. In addition to the Browning, a Bren gun (originally .303 caliber, although later variants were 7.62mm) could be mounted on an anti-aircraft ring-mount that was accessed through a roof hatch. Ports were also installed in the side panels to allow troops to use their personal weapons.

The Saladin was the armored car of the FV600 series, using similar suspension and the six-wheel drive-train of the Saracen. Its main armament was the reliable 75mm L5A1 cannon. Armor was 32mm thick and secondary armament consisted of two M1919A4 machine guns. It had a top speed of 45 mph and a crew of three (commander, driver and

**Saracen personnel carrier, made by Alvis and using the same chassis and engine as the Saladin.**

**Ferret armored car. Used by the New Zealand army in Vietnam, the sale of these suggested by the Americans was also never agreed on.**

## 15. Military Hardware

**Ferret armored cars in use by UN forces and painted in the standard white used for vehicles belonging to that organization.**

gunner). The Ferret, being smaller and faster than the Saladin, was particularly well adapted for use in urban combat situations. It was fitted with a 130 horsepower, six-cylinder Rolls-Royce petrol engine (giving a top speed of 60 mph), four-wheel drive and a single .30 caliber Browning machine gun. It had a crew of two (commander/gunner and driver).

## The Sale

The DOD initially wanted to order 150–200 Saracens, 100 Saladins and 100 Ferrets. Although, as usual, no mention was made of where the vehicles would be used, it seemed clear to government officials that they were intended for Vietnam. Delivery would not be possible until 1968, however, which meant, since government policy on arms supply for use in Vietnam was still governed by the "Jay" rule, the tender could be allowed. It also meant, as one official explained, "that a choice has been made in favor of allowing the deal to proceed in the hope that the war in Vietnam will have ended before delivery is made."

At the time there was certainly some trepidation about this sale. One official gave a very clear appreciation of the situation:

> The Saladins, Saracens and Ferrets are for delivery after 1.1.68 and thus, despite their probable Vietnam destination, pass the test of the "Jay" rule. The M.O.D have accordingly submitted tenders to the Americans. We cannot now retract those tenders without disclosing to the U.S. Government that we are being selective about what we sell. Such disclosure would land us in very serious political trouble with the U.S. and probably in wider commercial loss. If the vehicles turned up in Vietnam, we might likewise be exposed to embarrassment. There is no obvious

way out of this dilemma and it looks as though we can only deal with this contingency in the light of circumstances if it arises.[18]

What happened to this sale is difficult to determine. No record exists in the relevant literature on military vehicles to show that any of the three types were ever used by American forces, so the deal may have been scrapped after the F-111K arrangement was canceled. However, all these vehicles saw extensive service with the Australian military, although only the Ferret was in use with the New Zealand army.

## Buses

Early in January 1968 the British Embassy in Saigon received an inquiry from the General Trading Corporation regarding the purchase of some buses for the U.S. military in Vietnam. The corporation was a Formosa-registered company owned by a Chinese businessman, and although the embassy officials were not entirely happy about his credentials (one telegram in particular refers to him as a "smooth talker and a bit of a 'wide boy'" [i.e., con man]), they felt he should be able to secure the contract.

### The Sale

The request itself was for two separate consignments of vehicles:

- 383 secondhand or new single-decker, two-door buses capable of seating no less than 36 adults; their (the buses') average age should not be greater than two years, nor earlier than the 1964 model, and 20 should be air-conditioned.
- 50 new buses of similar design.

Both consignments were required for delivery at Saigon port no later than 10 June 1968.[19]

The relevant government files have only a notification that the request was made, and there is no record of a tender for the contract(s) or any indication that the buses were supplied by a British company.

## Armored Recovery Vehicles

At the end of January 1968 the U.S. Embassy in London asked for information on the price and availability of Centurion ARVs (Armored Recovery Vehicles), either new or secondhand. As their name suggests, these are armored vehicles based on an existing tank chassis and specifically designed to recover tanks or other armored vehicles that have been damaged in combat.[20]

### The Sale

The order was for 53 vehicles to be delivered within roughly 2 years (1970–1971), for a total of £5,300,000 (£100,000 each). The Defence Supply Department of the FCO agreed to a price being quoted, despite the possibility of the vehicles being used in Vietnam, and there the government record ends. American military literature does not describe British-made Centurion ARVs as having any role with American units in Southeast Asia, although they did see action with the Australian 1st Armoured Regiment (C Squadron).[21]

## Self-Propelled Guns

In June 1969, the U.S. Department of Defense agreed to allow Vickers Limited to tender as the main contractor to supply the U.S. Army with a number of complete armored vehicles of the following types:

- 102 vehicles of the M107 type 175mm self-propelled gun. These weapons had a maximum range of approximately 15 miles and could maintain a sustained rate of fire of one round every two minutes.
- 31 vehicles of the M110 type 8-inch self-propelled howitzers. These weapons had a maximum range of approximately 30 miles and could maintain a sustained rate of fire of one round every two minutes.
- 121 vehicles of the M578 type. These are lightly armored recovery vehicles, capable of recovering heavy lorries but not large enough to use for tanks.

### The Sale

The contract specified that Vickers would make the chassis, and then fit guns and armor that were to be supplied by the United States. Complete vehicles would then be shipped back to America for testing and acceptance. Although it was considered possible that the vehicles might be used in Vietnam, since no part of the armament or armor was being produced in Britain, the contract, which was worth around £10 million, seemed acceptable (read: not politically embarrassing). The usual arguments about the nature of the war being very different before these vehicles were delivered in 1971 and the non-offensive nature of the parts being made in Britain were advanced, and, after some objections from the SEAD on political grounds, Vickers was allowed to submit a tender. PRO records do not indicate whether the tender was successful, but none of these vehicles are described as produced by Vickers in the relevant American literature on military vehicles, so presumably the bid failed.[22]

## *Boats*

### Fast Patrol Boats

This appears to have been another request that ultimately came to nothing. Early in March 1968, the chairman of the Arms Working Party received notification from the Navy Department that it had received an inquiry from the Americans about the possibility of buying a number of FPBs (Fast Patrol Boats).

### The Sale

The navy considered it likely that these vessels were intended for use in Vietnam and requested ministerial approval, since they were "politically sensitive." Once again the time delay on the order made it seem possible to allow a tender from a British company, Vospers being suggested. The last entry in PRO records states that the program for acquisition of FPBs was "in abeyance for further political and financial consideration."

In this context, it is relevant to record that Byrne's bill prohibiting money from being spent in foreign shipyards had been passed on 13 September 1967. No further record exists to show that there was either a tender or a sale by a British company, and the army's requirement may well have been adequately filled by its earlier purchase of PCFs (Patrol Craft, Fast), which entered service in August 1965.[23]

## Rifles, Ammunition and Other "Sharp" Weapons

Before 1966, American troops, wherever they were serving, were all issued with the M-14 rifle chambered for the 7.62×51mm NATO cartridge, the same cartridge that was used by the British, Australian and New Zealand armies in their ultra-reliable L1A1 SLR (self-loading rifle). After 1967, American troops in Vietnam received a new weapon, the Colt M-16 semi-automatic rifle, chambered for the smaller 5.56×45mm NATO cartridge, although U.S. troops in all other theaters retained the older M-14, in some cases until 1970. Reliability problems with the original M-16 rifle, the XM16E1, led to the adoption of later, improved variants—the XM16A1 and XM16A2.

### Proposed Manufacture of M-16 Rifles by Sterling Engineering

The Sterling Armaments Company (a.k.a. Sterling Engineering) was an arms manufacturer based in Dagenham, London, and best known for manufacturing the L2A3, usually referred to simply as "the Sterling," a "blow-back"-operated sub-machine gun with a 30-round magazine chambered for the ubiquitous 9×19mm Parabellum cartridge. The Sterling replaced the far inferior STEN gun within the British Army from 1947, being retained in service until 1994, when it was replaced in turn by the L85A1 assault rifle. Among the less well-known guns Sterling produced were the Armalite AR18 (an improved version of the M-16 rifle, produced under license from ArmaLite, Inc.) and the unpopular SAR-87 assault rifles. The company was bought out by BAe/Royal Ordnance in 1988 and its factory closed.

**The Sale**

On the 15 September 1967, a letter was received in the MOD from the Sterling Engineering Company of Dagenham. It was from the managing director of the company, explaining that Sterling had for some time been negotiating with Colt Industries in an attempt to obtain sub-contract work manufacturing parts for the M-16 rifle (probably the XM16E1, although the exact variant is not specified). Since the DOD was now looking for an alternative manufacturer for the M-16, Sterling's managing director asked for the MOD to ensure that its name was placed on the list of companies allowed to tender for this work, claiming the contract "could amount to 1½ million dollars a month over a considerable period"—effectively, between 5,000 and 10,000 M-16 rifles every month at around $100 for each rifle. Unfortunately, the U.S. government had already made it abundantly clear that only American firms would be allowed to tender for the contract to produce the M-16, because one of the conditions under which it had purchased the right to produce the rifle from Colt was that only U.S. manufacturers would serve as any second source of supply.

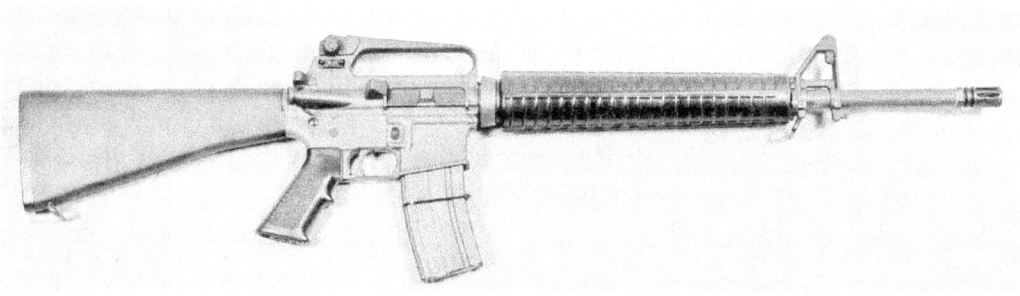

**Colt M-16A2 semi-automatic rifle from the right side. The issue long-arm for U.S. troops fighting in Vietnam.**

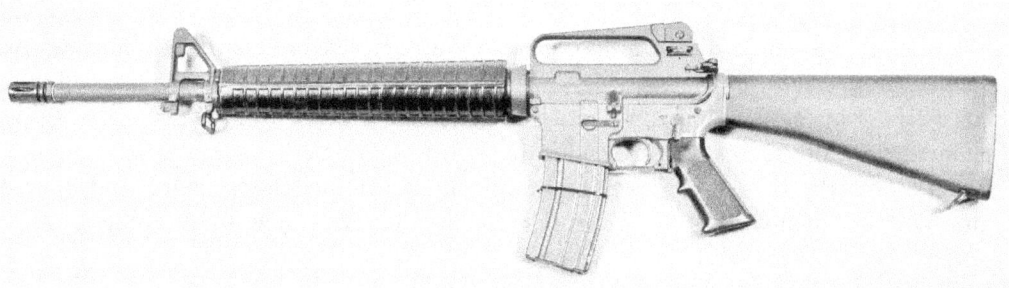

**Colt M-16A2 semi-automatic rifle from the left side. Chambered for the 5.56×45mm NATO cartridge, the initial version was prone to stoppages because of a fault in the design of the firing chamber and consequently was unpopular with many troops serving in Vietnam.**

Moreover, the Americans had not included the M-16 on their "shopping list" of tenders for September 1966, and even if they had, it would have been politically difficult for the government to allow such a contract, with arms and ammunition now being on the "sensitive" list.

Sterling was informed of all these strictures on 27 September 1967; however, despite it being made clear that a deal of any sort would be extremely unlikely, the company sent its representative to the MOD on the following day, 28 September. At this meeting, he asked for help in his sales campaign and, in particular, admittance to a briefing conference for potential suppliers at the Rock Island Arsenal on 4 October. The MOD politely declined to help, as officials felt a contract to supply the M-16 that involved a British firm would be politically embarrassing. They also informed the representative that he was unlikely to be admitted to the conference, as the Americans enforced a strict rule that thirty days' notice was required for any meeting of this sort. He immediately informed the press of the MOD decision, which resulted in a story in the *Daily Telegraph* in which certain details were incorrect, including the implication that the government was attempting to sabotage Sterling's sales bid. By the time this story appeared, Sterling's man was in New York, where the embassy also informed him of the thirty days' notice rule and declined to try and pressure the Americans into allowing him into the conference. Once more he went to the press and it was his version of events that was published again, this time in the *Daily Express* of 3 October 1967. In this account, he claimed that all he had wanted was for the embassy to confirm he worked for a "highly reputable" British firm and that they had refused to do this. His story again implied that the sale had not been encouraged, this time because of potential embarrassment to the Wilson government.

Subsequently, the situation cooled down and Sterling modified its plans, intending to try and secure some sub-contract work for parts from Colt, rather than manufacturing complete weapons, and also discussing the possibility of making the M-16 for British and Commonwealth forces. Government records contain no further reference to M-16 manufacture by Sterling, either of parts under sub-contract or of complete weapons, although the company did manufacture ArmaLite's AR18 rifle under license between 1975 and 1983. Despite being a good weapon, the AR18 never became a standard service rifle in any country's armed forces and so failed to save Sterling from bankruptcy and eventual closure.[24]

## 7.62 Cartridges and Links

Although the standard U.S. military rifle in Vietnam was now chambered for the new, lighter 5.56mm (.223 caliber) cartridge, American troops there were still equipped with their excellent M-60 machine guns, which used the same 7.62×51mm NATO cartridge as the Commonwealth forces, together with their own M-13 link. This link was essential to the operation of the M-60, since it was the component that joined the cartridges and allowed them to be continually fed to the weapon, replacing the canvas belt used in older guns.

### The Sale

A number of requests from the Americans for ammunition appear in government files for 1968. The sales described were not especially valuable (only around £11 million), and the recommendation by the Foreign and Commonwealth Office was that most of them should be declined, including a request for 105mm HESH (High Explosive Squash Head) shells, on the grounds that they conflicted with government policy on the supply of arms and ammunition that might be used in Vietnam. There was one exception, however.

On 1 May 1968, the MOD sought ministerial approval for the sale of a quantity of 7.62mm ammunition and the associated links to the U.S. Army, an order worth around £4.25 million, ordnance clearly intended to be used in the U.S. Army's M-60 general-purpose machine guns. The request came from the U.S. Army Procurement Center at Frankfurt and asked for an estimated price for 250 million links and 51 million rounds of ammunition. The MOD was optimistic about convincing the relevant authorities to allow a tender for the sale to be offered to the Americans because:

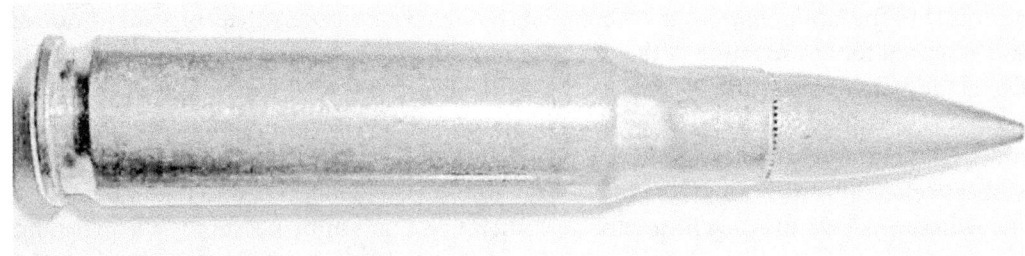

**7.62×51mm NATO cartridge, used in the LA1A1 self-loading rifle issued to Australian and New Zealand troops and the M-60 GPMG used by American forces.**

- the origin of the order indicated that the ammunition was intended for U.S. troops in Europe, not Vietnam; and
- the ammunition could not be made available until 1970 at the earliest.

Foreign Office staff considered the request, and subsequently a paper was written, recommending that the request for ammunition be declined, although the sale of links could be allowed. The reasons given were the extreme political sensitivity of such a sale and, more significantly, because the Frankfurt Procurement Center covered the requirements of the whole of the U.S. Army, not just units in Europe. Consequently, the ammunition might well be sent to Vietnam for use in the army's M-60 machine guns, and, more importantly, it might be identified as being of British origin. The origin of the links could not be identified in a similar way, which was given as another reason for allowing their sale.

This paper was seen by a number of senior officials, who added their own comments. One of these responses indicates the changing attitude within the government regarding sales of military hardware to the Americans and the reasons behind it. The minute includes the following passage:

> Given our acute need to export and earn, I should be sorry to see us pass up this opportunity of earning £4¼ m for small arms ammunition, and wonder whether we cannot perhaps let ourselves be taken in by the Frankfurt address—if we lose the order on price, too bad.

Head stamp of British-made 7.62×51mm NATO cartridge.
Letter code designations are:
- **L42A3**—Cartridge type (in this case, 155 grain Sniper MATCH).
- **RG**—Made at Royal Ordnance Factory Radway Green, UK.
- **08**—Year of manufacture.
- **Cross enclosed in circle (+)**—Cartridge meets NATO specifications.

Since this sort of information is included on every cartridge manufactured in Britain, the origins of such ammunition would be readily apparent to experienced military personnel and British involvement in the supply of these cartridges could not be denied.

There is no record in the relevant government file of whether the sale was agreed to, although it probably was not, Eastern European ammunition being cheaper and more easily available at the time. Moreover, "head" stamps on the cartridge cases manufactured by

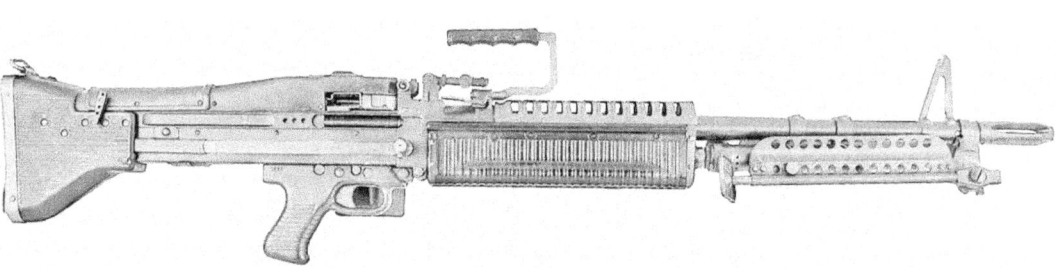

**M-60 general-purpose machine gun (GPMG). Chambered for the 7.62×51mm NATO cartridge and used extensively by U.S. forces in Vietnam (Wikipedia; Creative Commons).**

British ordnance factories would have made them readily identifiable as being of British origin. However, whether or not the sale was agreed, the attached minute does indicate the levels of cynicism prevalent in the Foreign and Commonwealth Office over government arms policy, especially because underneath the handwritten minute suggesting they allow themselves to be taken in, several senior officials who were also asked for their opinions about the sale simply wrote, "I agree."[25]

## CS Gas

CS gas (active constituent: 2-chlorobenzalmalononitrile) is a riot-control gas, of the type commonly known as "tear" gas, originally developed by two Americans, Ben Corson and Roger Stoughton. The name given to the gas is derived from the first two initials of their surnames, and although it was an American invention, the major development work that resulted in the gas being used as a riot-control measure was done in England at Porton Down in the 1950s and 1960s. This included the development of a delivery system, which received a British Patent in 1960 (Brit.Pat. 967660/1960).

Claims that CS gas was used in Vietnam were made in the *Observer* in February 1968, and on 26 February 1968 Mr. Tam Dayell submitted a written question to Mr. Roy Mason, then Minister of Defence (Equipment), about the terms under which the Americans were allowed to manufacture CS gas. The exchange between Dayell and Mason is recorded here:

> **Mr. Dayell:** Asked the Secretary of State for Defence if he will state the terms of the licence under which the gas CS is manufactured in the United States of America under licence from the Microbiological Research Establishment at Porton.
> **Mr. Mason:** No exclusive rights in respect of CS itself are vested in Her Majesty's Government and it was not developed at the Microbiological Research Establishment, Porton. Riot-control apparatus suitable as a container for anti-riot agents such as CS is the subject of United Kingdom patent 967660 of 1960, but it is not patented in the United States. In neither case, therefore, does the question of a licence arise.[26]

Mason's argument was essentially true, but what he had not told the House was revealed in a government memo referring to CS gas and its containers, also dated 26 February 1968. The relevant passage reads, "(2) (not for publication) Manufacturing know-how was released to the U.S. under the confidential exchange of military information."[27] It is not clear from this statement whether the "know-how" referred to manufacture of the CS gas itself or the delivery system, although "Chemical and Biological warfare agents of all kinds," which must presumably include riot gas, were on the Strategic Export Committee's "Sensitive" list. Consequently, they should not have been sold or traded for use in Vietnam without, at least, a ministerial decision.

## "Point Focal" Charge

This item is a small, self-contained explosive device designed to neutralize mines on land or in the sea, with minimal damage to the mine-activating mechanism. After initial development, these charges were offered to the USN in 1965, but an initial order for 200, worth only £800, was not placed until November 1967. Given their defensive nature and the small number requested, the sale was allowed.[28]

## 15. Military Hardware

**Table Ten: Proposed Equipment Sales between Britain and United States, Possibly Destined for Vietnam (1963–1976)**

### Aircraft and Aircraft Components (including hovercraft)

| Date | Equipment Requested | Value | Final Status |
|---|---|---|---|
| Initial approach: 1/1/1965 Delivery (for evaluation): 1965 | SR.N5 hovercraft, modified under license by Bell Aerosystems, after Saunders-Roe (later BHC). Initial order: 7 hulls for evaluation | £2 million | Sale confirmed; "Jay" rule still in effect. |
| Initial approach: 1/5/1969 | 9 SR.N 5 | $3.7 million | Decision not known but almost certainly the order was not endorsed by the United States. |
| Initial approach: 17/11/1966; Final contract: 1/1/1967; Delivery: 1968 | Rolls-Royce Spey engine parts for Allison TF41 jet engines; 1st order: supply of components and 500 engines; 2 order: 240 engines | $80 million (projected) | Sale confirmed; "Jay" rule still in effect. |
| Initial approach: 23/6/1967 | Handley-Page HP 137 Jetstream, small passenger aircraft designed for civilian use; intended for use by U.S. Army for executive and cargo transport 1st order: 171 aircraft | Aircraft: £95 million (1968–1972) Spares: £10 (1968–1983) | Sale lost due to delivery problems and cancellation of F-111K off-set agreement. |
| Initial approach: 8/11/1967 | Elliot Automation Limited "heads up" display equipment intended to be fitted to USAF A-7D Corsair | $40 million | Sale confirmed. |
| Initial approach: 4/12/1968; First delivery: 1971; Final delivery: 1976 | Hawker Siddeley Harrier jump-jets for USMC; 1st order: 12 aircraft; Final delivery: 110 aircraft | 1st order: £80 million Final order: £400 million | Sale confirmed. |
| Initial approach: January 1969 | Shorts Bros. Skyvan aircraft to Air Vietnam and the ARVN, with 200 aircraft suggested for Vietnamese military; Suggested order: 200 aircraft | | Sale not approved. |

### Arms and Ammunition

| Date | Equipment Requested | Value | Final Status |
|---|---|---|---|
| Initial approach: 18/6/1968 | Possible production of M-16 rifles by Sterling Engineering of Dagenham | £12 million | Tender never agreed by United States. |

| Date | Equipment Requested | Value | Final Status |
|---|---|---|---|
| Initial approach: 18/6/1968 | 175mm HE ammunition for U.S. Army and German Federal Government; 40,000 complete roads to United States; 130,000 empty cases to Germans | £7 million | Not known. |
| Initial approach: 1/5/1968 | 51 million rounds; 7.62 ammunition; 250 million; 7.62 links | Ammo: £1.75 million; Links: £2.5 million | Sale of links approved. Sale of ammo not confirmed. |
| Initial approach: 19/3/1968 | 105mm HE/SH ammunition for U.S. Army | | Sale not approved. |
| Initial approach: 4/4/1968 | 2,000 tons TNT to U.S. Army Munitions Command | Not known | Sale agreed in department and later confirmed. |

**Vehicles**

| Date | Equipment Requested | Value | Final Status |
|---|---|---|---|
| Initial approach: 1/4/1967; Delivery: after 1/1/1968 | Alvis Saracen armored personnel carriers 150–200 vehicles | £16,000 each; Total: £2.4–£3.2 million | Contract agreed but vehicles not supplied; "Jay" rule still in effect. |
| Initial approach: 1/4/1967; Delivery: after 1/1/1968 | Alvis Saladin armored cars; 100 vehicles | £25,000 each; Total: £2.5 million | Contract agreed but vehicles not supplied; "Jay" rule still in effect. |
| Initial approach: 1/4/1967; Delivery: after 1/1/1968 | Daimler Ferret armored (scout) car, Mk 2/3; 100 vehicles | £9,100 each; Total: £0.91 million | Contract agreed but vehicles not supplied; "Jay" rule still in effect. |
| Initial approach: 5/1/1968 | Civilian buses for General Trading Corporation; Secondhand: 383 vehicles, 20 air-conditioned; New: 50 vehicles | Not known | Not known. |
| Initial approach: 1/2/1968 | Centurion ARVs (Armored Recovery Vehicles); 53 vehicles | £5.3 million | Not known. |
| Initial approach: 22/3/1968 | Fast Patrol Boats (FPV) from Vosper | | Canceled by United States. |
| Initial approach: 23/6/1969 | Permission for Vickers to tender for supply to U.S. government of chassis for: M107—175mm self-propelled guns; 102 vehicles; M110—8-inch self-propelled howitzers; 31 vehicles; M578—Armored recovery vehicles (ARV); 121 vehicles | £10 million | Tender agreed in all Departments, except South East Asian Department. Final status not known. |

### Miscellaneous

| Date | Equipment Requested | Value | Final Status |
| --- | --- | --- | --- |
| Initial approach: not known | CS gas container (Brit Pat.). Manufacturing information released to United States in exchange for military intelligence | Not known | Not known. |
| Initial approach: 20/12/1967; Delivery: not known | Anglo-Swiss Screw Co.; Body of clockwork mechanism for shell fuse | £12 million | Sale approved. |
| Initial approach: 14/11/1967; Delivery: not known | Point Focal charges to U.S. Navy for use in neutralizing land or sea mines; 200 | £800 | Sale approved. |
| Initial approach: 22/11/1968 | Decca Navigator equipment | Not known | Sets and radio masts delivered. Decca also responsible for training. |

*Total value of potential and agreed sales, 1965–1976:* ~£634 million (~$1,522 million)
*Average value of sales each year (total/12):* ~£53 million (~$127 million)
*Average value of sales each year without Harriers:* ~£20 million (~$48 million)
*Exchange rate in 1968:* approx. $2.40 = £1.00
*Information in this table taken from PRO files: FCO 15/1085, FCO 46/204.*

## Britain's Arms Contribution to Australia and New Zealand

Traditionally, Britain had always been the major supplier of arms to both Australia and New Zealand, but Wilson's House of Commons statement about the supply of arms to countries fighting in Vietnam meant that these arrangements came in for closer scrutiny than had previously been the case. Although both countries had troops fighting in Vietnam, the history of their arms supply from Britain was of such long standing that ministers found it impossible to refuse to supply equipment to either country when it was ordered.[29] More-

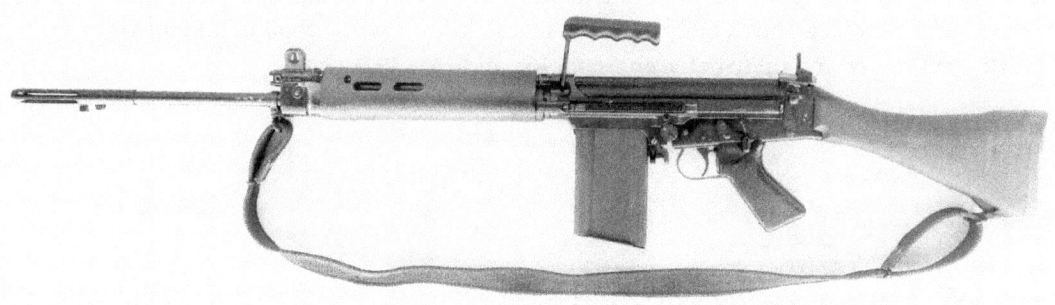

**SLR L1A1 semi-automatic rifle from the left side. Standard weapon for Australian and New Zealand troops in Vietnam. Chambered for the ubiquitous 7.62×51mm NATO cartridge, it was a reliable weapon, considered by many of its users to be far superior to the Colt M16.**

over, these requirements were likely to decrease in the future, as Australia was fast developing a domestic arms industry capable of supplying all its requirements (and probably those of New Zealand as well). With this loss of revenue in mind, the government must have been particularly anxious to facilitate any and all possible sales.[30]

Harold Wilson explained the official government position in a reply given in the House of Commons to Mr. Edward Heath, then leader of the opposition:

> The Australians have not asked for any arms specifically for use in Vietnam but, as I say, if we are supplying continuing orders of, shall we say, small arms ammunition, we obviously could not say with the next lot, "This particular batch should not be used in Vietnam."[31]

He also replied to another question in the House of Commons on the same day, in a further attempt to clarify the situation:

> If there were a situation, for example, in which the Australians were asking for bombs for bombing North Vietnam—and that is the whole issue that has given rise to all these questions—we would have to consider our position as Co-Chairman, and the decisions in the Commonwealth Prime Ministers Conference.[32]

The Australians did make a request for both 500-pound and 1,000-pound bombs in October 1967, their requirement being for a total of 60,000 pieces of this type of ordnance, to be used by their Canberra aircraft (No. 2 Squadron had been operating this aircraft in Vietnam since April 1967). The contract was valued at over £1 million, and both the Committee for Strategic Exports and the MOD agreed to the sale, with an official from the MOD noting, in response to a memo from the Foreign Office, "You assume the bombs are to be used in Vietnam. This is not the same as a specific request for bombs for use there which the Prime Minister had in mind in his answer to the supplementary Question on 14 July 1966."[33] Despite agreement being reached to supply the bombs, they never seem to have reached Vietnam, and any ordnance of this type that the Australians required for use there was supplied by the United States, although the RNZAF was sold some replacements for its FEAF stockpile by the MOD.[34]

During this period, 8,000 Australian troops routinely served in South Vietnam in the course of any single deployment (60,000 troops in total), so it is probable that a significant proportion of the equipment supplied to the Australian government, including ammunition and other ordnance, was used there. Canberra jet aircraft of No. 2 Squadron RAAF were also deployed with American forces and were involved in bombing operations in North Vietnam.[35] New Zealand's commitment was much less, with a total of 3,890 troops from various units serving there between May 1965 and May 1971.

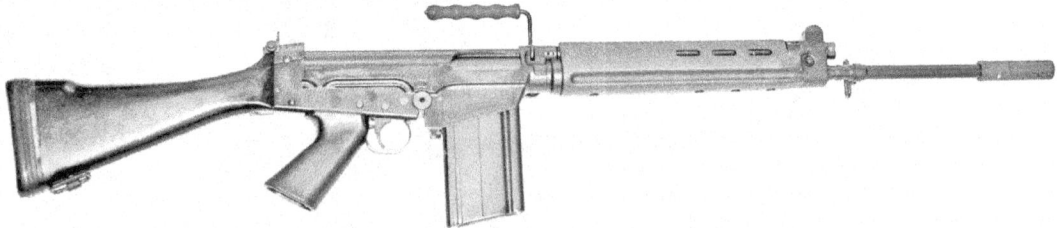

**Fabrique Nationale (FN) FAL semi-automatic rifle, of which the British SLR L1A1 is a variant.**

Centurion Mk III main battle tank. Powered by a Rolls-Royce Meteor engine, producing a top speed of 22 mph. The main armament is the vastly successful 105mm L7 rifled gun, which uses a 105×607mm shell, with a single .30 caliber Browning machine gun as secondary armament. Crew is 4: commander, gunner, loader and driver (Wikipedia; Creative Commons).

## RAAF Bombing Operations in Vietnam

Members of No. 2 Squadron RAAF were re-equipped with English Electric Canberras in 1953 and subsequently operated from RAAF Butterworth during the Malayan Emergency.

English Electric Canberra T.4. This aircraft is painted blue to represent the first prototype. Canberras of the RAAF flew over 12,000 sorties while serving in Vietnam between 1967 and 1971.

**Avon CA-27 Sabre fighter jet. The Australian 79 Squadron, RAAF, was equipped with these aircraft, and the unit's members stationed at RTAF Ubon during their tour in Vietnam.**

In April 1967, 8 Canberras from that squadron were sent to South Vietnam to become part of the U.S. 35th TFW (Tactical Fighter Wing), flying over 12,000 sorties between April 1967 and June 1971. These aircraft dropped more than 76,000 bombs, which killed over 780 enemy personnel, with another 3,300 possibly killed. The squadron is also credited with destroying approximately 8,600 "structures," 15,500 bunkers, 1,200 sampans and 74 bridges, for the loss of two aircraft and five crew members killed. Initially, bombs for raids by No. 2 Squadron were claimed to have come from bomb dumps of World War II weapons retained in Australia (total 27,568 bombs); when these supplies had been exhausted, ordnance was supplied by the USAF. The USAF bombs were larger than the World War II weapons the RAAF had used previously, and because the Canberras had to be modified to accept the modern U.S. ordnance, this may have precluded the use of any bombs supplied by the MOD, although this is by no means certain.[36]

In addition to No. 2 Squadron RAAF, the RAAF also deployed one squadron operating Bell UH-1B helicopters (No. 9 Squadron RAAF) and three squadrons operating transport aircraft (Nos. 35, 36 and 37 Squadrons RAAF) to Vietnam, with another squadron of CA-27 Avon Sabres (No. 79 Squadron RAAF) stationed at RTAF Ubon in central Thailand, near the Laotian border. Bell UH-1B helicopters were also operated by No. 723 Squadron RAN as part of the Experimental Military Unit in Vietnam during the war.

### Table Eleven: Arms Trade between Britain, Australia and New Zealand*
#### "Sensitive" Equipment Requested by Australia and New Zealand

**Australia**

| Date | Equipment Requested | Quantity | Value | Final Status |
|---|---|---|---|---|
| Initial approach: 15/9/1967 | 500-pound bombs | 45,000 | In excess of £1 million | Sale agreed but final status not known |
| Initial approach: 15/9/1967 | 1,000-pound bombs | 15,000 | | |

## 15. Military Hardware

| Date | Equipment Requested | Quantity | Value | Final Status |
|---|---|---|---|---|
| Initial approach: 1/1/1968 | Centurion tanks (offered to Australians by MOD) | 25 surplus vehicles | Not known | Not known |
| Initial approach: 1/2/1968 | Saladin armored cars and 76mm turrets | 20 vehicles and 20 turrets | Not known | Sale agreed |
| Initial approach: 21/3/1968 | RMG observing ammunition (used for calibrating sights on Centurion tanks) | 130,000 rounds | £40,000 | Sale agreed |
| Initial approach: 16/4/1968 | Infrared and RMG modification kits for Centurion tanks | Unspecified | Not known | Sale agreed |
| Initial approach: 24/8/1968; Delivery: at intervals until end of hostilities | Canberra bombers: supply of spares | 39 junction box tops: bomb gear; 28 unit releases: bomb gear; 72 rubber sealing rings: armament | Not known | Sale agreed |

### New Zealand

| Date | Equipment Requested | Quantity | Value | Final Status |
|---|---|---|---|---|
| Initial approach: 1/4/1968 | M557 fuses for American 105mm howitzer shells. | 4,308 | £33,000 | Sale agreed |
| Initial approach: 13/8/1968 | 1,000-pound high-explosive bombs as replacements for FEAF stocks. Not used in Vietnam, as RNZAF did not deploy bombers there. | 1,260 | Not known | Sale agreed |

*Included here are only those sales that were considered in government files to be non-routine sales. Clearly, many routine equipment sales to the Australian and New Zealand armed forces were also conducted during this period and not necessarily recorded.

### Value of Arms Sales to Australia and New Zealand (1962–1965)**

| Year | Australia (£m) | New Zealand (£m) | Total value (£m) |
|---|---|---|---|
| 1962 | 6.21 | 2.1 | 8.31 |
| 1963 | 7.88 | 2.19 | 10.07 |
| 1964 | 4.72 | 2.86 | 7.58 |
| 1965 | 6.05 | 3.12 | 9.17 |

**Arms sales to Australia for 1966–1970 were estimated at an average of £6 million each year, with sales to New Zealand being around £3 million, although precise figures from British government records are unavailable.

*Information for this table taken from PRO files: FCO 15/624, CAB 148/28/23.*

## Britain's Arms Contribution to the South Vietnamese

Britain began selling arms to South Vietnam in 1960, although the sales were fragmentary at best, because the Americans were supplying most of the requirements of the South Vietnamese during that period. Britain also traded with the North Vietnamese during the war, and details of all these transactions as recorded by the British government are included in Table Twelve.

### Table Twelve: Economic Information Relevant to Vietnam
### Equipment Requested by South Vietnam

| Date | Equipment Requested | Value | Final Status |
|---|---|---|---|
| Initial approach: 17/8/1960 | 1,915 .38 caliber Smith & Wesson revolvers | Not known | Approved |
| Initial approach: 13/10/1960 | 10,000 rounds, 25-pounder ammunition: HE and smoke | Not known | Approved |
| Initial approach: 4/11/1960 | VOICE aircraft, possibly Douglas DC-3 aircraft | Not known | Not known |
| Initial approach: 22/12/1960 | 200 "tanks" from a source in Malaya (possibly designed to stimulate the United States into supplying alternative equipment) | Not known | Not known |

### Value of Trade between Britain and North Vietnam

| Year | Exports to North Vietnam (£) | Imports from North Vietnam (£) |
|---|---|---|
| 1965 | 72,000 | 119,000 |
| 1966 | 33,000 | 91,000 |
| 1967 | 66,000 | 75,000 |

*Information for this table taken from PRO files: FCO 15/1085, FCO 15/773.*

### Table Thirteen: Value to UK Economy of Arms Sales to United States (1968)

| Potential "Sensitive" sales for 1968 ($); (Table 7 + 10) | Potential "Non-Sensitive" sales for 1968 ($) (Table 8) | Potential total sales (Sensitive + Non-Sensitive) ($) | Total value of exports for 1968 ($) | Potential arms sales to United States as percent of exports for 1968 |
|---|---|---|---|---|
| 72 million (24 + 48 million) | 74 million | 146 million (72 + 74 million) | 15,000 million (£6,537) | ~1.00 percent |

*Agreed total value of sales under F-111K "off-set" agreement: $325 million (1966–1978)*
*Value of arms sold between May 1966 and November 1967: $138 million*

## Perspectives

Sales between Britain and America of military hardware that could potentially be used in Vietnam certainly took place, and some of the equipment purchased did see service with the Americans in that country. Several of these proposed sales also breached the Committee for Strategic Exports' 1967 recommendations and, if the line taken in Wilson's statement of 17 June was to be followed implicitly, the government should have instructed the suppliers that these proposals were to be declined before even the initial negotiations began. These included:

- The Harriers and the Spey engines: Combat aircraft and the engines for them were specified by the Strategic Export Committee as "Sensitive."
- The 7.62mm ammunition, black powder and .45 caliber balls: All ammunition and its components were similarly specified as "Sensitive."
- The armored cars and personnel carriers: All armored vehicles were on the "Sensitive" list.
- The self-propelled guns: Although only the chassis were built in Britain, even assembly was prohibited, since armored fighting vehicles and guns were on the "Sensitive" list.

In addition, if Healey had not modified the British government's definition of "arms," many of the ancillary items should likewise have been declined, since they were military hardware. These included equipment such as the "heads-up" weapons display for the Corsair II A-7D, the Centurion ARVs and even some of the equipment included on the "Non-Sensitive" list, such as 5.56mm magazines, black powder and dynamite.

The usual government response if such agreements were made public was to imply that it was "not clear" that any arms being sold were explicitly intended for Vietnam, and that no assurances were ever asked from their American allies about where arms would be used once they were sold. Despite this public stance, Healey himself said that he thought much of the military hardware Britain sold to the Americans might "finish up in South Vietnam should the war be protracted." Harold Wilson had also given a clear indication to the Americans that he and his government were amenable to some sort of self-regulating arrangement as early as July 1966 in a statement to the House of Commons (the F-111K offset agreement having been signed in April 1966):

> Her Majesty's Government do not place any restrictions or conditions, for example on the future use or destination, on any arms sold to the United States of America. This is the position once we have agreed a sale. But obviously, when our American friends are considering what they want to buy from us and when we are considering whether a sale should be made our position as Geneva Co-Chairman must be taken into account. And since this is well-known to the United States Administration I do not foresee any practical difficulties in pursuing our normal sales arrangements with an ally.[37]

This is not quite in the same spirit as Wilson's statement on 17 May, because, in this later statement, there was no clear assurance that the Americans would need to inform the British about the intended destination of any arms they bought. Moreover, it is clear from a number of government memoranda that officials concerned in these sales not only specifically avoided asking the Americans where anything they were buying was going to be used but also occasionally suggested that they might ignore clear indications that certain arms might end up in Vietnam. Wilson's reply also suggests that the Americans could be trusted implicitly to refrain from asking for anything the British would not be able to supply under the terms of their own policy. This is significant, because the memo dated 11 April 1967, referring to the sale of armored cars, says specifically that there would be serious political consequences if the Americans found out the British were being selective in what they sold, which implies that the United States was not sympathetic to the British government's stance.[38]

There was certainly considerable room for maneuver within these arms sales agreements and they were worthy of Harold Wilson, whom Richard Crossman once described as "the master tactician and the super-opportunist." Britain was also the major supplier of arms to Australia and New Zealand during this period. Sales to those countries were not subject to any practical restrictions, because of Britain's historic role in supplying them, although both Australia and New Zealand were making a significant contribution to the war for the South Vietnamese.

Although a huge amount of equipment of every variety was deployed by the Americans and their allies during operations in Vietnam, hardware supplied by firms not based in the United States, including those in Britain, was negligible.[39] Despite the best efforts of government officials, revenue accrued from sales to the United States was only a small percentage of British exports, with the total *projected* revenue from arms sales to the United States for 1968 (before the cancellation of the F-111 agreement) being only $146 million (approx. £61 million), just under 1 percent of total exports for 1968 (this excluded the Harrier sales, the revenue for which would not be available until 1972).[40] Considering revenue from the off-set agreement alone, however, in the eighteen months between May 1966 and November 1967, British sales to the United States were $138 million, or $92 million per year, which would have made a total of $284 million by the end of 1968, including the $146 million of the 1968 estimate ($138 million + $146 million). This would certainly have been a respectable proportion of the $325 million in total sales that were intended to take place between 1966 and 1978, although it was still only 1.25 percent of total exports from Britain for that period.

Britain's policy on arms sales, in reality, paralleled that on training and troop commitments, with successive governments committing themselves to as little support as was found to be expedient and profitable. Sales that were lucrative enough and could be conducted without political embarrassment were allowed to proceed with minimal publicity, while Britain outwardly took a public stance, as Chairman of the Geneva Conference, not to supply arms to its most important ally for use against the Communist countries of the Far East. Almost certainly, if more contracts of a value similar to that of the Harriers could have been negotiated without political consequences, there is no reason to suppose that the government would not have allowed them to proceed as well, given its previous record.

The level of cynicism shown by some government officials and the lengths they went to when accommodating the Americans over the sale of arms is not really so surprising. The British economy was in serious trouble, and, as one government official explained in a minute attached a paper about the supply of 105mm ammunition to the United States (which was subsequently declined), "The Treasury want the money more than the morality!"[41] This seems characteristic of the attitude of many within the government after 1967, in the wake of the devaluation of the pound and an unsuccessful "prices and incomes" policy, and such a response to what amounted to a financial crisis was at least understandable, if not wholly excusable in light of their often reiterated policy on arms sales for use in Vietnam. Certain government officials apparently advocated a response that was both politically and financially expedient, given the need to increase dollar sales and, consequently, not risk offending the Americans. In this attitude they did not differ significantly from the general run of politicians of any other country or political persuasion during that period, including the United States and North Vietnam. President Johnson manipulated the U.S. budget to hide the cost of the war from his voters and Congress, and Hồ Chí Mính was well known to have turned to the Communists for a supply of arms only as a last resort, after both the French and the Americans refused to negotiate with him.

# 16

# Intelligence Support, or:
## *What Was Britain Telling the Americans That They Didn't Know Already?*

## *Military Intelligence*

Military intelligence is concerned with the collection of information and its subsequent analysis, in order to accurately inform military commanders and allow them to make effective use of the resources at their disposal. There are five basic types of potentially useful intelligence information, described by the sources from which they originate:

- SIGINT (signals intelligence) refers to information derived from intercepted communications, radar, and telemetry.
- IMINT (imagery intelligence) includes images from both overhead and ground sources.
- MASINT (measurement and signature intelligence) is technically derived information other than IMINT and SIGINT. It uses information collected by a range of techniques derived from nuclear, optical, radio frequency, acoustics, seismic, and materials sciences.
- HUMINT (human-source intelligence) involves clandestine and overt collection techniques to obtain information from human sources, including covert acquisition of secrets, debriefing of persons of interest and acquisition of information from friendly foreign intelligence services (SIS-CIA liaison).
- OPSINT (open-source intelligence) is publicly available information appearing in print or electronic form.[1]

## *The Scope of Intelligence Operations*

A military intelligence operation begins by identifying the information requirements for a particular situation. Based on this assessment, a process of information collection is then instituted using the five sources described previously, with the collated information subsequently being analyzed and finally disseminated to the appropriate recipients as an intelligence assessment. Intelligence information is usually shared between services and civilian organizations at the appropriate levels.

In Vietnam, the usual source for HUMINT and OPSINT about the North was the consulate in Hanoi, via the British Embassy in Saigon.² SIGINT was also coming from the monitoring equipment installed in the Saigon Embassy and operated by DWS staff, as well as from sources within the People's Republic of China, obtained by the Hong Kong monitoring stations and passed on as a matter of routine to the Americans. Information from the Hong Kong stations would have included information about North Vietnam but would not have been confined to that area, as the SIS and the American intelligence agencies (OSS and, subsequently, the CIA) had an agreement to share relevant information that dated back to an informal arrangement included in the Atlantic Treaty of 1941. This arrangement was formalized in 1946, with the adoption of a UK-USA Communication Intelligence Agreement, which described the association of the two countries in the following way:

The parties agree to the exchange of the products of the following operations relating to foreign communications:

- Collection of traffic
- Acquisition of communications documents and equipment
- Traffic analysis
- Cryptanalysis
- Decryption and translation
- Acquisition of information regarding communications organizations, procedures, practices and equipment

The agreement also stated, "It will be contrary to this agreement to reveal its existence to any third party whatsoever."³

Under this agreement British GCHQ (General Communication Headquarters) and the American NSA (National Security Agency) shared information about the Soviet Union, the People's Republic of China and several Eastern European countries. It was extended to include Canada in 1948, Norway in 1952, Denmark in 1954, West Germany in 1955, and Australia and New Zealand in 1956, although the agreement itself was not public knowledge until 2010. The British do not appear to have had any sources for either IMINT or MASINT from Vietnam and so could not have been passing on these types of information.

## France's War (1946–1954)

For most of the period French forces operated in Vietnam, they were in the north of that country, often close to Hanoi, and their own intelligence network, which included the Vietnamese Surete, probably supplied all their military information without needing to consult the British Consulate. There is no official government record from that period describing any intelligence apparatus for passing on information collected about Vietnam to the French.

Initially, the Việt Minh used captured French communications equipment and their first messages were sent *en clair* ("in clear"—uncoded). A Military Cryptographic Section was established in Hanoi on 12 September 1945, and by early 1946 the Việt Minh had established a crude radio network, although this was still transmitting with minimal communications security. Unfortunately for the Vietnamese, the French had developed a system for direction-finding and were able to both identify the Việt Minh networks and analyze their communications traffic (although the analysis of this SIGINT was limited because of the small number of Vietnamese or Chinese speakers they employed). During this period, between 1946 and 1950, they were also monitoring Nationalist and Communist Chinese, British, Dutch and Indonesian communications. Subsequently, with the arrival of military communications equipment from China and the Soviet Union, Việt Cộng equipment and protocols would probably have been comparable to those available to French forces, with both sides monitoring communications and analyzing the results. French operations, however, were said to be continually limited by the lack of Vietnamese speakers, even in this later period.[4]

## America's War (April 1954–August 1975)

During the period of U.S. operations in Vietnam, enemy SIGINT interception was conducted principally by cryptographic units belonging to the Army Security Agency or Naval Security Group, although there was some central coordination from the NSA. When it was deemed necessary, certain military SIGINT personnel were also assigned to covert special operations and intelligence units. In the later stages of the war, South Vietnamese personnel, principally from the ARVN, were trained to intercept radio communications, although this information was always subsequently relayed to U.S. cryptographic and intelligence analysis units for interpretation. Radio direction-finding aircraft and ships were also used to target specific Việt Cộng installations. The main source for the HUMINT available to the U.S. Army in Vietnam came from operations conducted by the 525 MIG (Military Intelligence Group), which collected and collated information from U.S. military units and South Vietnamese sources, both military and civilian.[5]

## The British Embassy in Saigon and the Hanoi Consulate

During the period between 1963 and 1973, the British government maintained an embassy in Saigon and a consulate in Hanoi. The staff of the Saigon Embassy included a number of military attachés who were collecting intelligence information, while the consul-general in Hanoi was responsible for sending intelligence reports from that location (HUMINT and OPSINT). Defense attachés were also authorized to visit American headquarters and training establishments outside Saigon, but they were not to visit or observe units in action, although they might encounter operations en route, as the official background notes made clear.[6] These trips were intended to enable the embassy staff to obtain relevant information about the way the Americans were conducting the war, so the MOD could learn from American mistakes and exploit their successes.[7] Between 1961 and 1967, personnel attached to BRIAM were also present in Vietnam, assigned to various roles, including training the South Vietnamese police. BRIAM personnel were given quarters separate from the embassy and do not appear to have been involved extensively in intelligence work, although one officer was assigned to the South Vietnamese Special Branch.[8]

## The Attaché's Role and Visits by Senior Officers

Between 1963 and 1965, there were four service attachés on the staff of the ambassador in Saigon, two army and two RAF serving officers, as well as an RAF liaison officer, who was responsible for RAF traffic through the Tan Son Nhut airport in Saigon. With the increase in American military activity in South Vietnam starting 8 March 1965, when the initial wave of U.S. Marines came ashore at Danang, British military commanders found themselves in need of much more detailed information about events in that country than had previously been the case. Consequently, MOD asked that two more assistant defense attachés to be assigned to the embassy, together with a temporary naval attaché; these officers joined the Saigon staff in February 1966. The naval attaché was found to be so essential, however, that his appointment was made permanent in November 1966 and extended to November 1967. Since the attachés were now collecting most of the intelligence required by the MOD, this increase in the embassy's service staff meant that visits by senior British officers, which were becoming increasingly sensitive politically, could be kept to a minimum. Visits at a rate of 4 each year, or roughly one in every quarter, were still sanctioned, however, when discussions between either officers of high rank or those with specialist knowledge were required. When these visits were allowed by the FO (and, after 1968, the FCO), their purpose was invariably decided in considerable detail prior to the officer's arrival, as described in the following summaries.

This extract describes a proposed visit by an army intelligence officer:

### Visit by Brigadier, General Staff, Intelligence (3–7 July 1967):

BGS (Int) is attending a Far East Command Defence Attaches Conference in June and is thereafter making a tour of Far East countries of particular interest to the Defence Intelligence Staff. Because of the great importance which the DIS attach to the study of counter-insurgency and the influence of China on the North Vietnam techniques and equipments which are being employed in South Vietnam the Director General of Intelligence is particularly anxious that BGS (Int) should visit Saigon. It is intended that he would have discussions with the Ambassador and his staff, with the appropriate U.S. command and intelligence evaluating agencies and with the Australian contingent. The Defence Attaché has confirmed that he would welcome the visit and that the Ambassador agrees. BGS (Int) is the responsible authority for the annual report on the Defence Attaché.

This second extract describes the aims of a visit by a senior military officer:

### Visit by GOC 17 Division (after 24 September 1967 for 3 days):

The aim of this visit is to hold discussions at two U.S. Army Divisional Headquarters and the Headquarters of the Australian Task Force on tactical problems, concepts and procedures which could be applicable elsewhere in South East Asia. It is considered essential that the GOC should discuss these matters personally with his U.S. Army counterparts in order that he can obtain first hand information to evaluate it in light of what he sees and hears during his visit and of his past experience and to follow up aspects which may not have been covered in initial briefings. The Assistant Defence Attaches cannot substitute for the GOC in these matters as they do not have the requisite experience of command at divisional level, nor are the U.S. Divisional Staffs likely to release the same level of information as they would to the GOC.

The visit to the Australian Task force will enable the GOC to compare the U.S. Army methods with those of the Australian Forces, whose tactics and training are similar to those of the British Army, in assessing the relative merits of the two systems.

The GOC 17 Division is specifically charged with the task of carrying out revolutionary war studies in FARELF. The information gained from a visit to Vietnam would clearly be invaluable in the preparation of studies and exercises.[9]

The proposed aims of these particular visits were certainly very carefully formulated in advance, and, considering the detailed and extensive itinerary, the expectation must have been that a significant benefit was to be gained from them. How effective they were and the extent to which the Americans were forthcoming is debatable, however, especially during this period, with Johnson in the White House and British levels of cooperation being considered negligible by the Americans.

## Intelligence Transfer

In addition to facilitating the collection of information for the MOD, the Foreign Office (and the Foreign and Commonwealth Office in its turn) also had a well-developed protocol for passing information from the consulate in Hanoi to the U.S. State Department in Washington, which began to be developed from as early as 1963. The British consul-general in Hanoi was responsible for making periodic reports, which he passed to the British Embassy in Saigon, having first marked as "Sensitive" anything it was thought better not to pass on to the Americans. Upon reaching the embassy in Saigon, information was then usually passed in two directions—to the U.S. Embassy in Saigon and to the Foreign Office in London, where it eventually reached the SEAD (South East Asia Department). SEAD then passed it to the British Embassy in Washington (unless it had already been passed directly from the British Embassy, Saigon, as occasionally happened), and the Washington embassy would forward it to the U.S. State Department to be disseminated as they felt appropriate. In addition to that obtained by their own officials, intelligence was also passed to the British Embassy in Saigon from the Canadian permanent representative in Hanoi, via the Canadian commissioner in Saigon; from here it was also sent to SEAD at the Foreign Office and the U.S. Embassy in Saigon.

As usual, British officials were concerned that their role in supplying this information remain undisclosed. An official in the Washington embassy was very specific about this, in a communication to SEAD on 28 March 1967, which contained this passage:

> We in the Embassy had both the discretion and the responsibility to transmit information from [name of British consul-general, Hanoi, omitted], and we regarded it as being the responsibility of the recipients in the State Department then to disseminate it further within the American machine as might seem to them desirable, bearing in mind whatever *ad hoc* cautions we might attach and the general proviso that information of this sort should not be used publicly without specific clearance with us and every care should be taken to avoid giving either a specific indication or the general impression that the British Consulate-General in Hanoi was reporting to the Americans.[10]

## The Hong Kong Monitoring Stations

Hong Kong became an important center for SIGINT after World War II, with the development of a Royal Navy facility at Stonecutter's Island, and 367th and 743rd Signals Units of the RAF also operated sites for the interception of radio traffic. The Little Sai Wan RAF base served as the central operating station, with another out-station at Batty Belvedere on the Peak and direction-finding sites at Kong Wei RAF base and the Sek Kong airfield. From 1951, Australians from RAAF Pearce were attached to the 367th Signals Unit and were involved in various intelligence duties, including the provision of Chinese and Vietnamese speakers. Civilian GCHQ operators began replacing the military at many of these listening posts starting in 1962; this eventually included Little Sai Wan, which became the responsibility of GCHQ in 1964. SIGINT from this source would have been communicated routinely to the Pentagon under the 1946 Communication Intelligence Agreement, although U.S. intelligence services were also operating both airborne and shipborne monitoring stations in the region during this period. Consequently, it is doubtful if information relayed by the British from these Hong Kong stations revealed anything the NSA was not already aware of.[11]

## The Singapore Intelligence Center

No record has been located so far describing the nature of this institution. One of the few references to it is made in a confidential paper contained in a file on the Jungle Warfare School. The relevant passage reads:

> (Confidential) Personnel from a number of countries, including Vietnam and Thailand, attend courses from time to time at the Intelligence Centre at Singapore, this has never been made public and should not be referred to unless there is an unavoidable direct question specifically mentioning Singapore as opposed to Malaysia.[12]

## Perspectives

Intelligence information was certainly being passed from various British sources to the Americans during the period of the Vietnam War, and Britain was monitoring both Chinese communications in Hong Kong and Việt Cộng traffic in Saigon during the same period. However, all this information seems to have been transferred as a matter of routine, related to the 1946 agreement between the United Kingdom and the United States, and was concerned only incidentally with events in Vietnam. Specific information about North Vietnam was also being passed to the Pentagon from both the Hanoi consulate and the Saigon embassy, but it is unlikely that the British would have been able to tell the United States anything the CIA had not become aware of independently, especially since the various American intelligence agencies had such vast resources at their disposal. British HUMINT and SIGINT was probably a source of corroborative information rather than original intelligence, and it is certain that the CIA had its own sources in Hanoi. This was demonstrated very clearly in April 1968 by the depth of knowledge displayed in the report about "Free World" shipping visiting the port of Haiphong, which served Hanoi.[13]

The British SIS agents were probably passing intelligence about Vietnam to the Americans as a gesture of good will rather than because it was original information. Like the stance on troop deployments and arms sales, this is another example of the British government's desire to be seen as helping the American war effort while expending as little in the way of real resources as possible.

# 17

# Medals and Myths

## Medals and Awards to British Military Personnel

### THE GSM (1962) WITH VIETNAM CLASP

Britain's General Service Medal, also known as the Campaign Service Medal, was introduced in 1962 and awarded to army, navy and RAF personnel for service in minor military operations for which no separate medal was issued. Clasps are awarded with the medal indicating the campaign in which the recipient served, and all GSMs have the name, rank, service number and regiment or corps of the recipient stamped on the rim of the medal.

Confusion and a certain amount of speculation has arisen because the GSM (1962) has a South Vietnam clasp. Unfortunately for the conspiracy theorists, this clasp was instituted with royal approval on 16 December 1965 for "members of our Australian Armed Forces who qualify by participation in operations in defence of the Republic of Vietnam as from 24 December 1962, and to a date to be determined." The eventual qualifying date was 24 December 1962–29 May 1964, and one of the following was required:

*Left:* Obverse of General Service Medal (GSM), 1962, showing the crowned head of Queen Elizabeth II. The rim of such a medal is always inscribed with the name, rank and unit of the holder. *Right:* Reverse of GSM (1962), showing the words FOR CAMPAIGN SERVICE under a crown, surrounded by a wreath of oak leaves.

- 30 days' service in ships operating in inland waters or off the Vietnamese coast
- One day in the service of a land unit
- One operational sortie
- 30 days' service on an official visit

Only 68 men qualified, all members of the AATTV (Australian Army Training Team Vietnam), who provided training and assistance to South Vietnamese forces, although the award had originally been intended to include 232 members of the RAAF Transport Flight (Vietnam). All the medals issued with this clasp are accounted for, and none went to British servicemen, clandestinely or otherwise. Eighty-five British citizens did serve with the AATTV between 1964 and 1971, although they were all too late to qualify for the medal, and members of the Australian and New Zealand forces serving after 29 May 1964 were awarded the Vietnam Medal, which would have included British volunteers and conscripts.[1]

## THE GSM (1918) WITH SOUTHEAST ASIA CLASP 1945–1946

There is also a Southeast Asia 1945–1946 clasp for the General Service Medal (1918), and this was awarded to British personnel who served in Southeast Asia after the Japanese surrender on 15 August 1945. Specifically, that means Gracey's men of the 20th Division who served in Vietnam, as well as British troops who reoccupied Indonesia, Malaya, Burma and Singapore. This was the only medal awarded to British military personnel for service in Southeast Asia, although, of course, there were numerous awards for gallantry and distinguished service that were not specific to any campaign.[2]

*Left:* Obverse of GSM (1918), showing the uncrowned head of King George IV. The rim of such a medal is always inscribed with the name, rank and unit of the holder. *Right:* Reverse of GSM (1918), showing winged Victory in a Corinthian helmet, carrying a trident and bestowing a wreath on either a sword (GSM for army personnel) or wings (GSM for RAF personnel).

## American Awards to British Citizens

### SILVER STAR

Newspaper reports include a number of accounts of British citizens who received gallantry awards while fighting with the Americans and Australians. An article in the *Daily Mail* of 10 October 1967 gives the names of a number of British nationals serving with United States forces in Vietnam, one of whom was awarded the Silver Star (equivalent to the Distinguished Conduct Medal).[3] There is also one instance of a British citizen serving in Vietnam being awarded the Air Medal with Oak Leaf cluster "for services performed while flying."[4]

## Media Myths

Britain's role in the fighting in Southeast Asia has been subject, from time to time, to a number of startling media "revelations." The most common and recurrent of these are described here, together with the source from which they originated (where it has been possible to reliably determine any origin at all).

### "BRITONS" FIGHTING IN VIETNAM

Although there seems to be no basis in fact for such an estimate, it is often claimed that approximately 2,000 "Britons" were actively involved in the Vietnam War.[5] It is difficult to know what the term "Briton" means in this context, although those in such a group might perhaps be thought to fall into the following main sub-categories:

- UK passport holders resident in the United Kingdom before moving to Vietnam and fighting there.
- UK passport holders who emigrated to one of the countries fighting in Vietnam and who subsequently joined or were conscripted into that country's armed forces.

At any rate, this figure is certainly a considerable underestimate, since government figures for individuals giving the United Kingdom as their place of birth when joining Australian and New Zealand forces alone numbered nearly 4,500.[6]

### BRITISH REGIMENTS FIGHTING IN VIETNAM

Periodically, during the time of their involvement in Vietnam, stories appeared in the media on both sides of the Atlantic claiming that the Americans had demanded or suggested that certain regiments of British troops be made available for service in Southeast Asia. Most commonly, these stories involved the Black Watch (the Royal Highland Regiment: 3rd Bttn. Royal Regiment of Scotland) or one of the Gurkha units. The origin of these rumors is described below, as far as has been possible to trace them.

#### The Black Watch (Royal Highland Regiment)

President Johnson certainly asked Harold Wilson if the Black Watch could be deployed to Vietnam at his meeting with the prime minister in December 1964, ostensibly because of their experience against Malaysian terrorists.[7] Johnson's secretary of state, Dean Rusk, also made a statement to Louis Heren, the London *Times* American editor, that included the passage, "All we needed was one regiment, The Black Watch would have done. Just one regiment, but you wouldn't."[8]

Between 1965 and 1969, the Black Watch was deployed with the BAOR (British Army of the Rhine), and from 1969 onward, its members were in Northern Ireland as part of Operation "Banner." Perhaps needless to say, no official record exists of any enlisted member or unit of the Black Watch serving with the Americans in Vietnam between 1963 and 1973.[9] Another variant of this story suggests it was the Argyll and Sutherland Highlanders who were requested, although Johnson certainly appears never to have mentioned this regiment.

## The Gurkha "Divisions"

Government records contain a letter from the British Embassy in Washington, D.C., dated 22 March 1968, recording the remarks a Democratic Party congressman from Florida called Sikes had made about the supply of troops to Vietnam. He described an "untapped source ... the 'six divisions of well trained and highly efficient Gurkha troops'" then enlisted in the British Army, thinking that this was possibly a way of involving British troops who were being demobilized and sent home. Foreign Office staff were derisory, to say the least, about the congressman's suggestion, minuting that the figure was more likely to be "six battalions," and no further action appears to have been taken by either party. Certainly, no record exists of any enlisted Gurkha or Gurkha unit serving with the Americans in Vietnam between 1963 and 1973, nor of any offer being made to individual Gurkhas by the U.S. government.[10] Retired Gurkhas were employed, however, guarding both the British Embassy in Saigon and the consulate in Hanoi.

### BRITISH EMBASSY STAFF IN SAIGON

It has also been suggested that some or all of the military attachés in Saigon were serving SAS personnel, placed there to conduct clandestine military operations.[11] While this is entirely possible, it would have contravened the DCI issued with regard to the conduct of British service personnel in Vietnam, and it is difficult to understand what purpose such a team could have served, unless it was liaising with the Americans. Moreover, if these men were conducting such operations, the White House might well have publicized their operations in a general way, given the previous demands for British troops and the advantageous political consequences for the Americans of being able to demonstrate official British army involvement. No confirmation of an SAS presence has so far been located in any government record of the period, and it is perhaps suggestive that the nature of the attaché's role meant that personnel with typical SAS training would not have been entirely appropriate.

### COVERT ARMS SUPPLY

Britain was also been accused, at various times by sources in the media, of covertly supplying huge quantities of arms, ammunition, bombs and even napalm and defoliants to the Americans and their Commonwealth allies. Britain did continue to sell Australia and New Zealand routine military necessities after their troops were deployed to Vietnam, and the government authorized those sales on the basis of Britain's traditional role in supplying arms to these two countries. Whatever the political and economic ramifications of this decision, both countries would have been seriously and unfairly inconvenienced if Britain had declined these sales, resulting in a deterioration in relations and potential difficulties in the ability of both Australia and New Zealand to respond effectively to external threats. This would hardly have been an acceptable or even sensible response by Britain to two of its most important allies in the Far East, especially during such a highly volatile period. The U.S. Army and USAF also requested small arms ammunition (but not weapons) and "bombs," but these items were probably never delivered, since they were both included on the June 1967 "Sensitive" list and these particular munitions were also to have been purchased as part of the canceled F-111 off-set agreement.[12] Other, more specific requests for ammunition of several types were also made after the termination of the F-111 agreement, but all of those sales were declined, as was the previous request for herbicides. Napalm was not on the "shopping list," and it almost certainly would not have been supplied due to the political and humanitarian implications involved in its use. Moreover, Napalm-B was an American invention and the subject of U.S. Patent 2,606,107, owned by the Dow Chemical Company, so the Americans would hardly have needed British help to either make or transport it. In any case, a British company would have required a license from Dow for its manufacture, which, given the competitive nature of the chemical industry, would probably not have been granted.

# 18

# What Was British Involvement in Vietnam Between 1946 and 1973?

That is the question this book set out to resolve, and the real answer is: Not very much.

The last organized British forces left Vietnam in June 1946, and no official forces at unit strength were deployed there again after that date. Subsequent military involvement consisted of some instances of British citizens volunteering to fight and what amounted to normal duties for members of the armed forces (in the form of secondments or technical visits). Relatively small numbers of Americans and South Vietnamese were trained at the British army's Jungle Warfare School in Malaysia and, although the dog handler and combat tracker training programs did make a significant contribution to the American campaign, it was far too little and much, much too late. Ships of the Royal Navy certainly made regular official visits to Saigon, but only until 1963, and the RFA was involved in some minor supply operations, while the RAF flew four major relief missions and a number of smaller ones in the country, as well as staging refueling stops through the capital. Robert Thompson played an initial role in the "Strategic Hamlets" program as an adviser, and members of BRIAM, which he led, also trained some of the South Vietnamese police and Special Branch officers.

A little material help was given to the French while they were fighting in Vietnam and, despite Harold Wilson's assurances, equipment that was later used there was also sold to the U.S. and Commonwealth armed forces by British companies. These sales were made as part of normal military contracts, however, with many of those to the United States falling under the umbrella of the F-111 off-set agreement. British government officials justified these sales by claiming to have no knowledge of the ultimate destination of any of this material. Since no country that bought military hardware, including the United States, ever disclosed where it was going to be used, and the government never asked for any assurances regarding its destination, this claim was ostensibly truthful, although the circumstances that allowed such a denial to be made were certainly very convenient. British officials were quite entitled to claim that nothing was sold to any country *specifically* for use in Vietnam, whatever those involved may have suspected (and perhaps occasionally ignored in order to encourage the flow of dollars and its positive effect on the UK balance of payments). Unfortunately, despite the government's best efforts, even before the cancellation of the F-111 agreement, these sales would have only amounted to a projected yearly total of approximately 1 percent of Britain's total exports, beginning in 1968 and excluding the Harrier sales. Moreover, by this time, foreign sales and good relations with the Far East had become so important that Britain even risked U.S. displeasure by allowing exports to North Vietnam and importing some of its manufactured goods.

Intelligence information was sent back by British officials and officers who served in both the Hanoi consulate and Saigon embassy, and this was shared with the Americans, together with much of the information passed on from various monitoring stations in Hong Kong. In addition, a number of South Vietnamese were trained at the intelligence school in Singapore. All of these exchanges, however, were part of a more extensive, overall agreement between the SIS and CIA to share any relevant information of joint interest (which the two services have been doing since World War II) and did not originate as a direct response to the situation in Vietnam.

So there was cooperation and, in some instances, more than the British government felt comfortable about publicizing, but that cannot reasonably be seen as constituting a wholesale conspiracy to support either the French or the Americans covertly with troops, munitions or intelligence. Certainly, the Americans believed that British involvement was very much less than it should have been. There were circumstances, perhaps inevitably, that have excited the suspicions of some conspiracy theorists, but, like so many of these "ghosts in the machine," once subjected to a search for evidence they seem to magically evaporate.

Consider one example—the story about the General Service Medal and its Vietnam clasp. Two General Service Medals were awarded to British service personnel, and both certainly do have a clasp for service in Southeast Asia. This has led some to conclude that the 1962 medal must have been a clandestine award for British military personnel serving covertly in Vietnam and whose function the government was keeping secret.

Sadly, the truth is a little more prosaic.

The earliest medal, the GSM (1918), has a clasp for "Southeast Asia 1945–1946," and it was awarded to the men of Gracey's 20th Division, among others, for guarding Japanese POWs and maintaining law and order in Cochinchina before the French took over. While the later medal, the GSM (1962), does have a "South Vietnam" clasp, it also has a Royal Warrant that very specifically limits it to Australian service personnel in the AATTV. British citizens did serve in the AATTV, but they all enlisted after 1964, and so were not eligible for receipt of this medal.

Accusations have also arisen at various times that Britain covertly supplied huge quantities of arms, ammunition, bombs and even napalm and herbicides to the Americans and their Commonwealth allies. Britain did supply routine military requirements for Australia and New Zealand because it was the traditional arms supplier to both countries, and so the British considered themselves justified in not refusing the lucrative contracts to supply ammunition, ancillary equipment and spare parts for the military hardware they had sold there in the past. The U.S. Army and USAF also tried to negotiate munitions and equipment sales at various times, although many proposals were refused as a consequence of government policy and because British-made ammunition and some equipment was thought to be too readily identifiable to be sold safely for possible use in Vietnam. Napalm, in particular, was never requested by the Americans, and, anyway, Napalm-B was the subject of a U.S. patent, so they would hardly have needed to use an additional supplier. Defoliants were certainly requested, but Britain declined to supply them because of the "political sensitivity" of such material. There were arms sales, but at hardly more than the normal commercial level, and many of those deals would have taken place regardless of the war in Vietnam. Indeed, a number of small but quite lucrative contracts were declined precisely because the British government was obliged to be seen as adhering to its policy of not selling arms to countries with troops deployed in Vietnam, and the British could not risk such a sale being detected.

Despite the regular resurgence of these "media myths" revolving around covert troop deployments and secret arms sales, in reality, many of the U.S. demands during the period of the third Vietnam war were a source of inconvenience, even embarrassment, for the British. From the earliest days of American military operations in Southeast Asia, successive British governments tried to subtly direct U.S. efforts toward a political, social and economic solution because a simple, overwhelming military response was seen as having little chance of success. Such an initiative was especially important because many in the government were sure that Britain could not avoid being dragged in if the United States went to war in Vietnam. These careful attempts at coercion began with BRIAM and the sponsorship of Robert Thompson's "Delta" Plan, and then developed, rather more feebly, into the various peace initiatives that the Wilson government attempted to organize. Unfortunately, Britain had such close ties with the United States that it would have been extremely difficult, even unwise, to have tried to exert a stronger influence on the Americans by either refusing outright support or trying to subtly distance itself from such a major ally. Britain, after all, was dependent upon the Americans for, among many other things, the hardware for its nuclear deterrent and economic support for the pound, as well as dollar revenue from the F-111 deal and other economic agreements. Consequently, it was perhaps inevitable that, when their efforts to influence the Americans had failed, successive British governments were forced to accommodate certain U.S. demands, although there was a nice consideration in the level of this support. More significantly, these accommodations certainly had nothing to do with ideology, cozy relations with the United States or a desire to sequester the "Red Menace." It was a combination of financial and political considerations at home and abroad that obliged the government to refuse any troop commitments and forced the unwelcome moderation in arms sales, although, as a direct consequence of that policy, expediency dictated the need for a certain amount of clandestine support, which was specifically aimed at appeasing the Americans. Moreover, since certain members of the U.S. Congress had clearly shown what their response might be if Britain was not wholly supportive of American activities in Vietnam (as in the case of Senator Gross' proposed amendment to the Foreign Assistance Bill), British officials can hardly be condemned for adopting such a policy of conciliation toward successive U.S. administrations, especially with the UK economy in such pressing need of dollar revenue.

Perhaps, in hindsight, British reluctance did serve the cause of the Vietnamese. If British troops, with their greater experience in jungle warfare and counter-insurgency, had been deployed in Southeast Asia, the war would have been conducted in quite a different way. In this scenario, it is anyone's guess how long it might have dragged on. Or, eventually, what it might have led to.

# Appendix I

# Chronology of the Vietnam Wars

## Britain's Vietnam War (1945–1946)

### 1945

*July*

          **Labour government elected; Clement Attlee is prime minister.**

*August*

13    Reoccupation priorities for Southeast Asia laid down by British Chiefs-of-Staff. French Indochina (FIC), Siam (Thailand), Java, Sumatra.
15    Japan accepts armistice.
16    Memo from PRO issued in which Britain and France agree on objectives in FIC. These are as follows: "Disarm Japanese forces, liberate French authorities and re-establish and/or maintain public order." In addition, an agreement is reached that the French will return and administer FIC. (Agreements are signed in September and October.) Control of HQ of Japanese Southern Army is seen as first priority.
19    MacArthur orders that Allied reoccupation of areas invaded by the Japanese must be delayed until he has accepted official surrender scheduled for 28 August. Ceremony, in fact, delayed until 2 September, giving Việt Minh opportunity to exploit power vacuum left by Japanese.
25–27    British send 20-man delegation to Rangoon to tell Japanese what is required of them, locations of POW camps and Japanese forces, etc.
26    Supply drops into Saigon by RAF begin.
27    Revolutionary Government (Communists and Việt Minh) proclaim Republic of Southern Vietnam.
28    Cease-fire agreement signed in Rangoon. Americans (Brigadier-General Timberman) claim it is "preferable" not to allow a U.S. signals party to accompany Saigon Control Commission, leaving Gracey without signals office for several weeks.

*September*

2    MacArthur receives Japanese surrender in Tokyo Bay aboard USS *Missouri*. Rioting in Saigon begins, inspired by Việt Minh. Reports are received from Hanoi, via radio, that 5,000 French officers and civilians were imprisoned in the Citadel.
4    After the death of several French citizens in Saigon, Gracey sends telegram to Terauchi, reminding him that he is responsible for law and order in FIC and protection of Allied nationals.

| | |
|---|---|
| 5 | First medical team parachutes into Saigon (Operation "Mastiff"). |
| 6 | First British troops arrive at the Tan Son Nhut airfield, outside Saigon. |
| 8 | Small detachments of British engineering and medical personnel arrive in Saigon. Meeting at SEAC, where Timberman objects to French involvement in reoccupation of Indochina (see also 28 August). |
| | RAF HQ set up at Tan Son Nhut airfield. (U.S. government seems to be avoiding difficulties associated with reoccupation.) |
| 11 | Advance units of 80th Indian Infantry Brigade, part of Major-General Gracey's 20th India Division, land by air in Saigon (Operation "Masterdom"). |
| 12 | Mountbatten accepts Japanese surrender in Singapore. In Saigon, a proportion of the French POWs are released, armed and supplied with alcohol by French civilians. Rioting ensues, with French civilians joining the POWs. |
| 13 | Gracey arrives in Saigon and is met by delegation of Việt Minh representing the "Southern Committee," which he ignores, since HMG did not recognize the committee and recognition would be interpreted politically, a situation Gracey had been ordered to avoid (see Slim's later amendment to his orders). |
| 14 | Brigadier Maunsell inspects Saigon from Terauchi's car. City appears peaceful. |
| 15 | Leaflet distribution begins. |
| 16 | Slim arrives for tour of inspection and immediately orders reinforcements be sent to Saigon (rest of 20th Div.). |
| 17 | Việt Minh proclaim the establishment of "The Independent Government of Vietnam." General strike called by Phạm Văn Bạch, in response to lack of progress in independence negotiations with French, represented by M. Jean Cédile. Gracey discusses surrender with Japanese commander-in-chief, Field-Marshal Terauchi. The Việt Minh action is thought by many, including Gracey, to be the beginning of a planned insurrection. |
| 19 | 273 Squadron Spitfires arrive in Saigon. 4/17 Dogra begin move to Saigon. Mountbatten (SACSEA) also orders Gracey to suppress Saigon Radio, although this is seen as a direct political measure, and thus not within SACSEA's responsibilities. |
| 21 | **Gracey issues proclamation of martial law in Saigon and surrounding area.** |
| | Gracey is clear at this point that his proclamation is intended to specify the duties and responsibilities of the Japanese and that the British will confine their activities to Saigon. |
| | **Mountbatten disagrees**, but subsequently supports Gracey's actions and suggests that it is necessary for Leclerc to reaffirm the proclamation and agree to assume control of FIC outside "key areas." Leclerc agrees but insists he cannot take control until he has sufficient troops in FIC. |
| | 1/19 Hyderbad take control of civil jail, two police stations (Police Commissariats) and Treasury from Việt Minh. 1/1 GR take control of Saigon Post and Telegraph office from Việt Minh. British troops also continue disarming Việt Minh police. (This was a build-up to the peaceful removal of Việt Minh from the civil administration of Saigon and their replacement by French officials in the planned coup d'état.) |
| 22 | Overnight, French take control of Việt Minh police posts and the Town Hall and place guards on five bridges over l'Arroyo de l'Avalanche. |
| 23 | **Saigon coup d'état takes place.** |
| | French 5th RIC, 11th RIC and civilians are involved. Việt Minh administration is replaced by French officials. 1/1 Hyderbads take control of Yokohama and Indochina banks. |

After control is established peacefully, subsequent problems occur because of French lack of discipline.

Casualties: 2 French killed, four wounded; no Vietnamese casualties.

24 General strike in Saigon and surrounding area as a result of French behavior during coup. Tan Son Nhut airfield, prison and central market attacked.

**Việt Minh sources date the beginning of the war from this day.**

**Overnight, Cité Heyraud incident occurs.** 150 French civilians are murdered and 100 captured and tortured, probably by Trotskyites, although initially Bình Xuyên is blamed. Main British concern is that Japanese guards appear to have allowed rioters into French residential areas, which they were supposed to be guarding.

25 Heavy fighting in Saigon. Brigadier Myers arrives to conduct survey of Vietnam situation. Gracey reiterates his understanding of his orders and current situation to Mountbatten.

26 Gracey telegraphs Mountbatten, explaining limits of his proclamation. Gracey also summons Field-Marshal Terauchi and emphasizes responsibilities of Japanese forces in FIC and the consequences if these obligations are not met. Road blocks in place around Saigon are cleared by British and Japanese forces.

**Lt. Col. Peter Dewey, OSS, killed in ambush.**

27 British troops still involved in heavy fighting and subjected to constant Việt Minh raids. Also large numbers of French civilian casualties, some involving torture and other atrocities, which affects attitude of British-Indian forces.

Brain's report sent to SEAC, suggesting covert Japanese organization is aiding Việt Minh.

28 Ton Son Nhut airport secured.

Singapore meeting, where Gracey confronts Mountbatten about failure to send 20th Division to Saigon as promised and offers another explanation of the proclamation. Gracey repeats that he never intended to move out of Saigon but issued his proclamation to inform Việt Minh behind the disorder that the Japanese were responsible for security and punishment of offenders. Mountbatten had previously decided to relieve Gracey, but is prevented by Slim's contention that if Gracey goes, so will he.

**Rest of 20th Division finally scheduled for deployment to Saigon.**

**Myers' report to SEAC during this period suggests that problems in FIC are mainly due to French intransigence.**

## October

1 Saigon Control Commission's Political Report: 2 Phase of Operations (23 September–1 October): "a period of rioting and bloodshed."

First meeting between South Vietnamese and British to establish a truce: real intention is to bring French and Việt Minh together to plan peaceful way forward, under UN guidelines. Gracey doubtful about French desire for discussion with Việt Minh and Việt Minh ability to guarantee their forces will observe conditions of truce. Gracey states that unless the French promise some form of autonomy to the Vietnamese, fighting is inevitable.

2 Truce comes into effect. Imperial General Staff (IGS) realize Gracey's difficulties and authorize him to operate outside Saigon. Mountbatten receives COSSEA 366 from IGS, confirming this order.

3 French and Việt Minh meet for discussions, with Brain present as Gracey's observer. Dr. Thach, the leading Việt Minh negotiator, tells Brain that the wilder Việt Minh

| | |
|---|---|
| | elements will not obey the political negotiators. Việt Minh occupy public buildings in Dalat (Japanese eject them on 6 October). |
| 5 | **General Philippe Leclerc and first contingent of French troops arrive in Saigon.** |
| 6 | Second meeting between French and Việt Minh, with Brain again present. No progress made; Việt Minh demand full sovereignty and deny knowledge of hostages, while French profess no power to negotiate on independence. New meeting for 8 October scheduled. Việt Minh ejected from public buildings in Dalat by Japanese. |
| 8 | **32nd Brigade begin to arrive Saigon by sea, along with other British troop and vehicle contingents.** |
| 9 | British forces sent to Cambodia to disarm Japanese forces. Meeting between British and Việt Minh takes place, at which Việt Minh are told British will occupy the northern suburbs of Saigon (Gia Định and Go Vap) but only in order to disarm Japanese. Việt Minh negotiators agree that this can be done peacefully. |
| 10 | **Truce broken,** when engineering party attacked, with loss of R E Adjutant, 1 VCO (Viceroy Commissioned Officer) and 2 IOR (Indian Other Ranks), with remainder wounded. Gurkha detachment also attacked at Ton Son Nhut airfield; this, together with a number of similar incidents, suggests a deliberate series of actions, designed to incite retaliation. |
| 11 | **32nd Brigade movement to South Vietnam complete.** |
| | Gracey reports attack on engineering party and states that he is ready to take "strong action." 32nd Brigade deployed in Saigon's northern suburbs, as agreed on 9 October, although British are fired upon by Việt Minh extremists, despite previous assurances. |
| 12 | Intense night fighting in Saigon, with most units involved. |
| 13 | Ton Son Nhut airfield attacked again. Attack beaten off but not before Việt Minh reach the doors of the radio station, within 300 yards of the control tower. (Ton Son Nhut is vital to British forces for supply of food, reinforcements, etc.). |
| | Japanese found to be fighting alongside Việt Minh. |
| | British now seen by many Vietnamese as acting as cover for French colonial policy in FIC, although Japanese troops are responsible for most of the security measures. This attitude is encouraged by Việt Minh propaganda. |
| 14 | Heavy fighting continues. |
| 15 | Heavy fighting still continues. Gen. Leclerc flies to Phnom Penh (Cambodia) and arrests pro-Japanese prime minister. Extremists are then rounded up and situation in Cambodia becomes settled. |
| 16 | **Control Commission begins dismantling of Japanese HQ organization.** |
| 17 | **100th Indian Infantry Brigade arrive in Saigon.** |
| | Gracey asks permission to send liaison officer to Hanoi, in order to facilitate contact with Chinese. |
| 23 | Arrival of 100th Brigade allows British forces to begin movement out of Saigon by securing northern suburbs of Thủ Đức, Biên Hòa and Thủ Dầu Một, intending to use this triangle to concentrate Japanese troops before repatriation via Cap St. Jacques. Force led by commander of 16th Light Cavalry and consists of 4/10 Gurkhas, 1/1 Gurkhas and 14/13 FFR. |
| | 4/10 Gurkha Rifles occupy Thủ Đức. |
| 24 | Operation "Moussac"—plan for French to break out of Saigon and occupy Mỹ Tho— begins. First operation in French attempt to reoccupy FIC. |
| | 14/13 FFR occupy Biên Hòa. |
| | Japanese complain about French attitude. |

| | |
|---|---|
| 25 | 1/1 GR occupy Thủ Dầu Một, completing Gracey's occupation plan. Only Russian "adviser" captured. Sapper from 92nd Indian Field Company shot dead in Cholon (the Chinese district in west Saigon) by sniper while guarding a well. His commanding officer receives permission to burn houses near the well. Fire gets slightly out of control but is exaggerated by certain parts of the press, particularly U.S. media, which describes British as "burning Saigon." |
| 26 | **Last detachment of 20th Indian Division arrives (3,000 men), completing the movement of 20th Division to Saigon. Gracey's forces now total 22,190 troops (French have 4,575 troops in FIC).** |
| | Brigadier Rodiam ordered to control Xuân Lộc area (NW Saigon) and arrange for a separate force to operate against the Việt Minh, with a British officer commanding. Major L.D. Gates of 14/13 FFR is selected; force is designated GATEFORCE and comprises Indian infantry, artillery and armored cars, together with a Japanese infantry battalion. |
| 29 | GATEFORCE begins operations, with Gates ordered to establish a base at Xuân Lộc, the main objective being to force the Việt Minh to move away from Saigon. Force arrives outside Xuân Lộc by late evening, but strategic considerations require another force to occupy Trảng Bom, protecting GATEFORCE's line of retreat. |
| 30 | Trảng Bom occupied and GATEFORCE in action at dawn, forcing Việt Minh to withdraw and entering Xuân Lộc. Patrols commence with armored cars. |
| 31 | Việt Minh force attacked near Xuân Lộc. 250 Việt Minh are killed in this 2-day operation, incapacitating Việt Minh organization in that area for a number of years. |
| | (Although involved in sporadic fighting in and around Saigon during November, by the beginning of December Gracey's men had forced the Việt Minh to move far enough from Saigon to allow Gracey to begin replacing the men of 32nd Brigade, who had been policing the northern suburbs, with French troops, prior to returning responsibility for South Vietnam to the French. The activities of GATEFORCE, the Japanese and the French resulted in widespread destruction of Việt Minh forces below the 16th Parallel and largely prevented their resumption of guerrilla activities in that region for a long period.) |

*November*

| | |
|---|---|
| | British are still committed to pacifying areas where Japanese troops are to be concentrated and disarmed, although, during November, the emphasis moves from peacekeeping (which becomes the French role) to disarming and repatriating Japanese forces. |
| | British are intent upon maintaining a high profile in the areas they control, so as to encourage a return to normality. |
| 8 | Combined British, French and Japanese forces sweep Ben Cat area (northwest of Thủ Dầu Một). |
| 18 | Long Kien operation begins, but British are forced to withdraw due to having insufficient forces. |
| 19 | Meeting in Saigon between British and Japanese staffs to discuss Japanese role in fomenting unrest in Java. |
| 22 | New assault on Long Kien, this time with two full companies from 3/1 GR and a troop of guns from 114 Field Regiment, RA. |
| | Life in Saigon now returning to normal as the French administration is reinstated. |
| 23 | Establishment of military control by French begins, with relief of British (9/12 FFR) |

in Cholon. 9/12 FFR now move to Cap St. Jacques to receive disarmed Japanese. 9/14 Punjab also relieved at Gia Định.
25 Surrender of negotiable South Vietnamese currency by Japanese begins. French also invalidate all 500 piaster notes as legal tender.
28 Large part of 32nd Brigade's sector, north of Saigon, comes under French control. Hanoi-Saigon communications link becomes operational.
In Thủ Đức, 4/10 GR begin to confiscate piasters and drugs (opium).
29 Mountbatten arrives in Saigon.
30 Mountbatten accepts Field-Marshal Terauchi's surrender at a private ceremony in Saigon. Subsequent discussion about future operations in FIC.

## *December*

French begin to assume responsibility for security in more areas, and with disarmament of the Japanese, confiscation of their Vietnamese money and concentration of their personnel in its final stages, the British withdrawal begins. DRV administration in Hanoi is reported as disorganized and failing.

1 Mountbatten leaves Saigon.
7 Meeting in Singapore between Mountbatten, Gracey and Leclerc, with Chief of IGS, Field-Marshal Sir Alan Brooke present (it was during this meeting that Brooke assured Gracey that the proclamation of 19/21 September had been correct).
French informed that 12 Mk VIII Spitfires are to be transferred to French control.
Claim by Việt Minh that Gracey has been assassinated by Indian troops.
9 Initial conference concerning 32nd Brigade's last major operation in Vietnam—an assault on island of Han Phu to be carried out by 4/2 GR and 9/14 Punjab, with battery of 114 FR (RA) in support.
15 Assault on Han Phu, which had been developed into a major Việt Minh guerrilla base. Island cleared, resulting in an immediate decrease in guerrilla activity in suburbs of north Saigon.
Report of political officer (Meiklereid) again emphasizes problems caused by behavior of French troops.
18 9/14 Punjab relieved in Go Vap by French.
19 4/2 GR and 3/8 GR relieved by French.
20 32nd Brigade declared "non-operational," prior to move to Borneo.
Repatriation of Japanese now proceeding.
25 **First contingent of 32nd Brigade (3/8 GR)** leaves Saigon for Borneo on MV *Highland Brigade*.
27 **Second contingent of 32nd Brigade (4/2 GR)** leaves Saigon on SS *Aronda*.
28 Lt. Col. Trevor-Wilson's report received from Hanoi, describing chaotic state of Communist-controlled government in power there.
**Last contingent of 32nd Brigade (9/14 Punjab)** leaves Saigon aboard SS *Lake Charles Victory*, an American "Victory" ship.

## 1946

Official beginning of first Vietnam war, involving the French, with later American assistance. Russia and Communist China provide military aid to Vietnamese, led by Hồ Chí Mính, with the army commanded by General V. N. Giap. The French, with British help, are in control of most of southern Vietnam except for the east coast. Resistance confined to scattered guerrilla units.

## January

1–5   Việt Minh reported to be planning coordinated offensive between 1 and 10 January, so preemptive strike made by British infantry on Việt Minh bases. During this period, patrols report much Việt Minh movement on roads at night, probably due to withdrawal of more numerous Japanese forces.

3   Attack on 14/13 Frontier Rifles at their camp in Biên Hòa. Attack repelled, with 100 Việt Minh dead (British report no losses).

5   32nd Brigade transferred to HQ ALFSEA command.

10   **114th Field Regiment, RA**, leave Vietnam for Malaya.

11   **80th Brigade** relieved by French and stand down.

12   **16th Light Cavalry, except "C" Squadron**, leave Vietnam for Malaya.

21   **80th Brigade embark.**

22   **80th Brigade sail.**

28   Gracey hands over command of French forces to Leclerc.
Main Headquarters, 20th Indian Division, closes and responsibility is transferred.
**Gracey leaves Saigon** after delivering final report: "Notes on Overall Situation in FIC."
British troops no longer involved in fighting. Brigadier Hirst left in command of remaining British troops (two battalions). These are only to be used either against mutinous Japanese or to protect British lives.
**54,000 Japanese are disarmed and concentrated in Cap St. Jacques by the end of January.**

## February

4   Remaining Japanese in Thủ Dầu Một, Biên Hòa and Thủ Đức relieved by Japanese naval personnel under French command and ordered to Cap St. Jacques.

5   4/10 GR (Thủ Dà Một), one company 2/8 Punjab (Tan Son Nhut airfield) and one Jat MG company at the Phu Tho petrol depot relieved by French.

8   **100th Brigade and its HQ embark** SS *Cameronia*, leaving behind 2/8 Punjab and 9/12 FFR.

10   French assume control of Cap St. Jacques.

15   Japanese relieved in Xuân Lộc.
RAF HQ, FIC, declared "non-operational."

## March

4   French assume full control of southern FIC at midnight (4/5).

15   French assume complete responsibility for Japanese administration.

18   Parade in Saigon held to mark termination of stay of British forces in FIC.

29   2/8 Punjab, without "B" Company, embark SS *Islami*, which then moves to Cap St. Jacques to collect 9/12 FFR.

30   SS *Islami* sails for India with 2/8 Punjab and 9/12 FFR aboard.

## May

14   Interservice Mission declared non-operational.

15   **Last British troops leave Saigon ("B" Company, 2/8 Punjab).**

## France's Vietnam War (1946–1954)

### 1945

*October*

- 5  **General Philippe Leclerc and first contingent of French troops arrive in Saigon.**
- 15  Heavy fighting still continues. Gen. Leclerc flies to Phnom Penh (Cambodia) and arrests pro–Japanese prime minister. Extremists are then rounded up and situation in Cambodia becomes settled.
- 24  Operation "Moussac"—plan for French to break out of Saigon and occupy Mỹ Tho—begins. First operation in French attempt to reoccupy FIC.

*November*

- 8  Combined British, French and Japanese forces sweep Ben Cat area (northwest of Thủ Dầu Một).

*December*

French begin to assume responsibility for security in more areas, and with disarmament of the Japanese, confiscation of their Vietnamese money and concentration of their personnel in its final stages, the British withdrawal begins. DRV administration in Hanoi is reported as disorganized and failing.

### 1946

Beginning of first Vietnam war, involving the French, with later American assistance. Russia and Communist China provide military aid to Vietnamese, led by Hồ Chí Mính, with the army commanded by General V. N. Giap. Leclerc relieved of command of CEFEO, being replaced by General J.E. Valluy.

*January*

- 28  Gracey hands over command of French forces to Leclerc.
  **Gracey leaves Saigon. British troops no longer involved in fighting.**

*May*

- 15  **Last British troops leave Saigon.**

*November*

- 23  French fleet bombards Haiphong. Việt Minh later attack city.

*December*

French and Việt Minh engaged in fighting in Hanoi. Việt Minh evacuate but continue guerrilla campaign. The French now appear to be in control everywhere, but control continues only as long as troops are present.
**Vietnam recognized as "free state" within French Union (Fourth Republic).**

### 1947

British troops deployed in India and Palestine.

General Giap moves his base to Tan Trao, which French later attack without success. Guerrilla war continues, and later in 1947 the French launch Operation "Lea." French begin negotiations to allow Bảo Đại to return as emperor. Bảo Đại proves uncooperative, and although he remains as puppet emperor, French appoint General Nguyễn Văn Xuân as prime minister.

### March

12  "Truman Doctrine" approved by U.S. Congress. (Marshall Plan in place later in same year.)

### April

**Operation "Papillon":** *aim*—air and ground assault on Việt Minh in Hoa Binh province.

### September

Bollaert, French High Commissioner to Vietnam, suggests a return to a "self-governing" Vietnam, but with France controlling its defense and diplomacy.

### October

Beginning of Cao Bang campaign.
7  Beginning of **Operation "Lea"** (ending 22 December): *aim*—capture of city of Bac Can, Hồ Chí Mính and his staff.

### November

20  **Operation "Ceinture":** *aim*—anti-infiltration campaign against Việt Minh.
29  My Trach Massacre occurs.

## 1948

**UK: India** (1945–1948). Partition begins.
**Palestine** (1945–1948).
**Malaya** (1948–1966).

### June

5  Halong Bay agreements between France and government of South Vietnam result in formation of State of Vietnam. Participants agree to partial autonomy of country as an associated state within the French Union (Fourth Republic).

## 1949

**Europe (Cold War)** (1949–1989).
United States recognizes South Vietnam and begins to supply French with military aid.
China becomes Communist under Mao Zedong and the supply of weapons to North Vietnamese forces is hugely increased. This growth in support allows Giap to reorganize his forces into conventional infantry battalions—five in all. Giap then takes the offensive.
France officially recognizes South Vietnam, although the country is still effectively

under French control. Later in 1949, South Vietnam government allowed to form Vietnamese National Army (VNA). French use VNA, Cao Đài, Hòa Hảo and Bình Xuyên for routine patrol and enforcement role.

**Élysée Accords** (intended to signify greater independence of Vietnam from France, resulting in United States supporting Bảo Đại).

Laos and Cambodia also granted independence within the French Union.

## 1950

**Korean war begins** (1950–1953).
United States continues to provide military and economic aid to French in Indochina.
Britain joins United States in supporting French-sponsored government of Emperor Bảo Đại. American MAAG advisers begin to be sent to Vietnam.

### *January*

14  Hồ Chí Mính declares Democratic Republic of Vietnam is the only legal government of Vietnam, recognized by the Soviet Union and China.

### *June*

14  Recognition of Bảo Đại's regime by United States and establishment of U.S. embassy in Saigon.

### *September*

Military operations by Việt Minh result in capture of Đông Khê in September, followed in rapid succession by Cao Bang, Lang Son, Lao Kay and finally Thai Ngu Yen. North Vietnamese army pushes French back to Red River Delta, where new French commander, J. M. de Lattre de Tassigny, builds a fortified line, "de Lattre line," that temporarily holds up the Việt Minh.

## 1951

**UK: Suez** (1951–1954).
**Vietnam:** Increasing opposition to war in Indochina in France.

### *January*

13  Việt Minh defeated at battle of Vinh Yen.

### *March*

23  Việt Minh defeated at Mao Khe.

### *May*

29  Việt Minh defeated again at Phu Ly. De Lattre organizes successful counterattack. Việt Minh casualties for whole period come to over 30,000 dead and wounded.

### *July*

31  French General Chanson assassinated at Sa Dec, South Vietnam.

### *October*

15  **Conservative government elected with Winston Churchill as prime minister.**

## November

14   French occupy Hòa Bình, thereby expanding their perimeter westward.

## 1952

**UK: Kenya** (1952–1960). Operations against Mau-Mau.

## January

25   Việt Minh force French out of Hòa Bình and back to their 1951 positions. Việt Minh concentrate on attacking French supply lines.

## October

Việt Minh attack garrisons north of de Lattre line. French launch counteroffensive, Operation "Lorraine," aimed at drawing out Việt Minh forces and decimating them in conditions that would favor the French. Việt Minh refuse to respond as expected and the French retreat, leaving the Việt Minh logistical network intact.

## November

4   Eisenhower elected U.S. president.

## 1953

**Korean War ends.**
France grants Laos independence, and hopes for negotiated settlement in Vietnam. Ho claims to be ready to discuss peace terms. French occupy Dien Bien Phu.

## 1954

## May

7   French defeated by Việt Minh at Dien Bien Phu after a 55-day siege. The defeat signals an end to the French presence in Indochina.

## June

Pierre Mendès France forms new government in France and immediately opens negotiations with Hồ Chí Mính.
Ngô Đình Diệm appointed prime minister of South Vietnam.

## July

**End of first Vietnam war.**
At Geneva Conference, agreement reached to split country at 17th Parallel into Communist North (Democratic Republic of Vietnam), administered by Hồ Chí Mính, and anti–Communist South (State of Vietnam, or South Vietnam), under control of Bảo Đại, with Diệm as prime minister. Both countries are to have separate, but temporary, governments, because the agreement includes plans to hold a reunification election in two years.

## October

9   French leave Hanoi. Thousands of ordinary Vietnamese also leave Hanoi, after the return of the Communists, under America's "Passage to Freedom" initiative (estimates of those leaving—between 600,000 and one million people).

# America's Vietnam War (1955–1975)

## 1955

**UK: Sir Anthony Eden elected prime minister (Conservative).**
**Cyprus** (1955–1959).
**Aden** (1955–1967).
Diệm's cooperation allows United States to begin directly aiding the South Vietnamese government and training the South Vietnamese army. United States said to have blocked reunification elections, because of fears that Ho would win by large margin.
Ho introduces ill-considered land reform in North Vietnam.
American advisers from MAAG begin to operate with ARVN (South Vietnamese Army).

### April

27–28    **Beginning of "Battle of Saigon."** Diệm destroys power of Bình Xuyên.

### July

16    Diệm rejects reunification elections, a decision backed by United States. He removes Bảo Đại and assumes control of government of South Vietnam as president.

### October

6    Election date announced: 23 October.
23    Diệm wins election (almost certainly by illegal methods).
26    Diệm announces formation of Republic of Vietnam.

## 1956

### November

**UK: Suez crisis** (Operation "Musketeer").
Americans force withdrawal of British forces via UN, causing deterioration in Anglo-American relations.
Diệm begins purge of Việt Minh (Việt Cộng) and other dissidents.

## 1957

**UK:** Eden resigns on health grounds.
**Harold Macmillan becomes prime minister (Conservative).**

### January

Soviet Union proposes North and South Vietnam enter UN as separate states.

### September

South Vietnam's President Ngô Đình Diệm visits Australia. Menzies government reaffirms support.

### October

Communist insurgent activity begins in South Vietnam.

## 1958

Communists form coordinated command structure in Mekong Delta.
Anti-Communist government in Laos.

## 1959

**UK: Cyprus Emergency ends.**

*May*

North Vietnam forms Group 559, which begins moving weapons and men along the Hồ Chí Minh Trail.

*July*

Group 759 (North Vietnam) begins similar operation sending supplies south by sea.

*August*

Diệm introduces legislation to repress Communists and other dissidents.

*September*

Group 959 (North Vietnam) formed to supply Communists in Laos.

## 1960

*April*

North Vietnam imposes universal military conscription.
Coup d'état in Laos.

*November*

8   **John F. Kennedy elected U.S. president.**
11   South Vietnam army group attempts to remove Diệm from office in a coup led by Lt. Col. Vương Văn Đông.

*December*

    Laos attacks Vietnam.
20   Hanoi leaders form National Liberation Front for South Vietnam, which Saigon regime dubs **"Việt Cộng"** (meaning Communist Vietnamese).
    Diệm's future considered uncertain by many in White House.

## 1961

**700 U.S. advisers in Vietnam by end of 1961.**
**UK:** Macmillan agrees to the formation of British Advisory Mission (BRIAM), headed by Robert Thompson.
South Vietnamese begin using facilities at Jungle Warfare School, Johore, Malaysia.

*March*

Kennedy supports Laos, and Britain and Soviet Union suggest another international conference to resolve crisis.

*April*

        **Bay of Pigs.**

*May*

        Vice President Johnson visits South Vietnam and proposes more aid to Diệm regime. Geneva conference on Laos opens and eventually decides upon creation of neutral coalition in that country. Kennedy however, rejects neutrality for South Vietnam, even though Hanoi is prepared to accept it.

*October*

        Kennedy decides to send more equipment and advisers to South Vietnam.

*November*

    17    U.S. government seeks an indication through diplomatic channels of Australia's willingness to assist in Vietnam.
        "Strategic Hamlet" program promoted by U.S. and South Vietnam governments.

## 1962

**12,000 U.S. advisers in Vietnam by end of 1962.**
**UK: Borneo** (1962–1966). British operations begin in Brunei, prior to Indonesia Confrontation (1962–1966).

*February*

    8    U.S. Military Assistance Command, Vietnam (MACV), created to coordinate military aid being sent to South Vietnam.
    27    Diệm's palace bombed by South Vietnamese pilots.

*May*

        Communists begin to form battalion-size units in Central Vietnam.
    24    Australia's minister for defense, Athol Townley, announces 30 military advisers will be sent to Vietnam.

*June*

        **American advisers increased from 700 to 12,000.**
        **Implementation of "Strategic Hamlets" program begins.**

*July*

    31    First members of AATTV (Australian Army Training Team Vietnam) arrive in Saigon.

## 1963

**16,000 U.S. military advisers serving in Vietnam.**
**South Vietnam receives $500 million in U.S. aid.**

*January*

    2    **Battle of Ap Bac.** Việt Cộng defeat South Vietnamese army.

*May*

8     South Vietnamese army fires on Buddhist festival, killing nine civilians.
       More Australian advisers sent to Vietnam, in an initial group of 200.

*June*

1     An adviser, William Francis Hacking, becomes first Australian to die in Vietnam.
11     First occurrence of self-immolation (death by burning) by Buddhist monk.

*July*

4     United States learns of army plot to remove Diệm and agrees to support the plotters.

*October*

18     **Sir Alec Douglas-Home elected British prime minister (Conservative).**

*November*

1     South Vietnam's President Diệm and his brother Ngô Đình Nhu murdered in military coup (of which U.S. government had advance knowledge). South Vietnam now governed by military revolutionary council, headed by Dương Văn Minh.
       **North Vietnam increases level of fighting in south.**
22     **President John F. Kennedy assassinated in Dallas, Texas.**
       Lyndon Johnson becomes U.S. president after Kennedy's assassination and immediately announces United States will continue support for South Vietnam.

*May*

Crown airfield project reconnaissance begins in Leong Nok Tha district (Thailand).

*November*

Construction begins on Crown airfield.

# 1964

Americans begin using Jungle Warfare School for tactical training.
North Vietnamese start modernizing the old Hồ Chí Minh Trail.
New Zealand begins to send advisers to South Vietnam.

*January*

30     General Nguyễn Khánh seizes power in Saigon (South Vietnam).

*March*

United States offers support for Khánh.

*June*

Australian Prime Minister Menzies visits Washington, where talks center on Vietnam.

*August*

2     Attack on U.S. ships in Tonkin Gulf (Gulf of Tonkin Incident).
       United States begins bombing of North Vietnam.
7     **Gulf of Tonkin Resolution approved by U.S. Congress.** This legislation allows

Johnson to conduct the war in Southeast Asia, authorizing spending, military operations, and so on, without the agreement of Congress.
25  General Maxwell Taylor appointed U.S. ambassador to South Vietnam.

## *September*

"Sigma II" simulation shows futility of bombing campaign directed at North Vietnam.
13  Coup attempt in Saigon defeated by Nguyễn Cao Kỳ's threat to bomb the organizers.

## *October*

15  UK: Harold Wilson elected British Prime Minister (Labour)—4-seat majority.
30  Việt Cộng attack Biên Hòa air base. Johnson rejects retaliation.

## *November*

3  Johnson wins presidential election with biggest majority since 1820.
10  Australian government introduces barrel lottery conscription for two years of national service. Opposition to the war in Vietnam is not accepted as reason for exemption.

## *December*

**Johnson requests Black Watch regiment for service in Vietnam.**
20  President Quat and the prime minister, Tran Van Huong, deposed in coup by Khánh and Kỳ.
25  Việt Cộng bomb Brinks hotel in Saigon, which was being used to billet U.S. officers. Johnson again rejects retaliation.

## 1965

**200,000 U.S. troops deployed in Vietnam by end of year.**
Sir Robert Thompson, marginalized in both Washington and Saigon, resigns from BRIAM, and its operations are transferred to MACV.
**Saunders-Roe supplies seven SR.N5 hovercraft hulls to Bell Aerosystems for evaluation.**

## *February*

7  Việt Cộng attack U.S. installations. Johnson authorizes retaliation: Operations "Flaming Dart I" and "Flaming Dart II."
16  Khánh expelled from office in another coup and leaves Saigon for good.
18  Dr. Phan Huy Quat forms new Saigon government.

## *March*

2  Operation "Rolling Thunder" begins (extensive bombing of North Vietnam that lasts 44 months).
8  First U.S. combat troops come ashore at Danang, their role being to protect U.S. air bases.
William Fulbright warns against Vietnam involvement for the first time.

## *April*

7  **Johnson suggests peace plan.**
8  **Hanoi rejects Johnson peace plan.**

| | |
|---|---|
| 29 | Menzies government in Australia announces that combat troops will go to Vietnam; the 1st Infantry Battalion leaves in June. In September, the Morgan Gallup Poll in Australia finds 56 percent of those polled were in favor of continuing the war in Vietnam. A demonstration against the war in Sydney, held on October 22, results in 65 arrests. |

*May*

New series of Việt Cộng attacks.

*June*

U.S. troops in combat on routine basis, and a second draft of 40,000 troops is sent to Saigon.
**80,000 U.S. troops now in Vietnam.**
At the Commonwealth Conference, Wilson suggests that Commonwealth leaders should visit the capitals of all countries concerned in the war, to see whether a basis for a peaceful solution in Vietnam exists.
Australia deploys 1st Battalion Royal Australian Regiment to Vietnam.

| | |
|---|---|
| 11 | Nguyễn Cao Kỳ installed as prime minister, with General Nguyễn Văn Thiệu as head of state, removing previous civilian administration. |
| 26 | Việt Cộng attacks cause large South Vietnam troop losses. |

*July*

Hanoi rejects Commonwealth peace mission. Hồ Chí Minh quoted by *Daily Worker* as saying: "Mr. Wilson has not correctly carried out his obligations as co-chairman of the 1954 Geneva conference to Vietnam. He has tried to support U.S. imperialist aggression in Vietnam. He cannot engage in peace negotiations since he himself supported the U.S. policy of aggression and expansion of the war."

| | |
|---|---|
| 28 | Johnson approves Westmoreland's request for an additional 44 combat battalions in Vietnam, adding to the 18 already deployed. Americans attempt to coerce United Kingdom into giving them military aid in Vietnam, with McGeorge Bundy telling Johnson it makes "no sense whatsoever for us to rescue the pound in a situation in which there is no British flag in Vietnam." |

*September*

Chinese government states it will not intervene in Vietnam.

*October*

**Battle of La Drang Valley.** U.S. victory.

*December*

McNamara sent to Vietnam to report on conditions. On his return, McNamara reports that chances of complete victory are remote.
Wilson visits Washington.
**Johnson suspends bombing to induce Communists to negotiate.**

# 1966

**400,000 U.S. troops deployed by the end of the year.**

Indonesian Confrontation (Malaya) ends with death of President Sukarno after army coup led by General Suharto.

## January

**Johnson orders resumption of bombing campaign against North Vietnam.**
26   Harold Holt succeeds Menzies as Australian prime minister.

## February

8   Johnson and South Vietnam's leaders call for "pacification" in Vietnam.

## March

8   Australian Prime Minister Holt announces that the commitment of troops to Vietnam will be stepped up and will include conscripts.
10   Buddhist demonstrations in Hue and Danang.
Wilson calls general election.
31   **Harold Wilson elected prime minister:** Labour win with 96-seat majority.

## April

Britain and America sign contract for F-111 fighter, which includes the "off-set" agreement.

## May

17   **Wilson issues first statement about arms supply to the United States in the House of Commons:** "We are not supplying arms directly or indirectly for the fighting in Vietnam."
23   South Vietnamese troops take over Danang.

## June

1st Battalion RAR return to Australia. Its role in Vietnam is taken over by 1st Australian Task Force, which serves in Phuoc Tuy Province from June 1966 to December 1971.
16   South Vietnamese troops occupy Hue.
27   Healey proposes new definition of "arms" at meeting of Defence and Overseas Policy Committee.
29   U.S. aircraft bomb oil depots near Hanoi and Haiphong.
Wilson issues statement criticizing U.S. bombing operation.
30   Australian Prime Minister Holt pledges to go "all the way with LBJ."

## August

RFA *Tidespring* involved in RAS with USS *Coral Sea*.
8   Training for U.S. Combat Tracker teams at Jungle Warfare School agreed by Wilson.

## September

De Gaulle visits Cambodia, calling for U.S. withdrawal from Vietnam.

## October

McNamara returns to South Vietnam and devises a plan based on negotiation, while a second group based in the White House and Pentagon favors a more belligerent approach.

## November

17  Rolls-Royce and Allison sign agreement for building Spey engines.
19  Morgan Gallup Poll in Australia finds that 63 percent favor conscription, but only 37 percent favor sending national servicemen ("nashos") to Vietnam.

## 1967

**United States drops 800,000 tons of bombs on Vietnam throughout the year.**
**500,000 U.S. troops deployed by end of year.**
**Total American casualties by end of 1967: 9,000.**
Westmoreland's assessment: "Another 200,000 men to finish war in 2 years."
British leave Aden.

## January

USAF signs contract with Allison for its version of the Rolls-Royce Spey engine.
28  North Vietnamese foreign minister, N.D. Trinh, says United States must stop bombing before talks can begin.

## February

Harold Wilson and Alexei Kosygin attempt to organize peace talks, without success.
2  Meeting of British government's Committee for Strategic Exports introduces "Jay" rule, authorizing sale of military equipment if it is not due to be delivered before 1 January 1968.

## March

**North Vietnamese reveal exchange of letters between Johnson and Hồ Chí Mính.**

## May

Morgan Gallup Poll finds 62 percent of Australians favor continuing the war in Vietnam.

## June

12  British government's Committee for Strategic Exports abandons "Jay" rule as unworkable and generates list of "Sensitive" arms not to be sold to United States without ministerial approval.

## July

Denis Healey announces that Britain will give up the "East of Suez" bases.

## September

U.S. Secretary of Defense McNamara tells Senate sub-committee that bombing is ineffective.
3  Thiệu elected president of South Vietnam, with Kỳ as vice president, forming a regime that will last until 1973.
Việt Cộng start another major campaign. Fortification of Khe Sanh begins.

| | |
|---|---|
| 13 | U.S. House of Representatives passes bill prohibiting the purchase of warships built in foreign shipyards. |
| 29 | Johnson, in a speech in San Antonio, Texas, says he will stop bombing in exchange for "productive discussions." |

**Anti-war protests increase.**

## October

RAAF begins campaign to recruit British officers.

## November

**Australian army begins campaign to recruit 250 British officers.**

| | |
|---|---|
| 12 | Australian Premier Harold Holt drowns. |
| 18 | **Britain devalues pound by 14.3 percent.** **Exchange rate: £1.00 = $2.40.** |

## December

| | |
|---|---|
| 29 | Trinh: "Talks will begin with cessation of bombing." |

# 1968

**536,000 U.S. troops deployed to South Vietnam.**
**14,592 killed in action (KIA) this year.**
**UK:** Foreign and Commonwealth Office (FCO) formed by merger of the Commonwealth Office (created: 1966) and Foreign Office (created: March 1782).
Issue of DCI concerning involvement of British service personnel visiting South Vietnam.

## January

United States receives permission to pursue Việt Cộng into Cambodia.
**Wilson announces withdrawal from "East of Suez" bases by 1971 and cancellation of the F-111K purchase.**

| | |
|---|---|
| 10 | John Grey Gorton sworn in as prime minister of Australia. |
| 23 | USS *Pueblo* (ELINT and SIGINT ship) captured by North Korea. |
| 31 | **Tet Offensive** begins as Việt Cộng and North Vietnamese troops attack South Vietnamese cities and towns. Despite huge losses, Tet proves a propaganda coup for the Việt Cộng and a turning point in the war. |

## February

206,000 more troops requested; request subsequently rejected.
McNamara sacked and subsequently joins World Bank. Clark Clifford replaces McNamara as secretary of defense and produces a document whose conclusions parallel Nixon's later "Americanization" program.

| | |
|---|---|
| 12 | Gorton indicates that Australia will not increase its commitment to Vietnam, and the National Service Act is amended to impose a two-year civil jail term for draft evaders. |
| 25 | U.S. and South Vietnamese troops capture Hue. |

## March

| | |
|---|---|
| 16 | **Robert Kennedy announces presidential candidacy.** |

Massacre of civilians by U.S. soldiers at My Lai village; at least 450 unarmed Vietnamese are killed.
25 Johnson advised against escalation.
31 **Johnson announces partial bombing halt, offers talks, and states he will not run for reelection.**

*May*

10 Paris peace talks begin.

*June*

5 Robert Kennedy assassinated.

*October*

Opinion in United States turns massively toward a compromise with the Việt Cộng.
31 Johnson halts bombing.

*November*

2 Termination of bombing campaign, "Rolling Thunder," during which American air craft dropped an estimated 864,000 tons of bombs, at a cost of $900 million in aircraft lost alone. Adding the cost of ordnance and other consumables brings the total close to $3 billion dollars, or "ten dollars for every dollar's worth of damage."
5 **Richard Nixon elected U.S. president, with Spiro Agnew as vice-president.** His platform: **"end the war and win the peace."**

*December*

Royal Naval Dockyard, Singapore, handed over to Singapore government. Company operating dockyard tenders for contract to repair U.S. warships.
2 Kissinger appointed national security adviser.
4 **United States suggests purchase of Hawker Siddeley Harrier V/STOL jet from Britain for U.S. Marine Corps. British government agrees to order, then valued at £80 million.**

## 1969

**500,000 U.S. troops deployed.**

*January*

Paris talks expanded to include South Vietnamese government and Việt Cộng.

*March*

18 Secret bombing of Việt Cộng bases in Cambodia (Operation "Menu") begins on Nixon's orders and continues until May 1970.

*May*

14 Nixon proposes simultaneous withdrawal of United States and Việt Cộng from South Vietnam.
Story about Cambodian bombing appears in *New York Times*.

*June*

8 Nixon announces withdrawal of 25,000 U.S. troops.
10 General Creighton Abrams replaces Westmoreland.

## July

Nixon's ultimatum referring to "measures of great consequence" to be employed against Việt Cộng if they do not begin negotiations.

## August

Secret meeting between Kissinger and North Vietnamese negotiator, Xuan Thuy. Morgan Gallup Poll finds 55 percent of Australians want troops brought home from Vietnam.

## September

Nixon orders further troop withdrawals and a reduction in draft requirements.

**3 Hồ Chí Mính dies in Hanoi, aged 79.**

## October

4   Gallup Poll finds that 58 percent of Americans believe the war in Vietnam was a mistake.

15   Major anti-war demonstration in Washington.

## November

15   2 major anti-war demonstrations.

16   My Lai massacre revealed.

## December

**22   Press release details sale of Harrier V/STOL jets to United States; expected delivery date—January 1971.**

# 1970

**280,000 U.S. troops deployed in Vietnam.**

## February

21   Kissinger in secret talks with Le Duc Tho, representative of North Vietnamese government, without participation of Việt Cộng or Saigon government.

## March

25   Nixon orders Kissinger to devise a plan to aid Cambodian government.

## April

14   Cambodian Prime Minister Lon Nol appeals for help to the world community. By this time, American-trained Cambodian troops and equipment are already arriving in the capital, Phnom Penh.

**22   Australian government announces that a battalion will be withdrawn from Vietnam.**

30   Nixon reveals that U.S. troops are about to attack Việt Cộng bases in Cambodia.

## May

4   As large anti-war demonstrations spread across the United States, National Guardsmen kill four students at Kent State University in Ohio.

| | |
|---|---|
| 8 | Approximately 120,000 people throughout Australia demonstrate for an end to the war. The biggest of the moratorium marches is in Melbourne, where 70,000 people occupy the streets. |

*June*

| | |
|---|---|
| 18 | **Edward Heath elected British prime minister (Conservative).** |

*September*

| | |
|---|---|
| 18 | Approximately 100,000 people in Australia take part in a second moratorium. |

*October*

**U.S. KIAs only 24 this month, lowest since October 1965.**

| | |
|---|---|
| 7 | Nixon proposes "standstill" ceasefire. |

## 1971

**140,000 U.S. troops deployed.** This decrease from 1970 was due to draftees finishing their one-year tour and returning home, without new troops being sent to replace them.

*February*

South Vietnamese forces attack Hồ Chí Minh Trail from Laos, in Operation "Lamson 719."

*March*

| | |
|---|---|
| 10 | **Australia:** William McMahon replaces Gorton as Liberal leader and prime minister. |

*June*

Pentagon Papers published.

| | |
|---|---|
| 30 | Third and last of the big Australian anti-war rallies, with approximately 110,000 demonstrating in state capitals. |

*August*

| | |
|---|---|
| 18 | McMahon announces that most Australian troops will be home by Christmas. |

*October*

| | |
|---|---|
| 3 | Nguyễn Văn Thiệu reelected as South Vietnamese president. |

*December*

| | |
|---|---|
| 8 | Last Australian troops leave Vietnam—4th Battalion Royal Australian Regiment. "D" Company, 4th Battalion Royal Australian Regiment, remains until 12 March 1972 to provide security. |

## 1972

**100,000 American troops remaining in Vietnam.**

*January*

| | |
|---|---|
| 25 | Nixon reveals Kissinger's secret negotiations with North Vietnamese. |

*February*

21    Nixon flies to China for talks with its leaders.

*March*

12    "D" Company, 4th Battalion Royal Australian Regiment, leaves Vietnam.
30    New series of Communist attacks begins against South Vietnam, starting with North Vietnamese offensive across De-Militarized Zone (DMZ).
31    Nixon orders air raids against North Vietnamese targets, including Hanoi.

*April*

15    Nixon authorizes bombing near Hanoi and Haiphong.
20    Kissinger arrives in Moscow to arrange arms talks.

*May*

1    North Vietnamese capture Quang Tri.
5    Bombing of North Vietnam intensified.

*June*

17    **Watergate arrests.**

*August–October*

Kissinger in peace negotiations. South Vietnamese opposed.

*October*

8    Le Duc Tho offers new proposal, which he claims is "very simple and realistic." United States begins final negotiations on the basis of this proposal, without reference to objections from Saigon.
21    North Vietnamese approve draft agreement.

*November*

7    **Nixon reelected.**
20    Kissinger resumes peace talks.

*December*

2    Australian Labour Party elected to government.
5    Conscription in Australia ends. Draft resisters released from jail and pending prosecutions for draft resistance dropped.

18    Nixon orders renewed bombing of Hanoi-Haiphong area (Operation "Linebacker Two"), saying "U.S. will bomb North Vietnam to the peace table."

# 1973

*January*

3    Peace talks resume in Paris.
23    Nixon announces agreement has been reached for "peace with honor."
27    Cease-fire begins.

*February*

26   Australian Prime Minister Gough Whitlam announces establishment of diplomatic relations with Hanoi, but reiterates his government's recognition of South Vietnam's government on 29 March.

*March*

29   Last U.S. troops leave Vietnam.

*October*

Edward Heath places arms embargo on both sides in Yom Kippur war. This has most effect on the Israelis, America's most important allies in the region, as it prevents them from obtaining spare parts for their Centurion tanks.

## 1974

*January*

4   South Vietnam President Nguyễn Văn Thiệu declares that war has begun again.

*February*

28   **UK: Harold Wilson elected British prime minister.**

## 1975

*April*

17   In Cambodia, Phnom Penh falls to Khmer Rouge.
25   [**Anzac day**]: Australia closes its embassy in Saigon, completing withdrawal from Vietnam.
30   Communist forces capture Saigon as the last Americans leave in scenes of panic and confusion.

# Appendix II

# People and Organizations Associated with Vietnam: 1945–1975

## *British*

### ATTLEE, CLEMENT
(Prime Minister of Britain, 1945–1951)

Clement Attlee first came to prominence as deputy prime minister serving under Winston Churchill in Britain's wartime coalition government, while also acting as leader of the Labour Party. In 1945, Labour won the general election by a substantial majority, and Attlee embarked upon a policy entailing a huge number of social reforms that formed the basis for the considerable improvement in living conditions which British citizens enjoyed in the postwar years. The National Health Service and sickness, unemployment and child benefits were all introduced by Attlee's government. Pensions were increased to give recipients a reasonable income, an enormous program of public-sector house building was begun, and many core industries such as steel, electricity, gas, mining and transportation (including road transportation and the railways) were nationalized, on the principle that such monopolies would lead to more efficient use of physical and financial resources.

### CHURCHILL, SIR WINSTON
(Prime Minister of Britain, 1940–1945 and 1951–1955)

Winston Churchill's war service is too well publicized to need reiterating, but, in some ways, his most valuable contributions were the agreements he orchestrated between the Allied leaders, which determined much that happened after the war. These included the "Percentages Agreement" with Russia over the Balkans and the various boundary provisions that emerged from the 1945 Potsdam Conference.

Although Churchill is often perceived as the most exemplary of wartime leaders, this view was not held by many of his senior contemporaries, particularly those in the military. Of all his associates during those days, perhaps the one best placed to summarize Churchill's contradictory motivations and flawed character was the man most closely associated with him, Field-Marshal Alan Brooke, chief of the Imperial General Staff from December 1941 to 1946. Brooke's diary entry for 10 September 1944 is particularly revealing:

And the wonderful thing is that ¾ of the population of the world imagine that Churchill is one of the Strategists of History, a second Marlborough, and the other ¼ have no idea what a public menace he is and has been throughout this war! It is far better that the world should never know, and never suspect the feet of clay of this otherwise superhuman being. Without him England was lost for a certainty, with him England has been on the verge of disaster time and again.... Never have I admired and despised a man simultaneously to the same extent. Never have such opposite extremes been combined in the same human being.

Having served six years as leader of the opposition, Churchill was elected prime minister once again in October 1951 and also held the post of minister of defence between October 1951 and January 1952. Attlee's program of social reform was continued during Churchill's term of office, albeit on a significantly reduced scale.

Reforms during his party's time in government included legislation to limit the employment of women and young persons in mines and quarries (Mines and Quarries Act, 1954) and a new Housing Act, specifying a minimum level of repair below which housing became "unfit for human habitation" (Housing Repairs and Rent Act, 1955). The threshold for taxable income was also raised, pensions and national insurance benefits increased and the program for the construction of council housing accelerated (this last being the responsibility of Harold Macmillan, then minister of housing).

## The "Special Relationship"

Much has been written by commentators on both sides of the Atlantic about the "special relationship" between Britain and America, ever since Churchill coined the phrase for his "Sinews of Peace" address in 1946. Depending upon the nature of the leaders then in power and their relationship, it has been a more or less useful association for both countries, but perhaps the most honest appraisal came from President Truman's secretary of state, Dean Acheson, when he said, "Of course a unique relation existed between Britain and America—our common language and history ensured that. But unique did not mean affectionate. We had fought England as an enemy as often as we had fought by her side as an ally."

### Colombo Plan

Proposed by the Indian ambassador to China, Mr. K.M. Panikkar, in 1949, this plan was intended to be a multilateral fund, financed by America, Britain, and Australia (among others), to help countries in Southeast Asia resist Communist influence. Its most singular feature lay in providing not just financial aid and technology but also training programs to parallel the improvements in infrastructure and so allow a country's residents to manage their improved facilities. Britain was a founding member in 1951, until its resignation in 1991.

### Douglas-Home, Sir Alex
(Prime Minister of Britain, 1963–1964)

Appointed foreign secretary in 1960, Sir Alex Douglas-Home strongly supported Kennedy in his stance during the Cuban Missile Crisis. Prime Minister Macmillan was taken ill in October 1963, just before the Conservative Party Conference, and after some behind-the-scenes manipulation, Douglas-Home was appointed prime minister on 19 October 1963. He was not a popular choice with his own party, but during his term of office Britain experienced a period of economic prosperity, with an increase in exports and the economy growing by 4 percent annually. Only one significant piece of legislation was enacted during his premiership—the abolition of retail price maintenance, denying manufacturers and suppliers the power to fix the prices at which their goods could be sold by a retailer.

Douglas-Home was defeated in the 1964 general election, leaving office on 16 October 1964 and resigning as leader of the Conservative Party on 28 July 1965. He later served as secretary of state in the Foreign and Commonwealth Office from 20 June 1970 to 4 March 1974, during Edward Heath's premiership. Although strongly anti–Communist, he displayed a balanced, practical approach to negotiations with the Soviet Union, and Harold Macmillan wrote of him:

> Lord Home is clearly a man who represents the old governing class at its best…. He is not ambitious in the sense of wanting to scheme for power, although not foolish enough to resist honor when it comes to him…. He gives that impression by a curious mixture of great courtesy, and even if yielding to pressure, with underlying rigidity on matters of principle. It is interesting that he has proved himself so much liked by men like President Kennedy and Mr. Rusk and Mr. Gromyko.

## Eden, Sir Anthony
### (Prime Minister of Britain, 1955–1957)

Upon Churchill's retirement in 1955, he was succeeded in office by Sir Anthony Eden, who had previously served as his foreign secretary. Eden immediately called a general election, which took place on 27 May 1955 and increased the Conservative majority in the House of Commons from 17 to 60. Lacking experience in both domestic and economic affairs, he delegated these matters to better-qualified assistants like R.A.B. Butler and Harold Macmillan, who served as chancellor of the Exchequer. Domestic policy remained largely quiescent during Eden's term of office, and no major changes were made to the process of gradual improvement in living standards that had characterized the regimes of his predecessors. His period in office was dominated by the disaster of the Suez crisis and a consequent deterioration in relations with the Americans.

## Force 136

"Force 136" was the cover name given to a branch of the Special Operations Executive (SOE), especially tasked with conducting covert operations in enemy-occupied territory in Southeast Asia. Headed by Colin Mackenzie, Force 136 carried out insurgency operations in Malaya, China, Thailand and Burma, as well as having some minor involvement in French Indochina.[1]

## Gracey, Major-General D.D.

Commissioned into the Indian Army in 1915, Douglas Gracey fought in France during World War I and in Iraq and Burma during World War II, where he was responsible for raising the 20th Infantry Division. In August 1945, he was appointed Commander, Allied

Land Forces, South-East Asia (ALFSEA), with responsibility for maintaining law and order in the country as well as disarming and repatriating the 70,000 Japanese troops who were still present. Control of the country was returned to the French, in the person of General Philippe Leclerc, on 28 January 1946. Gracey was later appointed commander-in-chief of the Pakistan army in 1948, retiring in 1951. He died in 1964.

Many of his subordinates remarked upon Gracey's concern for his men and his humanity, although American commentators have been quick to condemn him for displaying intolerance and even callousness toward the Vietnamese. It has also been stated that he acted contrary to his orders in declaring martial law in Saigon and its surrounding area on 21 September 1945, although examination of the relevant document shows that this was not the case.[2]

Gracey's concern and respect for his men and his opinion of the French troops who were sent to Indochina in 1945 are made clear in this passage from a letter he sent to General Leclerc on 12 December 1945:

> The camaraderie which exists between officers of the Indian Army and their Gurkha and Indian soldiers must be explained to them [the French troops]. Our men, of whatever color, are our friends and not considered "black" men. They expect and deserve to be treated in every way as first-class soldiers, and their treatment should be, and is, exactly the same as white troops.[3]

His attitude to the Việt Minh may have been less than conciliatory since they were, after all, killing his men, and, moreover, he had been specifically ordered to enter into no political commitments with them that might embarrass the French or, most particularly, his own government. Despite the military necessities of his situation, Gracey was in no doubt as to where the real responsibility for South Vietnam's problems lay, and he was recorded as stating that the situation in Indochina was mostly a result of the French administration's initial intransigience.[4]

## HEALEY, DENIS WINSTON
### (Baron Healey, CH, MBE, PC)
### (Secretary of State for Defence from 1964 until 1970)

Appointed shadow defence secretary after the creation of the position in 1964, Healey became secretary of state for defence when Labour won the 1964 election, serving throughout the period of the Wilson government. He cut defense expenditures, scrapping aircraft carriers, the proposed CVA01 and the reconstructed HMS *Victorious*, the 150 TSR-2 aircraft and, finally, the F-111K "swing-wing" fighter-bomber. In the context of Vietnam, one of his most important contributions was the redefinition of the term "arms," which allowed extensive sales of military equipment to the United States after Wilson had stated that no arms would be sold to countries fighting in Vietnam. Healey also continued the previous government's policy of developing a strategic and tactical nuclear deterrent for the navy, RAF and West Germany. He remained as shadow defence secretary after Labour's defeat in June 1970.

## HEATH, EDWARD
### (Prime Minister of Britain, 1970–1974)

Edward Heath succeeded Harold Wilson as prime minister on 19 June 1970. His term in office included the introduction of decimalization in 1971, major reformation of the UK's system of local government in 1972, membership in the EEC in 1973 and the escalation of violence in Northern Ireland. Most famously, he also attempted to curb the power of trade unions with the Industrial Relations Act of 1971. In addition, he had intended to deregulate the economy and make a transfer from direct to indirect taxation. A rise in unemployment in 1972, however, made necessary a "reinflation" of the economy, resulting in higher inflation and the introduction of a "prices and incomes" policy to control spending.

In 1972, the 1971 Industrial Relations Act resulted, perhaps inevitably, in a confrontation with the NUM (National Union of Mineworkers). The second of the two miner strikes, in 1974, had much more serious consequences, resulting in the implementation of a three-day work week and domestic electricity cuts to conserve energy. Heath was eventually forced to call an election for February 1974 and attempted to win public support for his anti-union legislation with the election slogan "Who governs Britain?" Despite assiduous campaigning, the election resulted in a hung parliament and, following a failed attempt to establish a coalition government with the Liberal Party, Heath was forced to resign as prime minister in favor of Harold Wilson.

## INTERNATIONAL CONTROL COMMISSION FOR VIETNAM

Canada, India and Poland constituted the International Control Commission, which was put in place to monitor the 1954 cease-fire agreement. Officially, Canada did not have partisan involvement in the Vietnam War, and diplomatically it was "non-belligerent." However, several thousand Canadians served with the American forces in Vietnam (estimates range from 3,500 to 30,000 men), including one individual who was awarded the Medal of Honor.

## MACMILLAN, HAROLD
(Prime Minister of Britain, 1957–1963)

Macmillan was appointed prime minister in January 1957, after Eden's resignation in the aftermath of the Suez crisis. Once in office, his major concern in domestic policy was developing a strong economy that would result in high employment. This contrasted with the "monetarist" attitude of many in the Treasury, who took the view that support of sterling required the money supply to be controlled, resulting in an unavoidable rise in unemployment. Macmillan, refusing to be bullied, ignored Treasury advice, later referring to the loss of three of his Treasury ministers who resigned in protest at his stance (including Peter Thornycroft, then chancellor of the Exchequer) as "a little local difficulty."

International trading conditions helped his financial policy, with Britain experiencing a period of affluence, characterized by low unemployment and high (although uneven) growth, with average real pay for industrial workers in 1959 having risen by 20 percent since 1951. Macmillan was not naive enough to expect these favorable conditions to last, however, and issued a warning about the dangers of inflation caused by an unregulated money supply in a speech he gave at Bedford, Bedfordshire, in July 1957.

Under his leadership, the Conservative Party was reelected in 1959 for a second term, with an increased majority (going from 67 to 107 seats). Unfortunately, problems with the balance of payments in 1961 (there was a deficit of £545 million at the end of 1960) led first to a pay freeze and then, in July 1962, to a Cabinet reshuffle, known among Macmillan's contemporaries as the "Night of the Long Knives," because of his perceived betrayal of the Conservative Party. The end of Macmillan's term as prime minister was clouded by the Profumo and Vassal affairs and added to the pressures brought on by his declining health.

During his two terms in office, Macmillan's government was responsible for a number of social reforms, including the 1956 Clean Air Act, the 1957 Housing Act, the 1960 Offices Act, the 1960 Noise Abatement Act, the 1961 Factories Act, the introduction of a graduated pension scheme to provide an additional income for pensioners upon retirement, the establishment of a Child's Special Allowance for the orphaned children of divorced parents, and a reduction in the standard working week from 48 to 42 hours.

## MOUNTBATTEN, LORD LOUIS
### (KG, GCB, OM, GCSI, GCIE, GCVO, DSO, PC, FRS)

Mountbatten began his war service as commander of the 5th Destroyer Flotilla aboard HMS *Kelly*, before being promoted to captain of the aircraft carrier HMS *Illustrious* in August 1941. He was moved again in October 1941, taking over as chief of combined operations, which meant he was responsible for planning and organizing the raid on St. Nazaire and the disastrous attack on Dieppe. In August 1943 Churchill appointed him SAC-SEAC (Supreme Allied Commander, South-East Asia Command).

The SAC-SEAC's role was twofold. Initially, Mountbatten's forces were required to wear down the Japanese, especially the air force, thus compelling them to divert forces from the Pacific theater, where the Americans were making significant progress. Mountbatten's second objective, which became of increasing importance as the war progressed, was to improve relations with China. When the 14th Army under General William Slim began to drive the Japanese back into Burma in June 1944, it became clear to Mountbatten that a significant amount of pre-occupational work would need to be done before any attempt could be made to reoccupy FIC. He found himself at a disadvantage, though, because the Americans supported Chiang Kai-shek in assuming that both Thailand and Indochina would be under Chinese control. Mountbatten came to a "Gentleman's Agreement" with Chiang, whereby the British and Chinese would attack from the south and north, respectively, the final border being determined by the speed of advance of the respective forces; in return, the British would be allowed to put agents into the area to facilitate the occupation. Unfortunately, poor communications and difficulties with both Anglo-American and Franco-American relations meant that the campaign to reoccupy Thailand and Indochina took much longer than expected and was attended by largely unnecessary losses on the part of French colonial forces.

After the occupation of FIC by British forces, Mountbatten delayed sending Gracey the rest of the 20th Division, which Gracey had said from his first day in the country would be needed to maintain law and order below the 16th Parallel in southern Vietnam. Mountbatten seems to have chosen to prevent the troops' departure because he wanted to minimize the British role, in line with his orders from Whitehall. This delay increased Gracey's difficulties and resulted in the Japanese having to be deployed for peacekeeping, which delayed both their departure from Vietnam and the transfer of power to the French. The report Mountbatten's staff produced on the occupation in 1946, however, blamed Gracey for every mistake and credited Mountbatten with every success, when, in reality, the situation had deteriorated because of the SAC-SEAC's initial failure to make a determined, organized response in support of his forces in South Vietnam.[5] Mountbatten's period in command at SEAC is considered by some historians to have been less than successful, but he does seem to have been faced with American intransigence on a level that would have rendered even the most exemplary commander impotent.[6]

## NOONE, RICHARD

Richard Noone was a Secret Intelligence Service officer who served for a short period in Vietnam. He came to Malaya in 1939 to live with the indigenous tribes as part of his anthropological studies, and when World War II broke out in the Far East, Noone and his brother organized the local Malays into guerrilla groups responsible for conducting sabotage and insurgency operations against the occupying Japanese. It was operations of this type by Noone and others, incidentally, that generated a strong mutual respect between the Malays and their British counterparts, which was a determining factor in postwar operations against the Communists. After World War II, Noone was appointed head of the Malayan Department of Aborigines, and in this position he organized paramilitary forces from the local tribes who operated against the Communists. Later, during the Indonesian Confrontation, he served as commander of the special operations base in Sabah, Borneo.

During part of Noone's anthropological research, it had become clear that one of the local Malay tribes was closely related to the Montagnard tribes that lived in the central highlands of Vietnam. Emphasizing the potential of such a close relationship, he wrote a report to the Saigon Embassy and, early in 1963, he was appointed to lead a Special Forces team, made up of ethnic Malayo-Polynesian tribesmen, to operate in Vietnam with the Montagnards against the Việt Cộng. The two groups were so similar that virtually no linguistic or cultural barrier existed between them, but, unfortunately, the Vietnamese government attached an additional Vietnamese team to the expedition, and internal conflicts developed between the Vietnamese and Noone's men. This animosity became so intense that cooperation proved impossible, and Noone and his Malays had to be removed from Vietnam. He later became a counterinsurgency adviser to SEATO (the South East Asia Treaty Organization), dying in Bangkok, Thailand, in 1973.[7]

## SEATO (SOUTH EAST ASIA TREATY ORGANIZATION)

Formed as a Southeast Asian equivalent of NATO, in which the military forces of each member nation would be coordinated to provide for the collective defense of all countries in the organization. SEATO was headed by the secretary general, whose office was created in 1957 at a meeting in Canberra, with a council of representatives from member nations and committees for economics, security, and information. Its members included Australia, France, New Zealand, Pakistan (including East Pakistan, now Bangladesh), the Philippines, Thailand, the United Kingdom, and the United States.

In practice, SEATO proved largely ineffective, its main contribution being to provide a rationale for military intervention by the United States in Vietnam. The organization was

**SEATO committee at a meeting in 1966.** *From left to right:* **Prime Minister Nguyễn Cao Kỳ (South Vietnam), Prime Minister Harold Holt (Australia), President Park Chung Hee (Korea), President Ferdinand Marcos (Philippines), Prime Minister Keith Holyoake (New Zealand), Lt. Gen. Nguyễn Văn Thiệu (South Vietnam), Prime Minister Thanom Kittikachorn (Thailand), President Lyndon B. Johnson (United States).**

dissolved on 30 June 1977, after many members became dissatisfied with its operations and withdrew.

## Slim, Field-Marshal William Joseph, later 1st Viscount Slim

After a fairly conventional military career that included periods at several staff colleges and in command of regular troops, Slim was given command of Burma Corps in March 1942, being promoted to command of XV Corps later that year. XV Corps was then part of the Eastern Army, and after repeated clashes with his commander, Noel Irwin, Slim was superseded by Irwin, who took personal command of his Corps for an advance into the Arakan Peninsular. The operation was a disaster, resulting in mutual recriminations between Irwin and Slim and in Irwin finally being sent home. Slim was promoted to command the new Fourteenth Army, late in 1943, a force made up of a miscellaneous collection of Australian, Burmese, Canadian, British and African units. The Fourteenth Army's main component was from the Indian Army, which included the Gurkha regiments, and was the largest volunteer army in history.

Slim's innovative tactics, particularly his organization of supply drops by air, gave his troops a significant advantage over the poorly supplied Japanese. With the end of the Battle of Central Burma on 28 March 1945, and the reoccupation of Rangoon on 2 May, Fourteenth Army operations in Burma were successfully terminated and Slim turned his attention to reoccupying Malaya. He was promoted to Allied Commander, Land Forces South-East Asia, but before he could implement his plans for the invasion of Malaya, the Japanese surrendered.

He was still ACLFSEA when Gracey was sent to Vietnam, and Slim was unequivocal in his support of Gracey, both when Gracey was demanding that the rest of 20th Division to be sent to Saigon and later, when Mountbatten began his campaign of criticism. This culminated in the meeting of 28 September in Singapore, when Mountbatten told Slim he was relieving Gracey of his command. Slim's response was characteristically blunt and probably fueled by his disenchantment with Mountbatten's methods. He replied simply, "If he [Gracey] goes, I go!"

Slim returned to the United Kingdom at the end of 1945, and, after various civilian and military posts, including chief of the Imperial General Staff and governor-general of Australia, he retired in 1959. He died in London on 14 December 1970, aged 79.

Slim was one of the outstanding generals of World War II, and his period with the Fourteenth Army exemplified his innovative approach to new strategic situations. More than any other factor, his success was based on the trust he engendered in his officers and men, from divisional commanders to private soldiers. One eminent military historian, Max Hastings, wrote of him:

> In contrast to almost every other outstanding commander of the war, Slim was a disarmingly normal human being, possessed of notable self-knowledge. He was without pretension, devoted to his wife, Aileen, their family and the Indian Army. His calm, robust style of leadership and concern for the interests of his men won the admiration of all who served under him.... His blunt honesty, lack of bombast and unwillingness to play courtier did him few favors in the corridors of power. Only his soldiers never wavered in their devotion.[8]

This is made particularly clear in a description of Slim by a soldier of the Fourteenth Army, who said:

> His appearance was plain enough: large, heavily built, grim-faced, with that hard mouth and bulldog chin; the rakish Gurkha hat at odds with the slung carbine and untidy trouser bottoms; he might have been a yard foreman who became a managing director, or a prosperous farmer who'd boxed in his youth.

Perhaps the most sincere tribute came from the late George MacDonald Fraser, who served in the Fourteenth Army as a very young lance-corporal:

> But the biggest boost to morale was the burly man who came to talk to the assembled battalion ... it was unforgettable. Slim was like that: the only man I've ever seen who had a force that came out of him.... British soldiers don't love their commanders, much less worship them; Fourteenth Army trusted Slim and thought of him as one of themselves, and perhaps his real secret was that the feeling was mutual.[9]

## THOMPSON, SIR ROBERT
### (KBE, CMG, DSO, MC)

Robert Thompson was a counterinsurgency expert who had served with Orde Wingate's Chindits and on the staff of the British Director of Operations during the Malayan Emergency. After independence, he was appointed Malayan permanent secretary for defence in 1959, and, in response to a request from South Vietnam's president, Ngô Đình Diệm, the Malayan prime minister sent Thompson to advise the South Vietnamese on counterinsurgency techniques. Diệm asked for Thompson to be seconded to Saigon as an advisor, and subsequently, in August 1961, Macmillan appointed him to head BRIAM, where he was responsible for liaising with both Saigon and Washington. Initially, Thompson was well received in Washington, but after Kennedy's death, the failure of the "Strategic Hamlets" program and the beginning of major troop deployments, his advice became less acceptable and his influence in the White House diminished. He left BRIAM in 1965 and its remaining members were transferred to the Americans. Thompson returned to assisting the American government in 1969 when he became a special adviser on "pacification" to President Nixon. After leaving this post, he wrote extensively on the role of Special Forces and aspects of counterinsurgency, before his death in 1992, aged 76.[10]

### WILSON, HAROLD
(Prime Minister of Britain, 1964–1970 and 1974–1976)

Elected in 1964 with a 4-seat majority in the House of Commons, which he increased to 96 seats in the 1966 election, Wilson's main concern in his first three years was the economy and, more specifically, how to decrease the enormous balance-of-payment deficit he had inherited from Macmillan and Douglas-Home. Eventually, despite American intervention, he was obliged to announce the devaluation of the pound in 1967, which was followed by rapid increases in personal taxation. Labour's identification with high tax rates is considered by some political analysts to be the main factor that ensured that the Conservatives under Margaret Thatcher and, subsequently, John Major dominated British politics from 1979 until 1995. Wilson's social legislation included an easing and liberalization of the laws on censorship, divorce, homosexuality, immigration and abortion.[11]

## *French*

### D'ARGENLIEU, ADMIRAL GEORGES THIERRY

During World War I, d'Argenlieu served in the French navy, and after the war he began his religious studies, which culminated in ordination in 1925. He served with de Gaulle during World War II, and after the defeat of Japan he was sent to French Indochina. While there as high commissioner, he repudiated the Ho-Sainteny Agreement in 1946, which had recognized Vietnam as a "free state" within the French Union, and subsequently ordered the bombing of Haiphong. This action has been said by some historians to be the main cause of the "First" Indochina War. He was replaced as high commissioner by Émile Bollaert in January 1947.[12]

### CORPS LÉGER D'INTERVENTION (CLI), LATER THE 5TH RIC (REGIMENT D'INFANTERIE COLONIALE)

Created in French Algeria on 4 November 1943, the first detachment of this unit consisted of 500 volunteers commanded by Colonel Paul Huard, originally tasked with reinforcing resistance to the Japanese in French Indochina. Later renamed the 5th RIC and modeled loosely upon Wingate's Chindits, its members were fluent in Indochinese languages and had various military skills. Colin Mackenzie, head of Force 136 and the CLI's prospective theater commander, was clear that their tasks would be both military and political, including sabotage and the re-establishment of French sovereignty. Unfortunately, the Americans who were, intent upon stifling what they saw as British and French postwar colonial ambitions, refused to support the French resistance movement in FIC, and this specialist French force remained in Algeria for much of World War II.[13] In 1945, the 5th RIC were transported to Vietnam and extensively involved in the ensuing heavy fighting.

## DE GAULLE, CHARLES

Leader of the Free French forces between June 1940 and July 1944, de Gaulle became chairman of the Provisional Government of the French Republic in August 1944. In July 1945, the Potsdam Conference, to which de Gaulle had not been invited, decided to partition French Indochina into two sectors, a northern sector controlled by the Chinese and a southern sector administered by the British (although the intention was that the sectors should eventually combine and return to French control). Soon after the surrender of Japan in August 1945, de Gaulle sent the French Far East Expeditionary Corps to re-establish French sovereignty in French Indochina, making Admiral d'Argenlieu high commissioner and General Leclerc commander-in-chief of the expeditionary corps. Elections in France saw de Gaulle at the head of the government of the New Fourth Republic, but his refusal to share power with the new Constituent Assembly led to his resignation in January 1946. His subsequent return to politics in 1958 had little influence upon events in Vietnam before that date.

## DE LATTRE DE TASSIGNY, GENERAL JEAN MARIE

After distinguished service in World War II, including command of the Sixth Army Group, which invaded southern France (Operation "Dragoon"), de Lattre was sent to command French forces in Vietnam in 1950. He achieved some significant successes against the Việt Minh, most notably after building a defensive line from Hanoi across the Red River Delta to the Gulf of Tonkin, which was known as the "Lattre" line. Illness forced him to relinquish his command and return to Paris in 1951, where he died in January 1952.

## LECLERC, GENERAL JACQUES PHILIPPE

Leclerc rose to fame as de Gaulle's favorite tank commander when he led the tank corps that liberated Paris. Officially taking command of CEFEO (Far East Expeditionary Corps) on 15 August 1945, he began the southward drive out of Saigon in October 1945, which established the initial French domination of Vietnam's major cities. He was quick to perceive the necessity for a political settlement negotiated with the Việt Minh because, like the Americans, the French found they could conquer Vietnamese territory with relative ease, but could never manage to hold on to their gains. While deputizing for d'Argenlieu as high commissioner, Leclerc authorized Jean Sainteny to begin negotiations with Hồ Chí Mính in 1946, at the same time sending a flotilla containing large numbers of French troops into the Gulf of Tonkin as further encouragement to strike a deal. Lacking support from the Soviets, Chinese or French Communist Party, Ho negotiated a settlement that recognized Vietnam as a free state in the French Union and allowed France to base 25,000 troops in Vietnam for five years.[14] Unfortunately, upon his return from Paris, d'Argenlieu repudiated this agreement, establishing the French-controlled Republic of Cochinchina and committing the French to a war that lasted for the next seven years. Leclerc was replaced by J. E. Valluy in 1946 and died in a plane crash in French Algeria in 1947.

### Mendès France, Pierre

French politician who served as president of the Council of Ministers, effectively prime minister of France from 1954 to 1955. It was under his leadership that the cease-fire and eventual withdrawal from Vietnam by French forces was negotiated.[15]

### Sainteny, Jean

Former Hanoi banker and son-in-law to the retired governor of Indochina, Albert Sarraut. Appointed de Gaulle's representative in August 1945, Sainteny tried to negotiate a peace settlement between Ho and the French, but he was suborned by d'Argenlieu after Ho had been inveigled to Paris, ostensibly for further negotiations.[16]

## *American*

### Abrams, General Creighton Williams

After service during World War II and in Korea, Abrams replaced Westmoreland as head of the Military Assistance Command in Vietnam in June 1968. Under Abrams, the huge search and destroy operations were discontinued and replaced by operations that concentrated upon training and equipping the ARVN. When Nixon was elected president, this strategy began to be extended and referred to as "Vietnamization," a policy intended to gradually decrease U.S. involvement in Vietnam and allow American troops to leave the country. Under Abrams, U.S. troop numbers decreased from 500,000 in 1969 to less than 50,000 in June 1972.

Abrams was particularly well known for his dislike of politicians like Robert McNamara and McGeorge Bundy, although he reserved his greatest contempt for defense contractors, accusing them of "war profiteering."

### Dewey, Lt. Colonel Peter

Lt. Col. Peter Dewey was an OSS officer sent to Saigon in September 1945. He had only a minor role in FIC, simply to watch over U.S. interests (including POW property) and assist British counterintelligence staff.[17] Despite this limited assignment, Dewey refused to confine himself to his specified activities and even refused to cooperate with the Allies or associate with them in any way. Patti in Hanoi was adopting a similar attitude, and both men were said to be cordially disliked by their Allied contemporaries as well as their subordinates.[18]

After ignoring a series of warnings from the British authorities about the dangers of traveling in certain areas, Dewey was ambushed and killed on his way back from the Tan Son Nhut airport on 26 September 1945.[19]

## Johnson, Lyndon B.
### (36th U.S. President)

Born into a poor family in northwestern Texas, Johnson's politics were concerned mainly with social reform, even during the years of the Vietnam War, although his biographer, Robert Caro, also said of him, "Johnson's ambition was uncommon—in the degree to which it was unencumbered by even the slightest excess weight of ideology, of philosophy, of principles, of beliefs."

Elected to the House of Representatives in 1937, he served until 1949, also contesting a U.S. Senate election and serving in the U.S. Naval Reserve between December 1941 and July 1942 (during which time he conducted a survey of America's conduct of the war for Roosevelt). He was elected to the U.S. Senate in 1948 after a controversial campaign and elected minority leader in 1952. Kennedy invited Johnson to serve as his running mate in the 1961 presidential election, principally to ensure the support of traditional Southern Democrats, and it is claimed that, paradoxically, it was Johnson who appears to have dictated the pace of social reform that characterized Kennedy's term in office.

Johnson was sworn in as president on 22 November 1963, just over two hours after Kennedy's assassination, and from his reelection in 1964 until Nixon's victory in 1968, the pace of the Vietnam War escalated, with a total of over 500,000 troops deployed in Vietnam by 1969. He left office in January 1969 and died four years later, in January 1973.[20]

## Kennedy, John F.
### (35th U.S. President)

Elected in the closest presidential election of the 20th century, beating Richard Nixon in the popular vote by only 0.2 percent, Kennedy's term is remembered particularly for his administration's support of the African American civil rights movement, the building of the Berlin Wall, the beginning of the Space Race, the Cuban Missile Crisis and America's increased involvement in Vietnam. Kennedy's policy toward South Vietnam rested on the assumption that Diệm and his forces ultimately had to defeat the guerrillas on their own. Kennedy was against the deployment of American combat troops and observed that "to introduce U.S. forces in large numbers there today, while it might have an initially favorable military impact, would almost certainly lead to adverse political and, in the long run, adverse military consequences." In April 1963, Kennedy again assessed the situation in Vietnam: "We don't have a prayer of staying in Vietnam. Those people hate us. They are going to throw our asses out of there at any point. But I can't give up that territory to the Communists and get the American people to re-elect me."

Despite his misgivings, Kennedy sanctioned the plot to remove Diệm, which resulted in the South Vietnamese president's death, although he subsequently signed NSAM 263 (National Security Action Memorandum), dated 11 October 1963, which ordered the withdrawal from Vietnam of 1,000 military personnel by the end of the year. This has led some commentators to conclude that the president was preparing to withdraw all U.S. forces from Vietnam, although at the time of his death no firm decision had been made about U.S. policy in that country. Kennedy was assassinated in Dallas on 22 November 1963, and Lyndon Johnson subsequently reversed the military situation in Vietnam by reaffirming America's policy of assistance to the South Vietnamese.

## Assassination Theories

Conspiracy theories associated with Kennedy's assassination have been prevalent since his murder in Dallas. Among those theories has been the suggestion that his death was orchestrated by a military-industrial entity intent upon forcing America into a war in Southeast Asia. It has also been suggested that President Johnson was a party to the plot and sought the help of this organization to ensure his reelection. The best that can be said about this claim is that it is no more or less fantastic than many other theories that have developed around Kennedy's death.[21]

## KISSINGER, DR. HENRY

While still employed in a teaching post in the Department of Government at Harvard University, Kissinger visited South Vietnam at the behest of the U.S. ambassador, Henry Cabot Lodge, in 1965. He became convinced that the only means whereby the United States would be able to withdraw its troops lay in strengthening the South Vietnamese sufficiently to render them independent of U.S. military and financial support. When Nixon was elected in 1968, he appointed Kissinger his national security adviser; subsequently, Kissinger and Le Duc Tho negotiated the settlement that ended the war in 1973. Kissinger was awarded the Nobel Peace Prize jointly with Le Duc Tho in 1973, although Tho rejected the award on the grounds that peace had not really been restored in South Vietnam.

**Dr. Henry Kissinger, Nixon's national security advisor from 1968 until 1974. He retained the post under Gerald Ford until 1975, serving concurrently as secretary of state from 1973 until 1977. He was mainly responsible for the negotiations ending the Vietnam War.**

## MCNAMARA, ROBERT

McNamara worked for the Ford Motor Company as an executive starting in 1946, served as secretary of defense from 1961 to 1968, and was responsible for much of the policy on Vietnam during the 1960s. McNamara visited Saigon in October 1966 and, upon his return, advocated a de-escalation of operations in Vietnam. This position brought about the end of his political career in a series of maneuvers orchestrated by Senator John Stennis and supported by Pentagon generals, all convinced that they only needed to hit the Việt Cộng harder in order to win.[22]

## Military Assistance Advisory Group (MAAG)

Military Assistance Advisory Group, Vietnam (MAAG), was the designation given to the groups of American military advisers sent to South Vietnam to assist in the training of the South Vietnamese armed forces and facilitate the provision of military aid to the Saigon government. MAAG personnel were considered technical staff attached to the U.S. diplomatic mission in Vietnam and, consequently, enjoyed the same privileges as embassy staff.

The MAAG was first sent to Vietnam in 1950 by Harry Truman to assist the French. Unfortunately, French policy would not allow the training of Vietnamese troops; by the time they were ready to acquiesce to this sort of liaison, the efforts of the MAAG were too late to be effective. When the French left Vietnam in 1956, the MAAG remained and took over responsibility for advising President Diệm and members of his regime. Numbers of American advisers showed a slow, but steady, increase until 1961, with Diệm becoming increasingly reluctant to appoint them to senior commands because he feared their influence on his troops. In 1961 Kennedy began rapidly increasing both financial aid to South Vietnam and the number of MAAG advisers in the country, which resulted in an increase in the strength of the ARVN and also improved Diệm's political position, although this did not prevent his assassination in 1963. In May 1964, the MAAG was absorbed by the MACV and renamed the Field Advisory Element, Vietnam.

## Military Assistance Command, Vietnam (MACV)

The U.S. Military Assistance Command, Vietnam, was a joint service command of the U.S. DOD (Department of Defense), created on 8 February 1962 to oversee the increasingly complex military assistance program then being implemented in South Vietnam. Its main command components were as follows:

- United States Army Vietnam (USARV)
- I Field Force, Vietnam (I FFV)
- II Field Force, Vietnam (II FFV)
- XXIV Corps
- III Marine Amphibious Force (III MAF)
- Naval Forces Vietnam (NAVFORV)
- Seventh Air Force (7AF)
- 5th Special Forces Group
- Civil Operations and Revolutionary Development Support (CORDS)
- Studies and Observations Group
- Field Advisory Element, MACV

## NIXON, RICHARD
(37th U.S. President)

Born in California, Nixon graduated from Duke University Law School and served as a naval officer in the Pacific during World War II. Incidentally, like Johnson before him, he also exaggerated his war record, particularly his combat involvement. He was elected to the House of Representatives in 1946 and the Senate four years later, in 1950, winning on both occasions by smearing his opponents as Communist sympathizers. This anti–Communist stance became a feature of his future political life, although Nixon himself admitted that it was more opportunistic than ideological.[23] Elected president in November 1968, he served one full term, being forced to resign before the end of his second to avoid impeachment over his conduct during the "Watergate" scandal.

## OSS (Office of Strategic Services)

The OSS was a United States intelligence agency created during World War II and the forerunner of the CIA (Central Intelligence Agency). U.S. military intelligence before Pearl Harbor was the responsibility of each of the separate military services; consequently, it was poorly organized and lacked proper direction. The OSS was organized to coordinate military intelligence activities, but the Americans lacked sufficient expertise in such matters, so the first OSS operatives were trained by the British SIS (Secret Intelligence Service, or MI6) and used British short-wave broadcasting facilities until American equipment and radio networks became available. The OSS helped arm and train a number of resistance movements in the Far East, particularly Hồ Chí Mính's Việt Minh forces, which were the responsibility of Archimedes Patti. The OSS was absorbed into the SSU (Strategic Services Unit), then subsequently into the CIG (Central Intelligence Group), which became the current CIA under the terms of the National Security Act (1947).

## PATTI, ARCHIMEDES

Patti joined the U.S. Army in 1941 and served in Europe as a liaison with various resistance movements in North Africa, Italy and Yugoslavia. He later transferred to the OSS and worked in China. He appears to have been sent to Vietnam to establish an intelligence network, but he was told to avoid giving any support to the French because of Roosevelt's anti-colonial stance, although Patti also claimed later that the French had been "unwilling or unable to assist him," which forced him to turn to the Việt Minh. This is a curious assertion, since the French were supplying the United States with much of its intelligence about conditions in Indochina during this period.[24] Pierre Messmer, who was dropped into North Vietnam as a member of one of the teams intended to return French sovereignty to the area, was not impressed with Patti: "We had heavy difficulties with the OSS.... In the north the OSS sent an officer to Hanoi, a Major Patti, who was sort of a counselor to Hồ Chí Mính. And Hồ Chí Mính thought it was easy for him to play American off against French, and later play French against Chinese when Leclerc was there."[25] Võ Nguyên Giáp was clear about the mistakes the Americans made during that period. About the Potsdam Conference, he wrote, "Under American pressure the French were left out of the operation.... But gradually the Americans came to realize that we were not pro-western 'nationalists' as they had expected."

Patti helped Ho draft his speech declaring independence and seems to have deliberately obstructed both French and British operations in Hanoi and the surrounding area, despite the U.S. agreement to cooperate with both countries in Vietnam. He left Hanoi in September 1945, after his activities had led the French to allege he was fomenting rebellion in the north.

## ROOSEVELT, FRANKLIN D.
### (32nd U.S. President)

After a early political career that included terms as a state senator (New York) and assistant secretary to the navy, Roosevelt contracted polio in 1921. Convinced of the necessity to conceal his illness if he wanted to gain election to high public office, he never allowed it to become common knowledge. As a consequence of this decision, photographs taken during this period only show him standing, never walking (which he could only do awkwardly and for short distances), or in the wheelchair he used in private.

In 1932, he was elected president of the United States for his first term, followed subsequently by reelection in 1937, 1941 and 1945, shortly before his death on 12 April 1945.

Roosevelt's first term (1932–1937) was characterized by his New Deal legislation, which introduced social security payments for all those in need, union rights at a federal level and the end of Prohibition. Foreign relations were marked by a policy of isolationism from the rest of the world, especially Europe, and culminated in the passing of the Neutrality Acts and an arms embargo (unfortunately during that period when Hitler and Mussolini were preparing for a second world war).

His second term (1937–1941) was marked by a period of financial consolidation and an increase in isolationist sentiment, which Roosevelt reinforced through a number of policy decisions, including a declaration that the United States would remain neutral if Hitler invaded Czechoslovakia. In 1939, he proclaimed France and Britain to be America's "first line of defense" and advocated financial aid for the two countries, although he also reiterated his position that the United States would not be dragged into another war. Following German successes in France and with the Battle of Britain at its height, on 2 September 1940, Roosevelt offered Britain the "Destroyers for Bases" agreement, whereby the British received fifty mothballed World War I destroyers in exchange for allowing the United States 99-year leases on land in the Caribbean Islands, Bermuda and Newfoundland on which to build military bases. America certainly got the best of this arrangement; one English admiral described the ships as the "worst destroyers I had ever seen." Ineffective preservation after being placed "in reserve" meant that most of the ships required an extensive overhaul, so that by May 1941 only 30 were in service. In Britain, this deal has always been perceived as yet another example of the United States exploiting its most useful European ally and, along with the Atlantic Charter, as part of the American plan to dismember Britain's empire and reduce it to a second-rate power. This finally happened after the Suez crisis, although it is extremely unlikely that Britain would have retained its empire in its pre-war form and its preeminent economic and political position after 1945, whatever America's involvement might have been. Despite these negative aspects, the "Destroyers for Bases" agreement and the later "Lend-Lease" arrangements were the beginning of an Anglo-American coalition that was to play an important part in defeating the Axis Powers.

The Japanese attack on Pearl Harbor (7 December 1941) brought the United States fully into the war on 8 December 1941 and eventually resulted in enormous quantities of equipment being supplied for Allied use from American arms factories (Roosevelt's so-called Arsenal of Democracy). It was this level of logistical support and the huge numbers of American troops involved that made the invasion of Europe possible, although Roosevelt himself died of a massive stroke just days before Allied forces entered Berlin.

His approach to Indochina and particularly the French reflected his life-long antipathy to colonialism, although his attitude was often inconsistent and, at worst, destructive.[26]

The day after Pearl Harbor, Roosevelt sent a message to Marshal Pétain, head of the Nazi-controlled Vichy government, describing how essential it was to American interests that the French Empire be preserved and continue to exercise control in its colonies. This support for the Vichy regime, which could by no stretch of the imagination be considered to represent the majority of French people, was symptomatic of a lack of understanding of the European situation on the part of Americans in general, and Roosevelt in particular. From the beginning, Roosevelt's intention was clear: "He had mapped out a grand scenario of [postwar] world events, which included the elimination of the British and French empires."[27]

By 1943, the Americans were openly hostile to the Gaullists, with Roosevelt taking every opportunity to disparage and insult the Free French, and especially their leader, Charles de Gaulle. On 16 December 1943, he went a step further, calling a meeting of a number of Allied countries, including Britain, at which he said, among other things, that he had "been working very hard to prevent Indochina being restored to France," despite having given repeated reassurances to the French between 1941 and 1943 about the integrity of their empire. Mountbatten, at that time trying to establish a resistance net in French Indochina and the surrounding area, was in no doubt about the effect of this statement when it was eventually leaked, which he considered inevitable. He predicted the result in no uncertain terms: "The French, far from collaborating half-heartedly with the Japanese as they are now, will do all they can to obstruct our entry." The ramifications of Roosevelt's meeting seemed endless. It was even considered possible that it might result in difficulties over French cooperation with the European invasion, then being planned for the summer of 1944, and the British were at some pains to apprise the president of this issue, although Churchill himself refused to become involved, considering that "on this point the President's views are particular to himself."[28]

However, when the Americans needed the use of France's Pacific island bases for their island-hopping campaign toward Japan, the president performed a complete volte-face, sending de Gaulle a fulsome note assuring him of Roosevelt's personal regard, despite having sent Churchill another note only four weeks earlier that included the passage, "I will not ever have it said by the French or by American or British commentators that I invited him to visit me in Washington."[29]

This inconsistent attitude characterized Roosevelt's relations with de Gaulle and the French throughout the Far East war, and it was also reflected by the American military.[30]

Among other things, senior American military personnel impeded Mountbatten's efforts to establish the proposed Indochinese resistance net, delayed the transportation of the CLI to Indochina until it was too late for them to be effective, and refused vital military supplies, and even food and ammunition, to French troops cut off and surrounded by the Japanese. It is little wonder that the attitude of many older Frenchmen and women toward America has been less than conciliatory since the end of World War II.[31]

### Westmoreland, General William

Westmoreland was appointed deputy commander of the MACV in January 1964, succeeding General Paul Harkins. As head of the MACV he began the escalation of fighting that eventually led to the deployment of over 500,000 U.S. troops in South Vietnam. Returning home in 1967, he made a speech to a joint session of Congress on 28 April 1967, which included the following passage:

> In evaluating the enemy strategy, it is evident to me that ... our Achilles heel is our resolve.... Your continued strong support is vital to the success of our mission.... Backed at home by resolve, confidence, patience, determination, and continued support, we will prevail in Vietnam over the Communist aggressor!

Unfortunately, the battles during the Tet Offensive and at Khe Sanh showed the American public that the Việt Cộng would be unlikely to capitulate, even in the face of massive U.S. military force, and this marked a change in U.S. opinion at home that resulted in the war becoming increasingly unpopular. This forced Johnson to limit the increase in troop numbers Westmoreland was demanding, and with his strategy clearly failing, Westmoreland was replaced by General Creighton Abrams in June 1968.

Westmoreland was convinced from the outset that the Việt Cộng and VPA (Vietnam People's Army) could be defeated by a war of attrition that would deplete both their manpower and their equipment to a sufficiently low level to render them literally unable to fight. Although he tried to bring this about by engaging the Vietnamese in large-scale battles where he could use his superior artillery and airpower against them, the Communists avoided these set-piece engagements and continued to employ guerrilla tactics to wear down both the American military's morale and the U.S. public's support for the war. Consequently, it was attrition by the Communists that eventually forced the Paris peace negotiations.

# *Vietnamese*

### Bảo Đại

Last hereditary emperor of the Vietnamese Nguyen Dynasty. He was king of Amman when that area was a French protectorate between 1926 and 1945, including the short period when the Japanese ruled the area, from March to September 1945. He abdicated in favor of Hồ Chí Mính's government in August 1945, but was approached by the French with a view to his reinstatement in 1947. Bảo Đại refused to participate in the farce, and the French appointed General Nguyễn Văn Xuân prime minister and head of the new puppet government. On the occasion of his proposed reinstatement, Bảo Đại said, "What they call a Bảo Đại solution turns out to be just a French solution."

When the French were forced to leave the country in 1954, Bảo Đại remained as "Head of State" but moved to Paris, appointing Ngô Đình Diệm as his prime minister. In 1955, however, Diệm had Đại voted out of office and installed himself as president of South Vietnam, announcing at the same time that he would not allow South Vietnam to participate in the unifying elections that had been agreed to as part of the 1954 Geneva Accords.

Bảo Đại supported the North Vietnamese in their attempts to expel the United States from his country, calling for all factions to "create a free, neutral peace-loving government which would resolve the tense situation in the country." He died in a military hospital in Paris, aged 83, on 30 July 1997.[32]

## Bình Xuyên

The Bình Xuyên was an independent military force within the Vietnamese National Army whose leaders once had lived outside the law and subsequently sided with the Việt Minh. It first emerged

Bảo Đại, last hereditary emperor of the Vietnamese Nguyen Dynasty, in an early picture.

in the early 1920s as a loose collection of laborers and criminals; during its heyday, Bình Xuyên funded itself through organized criminal activities in Saigon, while also fighting the invading Communist forces. Originally boasting only a few hundred members, it had grown by 1949 into an organization numbering in the thousands, although this did not prevent it from being wiped out during the battle for Saigon in 1955. Bay Vien, who was then head of the Bình Xuyên, subsequently fled to exile in France, where he died in Paris in 1970, aged 66.

## Cao Dao

This group was a Vietnamese politico-religious organization established in southern Vietnam in 1926. During the First and Second Indochina Wars, the Caodaists (along with several other Vietnamese sects, such as Hòa Hảo) were active in political and military struggles against both French colonial forces and South Vietnamese Prime Minister Ngô Đình Diệm. Their criticism of the Communists was a factor in their repression after the fall of Saigon in 1975, when the incoming Communist government proscribed the practice of Caodaism. In 1997, however, Caodaism was granted legal recognition and free practice once again.

## Chiang Kai-shek (Chinese)

Chiang Kai-shek was a Chinese military and political leader who served as head of the Republic of China from 1928 to 1975. Defeated by the Communists on the mainland, Chiang evacuated his government to Taiwan in December 1949 and then ruled the island securely as president of the Republic of China and general of the Kuomintang until his death in 1975, aged 87.

## Ngô Đình Diệm
### (Prime Minister of South Vietnam, 1954–1963)

An intense anti–Communist nationalist from a Catholic, Central Vietnamese family, Diệm was appointed prime minister by Bảo Đại in 1954, because the emperor felt he was the candidate most acceptable to the Americans, who helped him maintain his position. Diệm refused to participate in the country-wide elections to be held in 1956 according to the 1954 Geneva agreement, although he organized elections in the south in 1959, when he was elected president, collecting a 98 percent share of the vote. Increasingly isolated and out of touch with the situation in Vietnam, he was overthrown and murdered in November 1963 in a coup that began with his order to ruthlessly suppress a Buddhist religious meeting.

After months of insecurity, Diệm was finally removed from power in an operation led by Dương Văn Minh on 1 November 1963. That same day, with only the palace guard remaining to defend Diệm and his younger brother, Nhu, the rebellious generals telephoned the palace offering Diệm exile if he surrendered. Diệm prevaricated, and that evening he and his brother escaped via an underground passage to Cholon. They were captured the following morning and subsequently executed in an M-113 armored personnel carrier by Captain Nguyễn Văn Nhung, under orders from Dương Văn Minh, while en route to the Vietnamese Joint General Staff headquarters. Diệm was buried in an unmarked grave in a cemetery next to the house of the U.S. ambassador.[33]

## Võ Nguyên Giáp

Serving as both a general in the Vietnam People's Army and a politician, Giáp first came to prominence during World War II as military leader of the Việt Minh resistance against the Japanese occupation of Vietnam. He was a principal commander in both the First Indochina War against the French and the Vietnam War, serving also as an interior minister in Hồ Chí Mính's Việt Minh government and as defense minister. Later he wrote extensively about the wars and his military involvement.

## Hồ Chí Mính

Hồ Chí Mính was born Nguyễn Sinh Cung in 1890 in Hoang Tru, which was the village where his mother had her family home, although from 1895 onward he lived with his father and received a French education. Between 1908 and 1919, he traveled extensively in Europe and the United States, arriving in Paris in 1919, where he first began to develop an interest in politics.

## Early Politics

In Paris, Nguyễn became involved with a Nationalist Vietnamese group that was petitioning the French government to recognize Vietnamese civil rights, and he was also active later in the Socialist Party of France, in addition to contributing articles with political themes to newspapers and journals. He left Paris for Moscow in 1923, working there and later in China, where he tried to organize the Communist Party of Vietnam in Hong Kong during 1930. He then left Hong Kong, traveling and working first in Spain and then in the Soviet Union, returning to China in 1938 to serve as an adviser to Mao's Communist armed forces. Around 1940, he began calling himself "Hồ Chí Mính," a name indicating he was in a state of enlightenment.

## Vietnamese Politics

In 1941, Ho returned to Vietnam as leader of the Việt Minh, fighting both the Japanese and the Vichy French and supplied with arms by the OSS. In return, Ho supplied the United States with some low-grade intelligence in return for what he called "a line of communication with the Allies." On 19 August 1945, Ho's forces seized power in Hanoi, proclaiming the establishment of the Democratic Republic of Vietnam on 2 September 1945. Unfortunately, Ho's government did not receive international recognition, and with the breakdown of negotiations with the French in 1946, war began to look increasingly likely. Fighting broke out in Haiphong, and by February 1947, the French had pushed the poorly equipped Việt Minh out of Hanoi, although they could not conclusively defeat Ho's guerrilla army. In February 1950, after the Soviet Union had officially recognized Ho's government, military aid from China and the Soviet Union began to arrive in North Vietnam, allowing Giap to reorganize his predominantly guerrilla forces into more conventional formations. By 1954, the French had been beaten and the Geneva Accords left Ho as president of the Democratic Republic of Vietnam, with the promise of unifying elections in 1956.

Both before and after the establishment of the Geneva Accords, the Vietnamese Communist Party had imprisoned or executed most political opposition, and from 1954 onward, North Vietnam was also subjected to a program of land reform that resulted in the execution of many so-called "landlords." A similar program to eradicate Việt Minh sympathizers was also conducted in the south, and when it became clear that he could not hope to win a free vote, Prime Minister Diệm refused to sanction the elections promised in the 1954 Accords. This precipitated military operations by the Việt Minh against the south, which finally resulted in the major U.S. involvement that escalated into the Vietnam War.

Ho relinquished leadership of the Vietnamese Communist Party in 1960 in favor of Le Duan, although he still retained considerable influence with the Hanoi government and was even asked to give his final sanction to the Tet Offensive in January 1968. He died in Hanoi on 2 September 1969, aged 79.[34]

# HÒA HẢO

A Vietnamese politico-religious organization, based on Buddhism but with more austere manifestations of worship, forgoing, for example, much of the expensive ceremonial ritual and ornate buildings of the more conventional Buddhist sects.

During World War II the Hòa Hảo supported the Japanese and opposed the Việt Minh, and between 1949 and 1955 (the period of the State of Vietnam), the Hòa Hảo supported the emperor, while covertly opposing the French. In 1956, the movement was decimated by General Dương Văn Minh, marking the end of the Hòa Hảo as an armed, political force, although after the death of President Diệm, the group turned against the Communists. After the American withdrawal, the Hòa Hảo was allowed to continue its religious observances, but only under strict Communist control.

## Nguyễn Cao Kỳ

First came to prominence as a flamboyant air vice-marshal in the 1960s, before staging a military coup that made him prime minister in 1965. Deposed in 1967 by the election of Nguyễn Văn Thiệu, Kỳ served as vice-president until 1975, when he left Saigon, prior to the Communists' occupation.

## Ngô Đình Nhu

Brother of Ngô Đình Diệm, he was responsible for the scheme to set the army and Buddhists against each other that resulted in the brothers' ultimate downfall and murder.

## Nguyễn Văn Thiệu

After World War II, Thiệu joined the Việt Minh, but left after one year, claiming that the Việt Minh were simply Communists intent upon oppressing the Vietnamese people. He was commissioned in the VNA as a 2nd lieutenant, and thus began a rapid rise through the ranks of the army. He was a lieutenant-colonel in 1954 when the Republic of Vietnam was founded and later played a major part in the removal and murder of Diệm. For his part in the coup, Thiệu was made a general and also became a member of the 12-man junta that ruled South Vietnam. After a complex series of plots and counter-plots, Nguyễn Cao Kỳ became prime minister of South Vietnam, with Thiệu serving as his chief of state, although this was a position without any real power. After further machinations, Thiệu was elected president of South Vietnam, with Kỳ retained as his vice-president, in a regime that lasted until 1975. With the city about to fall into Communist hands, Thiệu resigned as president on 21 April 1975, leaving for Taiwan five days later. He lived in England before moving to the United States, where he died in 2001, aged 78.

## Southern Committee

Placed in control of Saigon in August 1945, it proved ineffective and was deposed by Gracey's coup of 23 September.

## Việt Cộng
### (National Liberation Front)

Việt Cộng was the Diệm regime's name for the National Liberation Front for South Vietnam, which replaced the Việt Minh in 1960. Shortened from "Vietnamese Communists," the Việt Cộng was originally thought to be an autonomous, southern movement. It has been shown, however, that its members had firm links with the Hanoi government and that the organization's leaders took their orders from North Vietnamese generals. Its origins were originally concealed to forestall any accusation by the Americans of military build-up in the south by the northern Communists, who were controlled by the Hanoi government.

## Việt Minh

Originally the Viet Nam Doc Lap Dong Minh (trans: the Vietnamese Independence League). Formed in 1941 by Phạm Văn Đồng and Võ Nguyễn Giáp, after a meeting with Hồ Chí Mính at Pac Bo. Its forces consisted of "patriots of all ages and types, peasants, workers, merchants and soldiers."

The Việt Minh fought the Japanese during World War II and the French after their return during the first Indochinese war. The South Vietnamese administration (backed by the United States) refused to hold the unifying elections agreed to in the original 1954 treaty, and the Việt Minh were powerless to stop them after internal upheavals and a disastrous land reform policy that had been put into operation in the north after the ceasefire. As a direct result of these policies, the Việt Minh organization lost its popularity and was replaced by the National Liberation Front (NLF, or Việt Cộng) in 1960.

# Appendix III

# Allied Contributions to the Vietnam War: 1963–1973

Thirty-nine nations provided support to South Vietnam in one form or another, in response to the Free World Assistance Program launched by U.S. President Lyndon B. Johnson. Only those listed below provided military forces, and only Australia and New Zealand covered their own expenses.[1]

| Country | Participation | Losses<br>Killed in Action [KIA]<br>Died in Service [DIS] |
|---|---|---|
| United Kingdom | 4,434 UK citizens with Australian forces. 26 UK citizens with NZ forces.<br>No British service personnel officially deployed, but some may have served in Vietnam while on secondment to U.S., Australian and NZ Special Forces. | 26 UK citizens DIS with Australian services<br>3 UK citizens DIS with NZ forces |
| Australia | 8,300 troops and advisers during any single period.<br>60,418 Australian troops (including UK citizens) served in Vietnam. | Approximately 500 KIA |
| Canada | No government involvement, but thousands of Canadians (estimated numbers vary greatly from anywhere between 3,500 and 30,000) served with the U.S. armed forces in Vietnam, including at least one Medal of Honor winner. | At least 103 KIA |
| Italy | Ten-man surgical team and civilian aid, including scholarships. | None |
| Japan | Substantial monetary aid chiefly through repatriations, medical goods, and the construction of a neurological ward in Saigon. | None |
| New Zealand | 534 soldiers—one battalion under Australian (1st Brigade) command during any single period. | 37 KIA |
| Philippines | 12,000 troops. | About 1,000 KIA |
| South Korea | Three divisions—48,000 soldiers. | Between 4,400 and 5,1000 KIA |

278

## Allied Contributions to the Vietnam War: 1963–1973

| Country | Participation | Losses<br>Killed in Action [KIA]<br>Died in Service [DIS] |
|---|---|---|
| Taiwan | Some involvement, but specific details not known. | Not known |
| Thailand | Over 20,000 troops, including 31 Special Forces. | 351 to 1,000 KIA |
| USA | Over 540,000 troops. | Approximately 58,000 KIA |
| West Germany | No troops were deployed, but a West German hospital ship (SS *Helgoland*) was docked at Danang. | None |

# Appendix IV

# British Forces in South Vietnam (September 1945–May 1946)[1]

## Composition of Infantry Divisions in the British-Indian Army, 1939–1945

An infantry division in the British army during World War II consisted of three infantry brigades, each with three infantry battalions. In Southeast Asia, one battalion in each brigade was usually British and two were Indian or Gurkha. Three brigades were raised consisting entirely of Gurkha battalions. Later in the war, as British infantry reinforcements became more scarce, particularly in the Southeast Asian theater, British battalions in brigades fighting in Burma were replaced by Indian units.

In a division with a standard MT (Mechanical Transport) establishment, the divisional units were a reconnaissance unit, provided by a mechanized cavalry regiment, and a heavy machine gun battalion armed with the Vickers machine gun (each regiment of the Indian army raised a machine gun battalion in addition to its infantry battalions). Divisional artillery consisted of three field artillery regiments, one anti-tank regiment and one anti-aircraft regiment. There were three engineer field companies and one engineer field park company, plus signals, medical and transport units. In April 1945, the 20th Division was also converted to a partially motorized establishment by acquiring the vehicles from a British division whose personnel were being withdrawn from Burma.

## 20th Division (August 1945)

**General Officer Commanding:** Major General Douglas Gracey
**Second in Command and Commander, Royal Artillery:** Brigadier J.A.E. Hirst
**32nd Indian Infantry Brigade:**
**Arrived/Departed, Saigon:** 8–11 October 1945/25–28 December 1945
**Commander:** Brigadier C.H. Woodford
Composed of:
  9th Battalion, 14th Punjab Regiment
  3rd Battalion, 8th Gurkha Rifles
  4th Battalion, 2nd Gurkha Rifles
**80th Indian Infantry Brigade:**
**Arrived/Departed, Saigon:** 11–24 September 1945/21 January 1946

**Commander:** Brigadier D.E. Taunton
Composed of:
   1st Battalion, 1st Gurkha Rifles (Lt. Col. C. Jarvis)
   1st Battalion, 3rd Gurkha Rifles (Lt. Col. Purcell)
   9th Battalion, 12th Frontier Force Regiment (Major Mian Hayauddin, MBE)
**100th Indian Infantry Brigade:**
**Arrived/Departed, Saigon:** 17 October 1945/8 February 1946
**Commander:** Brigadier C.H.B. Rodham
Composed of:
   2nd Battalion, 8th Punjab
   14th Battalion, 13th Frontier Force Rifles
   4th Battalion, 10th Gurkha Rifles
**Other Infantry Units:**
   4th Battalion, 17th Dogra Regiment
   1st Battalion, 19th Hyderbad Regiment

## *Divisional Units*

**Reconnaissance Units**
   16th Light Cavalry (armored cars)
   4th Battalion, 3rd Madras Regiment (divisional reconnaissance unit)
**Heavy Machine Gun Battalion**
   9th Jat Regiment (armed with Vickers medium machine guns)
**Divisional Artillery Units**
   9th Field Regiment, RA
   23th Mountain Regiment, IA (Indian Artillery)
   114th Field Regiment, RA (only British army unit to serve in Vietnam)
**Anti-Aircraft/Anti-Tank Unit**
   55th Light Anti-Aircraft/Anti-Tank Regiment, RA
**Engineer Units**
   92nd Field Company, IE (Indian Engineers)
   422nd Field Company, IE
   481st Field Company, IE
   309th Field Park Company, IE
**Signal Units**
   20th Indian Infantry Division Signal Regiment
**Transport Units**
   Not known
**Medical Units**
   Three field ambulances manned by personnel from the RAMC (Royal Army Medical Corps)
**Military Police Unit**
   604th Field Security Section

# Appendix V

# Equipment Lists for Forces Operating in Vietnam: 1945–1975[1]

## *British Forces (1945–1946)*

### SMALL ARMS (PISTOLS AND RIFLES)

| Manufacturer | Equipment |
|---|---|
| Webley & Scott Royal Small Arms factory, Enfield (RSAF) | Webley revolver, Mk VI; Six-shot, double-action, top-break revolver, with automatic cartridge ejection; .455 caliber cartridge (British) |
| Webley & Scott Royal Small Arms factory, Enfield (RSAF) | Webley revolver, Mk IV and Enfield No. 2, Mk I; Six-shot, double-action, top-break revolver, with automatic cartridge ejection; .38 caliber cartridge (British issue or Smith & Wesson) |
| RSAF Birmingham Small Arms Co. (BSA) | Lee Enfield Rifle; Model: Short Magazine, Lee Enfield Mk III*; .303 caliber bolt-action rifle; Chambered for .303 cartridge (British) |
| RSAF BSA | Lee Enfield Rifle; Model: No. 4, Mk I, Mk I*, Mk II; .303 caliber bolt-action rifle; Chambered for .303 cartridge (British) |
| RSAF BSA | Lee Enfield Rifle (jungle carbine); Model: No. 5, Mk I; .303 caliber bolt-action rifle; Chambered for .303 cartridge (British) |
| RSAF BSA; Various other British and Commonwealth manufacturers | STEN gun; Models: Mk I–Mk VI sub-machine gun; Chambered for 9×19mm Parabellum cartridge |
| BSA; Colt; Savage Arms | Thompson (SMG); 20- and 30-cartridge stick magazines; Fully and semi-automatic operation; Chambered for .45 caliber, ACP (Automatic Colt Pistol, as used in M1911A pistol) |

Undoubtedly, other, privately acquired arms were in use. Officers seem to have favored the Colt M1911A and Browning Hi-Power semi-automatic pistols, and there may also have been captured German small arms in use.

Browning Hi-Power semi-automatic pistol. Usually chambered for the very common 9×19mm Parabellum cartridge when used by the British, Australian and New Zealand armed forces, and also featuring a 13-round magazine, which added to its appeal (Wikipedia; Creative Commons).

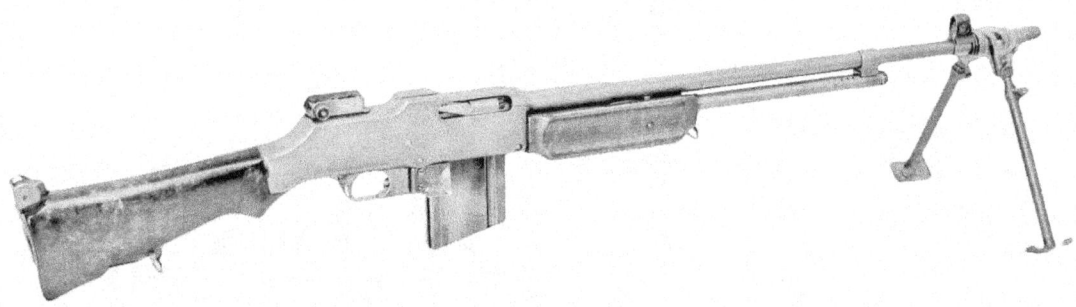

Browning Automatic Rifle (BAR), chambered for a variety of cartridges, including the 30-06 caliber Springfield and the .303 caliber British. By the time of the Vietnam War, the design was beginning to look distinctly tired, although it remained a popular weapon with many U.S. troops (courtesy Army Heritage Museum Collection).

## Machine Guns

| Manufacturer | Equipment |
|---|---|
| RSAF and others | Bren light machine gun (LMG); 30-round magazine (100-round in AA role); Fully and semi-automatic operation; Chambered for .303 cartridge (British) |
| RSAF and others | Vickers medium machine gun (in use 1912–1968); 250-cartridge canvas belt; Chambered for .303 cartridge (British) |

## Artillery (Mortars, Field Guns, AA Guns)

| Manufacturer | Equipment |
|---|---|
| Royal Ordnance factory | Ordnance QF 25-pdr field gun; Ammunition used: 25-lb shell in HE (high explosive), SMK (smoke), AT (anti-tank); British infantry divisions had 72 25-pdrs, in 3 field artillery regiments (24/Rgt) |

| Manufacturer | Equipment |
|---|---|
| Royal Ordnance factory | Ordnance SBML 2-inch mortar; 2.00 inches caliber; Rounds used: HE (high explosive), SMK (smoke), ILL (illuminating) |
| Royal Ordnance factory | Ordnance ML 3-inch mortar; 3.20 inches caliber |

## Aircraft

| Manufacturer | Equipment |
|---|---|
| Air frame: Supermarine; Engine: Rolls-Royce Merlin | Supermarine Spitfire; Single-seat fighter; Max speed ~400 mph; Armament: 8 Browning machine guns |
| Douglas Aircraft Company | Douglas; DC 3 "Dakota" (military variant: C-47 Skytrain); Twin-engine transport/cargo aircraft |
| Air frame: De Havilland Aircraft Company; Engines: Rolls-Royce Merlin | DH.98 Mosquito; Twin-engine fighter/bomber/reconnaissance aircraft; Max speed ~415 mph |

## Vehicles

| Manufacturer | Equipment |
|---|---|
| Rootes Group | Humber armored car (16th Light Cavalry) |
| Daimler | Daimler armored car (16th Light Cavalry) |
| Rootes Group | Morris Commercial C8 Field Artillery Tractor (Quad); 4-wheel-drive tractor used to tow 25-pdr gun |

## Logistic Supply/Rations

| Manufacturer | Equipment |
|---|---|
| UK govt. issue | **24-hour ration pack:** 1 tin of meat, plain biscuits, chocolate/sweets, tea blocks, sweet biscuits, matches, latrine paper, porridge, meat broth, chewing gum, sugar tablets, instructions/menu sheet |
| UK govt. issue (produced in Canada) | **Jungle ration pack:** Breakfast: oatmeal, tins of liver & bacon, fish & egg, cheese & egg; Dinner: meat pudding, ham or beef; Biscuits, cheese, jam, sweets, two bars of chocolate, chewing gum, salt tablets, tea, milk and sugar |

# *Vietnamese Forces (1945–1946)*

## Small Arms (Pistols, Rifles, LMG, HMG)

| Manufacturer | Equipment |
|---|---|
| Arisaka | Type 38 bolt-action rifle, with 5-round magazine (6.5×50mm Type 38 cartridge) |
| Arisaka | Type 99 bolt-action rifle, with 5-round magazine (7.7×58mm Type 99 cartridge) |

| Manufacturer | Equipment |
|---|---|
| Lebel | Model 1886 rifle; bolt-action, 8-round tubular magazine (8×50mm Lebel cartridge) |

Also supplied by the Americans prior to the Japanese surrender, so Vietnamese forces may also have been using M1 Garand, Thompson and Colt arms, although this has not been confirmed.

## Logistic Supply (Rations, Ammunition and Miscellaneous Requirements)

Supplies believed to have been obtained in most cases from local villagers. Almost certainly during this period the supply chain from the north did not operate, except to provide a small amount of ammunition.

# French Forces (1945–1955)

The weapons used by both the French Far East Expeditionary Corps and the French Foreign Legion units during the First Indochina War were practically all American World War II weapons, which were also used in the Korean War.

## Small Arms (Rifles, LMG, HMG)

| Manufacturer | Equipment |
|---|---|
| Springfield Armory (232,500 rifles supplied to France by the U.S. government [1950–1964]) | M1 Garand; Semi-automatic; 8-round, clip-loaded; Chambered for .30-06 (7.62×63mm) Springfield cartridge |
| Manufacture d'Armes de Tulle (MAT) in 1946 | MAT 49 (9mm); Semi-automatic machine gun; 20- or 32-round detachable box magazine; Chambered for 9×19mm Parabellum cartridge |
| Manufacture d'Armes de Saint-Étienne (MAS) | Model 36 rifle; Bolt-action, 5-round internal box magazine; Chambered for 7.5×54mm cartridge (French) |
| Colt Patent Firearms; Various other manufacturers | M1918A2 Browning automatic rifle; 20-round detachable box magazine; 30–06 (7.62×63mm) Springfield |
| BSA; Colt; Savage Arms | Thompson (SMG); Full and semi-automatic operation; 20- and 30-cartridge detachable box magazines; Chambered for .45 cal ACP (Automatic Colt Pistol, used in M1911A pistol) |
| Manufacture d'Armes de Châtellerault | FM 24/29 LMG; 25-round box magazine; Chambered for 7.5×54mm cartridge (French) |

## Artillery (Mortars, Field Guns)

| Manufacturer | Equipment |
|---|---|
| National armories | 105mm howitzers (various) |
| National armories | 155mm howitzers (various) |

| Manufacturer | Equipment |
|---|---|
| Rock Island Arsenal *(supplied by United States)* | U.S. M101 howitzer; 105mm cal.; Ammunition used: HE (high explosive), HEAT (high explosive, anti-tank), WP (white phosphorus), SMK (smoke) |

Although Britain sold France some 25-pounder ammunition and received a request for spare parts, there appears to be no indication in the relevant literature that the French army ever used British QF 25-pounder field guns in Vietnam.

## Vehicles (Tanks, Lorries, Motor Cycles)

| Manufacturer | Equipment |
|---|---|
| Cadillac, Massey-Harris *(supplied by United States)* | U.S. M24 "Chaffee" tank; Light tank; Armament: 75mm main gun; 1×50 cal. Browning HMG; 2×30.06 Browning M1919A LMGs |

Lorries, cars and motorcycles were probably supplied by the Americans and were of the usual military makes.

## Air Support (Helicopters, Fixed-Wing Aircraft)

| Manufacturer | Equipment |
|---|---|
| Air frame: Supermarine; Merlin engine: Rolls-Royce | Supermarine Spitfire (one squadron supplied to French by RAF in 1946); Single-seat fighter; Max speed ~400 mph; Armament: 8 Browning machine guns |
| Douglas Aircraft Company | Douglas: DC 3 "Dakota" (military variant: C-47 Skytrain: 1946–1954); Twin-engine transport/cargo aircraft (although some were modified as bombers and served until 1954); Max speed ~250 mph |
| Bell Aircraft Corporation | P-63 Kingcobra (Operational: 1946–1951); Single-seat fighter aircraft; Max speed ~400 mph; Armament: 37mm cannon firing through the nose cone; 4×.50 cal. M2 Browning Mgs, 2 in nose, 2 on wings; Bombs: 1,500-lb load distributed between fuselage and wings |
| Grumman Aircraft Engineering Corporation | F8F Bearcat (Operational: 1951–1954); Single-seat fighter aircraft; Max speed ~450 mph; Armament: either 4×.50 caliber machine guns, 4×20mm cannon, 4×5-inch rockets; A single 1,000-lb bomb could also be carried. |
| Douglas Aircraft Company | B-26 Invader; Twin-engine bomber; Max speed ~350 mph; Armament: .50 caliber Browning MGs, in groups in the nose, under wing pods and in remotely controlled upper and lower turrets; Bomb load: 6×1,000 lbs. |
| Aeroplanes Morane-Saulnier | MS 500 (Operational: 1946–1954); Light aircraft, copy of German Fiesler Storch |

| Manufacturer | Equipment |
|---|---|
| Fairchild Aircraft | C-119 (Flying Boxcar) (Operational: 1954); Transport aircraft with French markings but supplied by U.S. and flown by CIA pilots |
| Hiller Aircraft Corporation | OH-23 Raven; Multipurpose light helicopter; Used for casualty evacuation (CAS-VAC) |
| Sikorski Aircraft Corporation | UH-19 Chickasaw; Utility helicopters; Used for CAS-VAC |
| Piaseki Helicopter | CH-21C; Transport helicopter. Mainly used for troop insertions, although early trials were conducted to determine its usefulness as a ground attack craft |

Aéronavale (naval aviation) also operated older American aircraft during this period (F6F Hellcat, SB2C Helldiver, F4AU-1 Corsair and navalized B-24 Liberators).

## Logistic Supply (Rations, Ammunition and Miscellaneous Requirements)

| Supplier | Equipment |
|---|---|
| U.S. Army | U.S. field rations |

# Vietnamese Forces (1946–1955)

Many Việt Minh arms were captured French weapons, although after 1950 they began receiving supplies from both China and the Soviet Union. By 1954, however, the Việt Minh were extremely well organized and equipped so that, at Dien Bien Phu, they were able to deploy 140 field howitzers, 50 heavy mortars, 70–80 recoil-less guns, 36 anti-aircraft guns, and 12 Soviet-made Katyusha rocket launchers.

## Small Arms (Pistols, Rifles, LMG, HMG)

| Manufacturer | Equipment |
|---|---|
| Arisaka | Type 38 bolt-action rifle, with 5-round internal magazine; Chambered for 6.5×50mm SR Type 38 cartridge |
| Arisaka | Type 99 bolt-action rifle, with 5-round internal magazine; Chambered for 7.7×58mm Type 99 cartridge |
| Manufacture d'Armes de Tulle (MAT) in 1946 | MAT 49 (9mm); Semi-automatic machine gun; 20- or 32-round detachable box magazine; Chambered for 9×19mm Parabellum cartridge |
| Lebel | Model 1886 rifle; Bolt-action, 8-round tubular magazine; Chambered for 8×50mm R Lebel cartridge |
| Manufacture d'Armes de Saint-Étienne (MAS) | Model 36 rifle; Bolt-action, 5-round internal box magazine; Chambered for 7.5×54mm French cartridge |

| Manufacturer | Equipment |
|---|---|
| USSR *(claimed to have been obtained from China)* | SVT-40 rifle; Semi-automatic operation, with 10-round detachable box magazine; Chambered for 7.62×54mm R cartridge |
| IZHMASH (Izhevsk Machinebuilding Plant [USSR]) | Kalashnikov AK-47 assault rifle; Semi- or fully automatic operation with 10-, 20-, 30-, 40-round box magazines and 50- or 100-round drum magazines; Chambered for 7.62×39mm M43/M67 cartridge |

## ARTILLERY (MORTARS, FIELD GUNS, ROCKETS)

| Manufacturer | Equipment |
|---|---|
| USSR | Mortars were all probably World War II vintage; 50mm RM-39/40/41; 82mm PM-41; 120mm PM-43 |
| USSR | M1937 (ML-20); 152mm gun-howitzer; Ammunition: HE, CHEM (chemical), FRAG (fragmentation), ILLM (illumination) |
| USSR | Automatic air defense gun M1939 (61-K); 37mm anti-aircraft gun-howitzer; Ammunition: FRAG, HE, HVAP |
| USSR | Katyusha rocket launcher; Multiple rocket launcher, usually mounted on a lorry; 82mm rocket, although 132mm may have been supplied |

## LOGISTIC SUPPLY (RATIONS, AMMUNITION AND MISCELLANEOUS REQUIREMENTS)

| Supplier | Equipment |
|---|---|
| Locally acquired | Mostly fresh rations (rice, etc.) |
| China and USSR | Ammunition, radio equipment, medical supplies and fuel |

# *American and Allied Forces (1963–1975)*

## PISTOLS

| Manufacturer | Equipment | Issued to |
|---|---|---|
| Colt Manufacturing Co. and various other manufacturers depending upon origin | Browning Hi-Power pistol; Semi-automatic; 13-round butt magazine; Chambered for 9×19mm; Parabellum cartridge | Australian and New Zealand forces; also used on an unofficial basis by U.S. Reconnaissance and Special Forces units |
| Colt Manufacturing Co. and various other manufacturers depending upon origin | Colt M1911A1; Semi-automatic; 7-round butt magazine; Chambered for .45 cal ACP | U.S. Army's main sidearm; also used by some non–Commonwealth troops |

*Equipment Lists for Forces: 1945–1975 (American/Allied 1963–75)* 289

| Manufacturer | Equipment | Issued to |
|---|---|---|
| Colt Manufacturing Co. | Colt Model 1903 Pocket Hammerless | General officers (replaced by the Colt Commander in the mid-1960s) |
| Colt Manufacturing Co. | Colt Commander | General officers (replaced Colt M1903 pistol in the mid-1960s) |
| Smith & Wesson | Smith & Wesson Model 15 (USAF M15) | USAF security police units |
| Smith & Wesson | Smith & Wesson Model 12 | Helicopter pilots |
| Colt Manufacturing Co. | M1917 revolver | South Vietnamese and U.S. forces |
| High Standard | High Standard HDM (early type of suppressed pistol) | Special Forces units, such as SEALs |
| Smith & Wesson | Smith & Wesson Model 39 (later type of suppressed pistol) | Special Forces units, such as SEALs |
| Walther | Walther PPK (with suppressor) | Special Forces and covert operators |
| Smith & Wesson | Smith & Wesson Mark 22 Mod.0 "Hush Puppy"—Suppressed pistol | Special Forces units, such as SEALs |

## INFANTRY RIFLES AND AUTOMATIC WEAPONS

| Manufacturer | Equipment | Issued to |
|---|---|---|
| Lithgow Small Arms Factory (Australia) | L1A1 Self-Loading Rifle; Semi-automatic; 20- or 30-round detachable box magazine; Chambered for 7.62×51 NATO cartridge | Australian and New Zealand troops |
| Springfield Armory Winchester Repeating arms Co. | M1 Garand; Semi-automatic; Eight .30–06 cal. Springfield cartridges, clip loaded | Marine Corps, during the early stages of the war, and South Vietnamese, South Koreans and Laotians |
| Various military contractors | M1 carbine and M2 Carbine; Semi-automatic; Eight .30–06 cal. Springfield cartridges, clip loaded | South Vietnamese military, police and security forces, the Việt Cộng, and the U.S. military |
| Various military contractors | M14 rifle; 20-round, detachable box magazine; Chambered for 7.62×51 NATO cartridge | This rifle was issued to U.S. troops from the early stages of the war until 1967, when it was replaced by the M16. Also specialist sniper units. |
| Colt Manufacturing Co. (Licensed U.S. manufacturers) | XM16E1 and M16A1; Semi-automatic operation with 20 or 30 box or 100-round drum magazine; Chambered for 5.56×45mm NATO cartridge | Original XM16E1 was prone to stoppages, replaced by M16A1. XM16E1 issued from 1965. Replaced by M16A1 in 1967. |

| Manufacturer | Equipment | Issued to |
|---|---|---|
| Colt Manufacturing Co. | XM177E2 (shortened version of the M16 rifle) | MACV-SOG units (Special Forces reconnaissance units) |

A number of different types of sub-machine gun and shotguns were also used, mostly by Special Forces personnel.

## Machine Guns

| Manufacturer | Equipment | Issued to |
|---|---|---|
| Lithology Small Arms Factory (Australia) | L2A1 AR; Fully automatic version of the L1A1 SLR; Chambered for 7.62×51mm NATO cartridge | Australian and New Zealand troops |
| Cadillac Gage | Stoner M63a Commando & Mark 23 Mod.; 20- or 30-round box magazine or link fed; Chambered for 5.56×45mm NATO cartridge | U.S. Navy SEALs and tested by Force Recon |
| Saco Defense; U.S. Ordnance | M-60 machine gun GPMG (general purpose machine gun); Link fed; Chambered for 7.62×51 NATO cartridge | Main machine gun of the U.S. Army; also used as helicopter armament |
| Colt Patent Firearms; Various other manufacturers | M1918A2 Browning Automatic Rifle; Used in early stages but replaced by the Stoner 63 and M-60 machine guns; Chambered for .30–06 Springfield cartridge | U.S. troops |
| Various manufacturers | M1917 Browning machine gun; .50 caliber heavy machine gun | South Vietnamese Army and U.S. Army |
| Various manufacturers | M1919 Browning machine gun (replaced by the M-60 machine gun) | U.S. Army |
| Various manufacturers, including FN | Browning M2HB .50 cal Heavy Machine Gun; Link fed; Chambered for .50 BMG (12.7×99mm NATO) cartridge | U.S. Army, on vehicles and aircraft |

## Infantry Support Weapons and Artillery

| Manufacturer | Equipment | Issued to |
|---|---|---|
| Oto Melara (Italy) | L5 pack howitzer 105mm pack howitzer; Caliber: 105mm (HEAT) | Australia |
| Various manufacturers | M18 recoil-less rifle; Caliber: 57×303mm (HE, HEAT, WP) | U.S. Army and VC, supplied by China |
| Various manufacturers | M20 recoil-less rifle; Caliber: 75×408mm (HE, HEAT, SMK) | U.S. Army |

| Manufacturer | Equipment | Issued to |
|---|---|---|
| Various manufacturers | M67 recoil-less rifle; Caliber: 90×714mm; (HE, HEAT, APC [Armor Piercing Canister]) | U.S. Army |
| Various manufacturers | M40 recoil-less rifle; Caliber: 106×607mm (HEAT, HEAP, HEP, APC) | U.S. Army |
| Various manufacturers | M19 Mortar; Caliber: 60mm | U.S. Army |
| Various manufacturers | M29 Mortar; Caliber: 81mm | U.S. Army |
| Various manufacturers | 4-inch mortar; Caliber: 107mm (HE, WP, ILLM) | U.S. Army |
| Various manufacturers | M20 Super Bazooka; Recoil-less anti-tank rocket launcher (HEAT, HESH) | U.S. Marine Corps before introduction of M72 LAW |
| Hesse-Eastern | M72 LAW Light Anti-Tank Weapon; Caliber: 66mm | U.S. Army and Marine Corps |
| General Dynamics | FIM-43 Redeye MANPADS; Man-portable rocket launcher | U.S. Army |
| Rock Island Arsenal | 105mm Howitzer M2A1; Caliber: 105×372 R | U.S. Army |
| Rock Island Arsenal | 105mm Howitzer M102; Caliber: 105×372 R | U.S. Army |
| FMC Corporation | M107 Howitzer; Self-propelled 175mm howitzer; Caliber: 175mm (HE, HEAT) | U.S. Army |
| United Defense LP | M109 Howitzer; Self-propelled 155mm howitzer; Caliber: 155mm L/39 | U.S. Army |
| Various manufacturers | M110 Howitzer; Self-propelled 8-inch howitzer | U.S. Army |
| Various manufacturers | 75mm Pack Howitzer M1; Caliber: 75mm (HEAT) | U.S. Army |

## COMBAT AIRCRAFT

| Manufacturer | Equipment | Service with |
|---|---|---|
| English Electric | Canberra B.20; medium bomber | RAAF |
| Commonwealth Aircraft Corporation | Avon CA-27 Sabre; Australian-made variant of F-86F Sabre jet fighter | RAAF |
| Douglas Aircraft Company | A-1 Skyraider ground attack aircraft | USAF; USN; SVAF (South Vietnam Air Force) |
| Cessna Aircraft Company | A-37 Dragonfly ground attack aircraft | USAF; SVAF |
| Northrop Corporation | F-5 Freedom Fighter; light-weight, low-cost fighter used in strike aircraft role | USN |

| Manufacturer | Equipment | Service with |
| --- | --- | --- |
| Douglas Aircraft Company | A-4 Skyhawk; carrier-based strike aircraft | USN; USMC |
| Grumman Aircraft Engineering Corporation | A-6 Intruder; carrier-based all-weather strike aircraft | USN; USMC |
| LTV | A-7 Corsair II; carrier-based strike aircraft (later variants: A-7D and A-7E) | USAF; USN |
| Bell Helicopter | AH-1 Cobra; attack helicopter | U.S. Army |
| Douglas Aircraft Company | AC-47 Spooky Gunship (based on Douglas DC-3 Dakota) | 1st Air Cavalry Division |
| Lockheed Corporation | AC-130 "Spectre"; gunship | USAF |
| Fairchild Aircraft | AC-119G "Shadow"; gunship | USAF; SVAF |
| Fairchild Aircraft | AC-119K "Stinger"; gunship | USAF; SVAF |
| Boeing Company | B-52 Stratofortress; heavy bomber | USAF |
| Martin Company | B-57 Canberra; medium bomber | USAF |
| McDonnell Aircraft Corporation | F-4 Phantom II; carrier- and land-based fighter-bomber | USAF; USN; USMC |
| Vought | F-8 Crusader; carrier- and land-based fighter-bomber | USN; USMC |

**F-4 Phantom fighter bomber used by USAF, USN and USMC. A large, two-seater fighter/fighter bomber, the F-4 could reach a top speed of over Mach 2.2 while carrying a weapon load in excess of 18,000 pounds, which could include air-to-air missiles, air-to-ground missiles, and bombs of the most usual types then in use by American forces. It was deployed extensively during the Vietnam War as a fighter and in ground attack and reconnaissance roles.**

*Equipment Lists for Forces: 1945–1975 (American/Allied 1963–75)*  293

**F-4B Phantom II of USMC squadron VMFA-314 Black Knights returning to the Chu Lai airbase, South Vietnam, in September 1968.**

**F-4J Phantom showing the extensive weapon-carrying capability of these fighter bombers.**

| Manufacturer | Equipment | Service with |
|---|---|---|
| Republic Aviation | F-105 Thunderchief; fighter-bomber | USAF |
| North American Aviation | F-100 Super Sabre; fighter-bomber | USAF |
| McDonnell Aircraft Corporation | F-101 Voodoo (RF-101); fighter-bomber/ reconnaissance plane | USAF |

| Manufacturer | Equipment | Service with |
| --- | --- | --- |
| Convair | F-102 Delta Dagger; fighter | USAF |
| Lockheed Corporation | F-104 Starfighter; fighter | USAF |
| General Dynamics Corporation | F-111 Aardvark; medium bomber | USAF |
| Hughes Tool Co.; Aircraft Division | OH-6 Cayuse; transport/observation helicopter | U.S. Army |
| Bell Helicopter | UH-1 Iroquois "HUEY"; utility helicopter | U.S. Army; USAF; No. 9 Squadron RAAF |

## Air Support (Helicopters, Fixed-Wing Aircraft)

| Manufacturer | Equipment | Service with |
| --- | --- | --- |
| Lockheed Corporation | C-130 Hercules; tactical cargo aircraft | RAF; RAAF; RNZAF |
| Bristol Aeroplane Company | Type 170 Freighter; twin-engine transport aircraft designed to use unimproved airstrips | RAAF; RNZAF |
| Design by Chase Aircraft and subsequently built by Fairchild Aircraft | C-123 Provider; tactical cargo tactical cargo aircraft | USAF |
| Lockheed Corporation | C-141 Starlifter; strategic cargo aircraft | USAF |
| Boeing Rotorcraft Systems | CH-47 Chinook; medium lift helicopter | U.S. Army |
| Lockheed Corporation | C-5 Galaxy; strategic lift cargo aircraft | USAF |
| De Havilland Canada | C-7 Caribou; tactical cargo aircraft | USAF; RAAF |
| Boeing Vertol | CH-46 Sea Knight; rescue helicopter | U.S. Navy |
| Kaman Aircraft Corporation | H-2 Seasprite helicopter | U.S. Navy |
| Sikorski Aircraft Corporation | H-3 Sea King; rescue and recovery helicopter | U.S. Navy |
| Sikorski Aircraft Corporation | UH-34 Choctaw/seahorse; transport/cargo helicopter | U.S. Army; USN; USMC; RAN as Westland Wessex |
| Sikorski Aircraft Corporation | CH-53 Sea Stallion; medium lift helicopter | USMC |
| Sikorski Aircraft Corporation | CH-54 Skycrane; heavy lift helicopter | U.S. Army |
| Kaman Aircraft Corporation | H-43 Huskie; transport/cargo helicopter | U.S. Army; USN; USMC |
| Cessna | O-1 Bird Dog; observation aircraft | U.S. Army; USAF; SVAF |
| Cessna | O-2 Skymaster; observation aircraft | USAF; USN |

| Manufacturer | Equipment | Service with |
|---|---|---|
| Grumman | OV-1 Mohawk; battlefield surveillance and light strike aircraft | U.S. Army |
| Bell Helicopters | OH-58 Kiowa; transport/observation helicopter | U.S. Army |
| North American Rockwell | OV-10 Bronco; light attack/observation aircraft | USMC; USAF; USN |

## Tanks

| Manufacturer | Equipment | Service with |
|---|---|---|
| Various British manufacturers (produced in 13 variants, not including specialist vehicles) | Centurion; main battle tank; Armament: 105mm L7 main gun; .30 cal. Browning MG | Australian Army (1st Armored Rgt and "B" Squadron, 3rd Cavalry Rgt) |
| Cadillac, General Motors | M41 Walker Bulldog; light tank; Armament: 76mm M32 main gun; .50 cal. M2, .30 cal. M73 MG | South Vietnamese Army (ARVN) |

**M48 Patton tank, the U.S. Army's main battle tank during the Vietnam War. The main armament was a 90mm T54 tank gun, with secondary armament provided by .50 caliber and .30 caliber browning machine guns.**

| Manufacturer | Equipment | Service with |
|---|---|---|
| Chrysler, Ford Motor Company and others | M48 Patton; medium tank; Armament: 90mm T54 main gun or 105mm M68; .50 cal. M2, .30 cal. M73 MG | U.S. Army; USMC; ARVN |
| General Motors | M551 Sheridan; airborne reconnaissance assault vehicle/light tank; Armament: 152mm gun/missile launcher; cal. M2, .30 cal. M73 MG | U.S. Army |

## Armored Vehicles (Including Amphibious Vehicles)

| Manufacturer | Equipment | Service with |
|---|---|---|
| Alvis | Saracen APC; Armament: .30 Browning MG, .303 Bren LMG | Australian Army; New Zealand Army |
| Alvis | Saladin armored car; Armament: 76mm L5A1 main gun; Two .30 cal. Browning MGs | Australian Army; New Zealand Army |

**M8 Greyhound light armored car, declared obsolete by the U.S. Army in 1954, but given to the SVN for use in South Vietnam (Wikipedia; Collective Commons).**

| Manufacturer | Equipment | Service with |
| --- | --- | --- |
| Daimler | Ferret armored car; Armament: 7.6mm GPMG, .30 Browning MG | New Zealand Army |
| Food Machinery Corporation (FMC) | M113; armored personnel carrier; Armament: .50 cal. Browning MG | U.S. Army |
| Ford Motor Company | M8 Greyhound; Light armored car; Armament: 37mm main gun; .30 cal. MG, .50 cal. MG | ARVN |
| FMC | LVTP5 Landing craft | USMC |
| Allis-Chalmers | M50 Ontos; Self-propelled 106mm recoil-less rifle carrier | USMC |
| Cadillac Gage | V-100 Commando; amphibious armored car | USAF; ARVN |
| Not known | AMTRAC; amphibious tractor | USMC |
| Cadillac, GM | M114; reconnaissance vehicle | ARVN |
| GM; Cleveland Tank Plant | M42 Duster (self-propelled gun based on M41 light tank, with a twin 40mm anti-aircraft gun mounted on an open turret) | U.S. Army |

## BOATS AND AMPHIBIOUS VEHICLES

| Manufacturer | Equipment | Service with |
| --- | --- | --- |
| Various manufacturers | Monitor; flat-bottomed craft, armed with large-caliber guns designed for river use | USN "Brown Water" Navy; River Assault Flotilla One |
| Sewart Seacraft | Swift Boat; PCF (Patrol Craft, Fast) | USN; NRVN (SV Navy) |
| Various manufacturers | ASPB (Assault Support Patrol Boat) known as Alpha boats | USMC; USN |
| Various manufacturers | PBR (Patrol Boat, River); all-fiberglass boats propelled by twin water jets | USN; NRVN |
| Various manufacturers | USS *George Clymer* APA 27; troop transport | U.S. Army; USMC |
| Bell Aerosystems (under licence from British Hovercraft Corp.) | PACV (Patrol Air Cushion Vehicle); based on SR.N5 hovercraft, made under license by Bell as SK-5 | U.S. Navy River Patrol |
| Higgins Industries | LCVP (Landing Craft Vehicle Personal); landing craft designed to land troops | USMC; USN |
| Various manufacturers | LCM (Landing Craft Mechanized) landing craft designed to land vehicles | USMC; USN |

| Manufacturer | Equipment | Service with |
|---|---|---|
| Various manufacturers | Mark I PBR (Patrol Boat, River); armored river patrol boat | USN; NRVN |
| Various manufacturers | LARC-LX (a.k.a. BARC) amphibious lighter | USN |

## Logistic Support (Lorries and Jeeps)

| Manufacturer | Equipment | Service with |
|---|---|---|
| Willys, Ford MC | M38A1 ¼ ton Jeep | U.S. Army |
| Ford MC, AMG | Ford M151 MUTT ¼ ton Military Utility Tactical Truck (Jeep) | U.S. Army |
| Dodge | Dodge M37, ¾ ton truck | U.S. Army |
| Kaiser Motors | Kaiser-Jeep M715 1¼ ton truck | U.S. Army |
| Various | Truck, cargo/troops, 2½ ton (deuce and a half) | U.S. Army |
| Various | Truck, cargo/troops, 5 ton | U.S. Army |
| Caterpillar Inc. | M520 Goer Truck, cargo, 8 ton, 4×4 | U.S. Army |
| Rover Company | Land Rover, both short and long wheelbase types | Australian and New Zealand forces |
| GMC | M135 cargo/troop truck, 2½ ton | U.S. Army |
| GMC | M211 cargo/troop truck, 2½ ton | U.S. Army |

A variety of miscellaneous logistical vehicles not designed specifically for combat were sometimes armored and used in an escort role. These included:

- Gun trucks
- 2½ and 5 ton cargo trucks with quad .50 cal. machine guns mounted in the back
- M3 halftracks with quad .50 cal. machine guns in the back
- Jeeps with mounted M-60 machine guns
- Land Rovers with single and twin M-60 machine guns mounted (used by Australian and New Zealand forces)

## Logistic Supply (Rations, Ammunition and Miscellaneous Requirements)

In 1967, over 100 pounds of material were being moved into South Vietnam every day for every American stationed there, approximately one million tons each month. This included shaving foam, toilet rolls, aftershave and even U.S.-made clothes, cars and motorcycles, which were available from the U.S. Army's PX (Post Exchange).

# *Vietnamese Forces (1963–1975)*

All weapons are of Russian or Chinese manufacture or captured French, Japanese or American weapons.

## Pistols

| Manufacturer | Equipment |
|---|---|
| USSR government arsenals | Tokarev TT-33 handgun; Chambered for 7.62×25mm Tokarov cartridge |
| USSR government arsenals | Makarov PM handgun; Chambered for 9×18mm Makarov |
| USSR government arsenals | P-64 CZAK handgun; Chambered for 9×18mm Makarov |
| USSR government arsenals | Nagant M1895 revolver; Chambered for 7.62×38mm Nagant, Rimmed |
| Mauser | Mauser C96 handgun ("Broomhandle" Mauser); Chambered for 9×19mm Parabellum or 7.62×25mm Mauser |
| USSR government arsenals | CZ 52 handgun; Semi-automatic; 8-round butt magazine; Chambered for 7.62×25mm Tokarov cartridge |
| Tokyo Artillery Arsenal | Type 14 Nambu Pistol; Semi-automatic; 8-round butt magazine; Chambered for 8×22mm Nambu cartridge |

## Infantry Rifles and Automatic Weapons

| Manufacturer/Origin | Equipment |
|---|---|
| Japan | Type 99 Rifle; Chambered for 7.7×58 Arisaka |
| USSR government arsenals | SVD-63; Semi-automatic marksman rifle a.k.a. the "Dragunov" sniper rifle; Chambered for 7.62×54mm Rimmed |
| Soviet Union, Warsaw Pact countries, and the People's Republic of China | Mosin-Nagant bolt-action rifles and carbines; Chambered for 7.62×54mm Rimmed |
| Many of the Mausers used by the VPA and the NLF were rifles captured from the French during the First Indochina War and rifles provided by the Soviets as military aid | Mauser KAR 98K bolt-action rifle; Chambered for 7.92×57mm Mauser |
| Captured by the Soviets during World War II and provided to the VPA and the NLF as military aid | Sturmgewehr 44 assault rifle; Chambered for 7.92×33mm Kurz |
| USSR government arsenals | Kalashnikov AK-47 and AKM assault rifles; Chambered for 7.62×39mm M43/M67 |
| People's Republic of China government arsenals | Type 56 assault rifle; Chambered for 7.62×39mm M43 |
| People's Republic of China government arsenals | Vz. 58 assault rifle; Chambered for 7.62×39mm M43 |
| Chinese version of Russian PPSh-41, under license | K-50M sub-machine gun; Chambered for 7.62×25mm Tokarov |
| USSR government arsenals | PPSh-41 sub-machine gun; Chambered for; 7.62×25mm Tokarov |

Kalashnikov AK-47 assault rifle, this one the Type 2 variant, which had a machined receiver, rather than this component being stamped from sheet steel. Invented by Mikhail Kalashnikov, this weapon was adopted by the Soviet army in 1949 and has remained the most popular and widely used assault rifle in the world, principally because of its low production costs and reliability under even the worst conditions.

Kalashnikov AK-47 assault rifle, magazines, ammunition and ammo pouch. Although they are heavy, the early magazines mirrored the robust character of the AK-47, with some troops even having used them as hammers without inflicting significant damage on the magazine (Wikipedia; Creative Commons).

| *Manufacturer/Origin* | *Equipment* |
|---|---|
| Manufacture d'Armes de Tulle (MAT) in 1946 | MAT 49; Chambered for 9×19mm Parabellum |
| Czechoslovakia | Sa vz. 23 sub-machine gun; Chambered for 7.62×25mm Tokarov |
| Poland | PM-63 RAK sub-machine gun; Chambered for 9×18mm Makarov; 9×19mm Parabellum |
| Germany | MP40 sub-machine gun; Chambered for 9×19mm Parabellum |

*Equipment Lists for Forces: 1945–1975 (Vietnamese 1963–75)*

| Manufacturer/Origin | Equipment |
|---|---|
| USSR government arsenals | PPS-43 sub-machine gun; Chambered for 7.62×25mm Tokarov |
| People's Republic of China government arsenals | Type 63 assault rifle; Chambered for 7.62×39mm M43 |

## Machine Guns

| Manufacturer | Equipment |
|---|---|
| Used by Japanese forces in World War II and probably subsequently supplied to the Việt Minh | Type 99 LMG; Chambered for 7.7×58mm Arisaka cartridge |
| USSR government arsenals | RPD light machine gun; Chambered for 7.62×39mm M43 cartridge |
| USSR government arsenals | Degtyarev DP light machine gun; Chambered for Soviet 7.62×54mm cartridge |
| USSR government arsenals | RPK light machine gun; Designed by Mikhail Kalashnikov as part of a program to standardize arms supplied to the Red Army; Chambered for Soviet 7.62×39mm cartridge |
| Captured by the Soviets during World War II and provided to the VPA and the NLF as military aid | MG-34 light machine gun; Chambered for 7.92×57mm Mauser cartridge |
| Captured by the Soviets during World War II and provided to the VPA and the NLF as military aid | MG-42 light machine gun; Chambered for 7.92×57mm Mauser cartridge |
| Czechoslovakia | Uk vz. 59 general-purpose machine gun; Chambered for 7.62×54mm Rimmed cartridge; 7.62×51mm NATO |
| USSR government arsenals (equivalent to M2 Browning HMG) | DShK heavy machine gun; Chambered for 12.7×108mm USSR cartridge |

**RPK Soviet light machine gun. Based on the mechanism of the AK-47, it differs only in having a longer, chrome-lined barrel to allow extended periods of fire without overheating and a bipod support at the muzzle. Other minor changes include an improved front sight and strengthened receiver.**

| Manufacturer | Equipment |
|---|---|
| USSR government arsenals (in service since 1910, and carriage-mounted) | PM M1910 heavy machine gun; Chambered for 7.62×54mm Rimmed cartridge |
| USSR government arsenals | PK machine gun; Chambered for 7.62×54mm Rimmed cartridge |

## Artillery (Mortars, Field Guns, Anti-Aircraft Guns)

| Manufacturer | Equipment |
|---|---|
| USSR government arsenals | ZPU-4 quad 14.5mm anti-aircraft machine gun; 14.5mm full metal jacket cartridge, incendiary cartridge |
| USSR government arsenals | ZU-23 twin 23mm anti-aircraft cannon; 23mm AP (Armor Piercing), HE (High Explosive) |
| USSR government arsenals | M1939 37mm anti-aircraft gun; 37×250mm FRAG (Fragmentation), AP, HE, HVAP |
| USSR government arsenals | S-60 57mm anti-aircraft gun; 57mm AP, HE |

M1939 37mm automatic air defense gun (61-K). Soviet anti-aircraft gun developed in the 1930s and largely obsolete by the time of the Vietnam War, although many were sent to North Vietnam as part of the Soviets' military aid package.

| Manufacturer | Equipment |
|---|---|
| USSR government arsenals | 82mm, 107mm, and 120mm mortars; ammunition appropriate for caliber in HE |
| USSR government arsenals | 122mm Katyusha rockets |
| USSR government arsenals | 122mm gun 1931–1937; 121.92mm FRAG, HE, AP, CHEM |
| USSR government arsenals | 122mm howitzer M1938; 121.92mm HE, HEAT, FRAG, CHEM, SMK, ILLM |
| USSR government arsenals | 122mm D-74 field gun; 122mm HE, APHE |
| USSR government arsenals | 130mm M1954 field gun; 130mm FRAG, HE, AP, SMK, CHEM, ILLM |
| USSR government arsenals | 152mm howitzer; 152.4mm HE, HEAT, FRAG, CHEM, ILLM |
| USSR government arsenals | 152 howitzer M1955 (D-20); 152.4mm HE, CHEM, INCND |

## AIR SUPPORT (HELICOPTERS, FIXED-WING AIRCRAFT)

| Manufacturer | Equipment |
|---|---|
| Mikoyen-Gurevich OKB | MiG-21 jet fighter |
| Mikoyen-Gurevich OKB | MiG-19 jet fighter, used in limited numbers |
| Mikoyen-Gurevich OKB | MiG-17 jet fighter |
| Mikoyen-Gurevich OKB | MiG-15 jet fighter, used in limited numbers |
| Shenyang Aircraft Corporation | Shenyang J-6 jet fighter, PRC version of MiG-19 |

**MiG-15 single-seater jet fighter, used extensively in the Korean War. It was obsolete by the time of the Vietnam War, being largely replaced by the MiG-17 and MiG-19, although North Vietnam operated a number of MiG-15s and MiG-15UTIs for training purposes. The fighter never saw combat against American aircraft (Wikipedia; Creative Commons).**

MiG-17 landing. This aircraft saw extensive service with the North Vietnamese air force and was that entity's primary interceptor from 1965 (Wikipedia; Creative Commons).

MiG-21 jet fighter aircraft, designed for ground-controlled interception (GCI) sorties of short duration. It proved an effective adversary to the F-4 Phantoms of the USAF and USN.

**Mil Mi-4 transport helicopter, used extensively by the North Vietnamese.**

| Manufacturer | Equipment |
|---|---|
| Shenyang Aircraft Corporation | Shenyang J-5 jet fighter |
| Antonov Design Bureau | An-2 aircraft; utility and combat bi-plane |
| Mi Moscow Helicopter Plant | Mi-4 helicopter; (similar to Westland Whirlwind and Chicasaw H-19/S-55) |
| Mi Moscow Helicopter Plant | Mi-1 helicopter; light utility helicopter |
| Mi Moscow Helicopter Plant | Mi-2 helicopter; small transport and close-support helicopter |
| Mi Moscow Helicopter Plant | Mi-8 helicopter; large transport and close-support helicopter (also gunship versions) |

## Vehicles (Tanks and Personnel Carriers)

| Manufacturer | Equipment |
|---|---|
| Harbin First Machinery Building Group, 674 Factory (USSR) | Type 62; light tank; Armament: 85mm rifled main gun; 7.62mm and 12.5mm machine guns |
| Government factory (USSR) | T-34/85; medium tank (used in limited numbers); Armament: 76mm F-34 main gun; two 7.62mm machine guns |
| Government factory (USSR) | T-54; main battle tank; Armament: 100mm, D-10T; main gun; one 7.62 MMG, one 12.7mm HMG |
| Government factory (USSR) | Type 59 main battle tanks; Armament: 100mm main gun; two 7.62 MMG, one 12.7mm HMG |

**T-55 main battle tank, used extensively by the North Vietnamese Army. Armed with the D-10T 100mm rifle gun, this tank often did poorly against the M48 Patten tanks of the ARVN, although it did achieve considerable success against more lightly armored vehicles, particularly at Tan Canh in April 1972.**

| Manufacturer | Equipment |
| --- | --- |
| Government factory (USSR) | SU-100; Self-propelled guns (supplied in limited numbers); Armament: 100mm, D-10T main gun |
| VTF (Volgograd Tractor Factory); Kirov Plant (USSR) | PT-76; amphibious tank; Armament: 76.2mm rifled tank gun, 7.62mm machine gun |
| Harbin First Machinery Building Group, 674 Factory (USSR) | Type 62; light tank; 85mm rifled main gun; 7.62mm and 12.5mm machine guns |
| NORINCO (PRC) | Type 63; amphibious tank; light tank; Armament: 85mm rifled main gun; 7.62mm and 12.5mm machine guns |
| GAZ (USSR); Various manufacturers (PRC) | BTR-40; armored personnel carrier; Armament: 7.62mm medium machine gun |
| GAZ (USSR); Various manufacturers (PRC) | BTR-50; amphibious, tracked, armored personnel carrier; Armament: 7.62mm medium machine gun |
| Government factory (USSR) | BTR-152; armored personnel carrier; Armament: 7.62 mm medium machine gun |
| Government factory (USSR) | BRDM-1; armored reconnaissance/patrol vehicle; Armament: 7.62mm medium machine gun; Later models had 12.7mm or 14.5mm HMG |
| Government factory (PRC) | Type 63; armored personnel carrier; Armament: 12.7mm medium machine gun |
| Government factory (North Vietnam) | Type 63; Self-propelled anti-aircraft gun; Armament: Two 37mm AA auto-cannons |

BTR-40 armored personnel carrier, used by the North Vietnamese army in the later stages of the war. It could be equipped with three 7.62 medium machine guns (SGMB) and carried a crew of two (commander and driver), with the capability of holding up to eight fully equipped passengers (Wikipedia; Creative Commons).

| Manufacturer | Equipment |
| --- | --- |
| Government factory (USSR) | ZSU-57–2; Self-propelled anti-aircraft gun; Armament: Two 57mm AA auto-cannons |
| MMZ (Mytishchi Engineering Works) | ZSU-23–4; Self-propelled anti-aircraft gun; Armament: Four 23mm AA auto-cannons |

## Logistic Supply (Rations, Ammunition and Miscellaneous Requirements)

| Manufacturer/ Supplier | Equipment |
| --- | --- |
| Locally acquired | Mostly fresh rations (rice, etc.), and presumably much of what was stolen from the Americans |
| China and USSR | Ammunition, radio equipment, medical supplies and fuel |

Logistic support was provided by truck, bicycle, mule and human porters, down the Hồ Chí Minh Trail. In contrast to the Americans, the Việt Cộng used only 15 tons of supplies each day to maintain their efforts in the south, approximately 450 tons each month, compared to the U.S. supply of over 1 million tons each month, although the Soviet Union and China together were sending North Vietnam much more than this, approximately 180,000 tons of supplies each month (6,000 tons/day). One problem associated with logistic supply must have arisen over ammunition, since the NVA and NLA were using weapons chambered for at least ten different types of cartridge.

## British Arms Supply

As these lists clearly indicate, all the equipment used in Vietnam by American forces was produced by U.S. companies, with British companies responsible only for arms supplied to Commonwealth troops, mainly equipment such as the Chieftain main battle tank, the Alvis range of military vehicles and the Daimler Ferret. Nor did Britain supply Australia or New Zealand with the L1A1 self-loading rifles, these being made at the Lithgow Small Arms Factory, NSW. Britain did supply some of the 7.62×51mm NATO ammunition for which this rifle was chambered, although this cartridge was also produced in Australia as "Cartridge, Caliber 7.62mm, NATO, Ball, F4."

# Chapter Notes

## Abbreviations

PRO—Public Record Office (National Archives, UK). Public record office files are referred to by their file number, followed by their title.

HMSO—Her Majesty's Stationery Office.

*Hansard—Hansard* (the Official Report): edited verbatim report of proceedings of both the House of Commons and the House of Lords.

## Chapter 1

1. This is the origin of the term "Ammanite," which was sometimes wrongly applied to all ethnic Vietnamese. "Tonkinese" refers to people from North Vietnam.

2. British clandestine involvement in Vietnam during World War II and American (and particularly OSS) involvement in North Vietnam during this period is discussed in Peter Dunn, *The First Vietnam War* (London: C. Hurst, 1985), Chapter 2.

3. Stanley Karnow, *Vietnam: A History* (New York: Viking, 1983), p. 137.

4. Karnow, *Vietnam: A History*.

5. Dunn, *The First Vietnam War*, p. 43.

6. Karnow, *Vietnam: A History*.

7. F.S.V. Donnison, *British Military Administration in the Far East, 1943–1946* (London: HMSO, 1956).

8. Dunn, *The First Vietnam War*.

9. "Hồ Chí Mính," Appendix 2, "Participants."

10. Karnow, *Vietnam: A History*.

11. Dunn, *The First Vietnam War*, p. 256.

12. Dunn, *The First Vietnam War*, p. 120.

13. This statement has been widely, but quite wrongly, attributed to General Gracey before he left Rangoon. In fact, when dealing with the media, he carefully confined himself to simply repeating what had been said in their press statements by the Joint Planning Staff. See Dunn, *The First Vietnam War*, p. 141.

14. This included Major-General D.D. Gracey (20 Indian Div), Lt-General Stopford (12 Army), Lt-General Dempsey (14 Army), Lt-General Christison (15 Indian Corps) and Lt-General Roberts (34 Indian Corps). Dunn, *The First Vietnam War*.

15. Roosevelt's attitude to FIC and the French is described in Dunn, *The First Vietnam War*, p. 69. Incidentally, in a further demonstration of American antipathy to the colonial powers, many members of Roosevelt's team had opposed British participation in the Pacific Fleet, feeling this would also encourage a return to British colonial rule in the area.

16. The roles of Dewy and Patti are discussed in Dunn, *The First Vietnam War*. Dunn, who served as a colonel in the American Air Force, and fought in Vietnam, should be considered unbiased enough for most in this context. Details of the careers of Dewy and Patti will be found in Appendix II.

17. Dunn, *The First Vietnam War*, p. 51.

18. Ho's quote, "eating french shit," is from Karnow, *Vietnam: A History*, Chapter 2.

19. Dunn, *The First Vietnam War*.

20. Dunn, *The First Vietnam War*, p. 159 and p. 234–235.

21. Dunn, *The First Vietnam War*, p. 131.

22. Dunn, *The First Vietnam War*, p. 141.

23. Dunn, *The First Vietnam War*, p. 141.

24. Dunn, *The First Vietnam War*.

25. Dunn, *The First Vietnam War*, p. 143–144.

26. A complete discussion of British misgivings about their role and an assessment of the value of certain historical contributions is given in Dunn, *The First Vietnam War*, Chapters 6 and 7.

27. Dunn, *The First Vietnam War*, p. 146; PRO. WO 203/5644.

28. Dunn, *The First Vietnam War*, p. 197. This source also includes a full account of Gracey's dilemma and the official memos describing the return of Indochina to French control and U.S. involvement.

29. Dunn, *The First Vietnam War*, p. 134.

30. Dunn, *The First Vietnam War*.

31. In the British army, bodies of troops are designated by battalion/regiment. Thus, for example, 1/1 Gurkha Rifles means troops from the 1st Battalion of the 1st Regiment, Gurkha Rifles.

32. Dunn, *The First Vietnam War*, p. 150.

33. The Americans (Brigadier-General Timberman) claimed it was "preferable" not to allow U.S. signals party to accompany the Saigon Control Commission, leaving Gracey without a signals office for several weeks. Dunn, *The First Vietnam War*.

34. Dunn, *The First Vietnam War*, p. 151.

35. Control of Saigon was crucial to any military operation in South Vietnam, as the city dominated

the country's only international airport as well as the main rail and road links. It also controlled access to the city's deepwater port, which was one of the country's largest.

36. Dunn, *The First Vietnam War*, p. 170.
37. Dunn, *The First Vietnam War*, p. 146.
38. At this point, Gracey said he had not received Slim's amendment to his orders to restrict operations to key areas. He also said later, at a meeting with the SAC on 28 September, that although he interpreted his instructions as meaning his forces were confined to key areas, he could not simply absolve himself of responsibility for law and order below the 16th Parallel, where he was forced to rely on the Japanese to undertake those duties. Even had he not been inclined to do so on humane grounds, Britain's Manual of Military Law made him responsible for the safety of civilians in any area under his jurisdiction. Dunn, *The First Vietnam War*, p. 230.
39. Dunn, *The First Vietnam War*, p. 211.
40. Dunn, *The First Vietnam War*, p.173.
41. Dunn, *The First Vietnam War*, p. 164.
42. Dunn, *The First Vietnam War*, p. 177–179.
43. Dunn, *The First Vietnam War*, p.179–180.
44. Dunn, *The First Vietnam War*, p. 51.
45. Gracey's release from the SAC's restrictions was suggested by a member of the Foreign Office in a memo dated as early as 20 September, although it was not until 30 September that the Joint Chiefs received a JPS report confirming the situation and reiterating this suggestion. Incidentally, the Foreign Office also had significant misgivings about the effect any statement about British participation being "minimal" might have on encouraging the activities of the Việt Minh and thus further impeding the re-establishment of the French, perhaps fatally. See Dunn, *The First Vietnam War*, p. 182–183.
46. Dunn, *The First Vietnam War*, p. 202.
47. Dunn, *The First Vietnam War*, p. 208–209.
48. Dunn, *The First Vietnam War*, p. 198.
49. Dunn, *The First Vietnam War*, p.179.
50. Dunn, *The First Vietnam War*, p. 179.

## *Chapter 2*

1. Peter Dunn, *The First Vietnam War* (London: C. Hurst, 1985), p. 208–209.
2. Dunn, *The First Vietnam War*, p. 211–212.
3. Dunn, *The First Vietnam War*, p. 214–217; see also Appendix II of this book.
4. Dunn, *The First Vietnam War*, p. 224–226.
5. Dunn, *The First Vietnam War*, p. 226.
6. Dunn, *The First Vietnam War*, p. 227.
7. Dunn, *The First Vietnam War*, p. 230.
8. Dunn, *The First Vietnam War*, p. 233–235.
9. Dunn, *The First Vietnam War*, p. 239–241.
10. Dunn, *The First Vietnam War*, p. 249–251.
11. Dunn, *The First Vietnam War*, p. 257.
12. Dunn, *The First Vietnam War*, p. 259.
13. Dunn, *The First Vietnam War*, p. 265–267.
14. Dunn, *The First Vietnam War*, p. 264.
15. Dunn, *The First Vietnam War*, p. 269.
16. Dunn, *The First Vietnam War*, p. 273.
17. R. Harris Smith, *OSS* (Berkeley: University of California Press, 1972).
18. Dunn, *The First Vietnam War*, p. 277–278.
19. Dunn, *The First Vietnam War*, p. 280–284.
20. Dunn, *The First Vietnam War*, p. 290–291.
21. Dunn, *The First Vietnam War*, p. 293.
22. Dunn, *The First Vietnam War*, p. 293–300.
23. This was typical of Gracey, who regarded himself as personally responsible for the lives of the men he commanded in the 20th Division. He said on more than one occasion that it was not hard to be a great commander if the acceptance of unlimited casualties was of little importance. Dunn, *The First Vietnam War*, p. 326.
24. The Việt Minh were thought to be concentrated in four areas: (1) between Thủ Dầu Một and Ben Cat, (2) west and south-west of Bung, (3) around Ben Go, a town on the river 8 kilometer south of Biên Hòa and (4) north-west of Biên Hòa.
25. Dunn, *The First Vietnam War*, p. 332.
26. Despite the claims of some writers, Gracey did not rearm the Japanese troops under his command. He simply never disarmed them because he needed to use them for security duties, in line with Truman's directive.
27. See Trevor-Wilson's report, in Dunn, *The First Vietnam War*, p. 328.
28. See Dunn, *The First Vietnam War*, p. 161 and 343.
29. Dunn, *The First Vietnam War*, p. 161.
30. Dunn, *The First Vietnam War*, p. 263.
31. Dunn, *The First Vietnam War*, p. 195.
32. Stanley Karnow, *Vietnam: A History* (New York: Viking, 1983), p. 175.
33. With regard to reference sources in Chapters 1 and 2:

It may seem to some readers that the author has relied perhaps too heavily on Mr. Peter Dunn's book, *The First Vietnam War*. The reason for this is simple: Mr. Dunn's work is almost the only balanced, detailed report of the British Army's time in Vietnam between September 1945 and May 1946, and his account of that period is corroborated by reference to the British government's own records and Major-General Douglas Gracey's personal papers. In other words, he is that most invaluable and unusual journalistic source—a writer who can prove what he says, and who includes a list of verifiable references. The author can confirm the accuracy of Mr. Dunn's work, having checked most of the sources personally—hence the reliance placed on his publication.

## *Chapter 3*

1. Stanley Karnow, *Vietnam: A History* (New York: Viking, 1983), p. 150–151.
2. Karnow, *Vietnam: A History*, p. 153.
3. Karnow, *Vietnam: A History*, p. 156.

4. The Truman Doctrine was introduced on 12 March 1947, when President Truman asked Congress for funds to "support free peoples who are resisting subjugation by armed minorities or by outside pressures." What this came to mean was that funds were given to fight any faction the United States saw as undesirable. See Karnow, *Vietnam: A History*.

5. For a discussion of the later U.S. position in 1950 and the "domino effect," see Karnow, *Vietnam: A History*, p. 169–170.

6. Karnow, *Vietnam: A History*, p. 171.
7. Karnow, *Vietnam: A History*, p. 180.
8. Karnow, *Vietnam: A History*, p. 187.
9. Karnow, *Vietnam: A History*, p. 198–204.
10. Karnow, *Vietnam: A History*, p. 198.

## Chapter 4

1. Stanley Karnow, *Vietnam: A History* (New York: Viking, 1983), p. 223–224; see also "Ngô Đình Diệm" in Appendix 2.
2. Karnow, *Vietnam: A History*, p. 223–224.
3. Karnow, *Vietnam: A History*, p. 236.
4. Karnow, *Vietnam: A History*, p. 231–232.
5. Karnow, *Vietnam: A History*, p. 282.
6. Karnow, *Vietnam: A History*, p. 247–269. For more information on the British Advisory Mission to Vietnam, see Chapter 5 of this book.
7. Karnow, *Vietnam: A History*, p. 287.
8. Henry Cabot Lodge, *New York Times*, 30 June 1964.
9. "Ngô Đình Diệm," in Appendix 2.

## Chapter 5

1. Edward Heath, "Written Commons Answer," *Hansard*, 23 October 1961.
2. Peter Busch, *All the Way with JFK? Britain, the U.S., and the Vietnam War* (Oxford: Oxford University Press, 2003), p. 67.
3. Busch, *All the Way with JFK?*, p. 75.
4. Sir Robert Thompson, *No Exit from Vietnam* (New York: David McKay, 1969).
5. Busch, *All the Way with JFK?*
6. Busch, *All the Way with JFK?*
7. PRO. FO 371/180627, "Adverse 'Daily Mirror' Article on British Police Advisers in Vietnam."
8. See "Richard Noone," in Appendix II.
9. Richard Lamb, *The Macmillan Years 1957–1963* (London: John Murray Ltd., 1995).

## Chapter 6

1. Stanley Karnow, *Vietnam: A History* (New York: Viking, 1983), p. 326.
2. Johnson, despite his record in Vietnam, promoted some of the most progressive legislation in the field of social justice and economic and racial equality seen in the United States for many years. Some observers suggest that his early conduct of the war was an attempt to placate the more right-wing members of Congress so as to allow passage of this important social legislation. See Karnow, *Vietnam: A History* (New York: Viking, 1983), p. 320.

3. Karnow, *Vietnam: A History*, p. 325–326.
4. Karnow, *Vietnam: A History*, p. 331–332.
5. Karnow, *Vietnam: A History*, p. 401.
6. Karnow, *Vietnam: A History*, p. 362.
7. The DMZ was established after the first Indochina war as a boundary between North and South Vietnam, at the Ben Hai River, which enters the South China Sea at 17 degrees 0 minutes 54 seconds N latitude. The boundary followed the Ben Hai to its headwaters, about 55 kilometers WSW, and thence to the Laotian border. The area within 5 kilometer on either side of the border was declared a demilitarized zone and the troops of both governments were barred from this area.
8. Karnow, *Vietnam: A History*, p. 396.
9. Karnow, *Vietnam: A History*, p. 377.
10. Thiệu became president of South Vietnam in 1967, ruling until 1973. Kỳ was deposed as prime minister in 1967, but ruled as a figurehead vice-president, alongside Thiệu, until 1971.
11. "Rolling Thunder" resulted in the deaths of 90,000 Vietnamese, approximately 72,000 of these casualties being civilian. By 1 December 1967, after 33 months, 864,000 tons of bombs had been dropped, 996 U.S. aircraft had been lost, and approximately $530 million worth of damage had been done to North Vietnam's infrastructure and capital assets. Losses of U.S. aircraft alone had totaled $900 million, and when the figures for ordnance, wages and other consumables had been added, the estimated cost of "Rolling Thunder" was close to $3 billion, or "ten dollars for every dollar's worth of damage."
12. Karnow, *Vietnam: A History*, p. 413.
13. Karnow, *Vietnam: A History*, p. 418.
14. Karnow, *Vietnam: A History*, p. 436.
15. The degree of force being directed against the Việt Cộng is clearly demonstrated when one considers that the air traffic over South Vietnam during this period was heavier than in any other country in the world. Karnow, *Vietnam: A History*, p. 436–439.
16. Karnow, *Vietnam: A History*, p. 455.
17. Karnow, *Vietnam: A History*, p. 463.
18. Karnow, *Vietnam: A History*, p. 443.
19. Karnow, *Vietnam: A History*, p. 422.
20. Karnow, *Vietnam: A History*, p. 444.
21. Karnow, *Vietnam: A History*, p. 450–451.
22. Karnow, *Vietnam: A History*, p. 452.
23. For a discussion of the Communist military operation, see Karnow, *Vietnam: A History*, p. 460–463.
24. Karnow, *Vietnam: A History*, p. 460.
25. Karnow, *Vietnam: A History*, p. 466.
26. Ron Kovic, *Born on the Fourth of July* (New York: Akashic Books, 2005), p. 49.
27. Karnow, *Vietnam: A History*, p. 464–472.
28. Karnow, *Vietnam: A History*, p. 472.
29. Karnow, *Vietnam: A History*, p. 472–473.

30. Statistics illustrating this use of illegal narcotics are included in Chapter 7: "America's War (1968–1973)."

31. A survey published in October 1967 showed 46 percent of those polled regarded the war as "a mistake," while only 44 percent continued to back it. This was the first time the polls had shown those in favor of the war to be in a minority, although support had been dwindling since 1965. Karnow, *Vietnam: A History*, p. 488.

32. Karnow, *Vietnam: A History*, p. 483 and 492–496.

33. Karnow, *Vietnam: A History*, p. 490–491.

34. Karnow, *Vietnam: A History*, p. 501.

35. Karnow, *Vietnam: A History*, p. 502–504.

36. Karnow, *Vietnam: A History*, p. 505–507.

37. See "McNamara, Robert," in Appendix 2; Karnow, *Vietnam: A History*, p. 507–509.

38. Karnow, *Vietnam: A History*, p. 542–543.

39. For a list of towns and villages attacked, see Karnow, *Vietnam: A History*, p. 523–525 and 541–542.

40. Karnow, *Vietnam: A History*, p. 536.

41. Karnow, *Vietnam: A History*, p. 546.

42. Karnow, *Vietnam: A History*, p. 554.

43. Karnow, *Vietnam: A History*, p. 555–556.

44. Karnow, *Vietnam: A History*, p. 557–562.

45. Karnow, *Vietnam: A History*, p. 564–566.

## *Chapter 7*

1. At least, that is what the vice-president's supporters have always claimed. See Stanley Karnow, *Vietnam: A History* (New York: Viking, 1983), p. 580–582.

2. Karnow, *Vietnam: A History*, p. 582.

3. Karnow, *Vietnam: A History*, p. 577.

4. Karnow, *Vietnam: A History*, p. 585–587.

5. Karnow, *Vietnam: A History*, p. 590–591.

6. Karnow, *Vietnam: A History*, p. 597–598.

7. Karnow, *Vietnam: A History*, p. 598.

8. Karnow, *Vietnam: A History*, p. 600.

9. Helen Gahagan Douglas gave him this nickname during the 1950 U.S. Senate race in California, in reference to Nixon's alleged use of dirty tricks during the campaign.

10. The Khmer Rouge was the name given to the Cambodian Communist movement.

11. Karnow, *Vietnam: A History*, p. 611.

12. Karnow, *Vietnam: A History*, p. 623–625.

13. At the Geneva conference in 1954, the major powers had forced the Communists to stop fighting by holding out the expectation that free, nationwide elections would be held 2 years later. Later, those same powers conspired to prevent the elections, leaving Ngô Đình Diệm in power until his death in 1963.

14. Karnow, *Vietnam: A History*, pp. 175–178.

15. Karnow, *Vietnam: A History*, p. 629–630.

16. In 1970, U.S. Command in Saigon estimated 65,000 GIs were using narcotics (heroin, speed, LSD, or marijuana). In 1971, U.S. Army medical officers estimated that 10–15 percent of enlisted men were using heroin in some form (smoked, injected, etc.), mostly in response to the crackdown on marijuana use. By 1973, this proportion had risen to 34 percent. Karnow, *Vietnam: A History*, p. 631–632.

17. The Pentagon Papers were a huge collection of confidential government memoranda that had been compiled and analyzed by officials from the Defence Department during the Johnson administration. They were commissioned by Robert McNamara, although his purpose for doing so is not clear. Daniel Ellsberg, a former bureaucrat, later confessed to stealing and releasing the material. Karnow, *Vietnam: A History*, p. 633–634.

18. Karnow, *Vietnam: A History*, p. 634.

19. The Saigon regime had more than a million men in uniform, half regular troops and the rest in various local units, compared to one hundred and twenty thousand North Vietnamese regular troops and approximately eighty thousand Việt Cộng "irregulars."

20. Karnow, *Vietnam: A History*, p. 646.

21. Karnow, *Vietnam: A History*, p. 648.

22. Karnow, *Vietnam: A History*, p. 649.

23. Karnow, *Vietnam: A History*, p. 651–653.

24. Karnow, *Vietnam: A History*, p. 169.

25. Karnow, *Vietnam: A History* (New York: Viking, 1994), p. 16.

26. China became a Communist country after Mao Zedong declared the republic in October 1949.

27. Karnow, *Vietnam: A History*, p. 171, p. 175.

28. China's early involvement in Vietnam is discussed more fully in Karnow, *Vietnam: A History*, Chapter 3, "The Heritage of Vietnamese Nationalism."

29. The ambiguities of Johnson's approach are described in Karnow, *Vietnam: A History*, p. 395.

30. Graham Greene, *The Quiet American* (London: William Heinemann, 1955).

## *Chapter 8*

1. Sylvia Ellis, *Britain, America and the Vietnam War* (Santa Barbara, CA: Praeger, 2004); Jonathan Colman, *A "Special Relationship"? Harold Wilson, Lyndon B. Johnson and Anglo-American Relations "at the Summit," 1964–68* (Manchester: Manchester University Press, 2004); Richard Lamb, *The Macmillan Years 1957–1963* (London: John Murray Ltd., 1995).

2. See Chapter 1 of this book.

3. See "Corps Léger d'Intervention" in Appendix 2.

4. Peter Dunn, *The First Vietnam War* (London: C. Hurst, 1985), p. 28–30.

5. Dunn, *The First Vietnam War*, p. 79; "Mountbatten, Lord Louis," in Appendix 2.

6. Dunn, *The First Vietnam War*, p. 70.

7. Dunn, *The First Vietnam War*, p. 68–80; "Roosevelt, Franklin D.," Appendix 2.

8. Dunn, *The First Vietnam War*, p. 77.

9. Dunn, *The First Vietnam War*, p. 79.

10. PRO. FC 371/92400, " Annual Review of Events in Associated States of Vietnam, etc."
11. Lamb, *The Macmillan Years 1957–1963*, p. 379–381.
12. Lamb, *The Macmillan Years 1957–1963*.
13. Guy Laron, *Origins of the Suez Crisis: Postwar Development, Diplomacy and the Struggle over Third World Industrialization: 1945–1956* (Baltimore: John Hopkins University Press, 2013).
14. Harold Macmillan, *At the End of the Day* (London: Macmillan, 1973), p. 111.
15. John Dickie, *Special No More: Anglo-American Relations: Rhetoric and Reality* (London: Wiedenfeld and Nicholson, 1994), p. 105.
16. Alistair Horne, *Macmillan 1957–1986: Volume II of the Official Biography* (London: Macmillan, 1973), p. 304.
17. Dean Acheson, West Point speech, 1962.
18. Horne, *Macmillan 1957–1986: Volume II of the Official Biography*, p. 429.
19. Harold Macmillan, *At the End of the Day* (London: Macmillan, 1989), p. 339.
20. See Chapter 5 in this book, "BRIAM: The British Advisory Mission to Vietnam" Lamb, *The Macmillan Years 1957–1963*, p. 390–397.
21. Ellis, *Britain, America and the Vietnam War*, p. 7.
22. Stanley Karnow, *Vietnam: A History* (New York: Viking, 1983); Phillip Ziegler, *Wilson: The Authorised Life of Lord Wilson of Rievaulx* (London: Wiedenfeld & Nicolson, 1993), p. 222–227.
23. *Hansard*, 29 June 1966.
24. Ziegler, *Wilson*; Karnow, *Vietnam: A History*.
25. Ziegler, *Wilson*, p. 223; PRO. CAB 129/134, "Cabinet Minutes"; PRO. CAB 128/42, "Cabinet Minutes."
26. Ziegler, *Wilson*, p. 327.
27. PRO. CAB 128/45, "Cabinet Minutes."
28. Ziegler, *Wilson*, p. 327.
29. "Johnson 'Despised' Wilson," *London Times*, 5 August 1970.
30. Ziegler, *Wilson*, p. 222.
31. Dean Acheson, *Present at the Creation: My Years in the State Department* (New York: W.W. Norton, 1969), p. 387.

## Chapter 9

1. Richard Lamb, *The Macmillan Years 1957–1963* (London: John Murray Ltd., 1995).
2. Stanley Karnow, *Vietnam: A History* (New York: Viking, 1983), p. 250.
3. Karnow, *Vietnam: A History*; see also "BRIAM: The British Advisory Mission to Vietnam," Chapter 5 in this book.
4. Sylvia Ellis, *Britain, America and the Vietnam War* (Santa Barbara, CA: Praeger, 2004), p. 3.
5. Edward Heath, "Written Reply to Commons Question," *Hansard*, 29 November 1961.
6. Lamb, *The Macmillan Years 1957–1963*, p. 401.
7. Ellis, *Britain, America and the Vietnam War*, p. 5.
8. PRO. CAB 129/134, "Cabinet Minutes."
9. *Hansard*, 8 March 1966.
10. Ellis, *Britain, America and the Vietnam War*, pp. 6–7.
11. Karnow, *Vietnam: A History*.
12. Karnow, *Vietnam: A History*; Phillip Ziegler, *Wilson: The Authorised Life of Lord Wilson of Rievaulx* (London: Wiedenfeld & Nicolson, 1993), p. 222.
13. An earlier instance of near disaster from Macmillan's term is included in Lamb, *The Macmillan Years 1957–1963*, p. 4.
14. Ziegler, *Wilson*; *Hansard*, 21 April 1967.
15. *Hansard*, 5 April 1965; *Hansard*, 8 March 1966; *Hansard*, 3 May 1966; *Hansard*, 17 May 1966; *Hansard*, 22 June 1966; *Hansard*, 8 November 1967.
16. PRO. PREM 13/489, "Conflict in Vietnam: Labour MPs Sought Assurance that UK Forces Would Not Be Involved."
17. *Hansard*, 8 March 1966.
18. PRO. FCO 15/583. Vietnam. Defence, "British Service Personnel Involvement."
19. *Hansard*, 8 November 1967; PRO. FCO 15/583.
20. Defence Council Instructions (DCI): Defence Council Instructions are documents governing the conduct of British armed forces in a prescribed set of circumstances. They were introduced in 1963 to replace Admiralty Fleet Orders, Army Council Instructions and Air Ministry Orders. They are issued over the signature of the Permanent Secretary, Ministry of Defence. DCIs (General) affect all the services. See PRO. Defence Committee Instruction. DCI 221/68.
21. PRO. FCO 15/583; PRO. DEFE 4/235/4. Minutes of Meeting Number 4 of 1969. PART I 1), "Matters for Discussion by the Defence and Oversea Policy (Official) Committee on Wednesday 29th January 1969."

## Chapter 10

1. PRO. FCO 15/583. Vietnam. Defence, "British Service Personnel Involvement."
2. PRO. FCO 15/583.
3. See Table Four.
4. See Table Four.
5. PRO. FCO 15/583; PRO. FCO 15/625, "Visits by UK Personnel to South Vietnam"; *Hansard*, 4 May 1966.
6. PRO. FCO 15/583.
7. "The Naval Officer in Vietnamese Waters," *Times*, 9 November 1967; *Hansard*, 8 November 1967. See also Table Four.
8. PRO. FCO 15/785, "Training of U.S. and South Vietnamese Forces at UK Jungle Warfare School in Malaysia."
9. PRO. FO 371/186370, "UK Mercenary Force and U.S. Use of Gas."
10. "Jungle Warfare School, Johore, Malaysia." wingedsoldiers.co.uk/jungle-warfare-school.html.

11. "Jungle Warfare School, Johore, Malaysia."
12. PRO. FCO 15/785.
13. PRO. FCO 15/785.
14. PRO. FCO 15/785.
15. PRO. FCO 15/785.
16. PRO. FCO 15/785.
17. PRO. FCO 15/785.
18. "Written Reply to Commons Question," *Hansard*, 6 November 1967.
19. PRO. FCO 15/785.
20. PRO. FCO 42/139. Vietnam. Defence, "Armed Forces Training: Allied Troops: Malaysia."
21. PRO. FCO 15/785.
22. Army Rumour Services: www.arrse.co.uk/community/threads/did-any-british-forces-serve-in-vietnam.
23. PRO. WO 305/2281, "22 SAS."
24. PRO. FCO 15/583.
25. See Table Four.
26. PRO. FCO 15/583.

## Chapter 11

1. See Table Four.
2. See Table Four.
3. Australian Navy, "Naval Operations in Vietnam," http://www.navy.gov.au/history/feature-histories/naval-operations-vietnam.
4. PRO. FCO 15/583. Vietnam. Defence, "British Service Personnel Involvement"; "The Naval Officer in Vietnamese Waters," *Times*, 9 November 1967; *Hansard*, 8 November 1967.
5. *Hansard*, 4 May 1966.
6. Australian Navy, "Naval Operations in Vietnam."
7. PRO. FO 371/166753, "Visits by RN Ships."
8. PRO. FO 371/170138, " Visits by RN Ships: Joint Naval Exercises with South Vietnam"; PRO. PREM 13/2384. SERVICES, "Allegations that RN Ships and Personnel Had Taken Part in Operations Off Vietnam."
9. PRO. FCO 15/583.
10. PRO. FCO 15/583.
11. PRO. FCO 15/1086. Vietnam, "Combatants Use of British Bases."
12. Geoff Puddefoot, *The Fourth Force: The Untold Story of the Royal Fleet Auxiliary since 1945* (Barnsley: Seaforth, 2009), p. 71.
13. PRO. FCO 15/773, "British Shipping Visiting North Vietnam."
14. The Gross amendment would have prohibited the sale or purchase of arms from any country trading with Vietnam or allowing its ships or vehicles to transport goods to that country. "Mr. Healey Seeks Pledges," *Times*, 15 September 1967.
15. PRO. FCO 15/773; *Hansard*, 26 April 1967; PRO. FCO 15/774, "SS Dartford Incident at Haiphong."
16. PRO. FCO 46/204, "Policy on Politically Sensitive Arms to U.S. Which Could Be Used in Vietnam." Three accounts are also provided for British merchant ships off-loading at South Vietnamese ports: see Army Rumour Services, www.arrse.co.uk/community/threads/did-any-british-forces-serve-in-vietnam.

## Chapter 12

1. PRO. AIR 2/18352, "Report from FEAF on South Vietnam, Maintenance and Supply of U.S. Aircraft."
2. See Table Four.
3. PRO. FCO 15/583. Vietnam. Defence, "British Service Personnel Involvement."
4. See Table Four.
5. "RAF Flies Relief for Vietnam Children," *Times*, 20 January 1967.
6. "Hercules Relief Flights from Singapore," *Times*, 6 March 1968.
7. PRO. FCO 15/583.
8. PRO. FCO 15/583.
9. "The Naval Officer in Vietnamese Waters," *Times*, 9 November 1967; PRO. FCO 15/660, "Role of British Service Attaches at British Embassy in Saigon."
10. "Written Answer," *Hansard*, 10 May 1966.
11. Army Rumour Services, www.arrse.co.uk/community/threads/did-any-british-forces-serve-in-vietnam; Marc Tiley, "Britain, Vietnam and the Special Relationship," *History Today* (December 2013).
12. PRO. AIR 23/8682, "Leong Nok Tha Airfield, Thailand"; *Manual of Aerodrome Design & Safeguarding* (London: Military Aviation Authority, 1968), maa.mod.uk/mad.pdf.

## Chapter 13

1. "Reply to Commons Question," *Hansard*, 8 November 1967; *Times*, 9 November 1967; PRO. FCO 15/750. "Exchanges of Intelligence"; PRO. FCO 15/660, "Role of British Service Attaches at British Embassy in Saigon."
2. PRO. FCO 15/660.
3. PRO. FCO 15/591. "British Personnel Serving with Australian and U.S. Forces"; PRO. FCO 15/660.
4. "RAF Flies Relief for Vietnam Children," *Times*, 20 January 1967; "Appeal Issued on Vietnam," *Sydney Morning Herald*, 26 February 1974.
5. PRO. FCO 15/591; see also Table Four.
6. See Table Four.
7. PRO. FCO 15/593, "Mercenaries for South Vietnam."
8. Foreign Enlistment Act: 1870.
9. PRO. PREM 13/688. VIETNAM, "Alleged Recruitment of Mercenaries to Serve in Vietnam: Activities of Paul Daniels"; "British Volunteers Want Action in Vietnam," *Victoria Advocate*, 24 January 1966.
10. PRO. FCO 15/583. Vietnam. Defence, "British Service Personnel Involvement."
11. PRO. FCO 15/593.
12. Theresa Squatrito, "R&R: Military Policy on Prostitution," paper presented at the annual meeting of the American Political Science Association, University of Washington, 1–4 September 2005.
13. USS *Enterprise* (CVN-65): displacement: 93,000

tons, length × beam: 342m×40m, complement: 3,000 officers and ratings.
14. PRO. FCO 40/57. Hong Kong. Political Affairs, "External U.S Forces Facilities."

## Chapter 14

1. Peter Dunn, *The First Vietnam War* (London: C. Hurst, 1985).
2. PRO. FO 371/106792, "Supply, by Sale or Loan, of U.S. and UK Aircraft for the French Air Force."
3. See Table Six.
4. PRO. FO 371/106792.
5. PRO. FO 371/106792.
6. "Commons Reply," *Hansard*, 17 May 1966.
7. "Commons Reply," *Hansard*, 22 January 1968.
8. See Table Twelve.
9. "Commons Statement," *Hansard*, 11 May 1966.
10. PRO. FCO 46/207–214. These files refer to Britain's F-111 negotiations with the United States.
11. PRO. CAB 148/28/23: OPD (66)74. Memorandum by the Secretary of State for Defence, "Implications of the Vietnam War on Sales to the United States and Other Countries."
12. "Commons Question," *Hansard*, 3 August 1966.
13. "Commons Statement," *Hansard*, 8 November 1967.
14. Mark Phythian, *The Politics of British Arms Sales since 1964: To Secure Our Rightful Share* (Manchester: Manchester University Press, 2000); PRO. FCO 46/205, "Policy on Politically Sensitive Arms to U.S. Which Could Be Used in Vietnam."
15. PRO. FCO 46/205.
16. PRO. FCO 15/1085, "United Kingdom Defence Supplies."
17. PRO. FCO 15/1085 (confidential memo, 21 March 1969).
18. See Table Seven.
19. PRO. FCO 46/207, "F-111 Offset Arrangements. Policy."
20. See Table Eight.
21. PRO. FCO 46/204, "Policy on Politically Sensitive Arms to U.S. Which Could Be Used in Vietnam."
22. PRO. FCO 46/208, "F-111 Offset Arrangements. Policy."
23. See Appendix V.
24. *Times*, 14 September 1967.
25. PRO. FCO 15/773, "British Shipping Visiting North Vietnam."

## Chapter 15

1. PRO. FCO 15/1085, "United Kingdom Defence Supplies."
2. John W.R. Taylor, *Jane's All the World's Aircraft 1968–69* (London: Sampson Low, 1968).
3. PRO. FCO 15/1085.
4. "Commons Statement," *Hansard*, 8 November 1967.
5. PRO. FCO 46/207, "F-111 Offset Arrangements. Policy."
6. "HUDWAS System," *Flight International*, 14 November 1974.
7. PRO. FCO 46/207; PRO. FCO 46/217, "Possible Sale of UK Aircraft."
8. PRO. FCO 15/1085.
9. PRO. FCO 15/1085.
10. PRO. FCO 15/1085.
11. PRO. FCO 15/1085.
12. "Harriers for the U.S.," *Times*, 8 October 1970.
13. PRO. FCO 15/1085.
14. PRO. FCO 15/1085; *Times*, 25 October 1967.
15. PRO. FCO 15/1085.
16. Decca Navigator: http://www.jproc.ca/hyperbolic/decca_chains.html.
17. PRO. FCO 15/1085.
18. PRO. FCO 46/205.
19. PRO. FCO 46/205.
20. PRO. FCO 46/205.
21. For military vehicles in use by U.S. Army, see www.anzacsteel.hobbyvista.com.
22. PRO. FCO 15/1085.
23. PRO. FCO 46/205.
24. PRO. FCO 46/206, "Attempts by Sterling Engineering to Tender for Sub Contract Work for the M-16 Rifle."
25. PRO. FCO 46/205.
26. "Commons Question," *Hansard*, 26 February 1968.
27. PRO. FCO 46/205.
28. PRO. FCO 46/205.
29. See Table Eleven.
30. PRO. FCO 46/161, "Arms Sales: Australia: Aircraft, Bombs and Equipment."
31. "Commons Question," *Hansard*, 14 July 1966.
32. "Commons Question," *Hansard*, 14 July 1966.
33. PRO. FCO 46/161.
34. PRO. CAB 164/764. "Cabinet Minutes"; No. 2 Squadron, RAAF: airwarvietnam.com/raafno2.
35. Mark Phythian, *The Politics of British Arms Sales since 1964: To Secure Our Rightful Share* (Manchester: Manchester University Press, 2000).
36. No. 2 Squadron, RAAF: airwarvietnam.com/raafno2.
37. "Commons Statement," *Hansard*, 12 July 1966.
38. PRO. FCO 46/205.
39. See Appendix V. This appendix lists most of the equipment used by the United States in Vietnam and includes all equipment supplied by Britain that was used there.
40. See Table Thirteen.
41. PRO. FCO 15/1085.

## Chapter 16

1. "List of Intelligence Gathering Disciplines," www.wikipedia.org.
2. PRO. FCO 15/583. Vietnam. Defence, "British Service Personnel Involvement"; *Times*, 9 November 1967.
3. *The Guardian*, 25 June 2010; "UKUSA Agree-

ment," www.wikipedia.org; "U.S. Signals Intelligence in the Cold War," www.wikipedia.org.
 4. "U.S. Signals Intelligence in the Cold War."
 5. "U.S. Signals Intelligence in the Cold War."
 6. PRO. FCO 15/583.
 7. PRO. FCO 15/625, "Visits by UK Personnel to South Vietnam."
 8. PRO. FO 371/180627, "Adverse 'Daily Mirror' Article on British Police Advisers in Vietnam"; see also "BRIAM: The British Advisory Mission to Vietnam," Chapter 5 in this book.
 9. PRO. FCO 15/625.
 10. PRO. FCO 15/750, "Exchanges of Intelligence."
 11. Nigel West, *Historical Dictionary of Signals Intelligence* (Lanham, MD: Scarecrow, 2012).
 12. PRO. FCO 15/786, "Training of U.S. and South Vietnamese Forces at UK Jungle Warfare School in Malaysia."
 13. PRO. FCO 15/773, "British Shipping Visiting North Vietnam."

## Chapter 17

 1. See Table Four in this book, as well as J. Mackay and J. Mussell, eds., *Medals Yearbook—2006* (Devon: Token Publishing, 2006).
 2. Mackay and Mussell, *Medals Yearbook—2006*.
 3. PRO: FCO 15/593, "Mercenaries for South Vietnam."
 4. *Sunday Express*, 22 January 1967.
 5. See Army Rumour Services, www.arrse.co.uk/community/threads/did-any-british-forces-serve-in-vietnam; Marc Tiley, "Britain, Vietnam and the Special Relationship," *History Today* (December 2013).
 6. See Table Four.
 7. Phillip Ziegler, *Wilson: The Authorised Life of Lord Wilson of Rievaulx* (London: Wiedenfeld & Nicolson, 1993).
 8. *Times*, 5 August 1970.
 9. PRO. WO 305/3239, "1st Bn Black Watch."
 10. PRO. FCO 15/593.
 11. See www.arrse.co.uk/community/threads/did-any-british-forces-serve-in-vietnam.
 12. See Table Seven.

## Appendix II

 1. Peter Dunn, *The First Vietnam War* (London: C. Hurst, 1985), p. 28–32.
 2. Spencer C. Tucker, *The Encyclopedia of the Vietnam War: A Political, Social, and Military History* (Santa Barbara, CA: ABC-CLIO, 2011).
 3. Dunn, *The First Vietnam War*, p. 326.
 4. Dunn, *The First Vietnam War*, p. 235.
 5. Dunn, *The First Vietnam War*, p. 228–233.
 6. Dunn, *The First Vietnam War*, p. 79–112.
 7. Formerly in "Britain's Small Wars: Rumour Control." Website now defunct.
 8. Max Hastings, *Nemesis* (London: Harper Perennial, 2008).
 9. George MacDonald Fraser, *Quartered Safe Out Here* (London: HarperCollins, 2000).
 10. Peter Busch, *All the Way with JFK? Britain, the U.S., and the Vietnam War* (Oxford: Oxford University Press, 2003).
 11. Phillip Ziegler, *Wilson: The Authorised Life of Lord Wilson of Rievaulx* (London: Wiedenfeld & Nicolson, 1993).
 12. Stanley Karnow, *Vietnam: A History* (New York: Viking Press, 1983).
 13. Dunn, *The First Vietnam War*, p. 28.
 14. Karnow, *Vietnam: A History*.
 15. Karnow, *Vietnam: A History*.
 16. Karnow, *Vietnam: A History*.
 17. Dunn, *The First Vietnam War*, p. 155.
 18. Dunn, *The First Vietnam War*, p. 156.
 19. Dunn, *The First Vietnam War*, p. 214–221.
 20. Robert Caro, *The Years of Lyndon Johnson*, Vol. 4 (New York: Alfred A. Knopf, 2012).
 21. Robert Dallek, *An Unfinished Life: John F. Kennedy, 1917–1963* (New York: Little, Brown, 2003).
 22. Karnow, *Vietnam: A History*, p. 507–509.
 23. Karnow, *Vietnam: A History*, p. 577–578.
 24. Dunn, *The First Vietnam War*, p. 22–50.
 25. Dunn, *The First Vietnam War*, p. 42.
 26. Dunn, *The First Vietnam War*, p. 69–118.
 27. Dunn, *The First Vietnam War*, p. 70.
 28. Dunn, *The First Vietnam War*, p. 73–76.
 29. Dunn, *The First Vietnam War*, p. 77.
 30. Dunn, *The First Vietnam War*, p. 77–108.
 31. Dunn, *The First Vietnam War*. The chapter titled "Bitter Harvest: Roosevelt and Indo china" discusses in detail the events in Indochina during this period.
 32. Dunn, *The First Vietnam War*.
 33. Karnow, *Vietnam: A History*, p. 234.
 34. Any of the numerous biographies of Ho may be consulted for details of his life.

## Appendix III

 1. Britain's Small Wars, "Allied Contribution to Vietnam" (website now defunct).

## Appendix IV

 1. Compiled from official British army records and Peter Dunn, *The First Vietnam War* (London: C. Hurst, 1985).

## Appendix V

 1. The data in these tables is from various sources, including:
   List of World War II weapons of the United Kingdom (www.wikipedia.org).
   The Pacific Compo Ration (17thdivision.tripod.com).
   Weapons of the Vietnam War (www.wikipedia.org).

# Bibliography

## Books

Acheson, Dean. *Present at the Creation: My Years in the State Department.* New York: W. W. Norton, 1969.

Busch, Peter. *All the Way with JFK? Britain, the U.S., and the Vietnam War.* Oxford: Oxford University Press, 2003.

Caro, Robert. *The Years of Lyndon Johnson.* 5 vols. New York: Alfred A. Knopf, 1982-2012.

Colman, Jonathan. *A "Special Relationship"? Harold Wilson, Lyndon B. Johnson and Anglo-American Relations "at the Summit," 1964-68.* Manchester: Manchester University Press, 2004.

Dallek, Robert. *An Unfinished Life: John F. Kennedy, 1917-1963.* New York: Little, Brown, 2003.

Dickie, John. *Special No More: Anglo-American Relations: Rhetoric and Reality.* London: Wiedenfeld & Nicholson, 1994.

Donnison, F.S.V. *British Military Administration in the Far East, 1943-1946.* London: HMSO, 1956.

Dunn, Peter. *The First Vietnam War.* London: C. Hurst, 1985.

Ellis, Sylvia. *Britain, America and the Vietnam War.* Santa Barbara, CA: Praeger, 2004.

Fraser, George MacDonald. *Quartered Safe Out Here.* London: HarperCollins, 2000.

Greene, Graham. *The Quiet American.* London: William Heinemann, 1955.

Harris Smith, R. *OSS.* Berkeley: University of California Press, 1972.

Hastings, Max. *Nemesis.* London: Harper Perennial, 2008.

Horne, Alistair. *Macmillan 1957-1986: Volume II of the Official Biography.* London: Macmillan, 1989.

Karnow, Stanley. *Vietnam: A History.* New York: Viking Press, 1983.

Karnow, Stanley. *Vietnam: A History.* New York: Viking, 1994.

Kovic, Ron. *Born on the Fourth of July.* New York: Akashic Books, 2005.

Lamb, Richard. *The Macmillan Years 1957-1963.* London: John Murray Ltd., 1995.

Laron, Guy. *Origins of the Suez Crisis: Postwar Development, Diplomacy and the Struggle over Third World Industrialization, 1945-1956.* Baltimore: John Hopkins University Press, 2013.

Mackay, J., and Mussel, J., eds. *Medals Yearbook—2006.* Devon: Token Publishing, 2006.

Macmillan, Harold. *At the End of the Day.* London: Macmillan, 1973.

McGibbon, Ian. *New Zealand's Vietnam War.* Wollombi: Exisle Publishing, 2010.

Mountbatten, Vice Admiral, the Earl of Burma. *Post Surrender Tasks: Section "E" of the Report to the Combined Chiefs of Staff.* London: HMSO, 1969.

Phythian, Mark. *The Politics of British Arms Sales since 1964: To Secure Our Rightful Share.* Manchester: Manchester University Press, 2000.

Stiff, P. *See You in November: The Story of an SAS Assassin.* Alberton: Galago Publishing, 2002.

Taylor, John W.R. *Jane's All the World's Aircraft 1968-69.* London: Sampson Low, 1968.

Thompson, Sir Robert. *No Exit from Vietnam.* New York: David McKay, 1969.

Tucker, Spencer C. *The Encyclopedia of the Vietnam War: A Political, Social, and Military History.* Santa Barbara, CA: ABC-CLIO, 2011.

West, Nigel. *Historical Dictionary of Signals Intelligence.* Lanham, MD: Scarecrow, 2012.

Ziegler, Phillip. *Edward Heath: The Authorised Biography.* London: Harper, 2011.

\_\_\_\_\_. *Wilson: The Authorised Life of Lord Wilson of Rievaulx.* London: Wiedenfeld & Nicolson, 1993.

## Articles

Brush, Peter. "Higher and Higher: American Drug Use in Vietnam." *Vietnam Magazine* 15, no. 4 (December 2002).

Curtis, Mark. "Britain's Secret Support for U.S. Aggression: The Vietnam War." markcurtis.wordpress.com. 2006.

Squatrito, Theresa. "R&R: Military Policy on Prostitution." Paper presented at the annual meeting of the American Political Science Association, University of Washington, 1-4 September 2005.

Tiley, Marc. "Britain, Vietnam and the Special Relationship." *History Today* (December 2013).

## PRO Documents

AIR 2/18352. "Report from FEAF on South Vietnam Maintenance and Supply of U.S. Aircraft."
AIR 23/8682. "Leong Nok Tha Airfield, Thailand."
CAB 128/42. "Cabinet Minutes."
CAB 128/45. "Cabinet Minutes."
CAB 129/134. "Cabinet Minutes."
CAB 148/28/23. Memorandum by the Secretary of State for Defence. "Implications of the Vietnam War on Sales to the United States and Other Countries."
CAB 164/764 "Cabinet Minutes."
DEFE 4/235/4. Minutes of Meeting Number 4 of 1969. PART I 1). "Matters for Discussion by the Defence and Oversea Policy (Official) Committee on Wednesday 29th January 1969."
FCO 15/583. Vietnam. Defence. "British Service Personnel Involvement."
FCO 15/591. "British Personnel Serving with Australian and U.S. Forces."
FCO 15/593. "Mercenaries for South Vietnam."
FCO 15/624. "Vietnam War. Sale of UK Defence Equipment."
FCO 15/625. "Visits by UK Personnel to South Vietnam."
FCO 15/660. "Role of British Service Attaches at British Embassy in Saigon."
FCO 15/750. "Exchanges of Intelligence."
FCO 15/773. "British Shipping Visiting North Vietnam."
FCO 15/774. "SS Dartford Incident at Haiphong."
FCO 15/785. "Training of U.S. and South Vietnamese Forces at UK Jungle Warfare School in Malaysia."
FCO 15/786. "Training of U.S. and South Vietnamese Forces at UK Jungle Warfare School in Malaysia."
FCO 15/1085. "United Kingdom Defence Supplies."
FCO 15/1086. Vietnam. "Combatants Use of British Bases."
FCO 40/57. Hong Kong. Political Affairs. "External U.S. Forces Facilities."
FCO 40/58. Hong Kong. Political Affairs. "External U.S. Forces Facilities."
FCO 42/139. Vietnam. Defence. "Armed Forces Training: Allied Troops: Malaysia."
FCO 46/161. "Arms sales: Australia. Aircraft, Bombs and Equipment."
FCO 46/204. "Policy on Politically Sensitive Arms to U.S. Which Could Be Used in Vietnam."
FCO 46/205. "Policy on Politically Sensitive Arms to U.S. Which Could Be Used in Vietnam."
FCO 46/206. "Attempts by Sterling Engineering to Tender for Sub Contract Work for M-16 Rifle."
FCO 46/207. "F-111 Offset Arrangements. Policy."
FCO 46/208. "F-111 Offset Arrangements. Policy."
FCO 46/209. "F-111 Offset Arrangements. Policy."
FCO 46/210. "F-111 Offset Arrangements. Policy."
FCO 46/211. "F-111 Offset Arrangements. Policy."
FCO 46/212. "F-111 Offset Arrangements. Policy."
FCO 46/213. "F-111 Offset Arrangements. Policy."
FCO 46/214. "F-111 Offset Arrangements. Policy."
FCO 46/217. "Possible Sale of UK Aircraft."
FO 371/92400. "Annual Review of Events in Associated States of Vietnam, etc."
FO 371/106792. "Supply, by Sale or Loan, of U.S. and UK Aircraft for the French Air Force."
FO 371/166753. "Visits by RN Ships."
FO 371/170138. "Visits by RN Ships. Joint Naval Exercises with South Vietnam."
FO 371/180627. "Adverse 'Daily Mirror' Article on British Police Advisers in Vietnam."
FO 371/186370. "UK Mercenary Force and U.S. Use of Gas."
PREM 13/489. "Conflict in Vietnam: Labour MPs Sought Assurance that UK Forces Would Not Be Involved."
PREM 13/688. VIETNAM. "Alleged Recruitment of Mercenaries to Serve in Vietnam: Activities of Paul Daniels."
PREM 13/2384. SERVICES. "Allegations that RN Ships and Personnel Had Taken Part in Operations Off Vietnam."
WO 305/2281. "22 SAS."
WO 305/3239. "1st Bn Black Watch."

## Websites

Army Rumour Services. www.arrse.co.uk/community/threads/did-any-british-forces-serve-in-vietnam.
Australian Navy. "Naval Operations in Vietnam." http://www.navy.gov.au/history/feature-histories/naval-operations-vietnam.
Crown Airfield. op-crown.webs.com. The Coffelt Database of Vietnam Casualties. Coffeltdatabase.org.
Decca Navigator. http://www.jproc.ca/hyperbolic/decca_chains.html.
"Jungle Warfare School, Johore, Malaysia." wingedsoldiers.co.uk/jungle-warfare-school.html.
*Manual of Aerodrome Design & Safeguarding*. London: Military Aviation Authority, 1968. maa.mod.uk/mad.pdf.
No. 2 Squadron, RAAF. airwarvietnam.com/raafno2.
Wikipedia (www.wikipedia.org):
- List of Intelligence Gathering Disciplines
- Military Intelligence
- UKUSA Agreement
- U.S. Signals Intelligence in the Cold War

www.militaryfactory.com.
www.anzacsteel.hobbyvista.com.
www.vietnamroll.gov.au.

# Index

Acheson, Dean: on the "Special Relationship" 110; West Point speech 102
Agnew, Spiro 82; Vietnam protests 82
Allied Control Commission 11, 12
Allied Land Forces French Indochina 11, 12
American Foreign Assistance Act 178; Gross amendment 178
Ammonites 11
ammunition sales 200–202
Annam 7
armored recovery vehicles 196
arms sales: Australian 205–207; New Zealand 205–207; official policy 166; South Vietnamese 210; unofficial policy 167
Attlee, Clement 97–100
Australian troops: at Tan Son Nhut Air Base 113

B-52 bomber 80–81
Bảo Đại, Emperor of Vietnam 8, 42, 46–48
Bidault, Georges 41
Biên Hòa 26, 27
Bình Xuyên 46–47
Blackburn Beverley 135–137
Blum, Léon 41
Bollaert, Émile 42
Brain, Harry 11, 23, 24
BRIAM (British Advisory Mission to Vietnam) 50; later role in Vietnam 56
Briggs Plan 54
Brinks hotel bombing 65
Bristol freighter 140
British Army: exchanges 117; recruitment to Australian army 116; recruitment to New Zealand armed forces 117; recruitment to U.S. armed forces 116; Royal Army Medical Corps 124–125
British charity workers 149
British civilian employees 148–149
British Embassy staff 148
Buddhists 50–52
buses 196

Cambodia 7
Cao Đài 14, 46
Cédile, Jean 19, 23

Cholon fire 26
Churchill 95–99
CIA 8
Cité Heyraud 19
Clarke, Major R.W. 27, 28
CLARKOL 27
CLI (Corps Léger d' Intervention) 24, 96–97
Cochinchina 7
Committee on Strategic Exports 172
conscripts 149–150
Control Commission 10, 15
Corsair A-7E 181–183
COSVN (Central Office for South Vietnam) 60
coup d'état 18, 19
CS gas 202

d'Argenlieu, Admiral Georges Thierry 35–38
SS *Dartford* 134
Decca navigator 192
De Gaulle, Charles 11, 35–38, 96–97
de Langlade, François 96
de Lattre, General Jean 43
de Lattre line 43
Delta Plan 54
Democratic Republic of Vietnam (DRV) 8
Dening, Esler 13
Dewey, Richard 11
Diệm, Ngô Đình 44, 46–58
Điện Biên Phư 43, 44–56
Đôn, General Trần Văn 8, 51–52
Đồng, Phạm Văn 62, 66
Douglas Dakota transport aircraft 31
Douglas-Home, Sir Alex 103
Durbrow, Elbridge 48–50

Eden, Anthony 45, 97
80th Brigade 11
Elliot automation "Heads-Up" display 183–184
equipment 172–178
*Evening Standard* 130

F-111 off-set 168–171
Fairchild C119, The Flying Boxcar 35
fast patrol boats 197–198

Ferret armored car 193–196; sale 196
French equipment requests 163–165
French Far East Expeditionary Corps (Corps Expéditionnaire Français en Extrême-Orient, CEFEO) 35
fuel deliveries 134
Fulbright, William 66

GATEFORCE 26
Gates, Major L.D. 26, 27
General Dynamics F-111 166–168
General service medal/award 220
Geneva peace conference 45, 97
Giáp, General Võ Nguyên 40–45; Tet Offensive 76
Giàu, Trần Văn 16
Goldwater, Senator Barry 61
Gracey, Major-General Douglas 11–30
Gulf of Tonkin Incident 61–62
Gulf of Tonkin Resolution 61
Gurkha rifles regiment 15, 19

Haiphong 40
Handley-Page "Jetstream" 184–185
Hanoi 40
Hawker Siddeley Harrier "Jump Jet" 185–189
Heath, Edward 106
Hercules C-1 138–139
Hercules C-130 138
Hilsman, Roger 55
Hirst, Brigadier J.A.E. 12, 30
Hồ Chí Minh Trail 60
Hòa Hảo 14, 46
Hong Kong 152–153
Hovercraft 179–181
HUMINT (Human-Source Intelligence) 214
Humphrey, Hubert 78
Hyderbad regiment 15, 19

IMINT (Imagery Intelligence) 214
intelligence gathering: British Embassy 216; France 215; Hanoi consulate 216; Hong Kong monitoring stations 218–219; intelligence transfer 218; types of intelligence 214; U.S. 216
Iroquois UH-1 helicopter 64

Japanese Army 12
Japanese High Command 13
Jay rule 171
Johnson, Lyndon B. 56–68, 112, 114
Jungle Warfare School 118–123

Kai-shek, Chiang 9
Kempeitai 23
Kennedy, John F. 52–57, 111
Key areas 13, 14
Khánh, General Nguyễn 59, 63
Khmer Rouge 84
Khrushchev, Nikita 62
Kingcobra P-63, fighter-bomber 37
Kissinger, Dr. Henry 79–93
Kosygin, Alexei 65
Kovic, Ron 70
Kỳ, Nguyễn Cao 61–63, 69

Laird, Melvin 82–84
land reform 48–49
Laos 43–44
Lebel M1886 rifle 22
Leclerc, General Jacques 18, 24, 30, 35, 41
Leong Nok Tha crown air base 144–147
HMS Lion 128
Lodge, Henry Cabot 51

M-60 GPMG 201
M101 105mm howitzer 40
M2A2 howitzer 39
Mackenzie, Colin 96
Macmillan, Harold 100–102
martial law, proclamation of 17
MASINT (Measurement and Signature Intelligence) 214
Maunsell, M.S.K. 14
McNamara, Robert 72
Meiklereid, Ernest 25
HMAS Melbourne 127
mercenaries 150
mercenary units 151
Merchant Navy 133–134
Military Assistance Advisory Group (MAAG) 46, 53
Minh, General Dương Văn 59
Mính, Hồ Chí 7, 36–44
Montagnard operation 57
Mosquito fighter-bomber 29
Mountbatten, Lord Louis 11–27
Murray, Lt. Col. 19, 21, 25
Mỹ Tho 27
Myers, Brigadier M. 11, 21

Nhu, Ngô Dình 50–51
Nixon, Richard Milhous 78–89
Nolting, Frederick 55

North Vietnam 8, 9, 60, 64, 66, 68, 69, 71, 78, 85

Operation Flaming Dart I 65
Operation Flaming Dart II 65
Operation Lamson 719 86–88
Operation Lorraine 43
Operation Masterdom 14, 112, 230
Operation Rolling Thunder 65
OPSINT (Open-Source Intelligence) 214
OSS 8

Patti, Archimedes 11
Phantom F-4 jet fighter/bomber 71
point focal charge 202
Potsdam Conference 7, 11
Purcell, Lt. Col. 19, 21

RAAF operations in Vietnam 207–208
RAF stations 142–143
RAF, RAAF, RNZAF roundels 141
Ramadier, Paul 41
RAS (Refueling-At-Sea) 132
Raven OH-23 helicopter 38
Republic of Vietnam 47
Rifles 22, 199, 205; proposed sale 198–200
Rodham, Lt. Col. C.H.B. 26
Roosevelt, Franklin D. 96–97
Royal Air Force: aircraft in Vietnam 135–141
Royal Fleet Auxiliary 131
Royal Navy: clearance divers 129; secondments 126; visits 128; volunteers in the RAN 126; volunteers in the RNZN 126

Sainteny, Jean 36, 38
Saladin armored car 193–196
Salan, General Raoul 43
Saracen personnel carrier 193–196
self-propelled guns 197
Shawnee H-21C transport helicopter 36
Short Bros "Skyvan" 189–190
SIGINT (Signals Intelligence) 214
Sigma II 64–65
Sikorsky UH-19D helicopter 37
Singapore 131, 144, 152, 161, 219
Slim, General William 10, 12, 13
South East Asia Command (SEAC) 12
Southern Committee of the Việt Minh 15, 18
Special Forces 123–124, 223
"Special Relationship" between Britain and America 99
Spey jet engines 181–183

Spitfire 30
Strategic Hamlets 48–57; policy 55–57
Sydney 152

RFA Tarbatness 133
Taunton, Brigadier D.E. 11
Taylor, Gen. M. 54, 62; objection to increased troop numbers 66
Terauchi, Field Marshal 16, 21, 28
Tet offensive 75–77
Thant, U 62
Thiệu, Nguyễn Văn 62–69
Thọ, Lê Đức: peace negotiations 85, 89–91
Thompson, Sir Robert 53–57
Thủ Dầu Một 26
Thủ Đức 26
RFA Tidespring 132
Tonkin 7
training and secondments 115, 117
Trảng Bom 27
Trotskyites 18
Truman, Harry 10
Truman Doctrine 41
TSR-2 168
Twentieth 20th Indian Division 11, 12

urbanization, forced 68
U.S. forces, visits to by senior British officers 217
U.S. MSTS (Military Sea Transportation Service) 132

Văn Bạch, Phạm 16
Việt Cộng: formation 49; logistics supply 60–61
Việt Minh 8–25, 36–45
Việt Nam Quốc Dân Đảng (VNQDD) 9
Vietnam protests 74, 83–85
Vietnam War: cost to the U.S. 67, 68, 73

Westland S-51 Dragonfly helicopter 162
Westland Wessex 190
Westmoreland, General William: increase in troop numbers and strategy 66–68; search and destroy missions 67; further escalation 73
Wilson, Harold 103–107
Wreck-lifting barges 130

Xuân, General Nguyễn Văn 42
Xuân Lộc 27

Zedong, Mao 41

www.ingramcontent.com/pod-product-compliance
Lightning Source LLC
Chambersburg PA
CBHW081538300426
44116CB00015B/2677